Genders and Sexualities in History

Series Editors: **John H. Arnold, Joanna Bourke** and **Sean Brady**

Palgrave Macmillan's *Genders and Sexualities in History* series aims to accommodate and foster new approaches to historical research in the fields of genders and sexualities. The series will promote world-class scholarship that concentrates upon the interconnected themes of genders, sexualities, religions/religiosity, civil society, class formations, politics and war.

Historical studies of gender and sexuality have often been treated as disconnected fields, while in recent years historical analyses in these two areas have synthesized, creating new departures in historiography. By linking genders and sexualities with questions of religion, civil society, politics and the contexts of war and conflict, this series will reflect recent developments in scholarship, moving away from the previously dominant and narrow histories of science, scientific thought and legal processes. The result brings together scholarship from contemporary, modern, early modern, medieval, classical and non-Western history to provide a diachronic forum for scholarship that incorporates new approaches to genders and sexualities in history.

British Masculinity in the Gentleman's Magazine, *1731 to 1815* is a groundbreaking study of the 'world of the gentleman' represented in one of Britain's longest-running periodicals'. This fascinating and highly original book explores how new concepts of masculinity and notions of what it took to be a gentleman pervaded this unique, popular and vast miscellany. The *Gentleman's Magazine* was not so much a publication for the established gentry and aristocracy, but more a site of contestation and construction of notions of 'gentlemanliness' among Britain's emerging 'middling sorts'. Gillian Williamson's examination of masculinity through the lens of the *Gentleman's Magazine* challenges and reconceptualizes the periodization of gender and class formations in Britain. In common with all volumes in the *Genders and Sexualities in History* series, *British Masculinity in the* Gentleman's Magazine, *1731 to 1815* presents a multifaceted and meticulously researched scholarly study, and is a sophisticated contribution to our understanding of the past.

Titles include:

John H. Arnold and Sean Brady (*editors*)
WHAT IS MASCULINITY?
Historical Dynamics from Antiquity to the Contemporary World

Heike Bauer and Matthew Cook (*editors*)
QUEER 1950s

Cordelia Beattie and Kirsten A. Fenton (*editors*)
INTERSECTIONS OF GENDER, RELIGION AND ETHNICITY IN THE MIDDLE AGES

Valeria Babini, Chiara Beccalossi and Lucy Riall (*editors*)
ITALIAN SEXUALITIES UNCOVERED, 1789–1914

Chiara Beccalossi
FEMALE SEXUAL INVERSION
Same-Sex Desires in Italian and British Sexology, c. 1870–1920

Roberto Bizzocchi
A LADY'S MAN
The Cicisbei, Private Morals and National Identity in Italy

Raphaëlle Branche and Fabrice Virgili (editors)
RAPE IN WARTIME

Susan Broomhall
AUTHORITY, GENDER AND EMOTIONS IN LATE MEDIEVAL AND EARLY
MODERN ENGLAND

Matt Cook
QUEER DOMESTICITIES
Homosexuality and Home Life in Twentieth-Century London

Peter Cryle and Alison Moore
FRIGIDITY
An Intellectual History

Lucy Delap and Sue Morgan
MEN, MASCULINITIES AND RELIGIOUS CHANGE IN TWENTIETH
CENTURY BRITAIN

Jennifer V. Evans
LIFE AMONG THE RUINS
Cityscape and Sexuality in Cold War Berlin

Kate Fisher and Sarah Toulalan (editors)
BODIES, SEX AND DESIRE FROM THE RENAISSANCE TO THE PRESENT

Christopher E. Forth and Elinor Accampo (editors)
CONFRONTING MODERNITY IN FIN-DE-SIÈCLE FRANCE
Bodies, Minds and Gender

Rebecca Fraser
GENDER, RACE AND FAMILY IN NINETEENTH CENTURY AMERICA
From Northern Woman to Plantation Mistress

Alana Harris and Timothy Jones (editors)
LOVE AND ROMANCE IN BRITAIN, 1918–1970

Dagmar Herzog (editor)
BRUTALITY AND DESIRE
War and Sexuality in Europe's Twentieth Century

Josephine Hoegaerts
MASCULINITY AND NATIONHOOD, 1830–1910
Constructions of Identity and Citizenship in Belgium

Robert Hogg
MEN AND MANLINESS ON THE FRONTIER
Queensland and British Columbia in the Mid-Nineteenth Century

Tim Reinke-Williams
WOMEN, WORK AND SOCIABILITY IN EARLY MODERN LONDON

Gillian Williamson
BRITISH MASCULINITY IN THE *GENTLEMAN'S MAGAZINE*, 1731 TO 1815

Midori Yamaguchi
DAUGHTERS OF THE ANGLICAN CLERGY
Religion, Gender and Identity in Victorian England

Genders and Sexualities in History Series
Series Standing Order 978–0–230–55185–5 Hardback
978–0–230–55186–2 Paperback
(*outside North America only*)

You can receive future titles in this series as they are published by placing a standing order. Please contact your bookseller or, in case of difficulty, write to us at the address below with your name and address, the title of the series and the ISBN quoted above.

Customer Services Department, Macmillan Distribution Ltd, Houndmills, Basingstoke, Hampshire RG21 6XS, England

British Masculinity in the *Gentleman's Magazine,* 1731 to 1815

Gillian Williamson
Independent Scholar, UK

palgrave
macmillan

First published 2016 by
PALGRAVE MACMILLAN

Palgrave Macmillan in the UK is an imprint of Macmillan Publishers Limited, registered in England, company number 785998, of Houndmills, Basingstoke, Hampshire RG21 6XS.

Palgrave Macmillan in the US is a division of St Martin's Press LLC, 175 Fifth Avenue, New York, NY 10010.

Palgrave Macmillan is the global academic imprint of the above companies and has companies and representatives throughout the world.

Palgrave® and Macmillan® are registered trademarks in the United States, the United Kingdom, Europe and other countries.

ISBN 978–1–137–54232–8

This book is printed on paper suitable for recycling and made from fully managed and sustained forest sources. Logging, pulping and manufacturing processes are expected to conform to the environmental regulations of the country of origin.

A catalogue record for this book is available from the British Library.

Library of Congress Cataloging-in-Publication Data
Williamson, Gillian.
    British masculinity in the Gentleman's Magazine, 1731 to 1815 / Gillian Williamson.
        pages   cm. — (Genders and sexualities in history)
    ISBN 978–1–137–54232–8 (hardback)
    1. Gentleman's magazine (London, England)   2. Masculinity in literature.   3. Masculinity—Great Britain—History—18th century.
    4. Middle class men—Great Britain—History—18th century.   5. Great Britain—Intellectual life—18th century.   6. English periodicals—History—18th century.   I. Title.
    PN5130.G5W55 2015
    052—dc23   2015021882

Contents

Tables

Acknowledgements

I am most fortunate that Birkbeck College, University of London, gave me the luxury of a second opportunity to enjoy higher education, and provided funding for my postgraduate research. I owe special thanks to Dr Sean Brady and Prof. Jerry White for their guidance during my time there.

I am grateful for the support and encouragement of my colleagues and the historians I have met at seminars and conferences, in particular the members of the British History in the Long Eighteenth Century and Education in the Long Eighteenth Century seminars at the Institute of Historical Research, and the Women's Studies Group. Thanks go to Pene Corfield, Nick Draper, Matthew McCormack and Susan Whyman who read and commented on my work in whole or in part, and to Tim Hitchcock who suggested various additional sources.

I thank too the libraries, record offices and other archives where I pursued my research: Saffron Walden Town Library (an appropriate place to read the *Gentleman's Magazine*, as it was founded by the 'gentlemen' of this small, provincial town in 1832 as the Saffron Walden Literary and Scientific Institution); Cambridge University Library Rare Books Room; the John Johnson Collection at the Bodleian Library, Oxford; Dr Julian Pooley at the Surrey History Centre who made available his work-in-progress, the Nichols Archive Database, and Tom Boggis, Curator (Collections), London and East, English Heritage, who showed me the collection of the *Gentleman's Magazine* at Audley End House.

Finally there are my husband, Adrian, and children, Mary, Patrick and Tom, and their partners. They have endured the downs as well as the ups of the last five years and have always listened with fitting politeness to more information on the eighteenth century than I suspect they ever wanted.

Abbreviations

BL	British Library
BM	British Museum
Bodl.	Bodleian Library, Oxford
ESTC	English Short Title Catalogue
GM	*Gentleman's Magazine*
GSJ	*Grub Street Journal*
JJ	John Johnson Collection of Printed Ephemera
LM	*London Magazine*
MP	*Morning Post*
NAD	Nichols Archive Database
NPG	National Portrait Gallery
OBP	*Old Bailey Proceedings*, version 7.1, http://www.oldbailey online.org
ODNB	*Oxford Dictionary of National Biography*, http://www.oxford dnb.com
PC	Private collection
US	*Universal Spectator*

Notes

Biographical information	Unless otherwise stated, biographical information is from *ODNB*.
GM contributors	Unless otherwise stated, identifications of anonymous and pseudonymous correspondents are from Emily Lorraine De Montluzin, *Attributions of Authorship in the Gentleman's Magazine, 1731–1868* (see Bibliography).
NAD	Items are referenced by the shelfmark of the archive followed by the NAD reference number.
Predecimal British currency (pre-1971)	One pound (£) was divided into 20 shillings (s) or 240 pence (d). There were therefore 12 pence in a shilling. There were also coins representing a halfpenny and farthing (a quarter of a penny). A guinea was worth one pound one shilling (£1 1s).

Introduction

In 1823 William Hazlitt wrote:

> Who with the Gentleman's Magazine held carelessly in his hand, has notpassed minutes, hours, days, in *lackadaisical* triumph over *ennui*? Who has not taken it up in parlour window seats? Who has not ran [*sic*] it slightly through in reading rooms?[1]

He understood that pretty much the entire reading public was aware of the monthly miscellany periodical, the *Gentleman's Magazine*, and probably read it, at home or in a more public club or library, even if only dipping into it to kill time.

In 1823 the magazine was 92 years old. Throughout most of the previous century it had held a leading market position. In the 1750s some 15,000 copies were printed every month and sold to an even larger number of readers throughout Britain and beyond. Thousands of those readers also supported it by submitting compositions in prose and poetry.[2] This was astonishing in a bruisingly competitive publishing environment where periodicals usually survived only a few years and rarely outlived their founders. Indeed, as early as 1738 a *Gentleman's Magazine* editorial had gloated over the demise of 'almost twenty Imitations'.[3] Surviving copies of many are rare, some known only through incidental contemporary references.

The *Gentleman's Magazine*, by contrast, lasted until 1907. The hundreds of complete or long runs that were bound for preservation and kept in academic, public and private libraries in Britain and abroad are a tribute to its contemporary significance throughout the English-speaking world. Yet, despite this legacy, the *Gentleman's Magazine* has not received its due attention from historians of the eighteenth century as a cultural product in its own right.

It has suffered from a reputation established in the early nineteenth century for outdated stuffiness. To a rising generation of radicals, reformers or romantics, it represented the old-fashioned values of their fathers' and grandfathers' generations. They saw it as a rather dull, staid publication for a backward-looking readership. As of an aged relative, Hazlitt was fond of it ('we profess an affection') to the extent that he 'would almost wish some ill to those who can say any harm of it', but ultimately slightly damning of a title he regarded as past its sell-by date ('the last lingering remains of a former age').[4] Robert Southey agreed. He took the magazine in Keswick in 1804, excusing this as 'to enlighten a Portuguese student'.[5] He was actually both published in it and planned to use it for biographical notes for *Specimens of the English Poets*, yet called it 'a disgrace to the age and the country'.[6] In the privacy of his journal Sir Walter Scott noted that he had, as Hazlitt described, turned to an 'odd volume' of the *Gentleman's Magazine* because he had finished other books. It was like a pawnbroker's shop with interesting articles confused amid a jumble of nonsense. He was rather more complimentary when addressing the editor of the magazine directly.[7] It was the venerable old age of the *Gentleman's Magazine* that impressed printer Charles Timperley. His 1839 trade history dubbed it 'the Old Parr of periodicals'.[8] A decade later, in William Thackeray's historical satire *Vanity Fair*, set in the Napoleonic Wars, the *Gentleman's Magazine* symbolized an unattractive past as one of the unread 'standard works in stout gilt bindings' (alongside the *Annual Register*, Blair's *Sermons*, Hume and Smollett) in two glazed bookcases in the study of wealthy businessman and domestic tyrant, John Osborne.[9]

This book looks behind the nineteenth-century critical judgment to examine the huge and underexploited resource that the *Gentleman's Magazine* represents for its construction of British gentlemanly masculinity, from its launch in 1731 to 1815. It considers, as others have done its founder, Edward Cave, and his editorial successors, and its role within publishing and book history. But more importantly, it integrates the text with its readers, their understanding of their reading and their contributions, responses and reactions to the text. As a study of its readers' horizon of expectations, it also does for masculinity what Kathryn Shevelow's *Women and Print Culture* does for femininity.[10]

It therefore provides a bridge between a purely literary cultural approach to masculinity and the related social practices in which the readership engaged.[11] The active participation of correspondents both shaped the magazine, and helped to frame their understanding of the intertwined nature of eighteenth-century gender and class promised in the title: *Gentleman's Magazine*. Paradoxically perhaps, the group that emerges from this study is not the traditional gentlemen of the nobility or gentry, Samuel Johnson's 'men of Ancestry'.[12] It is, rather, 'gentlemen' of the middle class or 'middling sort'.

This is the story, then, of the rise and aspirations of this expanding and increasingly articulate eighteenth-century phenomenon identified by, among others, Penelope Corfield, Henry French, Margaret Hunt and Paul Langford.[13] It goes further, however. It is not so much the story of *who* these men (and women too) were, but of *how* they fashioned themselves as genteel and inserted themselves as a public in the nation's cultural and political life, by discussing and circulating through the magazine's pages the ideology of a new gentlemanly masculinity of merit achieved through industry and self-restraint. It extends considerably the time period of Shawn Lisa Maurer's *Proposing Men*. Maurer concentrates on the early-eighteenth-century *Spectator* and *Tatler* to argue that explicit periodical discourse about women also constructed a desirable masculine identity of the active, economically productive middling-sort man, exercising benevolent control over women in the setting of the household. Maurer indeed suggests that the *Gentleman's Magazine* deserved greater attention.[14]

The *Gentleman's Magazine* is unusually robust as a source. Unlike many texts used in cultural studies of eighteenth-century gender, it was available to readers throughout this whole time period of 84 years (and beyond), very widely disseminated and read throughout Britain and across the English-speaking world, and contained the multiple voices of thousands of real men and women outside elite and literary circles. It was a vast repository with a panoramic subject matter: an abridgement of the full range of Enlightenment fare, covering all the typical subject headings in a library catalogue of the time – divinity, philosophy, history, geography, scientific discovery, literature.[15]

It therefore provides an excellent opportunity to test through a longitudinal study the periodization and themes of the historiography of masculinity in the long eighteenth century. Here too it is a bridge: between the polite, metropolitan Whiggish world conjured in the earlier century by the *Spectator* and *Tatler* and the more class-conscious, gendered bourgeois values of the nineteenth century depicted in Leonore Davidoff and Catherine Hall's *Family Fortunes*.[16]

Given the vast scale of the total magazine archive (12 monthly numbers plus an annual supplement of 48 to 64 pages each year until 1783 and doubling in size thereafter), it has been sampled. The Preface (written retrospectively each year and providing editorial comment), January and July numbers have been read in full from 1731 (the launch of the magazine) to 1815 (the formal cessation of the world-wide military conflicts in which Britain was engaged for around half of those 84 years). As the magazine had a strongly serial flavour, with much cross-referencing and reader debates often stretching over several months, topics and arguments have inevitably sometimes been followed backwards and forwards into other numbers. The sampling includes quantification and analysis of the 21,583 family announcements (births, marriages and deaths).[17] These accounted for between four and 12 per cent of the magazine's content, on a rising basis over the time period studied and with an increasing element of reader contribution, especially for deaths. This is the first time the notices have been analyzed over such an extended period.[18]

Masculinities in the *Gentleman's Magazine* are always set in the wider context of representations both in other contemporary sources (many of which it reviewed) and in recorded experiences in diaries, memoirs, autobiographies and letters (recovering the extent to which men were able or willing to meet the standards of ideal or normative masculinity in their everyday lives and relationships). Case studies illustrate some themes in greater detail.

Chapter 1 considers eighteenth-century masculinity and its historiography. Chapter 2 introduces the magazine, its owners, editors and writers and the small changes to its format over the period of the study. Chapter 3 brings together and reassesses sources for the magazine's circulation and uses new empirical research to position its readership and reception as cutting across divisions between social ranks and geographical boundaries to form a national 'imagined community' of new gentlemanliness.[19] Chapters 4 to 6 are arranged in three chronological periods: 1731 to 1756, 1757 to 1789, and 1790 to 1815. This enables an analysis of the gentlemanly masculinities portrayed by the magazine in relationship to the historiography of crises and turning points. The Conclusion assesses the competing pull of traditional lineage gentlemanliness and its re-shaping along more inclusive, meritocratic lines.

1
Gentlemanly Masculinity

The *Gentleman's Magazine* and masculinity

The *Gentleman's Magazine*'s title was redolent of a traditional, superior masculine standing, evoking implied readers who were male rather than female, adult, and of high social status, Naomi Tadmor's 'lineage families' – the gentry, perhaps even loftier.[1] Their self-confidence was apparent in its contents, their ordered, hierarchical society represented in regular factual information of institutional promotions in the Church of England, army, navy, royal court and diplomatic service. The month's news chronicled the official engagements of the court, sessions of Parliament, meetings of directors of the Bank of England, of the South Sea Company and of the aldermen of the City of London and proceedings in the civil and criminal courts. Individual lives were inserted into this picture in lists of births, marriages and deaths, often featuring again the leading families from the news and promotions columns.

However, published statistics are 'neither totally neutral collections of facts nor simply ideological impositions', but rather 'ways of establishing the authority of certain visions of social order, of organizing perceptions of "experience"'. They become naturalized through repeated publication.[2] The magazine's 'facts' were not as value-free as they seemed at first glance. All the institutions featured in the magazine, including the family in the births, marriages and deaths, were organized by gender. It was, for example, only in certain elite male fields that it marked promotions and appointments. Births almost invariably acknowledged the father and sex of the child, rather than the mother's or child's name, unless they were of very high status indeed. Marriages almost always began with the groom. The deaths were highly selective, as comparison with the monthly Bill of Mortality for London, also a regular magazine feature, indicates. Unsurprisingly, approximately half the dead in the Bill were female, and over 40 per cent were minors, whereas the magazine's obituaries were dominated by adult males.[3] These obituaries marked not only the death but also the 'continuing "social being"' of the deceased. By differentiating one deceased person from another and the commemorated from those unworthy of record, they were contributing to the 'continuous production of the social order [...] proclaiming the posthumous existence of certain persons and the social values they represent'.[4] It was certain types of men and masculine values they emphasized.

Gender and, within this, masculinity are socially created and signify power.[5] Although the description 'gentleman' only rarely appeared in the personal announcements, the magazine consistently, and over a very long time period, represented and reinforced the importance of normative, institutional masculinity. Where masculinity was not the overt subject of an article or letter, there was still a subtext: the abiding entitlement to speak and act of educated, gentlemanly men. The magazine embodied a characteristic repeatedly identified as a key element of superior masculinity: its omnipresent, apparently timeless, yet invisible and unspoken nature. This was often concealed behind the apparently neutral and universalizing use of 'man' to mean 'human' and the deployment of certain masculine values as the yardstick of any person's worth.[6]

The magazine could then be read as a guide to how men were ranked as gentlemanly or not, male readers presumably expecting or hoping for inclusion. This seems to place the magazine's gentlemanliness close to Australian sociologist Raewyn Connell's model of 'hegemonic masculinity', that form of heterosexual masculinity which at any one time guarantees male dominance over women (patriarchy), and the dominance of some males over others.[7] Connell is criticized for failure to recognize on the one hand multiple and competing forms of masculinity both within and entirely outside the hegemonic ideal and, on the other, that the hegemonic ideal may be just that, rather than a lived reality. However, for the purposes of this study Connell's 'hegemony' is a useful reminder of the abiding power implicit in some masculinities, in this instance 'gentlemanliness'.[8]

A closer reading of the *Gentleman's Magazine* establishes that its masculinity was neither as stable nor confident as appears at first sight. Some reader contributions, especially the 'poetical essays' and the obituaries, betrayed a measure of private doubt amidst the public certainty, especially where the vagaries of men's personal lives (self-esteem, love, courtship and marriage) were concerned. Success in the gentleman's world the magazine depicted required constant effort and skilful navigation between the Scylla of relationships with women and the family (How do I know whether she loves me? Is the bachelor or the married family man happier? How can I reconcile myself to the death of my beloved child?) and the Charybdis of comparison with other men over rank, wealth, effeminacy and courage. The *Gentleman's Magazine* therefore not only upheld a version of hegemonic masculinity – apparently natural and universal, insinuated into all aspects of human society – but also captured the variety of relational 'lived experience and fantasy' that constituted gender and masculinity in everyday life for real individuals.[9]

There was too, as Connell's critics argue, variety in and dispute over exactly what qualities composed gentlemanly masculinity. These shifted over this study's 84 years as new sorts of gentlemen inserted themselves and their families into the magazine's announcements columns, measuring favourably their code of domestic respectability combined with hard-earned merit against aristocratic values. By 1815 there was a clear and increasingly self-identifying middling-sort tone to the magazine. It was a masculinity that some later used to justify claims to manhood suffrage.[10] Yet, for the upwardly mobile readers of the *Gentleman's Magazine*, the shock years of the 1790s and French Wars typically produced a retreat to conservatism and a defence of the constitutional *status quo*.[11] As they retreated, the magazine's cultural pull waned. It became the creature Hazlitt gently mocked. What had seemed sturdy and manly 50 years or more previously was dismissed by Southey and Scott as 'Oldwomania' by 'reverend old gentlewomen' correspondents.[12]

Eighteenth-century masculinity

Eighteenth-century British commentators recognized that Enlightenment thinking and the new social groups created by burgeoning commercialization had an impact on gentlemanly masculinity. The traditional gentlemanliness of the nobility (160 lords temporal who sat in the House of Lords) and gentry ('some 15,000 further landed families [...] lordlings, combining local clout and office with – for some at least – national stature as the backbone of the backbenchers') was based on inheritance and landed property.[13] Their position was justified as part of a divinely ordained patriarchal pyramid. God as the supreme father granted authority for analogous rule over their people by kings, and over their families and households by fathers. The system was upheld through a code of male honour, in which the control of female sexuality was key and the duel the ultimate sanction.[14]

From the seventeenth century this model was undermined as Enlightenment empiricism demanded a reasoned, scientific explanation of mankind's place in the universe that in this context can be termed 'modern'. John Locke (1632–1704) took anatomists' nerve theory, which privileged individuals' feelings and experiences, and applied it to government and education. If each person was subject to unique sensations, then the mind of a child might be conceived as a blank slate upon which good or bad upbringing formed the man (and Locke was thinking of men rather than women).[15] Locke was widely read throughout the following century (a collected volume published in 1714 was in its 13th edition by 1824). It was familiar to and admired by some *Gentleman's Magazine* correspondents.[16]

Locke's theory did not shake to the ground the concept of patriarchy. Rather, it relocated its justification in the individual and his family.[17] It opened to all, even those born well below the nobility and gentry, the possibility of attaining gentlemanliness and the power it conferred through education and socialization. This was attractive to the new social groups found in London and other growing cities and towns. Their occupations included finance (stockjobbers, bankers, speculators), the professions (lawyers, doctors) and trading in goods, especially new luxuries. Traders included both the great merchants and the many middling-sort retailers and shopkeepers.[18] These were occupations in which mental prowess and what we would call a 'client-facing' manner had greater value than physical masculinity: the aristocrat's libertinism and duelling or the manual worker's raw strength.[19]

In the early eighteenth century, Joseph Addison (1672–1719) and Richard Steele (1672–1729) provided guidance in the *Tatler* and *Spectator* to the requisite new behaviour: politeness a conversational ease in the company of strangers as well as family and friends. Both remained in print during the century as collected volumes that were regularly cited. Politeness could, then, be acquired, was accessible, and introduced new worlds of possibility for aspirational members of the new professional, commercial and even artisan classes. By mid-century, the period covered by Chapter 4, it was more or less synonymous with gentlemanliness.

Among historians of politeness, Philip Carter draws on a rich variety of material, including conduct literature, periodicals (especially the *Tatler* and *Spectator*), drama and the lived experience of individuals taken from published diaries, memoirs and letters. He concludes that polite masculinity was largely defined through social performance and against other men rather than women, and that restrained 'gentlemanly' conduct was the hegemonic norm with effeminate foppishness operating as a warning against exaggerated politeness rather than sexual orientation.[20] Some recent scholarship counsels against over-identification of politeness with the eighteenth century and masculinity. To be sure other forms of masculinity existed, but politeness remains a useful concept because it encompasses some of the key social and cultural changes of the period.[21] Analysis of the *Gentleman's Magazine* of 1731–56 goes beyond Carter because it reveals some of the ways in which polite ideals were transmitted to a broad national audience.

The process of self-education also produced fresh anxieties over both social origin and gender. Superficial politeness might conceal underlying vulgarity.[22] And politeness was not restricted to men. The civilizing influence of female conversation in mixed gatherings – at the tea table, in assembly rooms, public walks and gardens – was crucial. Yet too much frivolous interaction with women and the worlds of fashion and shopping associated with them could feminize a man. Such anxieties often lay at the heart of popular contemporary drama and fiction throughout the century, portrayed through stock characters, from the *nouveau riche* merchant Sterling and his sister Mrs Heidelberg in George Colman's and David Garrick's play *The Clandestine Marriage* to the malicious fop Mr Lovel in Frances Burney's *Evelina*.[23] These potential pitfalls are also examined in Chapter 4.

Chapter 5 begins in 1757 in order to capture an alleged 'gender panic' at the start of the Seven Years' War, when some contemporaries blamed the adverse effects of politeness for Britain's poor military performance. The key contemporary source for this interpretation is polemicist John Brown's popular *Estimate* of 1757 which attributed defeats to an effeminacy that had sapped men's military courage.[24] The *Gentleman's Magazine* responded immediately to Brown with excerpts and positive comment.[25] It also gave a voice to those who supported a revived militia aimed at re-injecting martial courage into the male citizen-soldier defending the nation, its women and children.[26]

With hindsight, 1759 ended as an *annus mirabilis*, with setbacks reversed. By 1763, victory was secured and a new sense of British nationalism was built on an unrivalled position as 'the most aggressive, the most affluent, and the most swiftly expanding power in the world'.[27] British manhood was vindicated and the superior, active male citizen was reconfigured as the 'independent man'. His virtue was generated by gendered personal attributes rather than inherited rank, for manly independence meant not only freedom from direct or indirect financial dependence on others but also 'the condition in which self-mastery, conscience and individual responsibility could be exercised'.[28] Taken together, the views of these men were 'public opinion', of which government was increasingly compelled to take note. The *Gentleman's Magazine* was one of the means by which this public opinion was disseminated.

Gender panic is said by some historians to have produced a sharper differentiation between men and women based on biology, one of the modern sciences.[29] They suggest that the new gentleman was compared not only to other British men but also to women, whose weaker nerve fibres rendered them incapable of the same degree of reason. Empire also opened up a new range of subordinate male 'others' against whom British masculinity was defined, through the development of 'scientific' racial and stadial theories.[30] This often manifested itself as the emasculation of non-European men or their definition as 'savages'. This study also challenges this interpretation of post-war masculinity.

Politeness was not abandoned, but the preferred version of gentlemanly masculinity metamorphosed into 'sensibility', in which brisk sincerity, candour and spontaneity reflected a man's true feelings.[31] The turn was evident in the negative public reaction to the posthumous 1774 publication of the noble Lord Chesterfield's *Letters to his Son*, which revealed the potential hypocrisy of outwardly good manners. The *Gentleman's Magazine* was in the vanguard of the critics. Its book reviewer praised the work's 'elegance and purity' of style but 'lamented' that 'sound principles of religion and morality are omitted in his system of education'.[32] Class conflict between aristocracy and middling-sort intruded on the gentlemanliness debate.

Sound principles of religion and morality were also what some Britons turned to after a second national crisis: the loss of the American colonies in 1783 following eight more years of war. The apparent withdrawal of divine approval for Britain's overseas ventures is seen as a key factor in the growth of evangelicalism, which sought to mend the Britain's broken relationship with God through a spiritual and moral revival of standards in public life.[33] Evangelicals relocated civic virtue in the Christian household, in the family life of rational, public men. Patriarchy was reconstructed as a mutually affectionate yet still unequal domestic conjugal bond between man and woman.[34]

Joanne Bailey notes that 'family sentiment and domesticity [...] can be traced throughout the long eighteenth century in major or minor forms', citing the widespread use of the ideal of the 'tender parent'.[35] At this particular conjunction, however, it took on a more political flavour. Together with sensibility's directness, it brought to further prominence the qualities required of the successful commercial and professional man: the possession of good character or moral credit, with its direct association with financial credit. One contemporary writer declared, 'True credit I call that which is founded upon a right Principle, the knowing and considering whom is to be trusted by his Character and Abilities'.[36] This ethic began to spread beyond the bourgeoisie. As Kate Retford points out in her study of eighteenth-century portraiture, private, domestic moral values were often enthusiastically displayed by the aristocracy, as politically useful when courting public opinion.[37] Nor was it absolute. The military nature of British success and the ongoing need to control the remaining colonies and trade routes meant that the image of the male soldier protecting a female Britannia remained powerful. The career of the populist independent politician John Wilkes (1725–97) also serves as a reminder of the co-existence of a masculinity founded on unrestrained sexual libertinism.[38] These various masculinities and their 'others' were all depicted in the magazine in the period covered by Chapter 5, which assesses their competing pull for the readership.

The final chronological chapter deals with the turbulent years of the French Revolution and subsequent wars, and radicalism and discontent at home. Although the Revolution was initially welcomed by many British observers, including magazine correspondents, the execution of Louis XVI in 1793 and the Terror revealed the potential for the total overthrow of both government and social structures. In Britain, the figure of the responsible male householder and head of the family was harnessed by some political reformers who sought a broader franchise as a means of averting the chaos and bloodshed seen across the Channel.[39] The result was a war-time hardening and polarization of positions in a bitter conflict between social conservatives and democratizing radicals. It was a climate in which the rather stately *Gentleman's Magazine* lost its edge.

The distinction between the gendered roles produced by this politicized yet domestic focus was epitomized by Revd Thomas Gisborne (1758–1846) in 1797:

> The science of legislation, of jurisprudence, of political economy; the conduct of government in all its executive functions; the abstruse researches of erudition [...] the knowledge indispensable in the wide field of commercial enterprise [...] these, and other studies, pursuits, and occupations, assigned chiefly or entirely to men, demand the efforts of a mind endued with the powers of close and comprehensive reasoning, and of intense and continued application.

Females, by contrast, possessed 'powers adapted to unbend the brow of the learned, to refresh the over-laboured faculties of the wise, and to diffuse, throughout the family circle, the enlivening and endearing smile of cheerfulness'.[40] In a sexual context this distinction recast men as naturally active, even predatory, and women as passive.[41]

This active and outward-looking masculinity and supportive femininity appear to corroborate Jürgen Habermas's concept of public and private spheres. Habermas describes how the needs of the emerging eighteenth-century capitalist economy opened up a political space, the 'public sphere', between the institutions of the state and the private sphere of the home, in which bourgeois private individuals came together to exchange information and engage in debate in ways that checked government activity. This space comprised the concrete – coffeehouses, taverns, clubs and assemblies – and print media.[42]

Although Habermas does not address gender directly, historians often associate the new public sphere almost exclusively with men, who 'straddled the public/private divide', and locate middling-sort women in the private sphere.[43] For over 20 years the seminal work in this field has been Davidoff and Hall's *Family Fortunes*. Their detailed empirical study of families and individuals in Birmingham and Essex deconstructs how class and gender operated together at a time of rapid economic, political and social change (1780–1850) to produce and articulate a nineteenth-century middle-class masculine public sphere of the market, workplace and political life and feminine private sphere of the home. They uncover the scale of the hidden contribution, written out of contemporary discourse, that women nonetheless made to men's public success through capital and contacts brought to a marriage and unpaid work in the household and business enterprise.[44] Looking forward to Victorian England, John Tosh also identifies a distinctly middle-class masculinity established through mastery within the three arenas of the private home, the public workplace and the male club or society.[45]

The concept of gendered separate spheres cannot be applied too strictly or crudely, however. Amanda Vickery cautions against a rigid interpretation of the exclusion of women from public life and reveals the intense longing of Georgian men for the comforts of domesticity.[46] Benjamin Heller uses daily diary entries of 45 propertied men and women to confirm the importance of the home as the prime location of social interaction for both sexes.[47] Heather Ellis points out the importance at early-nineteenth-century Oxford University of 'manliness' as a strand of hegemonic masculinity that derived its force not from the binary distinction between men and women but from distinctions of age: between boys and morally and intellectually mature men.[48]

Nevertheless, public and private spheres remain a useful way of capturing the longer term 'loose division of responsibilities between men and women'.[49] Habermas specifically noted the *Gentleman's Magazine* as a constituent of the British public sphere.[50] In *Family Fortunes*, Davidoff and Hall place the weight of their evidence for change in nineteenth-century sources, despite a starting point of 1780. The time period of this study permits a reconsideration of the roots of their argument for change.

2
The History of the *Gentleman's Magazine*, 1731 to 1815

Launch

The first, January, number of a new monthly periodical, *The Gentleman's Magazine, or, Trader's Monthly Intelligencer* was published in early February 1731. It was advertised in the London press and was to be sold by booksellers in London and the country, or sent direct to any address.[1] No periodical before this had called itself a 'magazine', so Edward Cave explained its purpose. It was an 'Abridgement' that gave:

> Monthly a View of all the pieces of Wit, Humour, or Intelligence, daily offer'd to the Publick in the News-papers, (which are of late so multiply'd as to render it impossible, unless a man makes it a business, to consult them all) and in the next place we shall join therewith some other matters of Use or Amusement that will be communicated to us.

He claimed that in the welter of print (over 200 London half-sheets per month and as many again in Britain's provincial towns) *'things deserving Attention'* were seen only *'by Accident'* before being thrown away. The *Gentleman's Magazine* would therefore be *'a Monthly Collection, to treasure up as in a* Magazine, *the most remarkable Pieces'* from this vast mass of material as a means of preserving them *'for universal Benefit and Information'*. It would be published more promptly than other monthlies and, at sixpence for 48 octavo pages, would offer better value than rival titles (typically twopence for a four-page quarto weekly newspaper).[2]

Both claims proved fair. The magazine always appeared within a week of the month's end.[3] It was closely-printed with two columns to a page in rather cramped typeface and generally, unlike most other periodicals and newspapers, did not carry advertisements inside, but only on the cheaper blue paper of the outer wrapper standard to unbound books of the period.[4] It was therefore genuinely denser in material than its competitors.

January 1731 opened with a title page summarizing the contents, naming 'Sylvanus Urban of Aldermanbury Gent.' as editor, and proclaiming his motto of *'prodesse et delectare'*: 'to be useful and to entertain'. The body of the magazine began with 'Weekly Essays' lifted from ten publications and accounting for 17 pages, a third of the total.[5] They were followed by four pages of 'Poetical Essays' (several again taken from elsewhere).

The 'back half' of the magazine was more factual in content. In the first number, 'The Monthly Intelligencer' contained nine pages of domestic news (from the Court, of crime, bad weather, an aristocratic duel, an archaeological find, supposed witchcraft in Pennsylvania, an Edinburgh ghost story from 1728, casualties and shipping). There were four pages of deaths, marriages and promotions (government, military, civil and ecclesiastical), a page of financial information (exchange rates and prices for stocks and commodities), the monthly Bill of Mortality for the City of London, two pages of 'Foreign Advices' (European news), a page of gardening tips, a list of bankrupts and two pages of January's new books and pamphlets. At the end of the year a supplement was issued containing an index to 'the principal subjects' of the 12 continuously-paginated monthly numbers, so that readers could take them to a book binder where, wrappers discarded, they could be made up into a durable volume. From 1732 the Supplement also contained a preface for the annual volume and often a pictorial frontispiece, typically in a classical style reminiscent of those found in encyclopaedias.

There was nothing new about these contents, standard fare in various types of journal for some time. 'Urban' frankly admitted the lifting from other publications. It was common practice at the time but nonetheless led the editor of the *Craftsman* to describe the *Gentleman's Magazine* as 'falsly [*sic*] so called'.[6] What 'Urban' had done was create a new formula for the presentation of this material as a miscellaneous collection for information, entertainment and reference. It was an instant success. From March 1731 the first number was already being reprinted, and reprints of other numbers were issued throughout the year.[7] By September 1731 the wrapper and title page carried what became the familiar woodcut of St John's Gate, Clerkenwell, where it was produced and printed.[8] The image was so familiar to American loyalist refugee Samuel Curwen that it was one of the first London sights he and a friend visited in 1775 and 'thought a just view'.[9]

The magazine spawned many imitators, but saw off both some exist-ing titles – the *Grub Street Journal*, which had commenced publication in January 1730, blamed its demise in December 1737 on 'the rise and progress of the *Gentleman's Magazine*' – and many of the newcomers, including in June 1785 its chief longer-term rival, the *London Magazine*.[10] Remaining successful against this competition over the long period cov-ered by this study – two or three generations of readers – required that the *Gentleman's Magazine* keep enough of its original format to ensure comforting familiarity, while altering in subtle ways that met the readership's changing needs and aspirations.

The obvious changes were relatively minor. A time-traveller from 1731 to 1815 or *vice versa* would have had no problem recognizing the product and its format. In particular, the external appearance and arrangement of material were the same in 1815 as in 1731. The edito-rial *persona* of 'Sylvanus Urban' survived the deaths of the founder and his successors, and the title-page woodcut of St John's Gate was retained when the operation moved elsewhere. Despite the higher production values of its main competitor, the *London Magazine*, the *Gentleman's Magazine* stubbornly persisted with its inelegant typesetting and layout. An exception was made in response to complaints about 'the smallness of the letter', when from 1778 it introduced 'a new and larger type for the contributions of our Correspondents'.[11]

A touch of luxury was, however, added by illustrations, a relative novelty in an age of 'image hunger', before the technology for mass reproduction of pictures.[12] The first was in March 1733, a small woodcut of condemned murderer Sarah Malcolm under 'Domestick Occurrences', adjacent to the report of her execution.[13] Woodcuts and plates, as fron-tispieces, to illustrate news stories and engraved from readers' sketches accompanying their letters, became a common feature. Especially popu-lar were maps. These had an explicitly educative purpose encompassing patriotism, military adventure and commerce:

> [...] that point out, e'en to Hovels and Sties,
> Where Battles are fought, that make Stocks fall or rise.[14]

In the 1750s some illustrations were even colour-washed, such as the plate of a coach-whip snake facing page eight in January 1755.[15]

In October 1737 music accompanied the words of a song, 'The Charmer'.[16] Again this was not an original idea (the late-seventeenth-century *Gentleman's Journal* contained music). It too proved popular with readers. In the November 1737 number was both a letter from

'Philalethes', 'a Lover of Musick' who had indeed been 'charm'd', and a further song.[17] Music, occasionally notated for dancing by several couples, was published throughout the period of this study, the last example being Swiss folk tune, 'Rans de Vach', submitted in February 1812 in reply to another reader's enquiry by self-educated naturalist and poet John Dovaston of Shropshire (1782–1854).[18]

Throughout the study period the magazine consisted of the front and back halves. Readers thought of it in this way.[19] The back half (where gardening tips were quietly dropped after a year) continued its coverage of domestic and foreign news, births, marriages and deaths (arranged chronologically), appointments and lists of factual information such as stock prices, books published and plays performed. This provided a reassuring backdrop to a reshaping of the front-half. Here original articles (including the not-strictly-legal parliamentary debates in the 1730s and 1740s) gradually replaced the 'Weekly Essays'. These were, in turn, supplemented by readers' contributions and correspondence, often written under pseudonyms or initials.[20] The opening article for January 1739 noted this change: 'I observe that the Extracts from the weekly Journalists, which made so large a part in your first Pamphlets, have, by a gradual Diminution, shrunk at length into a very few Columns, and made way for original Letters and Dissertations'.[21]

Again, other newspapers and periodicals had for some time contained reader correspondence. The 'Advertisement' in the first number had anticipated that the *Gentleman's Magazine* would be no different: 'any Pieces of Wit or entertainment proper to be inserted' could be delivered to St John's Gate. The point of difference was the significance of the correspondence, both in terms of the percentage of the pages it occupied and its importance to the readers. As early as January 1736 there was enough of this material for a section headed 'Dissertations, *and* Letters *to the* Author *from Correspondents*'. Nine issues of *Miscellaneous Correspondence,* containing items for which there had not been space in the magazine and generally also priced at sixpence, were published between 1742 and 1748.[22] Readers in the 1740s were also enthusiastic posers and solvers of mathematical problems and between 1745 and 1755 Cave produced a further, quarterly, spin-off: *Miscellanea Curiosa Mathematica.*[23]

By around 1750, readers' contributions dominated the front-half and the magazine, accounting for around half of each number, although the format remained flexible enough to allow excerpted material when the occasion arose (for example during the Wilkes and American Stamp

Act crises of the 1760s). In January 1783 the number of pages and price were doubled (to *c.* 96 and one shilling), apparently without complaint. In fact, the 1786 Preface claimed a 'very great Increase of Sale since the Enlargement of their Volumes'.[24] The primary importance of readers' contributions was signalled in January 1784 by moving the parliamentary reporting (dropped in 1747 after House of Lords action over reporting of the trial of Lord Lovat, but reintroduced in the magazine and other papers in 1770 at the time of Wilkes' freedom of the press case) from an opening item to somewhere near the end of the letters or after the poetry. It settled in the latter position in January 1802.[25]

Poetry remained a constant front-half feature. Again, it was a characteristic distinguishing the *Gentleman's Magazine* from its early rivals that an increasing proportion of this came from readers' own pens. This was deliberately stimulated by a series of seven prize competitions between 1733 and 1739.[26] Finally, although there had always been a list of new publications, some with editorial comment, a book review section was added in 1765. Qualitative book reviews, some including long extracts, typically took up eight to ten pages of the magazine. This was the only change described here made in direct response to competition. Two periodicals in which book reviews formed a major part of the content were launched during the 1740s and 1750s: the *Monthly* (1749) and *Critical Reviews* (1756). It proved a wise move. Each was a long-term and significant rival as the *Monthly's* high sales of 5,000 in 1797 to the *Gentleman's Magazine's* 4,550 demonstrate.[27]

In addition to continuity of form and content, there was an overall tone to the magazine which prevailed throughout the period of this study. The aim of entertaining, often supplied by excerpts from the *Universal Spectator* in the early years, was not entirely forgotten. In the back half some of the births, marriages and deaths were probably included for their comedy potential or curiosity value, such as two 1737 announcements: 'A Woman at *Banagher King's County, Ireland,* – of two Children in her 59th Year; and 20 from her last Child bearing' and the marriage of octogenarian Jane Johnson to a 19-year-old fourth husband.[28] In the 'front half' some of the poetry was light and humorous: odes to love, epigrams and riddles in the early decades, and the 'Parodies of Shakespeare' series of 1792–1805 by 'Master Shallow' (Revd Thomas Ford), for example.[29]

Nevertheless, the magazine as a whole had a solemn, earnest feel to it. The ugly typography was perhaps a conscious contribution to this, representing a triumph of content over appearance: 'a badge of its fundamental sobriety and practicality'.[30] Cave had, of course, projected his magazine as a journal of record where 'things deserving Attention' were 'preserved for universal Benefit and Information'. 53 years later, the 1784 Preface declared that: 'The part which is interesting to all, and it may be presumed is read by all, is, respecting the transactions of the times'. And the 'transactions of the times' certainly made for sobering reading: wars, horrible crimes, devastating fires and other catastrophes.

In furtherance of 'usefulness', the magazine deliberately eschewed the serialized fiction, scandal and gossip of the town that formed the mainstay of some mid-century competitors. The *Town and Country Magazine* was the most successful of these fiction-and-gossip periodicals. Published from 1769 to 1795, it took readers from both *London* and *Gentleman's Magazines*, selling an alleged 11,000 copies in 1770, 14,000 in 1772 and 20,000 in the 1780s (a more realistic estimate is 2,000 to 3,000 sold per month with double this number of readers). A particularly distinctive and regular feature was its 'Tête à Têtes', 'histories' of society love affairs under paired miniature oval portraits of the couple discussed. After initial resistance, both the *Universal* (1747–1815) and *London Magazines* carried serialized fiction from the 1760s and the *London* paid more attention to novels in its 'Register of Books' than did the *Gentleman's Magazine*.[31] At the risk of losing readers, the *Gentleman's* refused to concede. To those who objected that it contained: 'little or none of that fine sprightly kind of composition calculated to fill time, and furnish fashionable conversation; none of those select novels, love-stories those brilliant sallies of wit and humour, that captivate the young, and delight the gay', the 1784 Preface replied that they should turn elsewhere: 'We must observe, however, that persons of a certain gay way of thinking have Magazines professedly adapted to their taste; and those we are ambitious to please, know where to apply for more refined entertainment'.

An important aspect of this seriousness was a professed neutral stance. 'We shall always preserve our Impartiality' stated an advertisement of 1733.[32] Unlike other editors, 'Sylvanus Urban' neither participated overtly in magazine debates nor answered readers' queries directly. This was in marked contrast to the seventeenth-century *Athenian Mercury*, and *Tatler* and *Spectator*.[33] He was instead a master of ceremonies, coordinating and facilitating readers' questions, answers and expressions of opinion, and sometimes declaring a subject closed. When abridgements from other publications formed the bulk of the front half, the magazine presented each side of a case in roughly equal measure and without editorial comment, a policy aimed at maximizing long-term circulation.[34] Later editors were not even afraid of reader-led debates that were critical of the magazine or those involved with it, such as Anna Seward's critique of Samuel Johnson's character after his death in 1784.[35] Closely linked to the claim of impartiality was a repudiation of corruption ('The invariable rule of this Magazine is, never to receive a bribe for what is either inserted or omitted') and the avoidance of unpleasantness or excessive contention in the style of contributions ('We detest personal abuse' and 'we shall never, with our Eyes open; admit papers written with Anger or Animosity').[36] This was the chief stated reason for excluding material: all submissions were '*intended* to be used' eventually, except that 'in all cases where articles are *wholly improper*, we regularly point them out'.[37]

Editors, owners and writers

Although this study focusses on the agency of the readership of the *Gentleman's Magazine* in constructing gentlemanliness, it is important to consider issues of ownership and editorial direction. The editors and 'professional' writers involved in the production of the magazine were responsible for its appearance, the organization of material and article selection, even if they ceded to readers some control of the subject matter and overall tone. The following account is arranged for convenience in chronological order by editorship. All the editors in the period were first and foremost printer-publishers rather than 'journalists'. The *Gentleman's Magazine* was only one of the publications which they produced. Edward Cave, David Henry and many of those who wrote professionally for the magazine shared the experience of being migrants to London.[38] In the light of the magazine's claimed impartiality, it is also noteworthy that there was among them no dominant religious or political affiliation.

Edward Cave (1731–54)

The founder and first 'Sylvanus Urban' was Edward Cave. The chief account of his life, on which all others draw, is Samuel Johnson's four-page biography, published in the magazine immediately after Cave's death in 1754.[39] This is supplemented by 'The Autobiography of Sylvanus Urban' which appeared over several numbers of the *Gentleman's Magazine* in 1856–7.[40] Anonymous, it is attributed to John Gough Nichols, grandson of John Nichols, part-owner of the magazine from 1778 and sole editor from 1792, and himself editor between 1850 and its sale in 1856. It was exhaustive; making considerable use of primary sources, including Cave's correspondence with Thomas Birch, and attempted to place the magazine in the context of other periodicals published both before its launch and in competition to it.[41] There are also contemporary references to the Cave era of the magazine in both Hawkins' and Boswell's *Lives* of Samuel Johnson.

Cave was originally a Midlander, born in Warwickshire in 1691. His pre-1731 career was chequered and varied. His downwardly-mobile father, Joseph, worked as a shoemaker in Rugby but was affluent enough to send his nine-year-old eldest son to Rugby School.[42] It seems that a misjudged schoolboy prank forced Cave to leave early. He was next found a position as clerk to a travelling exciseman. Tired of this, and still in his teens, he followed a well-trodden path for young people at the start of their working lives: a move to London. He was initially employed by a timber merchant on Bankside before, in 1710, being bound apprentice to the printer Alderman Mr Collins. In 1712 Collins sent him, aged only 21, to Norwich to run his operations there. These included the *Norwich Post* newspaper. Returning to London on Collins' death in 1713, Cave fell out with Widow Collins and moved to the printshop of well-known City Tory politician John Barber as a journeyman printer, undertaking for him some copywriting assignments on *Mist's Weekly Journal*, a leading anti-Whig, anti-Walpole newspaper. Little is known of Cave's own political views which were not reflected in the *Gentleman's Magazine*. Samuel Johnson thought him influenced by Barber while employed there, moving later to a moderate Whig position: 'But as interest is powerful, and conversation, however mean, in time persuasive, he by degrees inclined to another party; in which, however, he was always moderate, though steady and determined'.[43]

In 1716 Cave married a widow, Susannah Newton. He gained his freedom of the Stationers' Company in 1717 and was running his own jobbing printing house by the 1720s. In 1721 he obtained, through Susannah's contacts, a salaried position in the Lombard Street sorting office of the General Post Office. In 1723 he was promoted to Inspector of Franks (franks were a much-abused statutory privilege, whereby Members of Parliament and other government officials sent mail free of charge). Through his Post Office surveillance role, only resigned in 1745, he acquired a thorough understanding of the scale, nature and timing of the rising traffic of newsletters, newspapers and other unpaid correspondence and mail into and out of the capital and across the country.[44]

Cave was already exploiting his access to material that crossed his post office desk before 1731, routinely selling news stories from the provincial to the London press. In 1727 he was arraigned before the House of Commons and imprisoned for 11 days for selling reports of its proceedings to Robert Raikes' *Gloucester Journal*. Cave maintained his country links once the *Gentleman's Magazine* was established. Gloucester and Norwich were among the provincial towns on the title page, Raikes was listed as a bookseller who stocked the magazine and the *Gloucester Journal* was among the few provincial sources from which Cave took articles.[45]

Even at the height of his national fame and success as owner-editor of the *Gentleman's Magazine*, Cave was unashamed of his modest provincial background, relishing his Rugby nickname of 'Ned Cave the Cobler'.[46] In fact, it was a strength. The combination of middling-sort provincial roots and contacts, active involvement in the print trade in London and beyond, sufficient experience on the fringe of City politics to be aware of pitfalls to be negotiated in maintaining neutrality, and the Post Office position were crucial to his conception and execution of *Gentleman's Magazine* project. They enabled him to understand, capture and bind together both the London and provincial markets. His other business ventures, which were more capital-intensive and where he did not have relevant experience, were all much less successful: a luxury serial edition of Du Halde's *A Description of the Empire of China* and investments in the cotton-spinning industry, for instance.[47]

Cave composed some magazine material himself (a 'speciality' being doggerel poetry such as 'Ralph Rhymer's Chronicle', a rhyming version of the domestic news for December 1735 'Inserted for Variety sake, and to divert the Reader at this Season').[48] He also relied on the new breed of professional writers to supply copy, especially from the late 1730s when press excerpts were reducing. Some were already established in the literary world, others at the start of their careers, but none wrote under a by-line.

William Guthrie (*c.* 1708–70) composed the parliamentary debates in the 1730s. He was responsible in 1739 for introducing the 'Senate of Lilliput' conceit to circumvent the April 1738 House of Commons resolution enforcing the standing order prohibiting the printing or publishing of parliamentary proceedings.[49] The son of a Scottish Episcopalian clergyman, work on the *Gentleman's Magazine* was among Guthrie's early literary forays after moving to London in around 1730. On leaving the magazine in 1740 he became better-known as a journalist ('Jeffrey Broadbottom' in the Whig *Old England*) and historian. His Whig views may not have been especially firm, however. Although Pelham rewarded him with a government pension of £200 *per annum* in 1745, this was renewed under Lord Bute's Tory administration in 1762.

On Guthrie's departure, Samuel Johnson (1709–84) took over the parliamentary reporting. His first known contact with Cave was a letter dated 25 November 1734, sent when he was an unemployed 25-year-old

in Birmingham. Already a reader of the magazine, he offered 'on reasonable terms, sometimes to fill a column'.[50] Johnson also placed an
advertisement in the June 1736 magazine for his school in Edial,
Staffordshire (which failed for lack of pupils the following January).[51]
His first published piece was a Latin poem 'Ad Urbanum' by 'S.J.' in
March 1738, followed in November by a short life of Father Paolo
Sarpi.[52] From this point he seems to have worked regularly and intensively for Cave, probably unsalaried, as an editorial assistant, poet and
writer, most famously of the 'Debates in the Senate of Lilliput' which
he composed from 1740 to 1743 (ceasing when offered more lucrative
work by bookseller Thomas Osborne, editing the Harley Collection catalogue). A stout defender of tradition, Johnson is often regarded as a
Tory. Any trenchant views did not, however, disturb the *Gentleman's
Magazine*'s impartiality.[53]

Johnson continued to contribute, assist with and influence the
magazine after 1743, but on a reduced basis.[54] Members of Cave's
and Johnson's literary circle, men such as John Hawkesworth, Sir
John Hawkins and Richard Savage, also wrote for the magazine.[55]
Hawkesworth (1720–73) was born in Tottenham to a dissenting watch-
engraver-turned-French-teacher, but baptized in the Church of England.
He contributed poetic fables from 1741 and assumed several of
Johnson's tasks on the magazine, including the parliamentary debates,
from the mid-1740s. James Beattie heard that the magazine was his chief
means of support before the launch of the *Adventurer* in 1752, he having
'sole management wt. a salary of £100 pr. Ann'.[56] Hawkins (1719–89),
lawyer and musical scholar, was also a Londoner, probably of humble origins (although he liked to claim descent from the Elizabethan
admiral). He contributed articles from March 1739. Savage (1698–1743)
contributed poetry. Other contemporary poets whose verses appeared
regularly in the magazine and could be considered among its circle
included Mark Akenside (1721–70), Thomas Beach (d. 1737), Moses
Browne (1704–87) who swept the board in the poetry contests, and,
a key distinction between poetical and journalist contributors, several
women: Jane Brereton (1685–1740), Elizabeth Carter (1717–1806) and
Elizabeth Rowe (1674–1737). These poets shared Cave's provincial, trading background: Akenside was a butcher's son from Newcastle, Beach
a Denbighshire wine merchant, Browne was originally from Worcester
and worked in Clerkenwell as a pen-cutter before ordination in the
Church of England in his late forties, Brereton was from Flintshire,
Carter from Kent, and Rowe, Somerset. Their religious backgrounds
were also varied. Both Rowe and Akenside were from non-conformist

families. Akenside had initially studied at Edinburgh University with the intention of entering the ministry, switching instead to medicine.

There is little surviving information on the production side of the magazine from this Cave era. Apart from scattered correspondence to him as editor and the occasional note from him, no archive survives.[57] Cave seems initially to have been assisted by printer Jacob Ilive (1705–63).[58] By 1736 the two men had fallen out, possibly because Ilive's activities as a radical religious lecturer and polemicist, deist writer did not sit well with the magazine's policy of stately neutrality. Ilive started his own publication with a title designed to confuse: *The Gentleman's Magazine and Monthly Oracle*.[59] The vicious knocking-copy of an advertisement for his ninth number indicates how far their relationship had deteriorated.[60] Ilive claimed he had been editing the *Gentleman's Magazine* almost single-handed but with constant interference from Cave who had a 'capricious and whimsical Temper'. He painted a picture of an exhausting, highly pressurized working environment, especially towards the end of the month as the publication deadline loomed, when he sat up all night for '30, 40 and 50 hours on a Stretch, without Rest or Sleep'.[61]

It was of course one of Cave's selling points that his magazine always appeared in the shops just a few days after the month ended. The 1735 Preface opened with 'Mrs. Urban's Lecture', a comic poem complaining of the demands the hectic schedule made on the Cave household in the Gate: papers everywhere so that the place looked 'like a jakes', Cave late for meals and then eating 'with a paper in your hand' and only turning in for the night once fire and candle had both gone out.[62] The Gate was also a focal point for readers who dropped by in person, or where they sent interesting items (a preserved fish skin in 1753 and in 1755, a year after Cave's death, a piece of human leg-bone removed during surgery, for example) for engraving and so that other callers could take a look.[63] On several occasions 'Urban' apologized to readers for mislaying their letters and poetry. To the extent that this was true rather than a tactful excuse for non-publication, it adds to a suspicion that a chaotic office and poor record-keeping contributed to the lack of a business archive.[64]

Richard Cave (1754–66) and David Henry (1754–92)

Cave had more lasting success with assistants drawn from his family, perhaps unsurprisingly: they stood to benefit from the growth in the value of the magazine.[65] By 1731 he had a journeyman David Henry (1709–92) who, like himself, had migrated to London (in his case from Scotland) and entered the printing trade. In 1736 Henry married Cave's sister, Mary, and the couple moved to Reading where he founded a printing house and the *Reading Journal and Weekly Review*. On Edward Cave's death on 10 January 1754, Henry inherited a half share in the magazine with Cave's nephew Richard Cave (also a printer but of whom little else is known) and the St John's Gate property. The total estate was worth almost £9,000 and the *Gentleman's Magazine* some £3,000.[66] In 1755 a small outside interest was introduced with the sale of a one-twelfth share to fellow publisher Benjamin Collins of Salisbury (1715–85) for £333 6s 8d.

Henry and Richard Cave were joint proprietor-editors until Richard's death on 8 September 1766, both names appearing on the annual title pages. Neither man has left a trace of his political opinions, but in the 1755 Preface they pondered the general future direction of their magazine in seven humorous 'letters to the editor' each requesting more of some features and less of others. They concluded that that the magazine provided something for every taste and so 'the present plan ought to be pursued without the least alteration'. The 'plan' appears to have been put into action. Their most significant changes were the further reduction in press extracts and increased space given to readers' original contributions, and the creation of the book review section, with Owen Ruffhead (*c.* 1723–69, chiefly noted as a legal writer but who also penned political pamphlets against Bute in 1763, and against Wilkes and in support of the government in 1769) and Hawkesworth as early reviewers.

Johnson and Hawkins continued their association with the magazine. Others on the London literary circuit regularly involved were Sir John Hill (1714–75, a Cambridgeshire-born physician and actor with an interest in science who, like Guthrie and Johnson, benefitted from Bute's patronage); an Ephraim Chambers (perhaps a misprint as the encyclopaedist had died in 1740); Christopher Smart (1722–71, Fellow of Pembroke College, Cambridge, poet and reprobate); Dr Robert James (1703–76, Johnson's school-friend from Lichfield, fashionable physician and inventor of the best-selling 'James's Fever Powders') and his friend John Newbery (1713–67, publisher/bookseller and retailer of patent medicines, including the Powders, father-in-law of Smart, and a Reading contemporary of Henry's). Newbery at some stage acquired Collins' stake in the magazine.[67]

After Richard Cave's death, Henry remained the owner of St John's Gate and an active editor and contributor. He made no major changes to the magazine but saw the retirement of Hawkesworth and his replacement as book reviewer by Revd John Duncombe (1729–86), and the first contribution (as 'D.H.', the last letters of his names) from antiquary

Richard Gough (1735–1809).[68] Gough was from a more socially-elevated family than most of the magazine's writers. His father, Sir Harry, was a merchant and Member of Parliament for the rotten borough of Bramber, Sussex, and his mother's family were wealthy dissenting London brewers. He remained closely involved with the magazine for many years, in 1786 replacing Duncombe as reviewer and contributing as 'D.H.', 'H.D.', 'P.Q.' and 'Q'.

During 1767 Henry retired from the production side of the magazine and moved to Kent. The July 1767 title page indicates that Francis Newbery, nephew and successor to the printing business of John (who died later that year in December) now oversaw sales. Francis' widow Elizabeth published the magazine from his death in 1780 until 1800 when bookseller John Harris acquired her business.[69] Printing still took place at St John's Gate under a J. Lister and from 1771 to 1778 by David Bond who paid Lister £520 for the lease of the printing house from Henry.[70] Bond was responsible for the magazine and covers and 'Miss Cave' (probably Richard's daughter Mary) for the folding and stitching.[71] She had presumably inherited her father's share of the business, because in 1778 she sold out to John Nichols. At the same time, the printing was moved from the Gate (now dangerously dilapidated) and from October 1778 was shared equally (three half-sheets each) between Bond at Union Buildings, Leather Lane and Nichols at his printing house in Red Lion Passage, Holborn where he also undertook the folding and stitching.

In late 1780 this arrangement broke down in acrimony. Moving wet sheets between the two sites was inconvenient, but there were also allegations that Bond was slipshod in meeting the tight end-of-the-month deadlines.[72] In December 1780 Nichols, possibly without notice (but with the agreement of Henry), took control of all the printing, both cover and pages. For the rest of the period of this study the magazine was printed at Red Lion Passage. The concrete link with St John's Gate was broken, but the Gate itself remained an important part of the branding of the magazine, continuing to appear on the wrapper and title page each month.[73]

John Nichols (1778–1826)

John Nichols (1745–1826) was the magazine's first non-provincial proprietor-editor. Like his predecessors he came from a printing rather than writing or journalistic background. A baker's son from Islington, where he was also educated (at John Shield's academy), in 1759 he was bound apprentice to non-juring printer William Bowyer (1699–1777), owner of one of the largest printing houses in London. His advancement was rapid: made a freeman of the Stationers' Company in March 1766, taken into partnership by Bowyer a month later and owner of the business on Bowyer's death. Nichols, who had many other interests including City and Stationers' Company politics, devoted a great deal of energy to the *Gentleman's Magazine*, working alongside Henry until 1792 when the latter handed over editorial control just before his death the same year.[74] The final handover coincided with the collapse of the French Revolutionary National Assembly, the descent into civil war and the Terror.

Like Cave, Nichols was inundated with reader contributions, especially of letters and obituaries. In 1783 he doubled the size and price to accommodate more of these and longer book reviews. Poetry still accounted for three to four pages and so shrank as a proportion of the whole. In 1785 the excess of reader submissions over space was further tackled by the device of the 'Index Indicatorius': a brief account of articles received for which there was no room. This too became a regular feature. The price rose again in 1799 (to 18d) and 1809 (to two shillings), a result this time of outside forces: war-time increases in paper duty.[75] In 1813 the colour of the wrapper was changed from blue to buff to render it more legible.[76]

Bowyer had encouraged Nichols' interest in literature, antiquities and biography. In 1765, as 'J.N.', he submitted a poem, 'Spring', to the *Gentleman's Magazine* and as its editor remained a frequent contributor under various pseudonyms including 'M. Green' and 'Eusebia'.[77] His interests were reflected in the contacts he brought to the magazine and some redirection of its contents towards these subjects (already popular with correspondents). In September 1784 an anonymous correspondent with enthusiasms suspiciously similar to Nichols' own, proposed that the *Gentleman's Magazine* should devote a section specifically to a 'register or repertory' of antiquarian and topographical findings.[78] In the annual Preface Nichols drew attention to the letter, declaring his readiness to give 'free admission to such facts'.

The 1788 Preface discussed the obituaries. The number of births, marriages and deaths had all risen, but there were now many long obituaries, such that deaths often accounted for around ten pages, ten per cent of the magazine. They became a feature for which it was especially renowned, with Nichols 'professing to make our Miscellany a Record of Obits' in which 'most, if not all of them [i.e. the readers], will find [...] some individual recorded in whom they may have an interest'.[79] The extent to which they were widely accepted as authoritative memorials is indicated by an 1804 poet, who regarded a deceased friend as 'Embalm'd in URBAN's soul-researching page', and by the monumental inscription to Viscountess Downe, erected by her son in the North Quire Aisle of York Minster, which suggests to the more curious passer-by, 'For her character and other particulars see the *Gentleman's Magazine* for May MDCCCXII, from which the following is an extract'. A full-length print memorial was of course cheaper than stone.[80]

Obituaries were still taken from other papers (sometimes noted as such) and Nichols himself was the author of many, but, as with the front-half material, they were increasingly submitted by readers.[81] Some were presented and received as didactic, what 'Cultivator' called 'the real characters of men who have lived with utility to the publick, and honour to themselves', which 'stimulate[d] the rising generation to the pursuit of Virtue'.[82] Others tended to the embarrassingly 'rhapsodical' or 'panegyric'.[83] As a result they drew criticism and mockery from some literary quarters. 'Peter Pindar's' satirical poem addressed to Nichols pictured the dying begging to be spared a *Gentleman's Magazine* obituary:

> 'Oh save us from John Nichols!' is their cry:
> 'Let not that Death-hunter know where we lie'.[84]

On the other hand, some were noted for their frankness, at times amounting to 'lives villainous'.[85] These had shock value. Sometimes the subject was a stereotype plebeian. Beggarly hoarders and drunken sots were perennial favourites from the magazine's launch.[86] Others contained a moral warning, such as that of attorney Peter Defaile, 'one of the worst men that ever became the scourge of private life', whose every iniquity filled half a page in January 1783.[87]

In addition to writing *Gentleman's Magazine* articles and obituaries, Nichols was a published author on his favourite subjects. His first work was *The Buds of Parnassus: A Collection of Original Poems* (London, 1763). He continued to write throughout his life, notable examples being *Anecdotes Biographical and Literary of W. Bowyer, Printer* (London, 1778); *Biographical Anecdotes of Mr Hogarth, and a Catalogue of his Works, with Occasional Remarks* (London, 1781), and *The History and Antiquities of the County of Leicester* (London, 1780–90). He also documented the *Gentleman's Magazine*. In addition to the 'Prefatory Introduction' to the 1821 *General Index*, his *Literary Anecdotes of the Eighteenth Century* contained entries for Cave, Henry and his contributors and his correspondents.

Nichols' record-keeping was more meticulous than that of previous owners and editors and, although much of his stock and papers was destroyed in a fire at the Red Lion Passage printworks on the night of

8 February 1808, the Folger Library, Washington DC, holds a run of 213 editorial volumes of the magazine from 1731 to 1863 originating with Nichols and Gough.[88] These comprise a 'working file', inevitably primarily from the Nichols years, containing manuscript annotations and, tipped-in, associated documents, such as wrappers, letters, art work and inserted advertisements.[89]

Epilogue

Nichols remained editor until his death in 1826. His son John Bowyer Nichols (1779–1863), who had worked in the family business as a partner since 1800, supervizing the rebuilding work after the 1808 fire and the move of the printing works to Westminster, succeeded him. He purchased the Cave/Henry family stake in the magazine in 1833 but in 1834 transferred a share to publisher William Pickering. A new series of the magazine was begun under an editorial team that did not include Nichols, although the family retained ultimate control. In 1850 John Bowyer bought back the Pickering share and his son John Gough Nichols (1806–73) was editor until the magazine, by now of declining significance, was sold in 1856 to J.H. Parker of Oxford 'for a nominal sum'. It passed through the ownership of Bradbury & Evans (1865–8) and Chatto & Windus (from 1868) and ceased publication in September 1907.[90]

The historiography of the *Gentleman's Magazine*

Most works on the eighteenth-century British press and book market mention the *Gentleman's Magazine* in passing.[91] As a highly accessible, indexed (and now searchable digital) source, with contents ranging across a huge variety of subjects, it is routinely mined by historians, appearing in the bibliographies and indexes of many general works on the period.[92] Roy Porter's *English Society in the Eighteenth Century* contains ten index references to *Gentleman's Magazine* articles on parliamentary reporting, violence, humanity, print culture and drunkenness. Elsewhere it has been cited to support arguments about duelling, suicide and sexuality.[93] It is potentially a social history source book for the period as Emily de Montluzin's *Daily Life in Georgian England as Reported in the Gentleman's Magazine* recognizes.

Works on the *Gentleman's Magazine* itself, however, are in most cases rather historic themselves. All but one (Anthony Barker's unpublished 1981 Oxford thesis) have emerged from universities outside Britain, reflecting the ready availability of full runs in academic libraries around the world. They are limited in chronological scope and can be divided into two main categories. Scholars of literature explore the contributions of Samuel Johnson and others and review the quality of the poetry, literary and theatre criticism, often in tandem with an attempt to unlock the secrets of the pseudonyms to identify works by those who subsequently became canonical.[94] For example, despite arguing that poems printed in the magazine between 1731 and 1780 form a coherent body of generally freshly-published work representing contemporary popular taste, Calvin Yost excludes those forms he considered 'low' (*bouts-rimés*, graffiti and short epitaphs) and so skews his analysis towards the more elevated compositions (which he finds neo-classical with no early indications of romanticism).[95] He is unable to resist the temptation to compare the magazine's poets to the canon, dismissing them as imitative, showing 'a restriction of poetic inspiration, a definite loss of individualism both in invention and in execution'.[96] He therefore fails to capture fully the widespread eighteenth-century pleasure in and facility for versifying.

James Kuist's 1965 thesis reviews literary criticism submitted by *Gentleman's Magazine* readers over a longer time span (1731–1800).[97] Unlike Yost, he sets this more firmly within the context of the magazine's owners, editors and development, concluding that by 1800 the magazine was less concerned with contemporary affairs and more, scholarly.[98] Attending to the two-way relationship between readers/contributors and 'Sylvanus Urban', Kuist concludes, more optimistically than Yost, that contributors on literary subjects were 'highly literate and well-read [...] able to draw wide comparisons' and motivated above all by the 'spirit of discussion': keenest and most vigorous when writing in response to the views of other readers.[99]

Historians, on the other hand, largely concentrate on the agency of owners, editors and professional writers in the development of both the periodical and their later careers. Their studies are all restricted to the Edward Cave period. They tend to search for precedents for Cave's new venture and, in common with literary scholars, make much of what was, in the scheme of things, the relatively brief involvement of Samuel Johnson before he was a 'famous name'.

The history of the magazine under Cave is the subject of literary historian C. Lennart Carlson's *First Magazine*. Carlson adds to biographical knowledge of Cave with original research in the London General Post Office archives. He dates Cave's office-holding there more accurately than Johnson's obituary and illuminates the way in which experience of news-gathering and dissemination by the postal service assisted the magazine enterprise, especially in reaching provincial readers effectively.[100] His search for antecedents of Cave's 'magazine'

concept in the seventeenth- and early-eighteenth-century press identifies it as a fusion of two traditions: the elite-orientated literary periodical
aiming to entertain (such as Motteux' *Gentleman's Journal*) and the more
informative historical miscellany or compilation of facts directed at the
'new bourgeoisie' as a work of reference (Henry Rhodes' *Present State
of Europe*, monthly 1692 to *c*.1736; Samuel Buckley's *Monthly Register*,
1703–7; Abel Boyer's *Political State of Great Britain*, monthly 1711–40;
Isaac Kimber's *Monthly Chronicle*, 1728–32 and the *Grub Street Journal*).[101]

While it is important to recognize that the *Gentleman's Magazine* was
far from original – a certain familiarity was indeed probably among
the reasons for its rapid acceptance – it is surely its long-term success
and influence that is more historically significant. In the event Carlson
begs more questions than he answers, some of which this book tackles.
Although he concludes that key features in its success were flexibility,
responsiveness to the readership and the avoidance of political partiality, he does not define or explore that readership and its relationship
with the magazine. He is content to assert that the magazine was 'significant' in the 'liberation of middle-class England': stolid and uncritical of
social issues yet part of a national 'democratic movement' (rather than
'aristocratic sentiment') that accustomed the public to expect news that
was accurate, consistent and broadened their intellectual horizons.[102]

Albert Pailler and Titia Ram elaborate on Carlson's Cave era.[103] Pailler
rightly suggests that the roots of the magazine are less important than
what Cave did with established formats. He provides evidence supporting Carlson's conclusions on flexibility, responsiveness and the
contribution to a developing middling-sort self-awareness based on
cultural capital, information and personal expression.[104] Ram adds to
understanding of Cave's readership by studying the advertising aimed
at them on the surviving wrappers and the internal evidence of contents and contributors to argue that the magazine's success was owed
in large part to providing a 'national platform' for a broadly-defined
middle class: 'the modern, often provincial reader with sometimes
less than a university education and traditional ideas about culture
and literature'.[105] She recognizes that the role here of the *Gentleman's
Magazine* (and its imitators) in democratizing the reading audience is
as worthy of study as that of the novel and that conservatism and
neutrality, unattractive to Hazlitt and twentieth-century scholars, were
its strength and significance.[106]

Articles and chapters in edited volumes interrogate the *Gentleman's
Magazine* as 'the bellwether of genteel opinion'.[107] Jean Hunter reviews
material on women, their status, education and characteristics and

finds a 'startling division'. While one quarter of the articles, mainly press excerpts, supported the 'traditional' or 'conventional' eighteenth-century ideal of woman as the weaker sex relegated to the private, domestic sphere and subordinated to the needs of her husband, the majority acknowledged sympathetically the problems inequality of the sexes imposed on them: lack of educational and career opportunities, and the inherent difficulties of marriage for women as legal 'non-persons'.[108] She therefore draws attention to possible reformist tendencies in the magazine.

Roy Porter uses the *Gentleman's Magazine* to examine eighteenth-century lay and professional medical understanding.[109] He concludes that pre-nineteenth-century medical knowledge was 'integral to the public role of the well-informed, public-spirited, and responsible layman' and open: with 'no insuperable boundaries between lay and professional'.[110] In contrast to Hunter, he takes the gendered title at face value: 'it catered [...] above all, quite explicitly, only to one sex'.[111] His conclusion therefore ignores women's contributions and reading, and the part played by gender in the construction of medical understanding. De Montluzin also considers medical content in a short article on its scatological poetry, linking this ungenteel genre to a preoccupation with bodily functions and fluids resulting from popular cures such as purging.[112]

Finally, and most recently, William Stafford's two articles analyze gentlemanly masculinities and the social order depicted in the *Gentleman's Magazine*.[113] In each case, he confines himself to 1785 to 1815, prejudging these as crisis years when 'British society was profoundly affected by the French Revolution and the wars with France'.[114] He concludes that the representation in his chosen period was, probably as 'a deliberate rhetorical strategy', of a reassuringly stable society, hierarchical yet open to social mobility into the ranks of the genteel.[115] On masculinity, he identifies a preferred model, similar to Carter's, of a polite and Christian gentleman, rational, learned and self-controlled, defined as much against visible masculine variants, such as youthful irresponsibility or the rougher world of sport, gambling and rakishness, as against femininity. The model was nationalistic: sober, serious, simple, English manly style contrasted with French effeminacy.[116]

The chapters that follow therefore break new ground by placing the readers and their reading of this important periodical centre-stage and over a long timeframe that can challenge existing chronologies of crisis and change.

3
Readers and Contributors

Scholarship of the *Gentleman's Magazine* associates it with a genteel readership: variously the nobility and gentry, and the middling sort and bourgeoisie. For the latter two groups Carlson describes it as a significant, liberating and modernizing influence, part of a 'democratic movement'.[1] However, there is no detailed empirical work on the magazine's readers and contributors, and the ways in which they read it, to support these claims. This chapter examines the contemporary evidence for the *Gentleman's Magazine* readership, setting this in the wider contexts of literacy, geography, gender and reading practices.

Literacy in the eighteenth century

Eighteenth-century estimates of literacy were impressionistic. In 1790 Edmund Burke thought the reading public totalled 80,000, less than one per cent of the population.[2] Others thought the reading habit much more widespread. Samuel Johnson believed 'general literature [...] now pervades the nation through all its ranks'. In 1791 bookseller James Lackington took a similar view: 'In short, all ranks and degrees now READ' (later qualified when he found, while distributing free religious tracts, that 'some of the farmers and their children, and also three-fourths of the poor could not read').[3]

Modern scholars agree that reading was percolating down through the social hierarchy.[4] There was more to read, with growth in the number of new books published and an even more dramatic surge in newspaper titles: from 12 London titles in 1712 to 52 in 1811, and from 24 provincial titles in 1723 to 41 in 1745.[5] Formal educational provision may have stagnated in the eighteenth century (apart from the development of SPCK charity schools and, later, the Sunday school movement) but Margaret Spufford and Susan Whyman demonstrate that informal, local teaching of reading and writing to a functional level was common. A higher 'epistolary' level, the capacity to compose and receive letters between family and friends or for work purposes, was not unusual.[6] Finally, the ability to sign names in official documents such as wills, depositions and parish marriage registers indicates a rise in literacy levels to around 45 per cent of men and 25 per cent of women by the accession of George I, with a further advance by mid-century to 60 and 40 per cent (some four million people), and small additional gains before around 1840.[7] Literacy was higher across all groups (including, for example, servants) in London than in the provinces, in towns than in the countryside and in 'clean' occupations (e.g. retailing) than 'dirty' (e.g. blacksmithing). By the eighteenth century all the gentry, clergy and professionals and a very high proportion, over 90 per cent, of urban tradesmen could read and write.[8]

These people with Spufford's and Whyman's informally taught readers and letter-writers were potentially the *Gentleman's Magazine*'s market. Their participation in literate culture marked them out, for reading and writing was recognized as an important constituent of cultural and educational capital. It promoted occupational advancement and extended participation in Enlightenment modernity. In 1782, Presbyterian minister and writer Andrew Kippis (1725–95) explicitly linked this to engagement with periodical literature:

> The Magazines have opened a way for every kind of enquiry and information. The intelligence and discussion contained in them are very extensiveand various; and they have been the means of diffusing a general habit of reading through the Nation; which in a certain degree hath enlarged the public understanding.[9]

The *Gentleman's Magazine*: quantifying sales and readership

In the absence of a *Gentleman's Magazine* business archive, most estimates of the number of copies produced and sold each month have been based on editorial puffs. Edward Cave in particular enjoyed trumpeting his success, especially in the 1730s and 1740s when the magazine's reputation was building and the *London Magazine* posed serious competition. In the 1736 Preface a poem by 'Bardus' claimed that 'Ten Thousand Monthly for his Labours call'. Cave apologized in the 1746 Preface to 'country readers' who had not received their copies promptly due to 'an unexpected demand of 3,000 Magazines monthly' over the year. The increase, attributable to intense interest in the 1745 Jacobite invasion and its aftermath, resulted in the first impression selling out and an urgent reprint. In 1748 monthly sales were still 12,000:

> Still thrice four thousand shall impatient wait
> The sterling sense that's stamp'd with St John's Gate.[10]

Hawkins remarked that Cave 'increased the sale of his pamphlet from 10,000 to 15,000 copies a month' when Johnson wrote the 'Debates in the Senate of Lilliput.'[11] Boswell reported a 1778 remark by Johnson that 'Cave used to sell ten thousand of the *Gentleman's Magazine*'.[12] This level of sales, well above a typical edition size of no more than 2,000 for a non-subscription novel, is corroborated in John Byrom's journal.[13] He recorded a 1739 conversation with Dr John Hartley in which Hartley told him 'that the *Gentleman's Magazine* [...] printed 10,000 and the *London* 7,000'.[14]

A sceptical Carlson regards these figures as strategic exaggeration, but Todd's bibliographical research substantiates their credibility.[15] He calculates from Cave's stray editorial note on the guinea cost of producing each page that the 1734 monthly print run was indeed around 9,000 copies.[16] The surviving ledger of Charles Ackers, printer of the *London Magazine* from its launch in April 1732, provides edition sizes for this rival in the 1730s and 1740s. These match closely Johnson's and Byrom's estimates: beginning at 4,000 for the first seven months they climbed steadily to a peak of 8,000 in August 1739 and then fell back slightly, settling at around 7,000 per month.[17]

There is less information for the post-Cave period. 'The monthly numbers struck off we were told amount to more than 6,000', Samuel Curwen recorded in his diary after his 1775 St John's Gate visit.[18] Apart from the 1786 Preface noting the 'very great Increase of Sale' on doubling the magazine's size and price, Nichols did not mention figures in his writing on the *Gentleman's Magazine*, leaving only Timperley's 1797 figure of 4,550, a significant fall since the 1740s but still in third position, only slightly behind the two market leaders.

Monthly print runs do not tell the whole story, however. Firstly, there were frequent reprints both of monthly numbers that had sold out, as in 1746, and of the back run (such as the reprint from 1783 of each past annual volume on a monthly basis at a price, in boards, of 6s 6d).[19] Furthermore, while many, like correspondent 'Aged Matron', read each new number of the magazine as soon as it came out – 'On the arrival of the

Gentleman's Magazine, if I am reading any other book (save the book of God) I constantly close it, and opening the Magazine, instantly cast my eye over the *bill of fare*' – these numbers were not 'consumed' and finished but, especially in bound form, had a durable life. They were subject to a 'stream of acts of reading', often over several decades.[20] In 1805 Charles Fothergill (1782–1840) noted *Gentleman's Magazine* articles dating from his childhood: from 1790 (on yew trees) and 1787 (on using hedgehogs to kill black beetles in the house).[21] Correspondent Robert Bell Wheler (1785–1857, antiquary of Stratford-on-Avon) referred in an 1815 letter on busts of Shakespeare to one on the same subject published over 50 years before.[22]

Secondly, then as now, each copy of any paper or periodical was usually read by many more people than the original purchaser. Earlier in the century, Addison thought a multiple of 20 readers per copy sold reasonable for the *Spectator*.[23] Cave's claim, in the 1751 Preface, to have 'the pleasure of entertaining at least 50,000 readers', five readers per copy, is therefore entirely plausible.[24] There were multiple readers in inns, taverns, coffeehouses and barbers' shops where newspapers and periodicals, including the *Gentleman's Magazine*, were available for customers to read as they drank or waited to be shaved.[25] Correspondents sometimes used a coffeehouse address. 'F.Y.' wrote from Garraway's and Antony Sinnot from the Exchequer and the Chapter.[26] Fothergill read the yew tree article at the Cross Keys Inn, Middleton, Teesdale. In Cambridge, 'A Cantab.' (Revd Weeden Butler jun., author, 1772–1831) 'often read your excellent magazine in the Master of Arts coffeehouse'.[27] Provincial bookshops fulfilled some of the functions of the metropolitan coffeehouse.[28] Self-confessed 'old fashioned clergyman' Joseph Boerhadem told *Gentleman's Magazine* readers that he dipped into books in shops without purchasing as this was 'inconvenient for my scanty finances'.[29]

The magazine was also widely available in the different kinds of eighteenth-century libraries (institutional, private, circulating and subscription), and through book clubs and societies. Lichfield Cathedral Library had 'an almost complete set'.[30] In 1793 Homerton Academy (for dissenting ministers) held volumes from 1754 to 1756.[31] Another dissenting institution, the London Library Society, listed 13 volumes in its catalogue of 1785 (the year of its foundation).[32] Cirencester Book Club bought the 1789 supplement and the 12 numbers for 1790 in January 1791.[33] The Junior Combination Room of Corpus Christi College, Oxford was a subscriber in the 1790s.[34] Volumes 43 (1773) and 56 (1786) were missing from the Sheffield Book Society in 1798, indicating actual borrowing.[35]

In the home, purchasers did read the magazine to themselves as Hazlitt and Scott envisaged: 'alone in my Bower' in the summer or 'snug at my Hearth' in the winter.[36] An 1800 etching by H. Rogers depicts author and magazine correspondent John Holt of Liverpool (1743–1801) reading an unbound and so probably new number by the fireplace in a room furnished with books and a globe.[37] But these copies were then passed around other readers within the household and beyond.

A common means of sharing at home was by reading aloud.[38] Although some of the magazine's contents did not lend themselves to oral performance (tables, diagrams and lists, for example), interesting articles and letters did. The magazine was read to Thomas Percy, Bishop of Dromore (1729–1811), when his eyesight failed in old age.[39] 'Aged Matron' read her house-maid Mary a letter on how best to lay a fire.[40] Poetry, music and dancing was enjoyed as a family or when socializing, as a reply to a riddle, appended by 'Cocceius' to his own poem, suggested:

> I've read your last Mag. and my daughter *Jugg* says,
> That *C.D.*'s Aenig. means her new pair of *stays*.[41]

'J.S.', also answering in verse a riddle from the previous month, asked the reader to imagine him enjoying an evening stroll on the green with his sweetheart Polly, producing the magazine from his pocket and sharing the puzzle with her.[42] Pictures too could be shared. The poem in the 1749 Preface described their appeal to children at a mother's knee:

> And infants lisp, what pretty things are these!
> These shall, when rattles tire, with joy be seen,
> And children tease mamma for Magazine.

The magazine was also passed between friends. In 1735 Thomas Dod described his circle in Woore, rural north Shropshire, 'perusing it one after another' such that 'the month is at an end before 'tis well read over by them'.[43] In the 1770s John Baker, former Solicitor General in the Leeward Islands, shared copies with various friends.[44] Fothergill read the 1787 article on hedgehogs and beetles at the Yorkshire home of his friend Edward Tennant. John Grey wrote to Nichols from the Lottery Office in 1800 to arrange purchase on his own account when a friend's death ended a sharing arrangement.[45]

It is therefore entirely reasonable to estimate an immediate readership for each new monthly number of at least Cave's 50,000, though not of course exactly the same readers month-to-month or year-to-year. The total must then be adjusted upwards for multiple readings as the years and editions rolled on.

Readers and contributors

In 1743, Henry Fielding referred slyly to the *Gentleman's Magazine* Lilliputian parliamentary debates in *Jonathan Wild*: 'it may be doubted whether those inimitable Harangues (published in the Monthly *Magazines*) came literally from the Mouths of the HURGOS, &c.'. [46] His joke assumed that the novel-reading public knew the magazine and its contents well enough to understand the 'Hurgos' were the Lords, and suspect the reports were not transcriptions. The magazine's emphasis on reader participation certainly placed its regular audience at this more fluent end of the literacy spectrum: sophisticated at making out a text and able to compose. This section examines in greater detail how far the magazine's influence penetrated by social class, educational level and geography, and the extent to which this readership was, as the title suggested, primarily male.

Problems of identification: obscurity, anonymity and pseudonyms

Since the *Gentleman's Magazine* was chiefly sold through booksellers, there was never a consolidated list of purchasers. Nichols himself did not know who they were: 'we scarcely know the NAME of one in a hundred of our Readers'.[47] It is nevertheless possible to recover something of them from fugitive references in diaries, from bookseller and library records, from the thousands of reader contributions to the magazine and from private correspondence with the editors.

Even so, most contributors are not readily identifiable. Often they signed '*Mr Jackson*, or *Mr Thompson*, & c. without giving the Christian name of the person; as if there was no other person of that name in England but the party there spoken of'.[48] Many more chose the anonymity of initials or pseudonyms. This was neither unusual nor sinister: 80 per cent of novels published in Britain between 1750 and 1790 were anonymous or appeared under a fictive authorial name. It was standard practice when writing to newspapers and periodicals.[49] Reasons for anonymity included aristocratic or gendered reticence, modesty or anxiety about the public reaction, especially for those not already published, and shame or embarrassment where a personal matter was being revealed. More positively, it allowed writers to 'add to the worlds they exchanged with each other by peopling them with alternative senses of selves'.[50]

Magazine correspondent Abraham Hawkins of Alston, Devon, for example, told Nichols that he had previously corresponded as 'Alphonso' and wished to be 'A.H.' should his bird's-eye view of Kingsbridge, Devon be published, as he did not wish anyone in the town to know his identity.[51] For others it was a playful game, 'a private exercise of ingenuity, an act of obfuscation disguised as honest modesty'.[52] Regular contributor Samuel Pegge deployed multiple *personae*: the anagram 'Paul Gemsege', 'T. Row' ('The Rector Of Whittington') and 'L.E.' (the last letters of his names). Nichols and Gough's several pseudonyms, an editorial ploy of which most readers were probably unaware, created a denser sense of debate and conversation in the magazine's pages.

Some, like 'W.L.', 'thought it sufficient to give the initials to the public, (as I always do,) and my name at length to the printer'.[53] Nichols was therefore able to remedy somewhat his deficiency in knowledge from his files. He printed a list of 521 of the more eminent contributors in the 'Prefatory Introduction', a few with their pseudonyms, and he and family members annotated, not always accurately, their editorial volumes of the magazine.[54] For example, an article by 'Scrutator' in 1809 was identified as 'The Last Communication of John Loveday DCL' and a 1793 letter from 'M.' as 'By Dr. Mavor of Blenham'.[55]

Kuist's catalogue of manuscript attributions and letters tipped into the editorial volumes is corrected and augmented by De Montluzin in a database covering 1731–1868. This identifies 2,362 authors of 25,585 letters, articles, reviews, poems and other items, still only the tip of the iceberg.[56] Its focus is inevitably on correspondents who are easier to trace because they held official positions (clergy and college fellows for example), were published writers, or achieved some lasting distinction, perhaps marked by an entry in the *Dictionary of National Biography*. Most contributors are doomed to obscurity, leaving only occasional clues to their backgrounds in pseudonyms which indicate a profession, such as 'Chirurgus' (surgeon) or 'Clericus' (clergyman), or location: 'Norfolciensis', 'Hullensis' or 'Oxoniensis'.

Perhaps most caution must be exercised around pseudonyms implying gender. Readers expected correspondence gendered as male would be taken more seriously. When Mary Streeter submitted observations on spiders in December 1765, 'A.Y.' accused her of being a man in 'female disguise', which she vigorously denied in July 1766.[57] Anna Seward corresponded as 'Benvolio' because she feared the consequences for 'an unlearned female entering the lists of criticism against the mighty

Johnson'.[58] Women may also have felt that publication represented indecency and immodesty, a fear which had prompted anonymous queries on emotional matters to the *Athenian Mercury* in the previous century.[59]

Although men could equally have used female disguise as a strategy to avoid accusations of effeminacy when writing on a subject traditionally gendered as female, or as a game (Nichols as female antiquary 'Eusebia', or travel writer Philip Thicknesse (1719–92) as Trojan princess 'Polyxena'), it is likely that taking the gender of a pseudonym as representative of reality underestimates contributions from women.[60]

The implied reader

As well as this direct evidence of the readership, there is the implied reader recovered from the internal evidence of the magazine: its title, format and content, the advertizing on its wrappers, and, during Nichols' editorship, on enclosed leaflets and flyers.[61] Although the latter material was ephemeral, it was read: many personal letters to Nichols mentioned books advertised on the wrappers.[62] In July 1799 'Amicus Patriae' chose as his subject of correspondence a notice on 'the Blue Covers' about the Royal Humane Society campaign to save the lives of shipwrecked sailors.[63] It was in response to requests from 'several respectable Correspondents' for greater legibility that the wrapper colour was changed to buff so 'that the Advertisements may be more distinctly seen.'[64]

Only a very small fraction of the 1,092 wrappers (13 a year: 12 monthly issues and the supplement) for the 84 years of this study survives: 132, around 12 per cent of the total, in archives in this country.[65] Each decade is represented but some very thinly. There is one from the 1730s, on the only known copy of the magazine still in its wrapper.[66] From 1754 to 1778, when the production was shared between Richard Cave, David Henry and latterly John Nichols, there are 15. Generally a wrapper consisted of a quarto sheet folded in half, printed on each of the resulting four pages with a woodcut of St John's Gate on the front, stitched and tied with linen thread through the folded white pages of the magazine. From August 1788 some are folio sheets folded twice, giving eight octavo pages. To date, only Ram has studied the wrappers, and this only for Cave's editorship.[67]

Gentlemen and traders

The title *Gentleman's Magazine* alone led Stafford to describe editorial strategy as 'the explicit targeting of an audience defined by social status' and Jon Klancher to state it 'carved its audience among the landed gentry and the upper middle class'.[68] Empirical work shows this to be far from the case.

(i) 'Gentlemen'

Landed gentlemen did take the magazine. It is still widely found in country house and 'stately home' libraries. The names of members of the Brydges family of Presteigne and Sir Justinian Isham of Lamport, Northamptonshire are written in manuscript on some wrapper covers.[69] A bound volume for 1736 in Trinity College Library, Cambridge carries the bookplate of John, Lord Sheffield, of Sheffield Place, Sussex.[70] Horace Walpole (1717–97) mentioned the magazine in his correspondence, referring to literary articles and those citing his name.[71] In the 1730s and 1740s there was a luxurious and expensive version of the magazine advertised as 'printed on fine Royal Paper, *large Margin*, for the Curious, at 1s. each Month' for these purchasers.[72] A 1733 poem to 'Urban' rejoicing at the 'death' of the *Weekly Magazine*, contrasted its fate to that of the 'Royal Paper, Gilt and Letter'd' special editions, lovingly pictured 'in bright order rang'd by princely hand' in the libraries of the Prince of Wales and his brother the Duke of Cumberland.[73]

This is, however, a tiny sample biased towards those who bound and kept their monthly numbers, unrepresentative of the readership as a whole. A far more substantial body of evidence demonstrates that the *Gentleman's Magazine* was not primarily aimed at those who were already gentlemen by birth, but rather deliberately and successfully sought its readers among the aspirational 'middling sort'.

(ii) The 'middling sort'

The 'middling sort' was that segment of British society which from the seventeenth century did not fit neatly into the traditional binary classifications of the landed interest and the rest, patrician *versus* plebeian, rich and poor.[74] At first the term was rarely used as self-description by the middling sort themselves, but more often deployed in critiques of social mobility.[75] Adopted as an analytical category by historians, it has proved problematic and complex. Attempts to establish its boundaries and size use 'exterior' measures (wealth, occupation and parish office-holding) and, more recently, an 'interior' approach that examines the language of hierarchies and collective activity (literacy, as described above, or civic, leisure, family and economic networks) to establish the shared ethics that constructed and articulated the identity.[76]

Exterior measures result in a class almost too broad to be helpful: an annual income of £40–£200; assets at death of £500–£5,000; one million people in a population of seven million; around half the nation's households or 'independent trading households' engaged in 'the translating of work into money' (professionals, dealers and retailers for example).[77] The cultural approach isolates common values such as self-interest, insularity and self-discipline.[78] Historians often gender the identity by equating it with certain male occupations, especially the professions, finance, dealing trades and, sometimes, specialist, skilled artisans, while categorizing women through their male relatives.

The commercial and social changes that produced this middling sort also affected the definition of a gentleman. This had 'moved away from a strict definition by external status towards a more personalized qualification'.[79] Thus, in his *Dictionary*, Johnson added a further definition of gentleman to his 'Man of Ancestry': 'A man raised above the vulgar by his character or post'.[80] This held out the possibility of attaining gentlemanly status through work and the social negotiation of politeness, Corfield's 'sufficiently confident display'.[81] In 1728/9 Daniel Defoe believed a man could become a gentleman through the possession of sufficient wealth combined with 'an originall fund of wealth, wit, sence, courage, virtue, and good humour [...] set apart by a liberall education'.[82] By 1769 Elizabeth Marsh, whose father was originally a ship's carpenter, could pronounce confidently 'I was the daughter of a gentleman'.[83]

(iii) Middling-sort Gentleman's Magazine readers

Some magazine contributors indicated middling status in their pseudonyms or letters. 'L.G.', who wrote in 1745 advocating a war-time boycott of French goods, had an annual expenditure of £175 for a household consisting of himself, his wife, three sons and four daughters.[84] Ram identifies 77 magazine poets from 1731 to 1754 who either gave their occupation or used an occupational pseudonym. Eight were members of the aristocracy, but 80 per cent were professionals (33 clerics, 26 academics, teachers and students, and three lawyers). Lower down the social scale were a 'Journeyman Bricklayer' (Irish poet and playwright Henry Jones, 1721–70, who had indeed served an apprenticeship as a bricklayer), a 'Tradesman from Chester', 'Cantius a Yeoman of Kent' and a soldier ('Soldado').[85] Still in the Cave era, Pailler concludes that around a fifth of contributors were clergymen, Anglican and dissenting, with physicians, surgeons and farmers also among the readership.[86] Clergymen, schoolmasters and medics continued to feature among the named occupations to 1815.[87] Stafford notes a 'two tier' approach in 1785 to 1815, with the subjects of the 'Deaths' markedly less genteel than those of either the 'Births' and 'Marriages', or the contributors. He describes the obituaries as illustrating a 'more broad and generous category of gentility' with a small but significant number drawn from the lesser clergy, professionals and their clerks and apprentices, farmers, graziers, upper servants and tradesmen including a hog butcher, cheesemonger, slopseller and tripe merchant.[88]

Diarists and memoirists who read the magazine also came from a broad spectrum of eighteenth-century literate society. Among the gentry, Buckinghamshire landowner Henry Purefoy (1697–1762), took the magazine regularly and recorded taking his 12 numbers and supplement for 1736 for binding. Professional man, Benjamin Rogers (1686–1771), Anglican rector of Carlton, Bedfordshire, copied out medical recipes in the 1730s. They were joined, however, by young journeyman stocking-maker William Hutton (1723–1815), James Bisset of Perth (*c.* 1762–1832, bound apprentice to an artist at age 15) who bought it with pocket-money from his uncle, Sheffield apprentice cutler Joseph Hunter, who borrowed the magazine from a subscription library in the 1790s, and Charles Fothergill, who aspired to leave the family ironmongery business and become a gentleman scholar.[89]

Edward Cave, middling-sort himself, had previous experience of publishing aimed squarely at their reading needs and tastes. The introduction to his 1729 *Adventures of Abdallah* announced that it was translated from French and abridged for 'Persons of a middle Rank' who 'have not so much Leisure'. Like the *Gentleman's Magazine*, it was 'useful as well as diverting'.[90] 'Mrs Urban's' lecture in the 1735 Preface contrasted the customers for the magazine and du Halde's *China*: 'Unless the middling rank, you seem'd to depend so much upon, come in a little better'.[91]

That Cave primarily aimed the *Gentleman's Magazine* at them, and only secondarily at the elite, is strongly implied by its plain and serviceable appearance and by its format and contents. The luxury editions were limited. 'Everyman' seemed quite happy with the basic and arguably ugly sixpenny issue. The magazine's 1731 sub-title was even 'Trader's Monthly Intelligencer'. However, the gentlemanly aspirations of the traders were to the fore in its swift abandoning: according to the *Grub Street Journal* it was 'too mechanical'. Its loss gave the magazine 'a more genteel and elegant Turn'.[92]

Shorn of 'Trader's', 'magazine' in itself still carried a meaning of particular significance for the middling sort. It is a commonplace, encapsulated in Carlson's title, that though Cave was derivative in selecting the contents of his new venture, he was original in the metaphorical use of the military word 'magazine' for a periodical miscellany. His erstwhile employee, Johnson, attributed to him this change in meaning:

MAGAZINE   1. A store-house, commonly an arsenal or armoury, or repository of provisions [...]

2. Of late, this word has signified a miscellaneous pamphlet, from a periodical miscellany called the Gentleman's Magazine, and published under the name of *Sylvanus Urban*, by *Edward Cave*.[93]

But the word 'magazine' had a much longer metaphorical history in the publishing business than either Johnson or Carlson allows.[94] Early English Books Online contains nine titles styled 'magazines', the earliest Robert Ward's 1639 *Anima'dversions of Warre: Or, A Militarie Magazine*. The ESTC contains an additional nine predating the *Gentleman's Magazine* launch.[95] The subject matter of the 18 titles is varied: from Ward's military manual, a context where the new use of 'magazine' probably suggested itself naturally, to the correct titles and law relating to the peerage, religion, navigation, spelling reform and the art of courtship, as is their scale, from folio to pocket-sized duodecimo, from book to pamphlet. What they have in common is their classification among reference or technical works and manuals, addressing directly middling-sort occupational needs of tradesmen.[96]

A good example of the genre is Edward Hatton's *Merchant's Magazine*. First published in 1695 and in print until at least 1799, the title page describes it as 'useful for Schools, Bankers, Diversion of Gentlemen, Business of Mechanicks, and Officers of the Queen's Custom and Excise', recommending it to 'the middling sort and not a few of the Gentry' whose education 'runs towards Trade and Merchandize', their children and servants, and schoolmasters. It contained writing exercises, *pro forma* letters and information on accounts and book-keeping, bills of exchange, overseas commodities and postal services. The template 'Book of Household Expences' conjured the highly gendered domestic spending arrangements of a householder with a fashion-loving wife and a (feckless) housekeeper:

To *Cash* paid my Wife for Apparel, &c.   £50 1/–
To *Cash* paid *Su. Savenone*, the Housekeeper,   £50 4/6.
   for this Month

(His own pocket-money was a modest £8.)[97]

'Magazines' were, then, well-established by 1731. For book-buying, middling-sort tradesmen the term had a particular, gendered resonance: a current, reliable, factual work of reference useful in business and domestic life.[98] It would be surprising were Cave, 20 years in the printing trade, unaware of this heritage.

As a miscellany, his *Gentleman's Magazine* was different, but there was an overlap in content, especially in the early numbers: 'A short RULE to determine the Value of BAR-SILVER', 'The COURSE of EXCHANGE balanc'd, showing how to Draw and Remit to Advantage' and 'A TABLE of Stamps', for example.[99] Its layout, too, met the needs of busy tradesmen: compact, abridged, indexed, cross-referenced, categorized and, in the 'back half', relatively standardized with tabulated or listed factual material: the Bills of Mortality, stock and commodity prices, and lists of bankrupts.[100] The *Gentleman's Magazine* was therefore located firmly within Altick's 'books of utility' meeting new demands brought about by changes in markets, products, law and agriculture.[101]

Wrapper advertising further confirms the intended middling-sort reader. Ram notes the predominance of advertisements for books, in contrast to other eighteenth-century periodicals and papers with their multitude of notices about medicines, houses to let, runaway servants and lost horses. She identifies 353 different book advertisements and only five for 'non-literary material' (in fact six: three lotteries, Tomlinson Busby soaps, a tincture of bark fever medication and Mountain Wine.)[102]

Advertised books were heavily weighted towards serious works with a moral or scholarly tone, suggesting a readership of formally educated men such as the clergy, school-masters and students. But some were explicitly aimed at the less-educated. *A New General English Dictionary* was 'as well for the entertainment of the Curious, as the information of the Ignorant, and for the Benefit of young students, Artificers, Tradesmen, and Foreigners, who are desirous thoroughly to understand what they Speak, Read or Write', for example.[103] Others were directed at specific middling-sort occupations: farming (monthly serial *The Modern Husbandman*), the law (*The Attorney's Compleat Pocket-Book* and *Precedents in Chancery*) and trade (*The Royal Gauger*, on excise calculations, and *Dr. Bracken's Traveller's Pocket-Farrier*, 'useful for all Gentlemen and Tradesmen who are obliged to Travel the Countries').[104]

This pattern continued after 1754, with book and pamphlet advertisements far outnumbering the 72 for other products and services.[105] Of the 206 inserted documents to 1815 catalogued by Kuist, 19 were advertisements for products and services, one for a set of illustrations, and seven addresses to the electorate of the Ward of Farringdon Without from an 1810 Common Council election. The remainder was again for books, pamphlets and serial and periodical publications.[106]

Publications advertised in this later period covered all the subject categories by which library collections of the period were classified (ancients, history, divinity, travel, poetry and plays, natural philosophy, fiction) again with a bias towards the factual and serious.[107] Some titles (Lowndes' pre-printed marriage registers for use after Hardwicke's Act, the many works for use in schools, Burn's *Justice of the Peace*) were tailored for the clergy, school-masters and other professionals Ram and Pailler identify as readers.[108] Others indicate a readership among traders and manufacturers: the 15th edition of an interest rate calculator by accountant Richard Hayes; George Fisher's *Young Man's Best Companion*, with sections on spelling, accounts and how to measure and price building works; *The Briton's Friend: or, Moral and Economical Register*, 'particularly addressed to the middle and lower classes of society' which encouraged religious observance and recommended sources of employment conducive to 'industry and good order'.[109]

The example that best illustrates the likely range of readers' circumstances, expectations and, above all, values, is *The Economist: Shewing in a Variety of Estimates, from Fourscore Pounds a Year to upwards of 800l., How a Family May Live with Frugality, for a Little Money*, by an anonymous 'Gentleman of Experience' and addressed to 'the mercantile and middling class, who stand most in need of advice'. It was a popular work: when advertised in December 1774 this one-shilling pocket-sized guide to household budgeting was in its 10th edition. Its emphasis was on maintaining gentility at the lower end of the title's income-range. The (inevitably male) householder was shown how to 'make an appearance in life equal to a person of twice his fortune' such as keeping a maid-servant, perhaps even a horse and carriage, while at the same time putting aside savings for a widow's and children's futures. The secret was thrifty buying 'at first hand' and 'for ready money', home brewing and pickling, dressing one's own hair and home-educating if necessary, the 'mistress' always keeping 'a weekly book' so that retrenchment could follow an extravagant week.[110] The implied reader here was very close indeed to Hunt's struggling, self-disciplining, commercial middling sort consciously deploying self-presentation to gloss over the difficulties inherent in their lives.[111]

(iv) 'Residual readers'

In the 1770s and 1780s Simon Edy, a regular beggar near St Giles in London, entertained passers-by with information gleaned from bits of old newspaper, including 'three or four greasy thumbed numbers of the *Gentleman's Magazine*'.[112] Jonathan Rose details the often random way in which texts were available to the nineteenth-century working class.[113] Edy reminds us that this was also true in the eighteenth century. It is important to acknowledge those below the middling sort who, like Edy, read, saw and were aware of the *Gentleman's Magazine*.

Pailler concludes that the *Gentleman's Magazine* did not penetrate as far as 'the submerged tenth'.[114] As Lackington had discovered, a few of the most poverty-stricken were able to read at all, or with anything approaching fluency. Still, there were various places and ways in which the less socially elevated such as Edy encountered the magazine. Some book clubs and libraries served clienteles from the 'inferior orders of society', the terminology of 'Z' of Lewes, Sussex, a *Gentleman's Magazine* correspondent who advocated subscription libraries to make expensive publications available to any 'above a state of penury'.[115] The inferior orders, such as 'Aged Matron's' maid, even if illiterate, might hear the magazine read out loud. 'For the greatest part of the *people* do not read *books*, most of them cannot *read* at all, but they will gather together about one that can *read*, and listen to an *Observer* or *Review*', remarked Charles Leslie in 1750.[116] In towns, texts and prints were displayed in shop windows and sometimes browsed without purchase (as did not only clergyman Joseph Boerhadem but the young Joseph Hunter).[117] Those handling the magazine's distribution, newsagents and the tradesmen who delivered papers and magazines to rural customers on their rounds, might also take a surreptitious glance.[118]

The less well-off bought single numbers and volumes second-hand. Three used, unbound volumes of the *Gentleman's Magazine* were William Hutton's first book purchases in 1746, and 'afforded a treat.' He bound them 'in a most cobbled style', his first exercise in this craft, rebinding them in 1748 and eventually setting up as a bookseller, binder and stationer.[119] Unemployed John Bates stole a volume of the *Gentleman's Magazine* worth four shillings from a Paternoster Row bookseller in 1810. He must have both recognized the product and knew it was saleable as he planned to turn it into cash to buy food for his wife and three children.[120]

The relative wealth of images inside could also be appreciated without reading. In fact, prints were often removed before numbers were sent for binding and many surviving volumes do not have the full complement. When John Goodford of Bath wrote to Nichols in 1814 seeking the 1773 back volume, he had to specify that it be 'with plates'.[121] Images from the magazine were framed and hung or pasted on walls as inexpensive interior decoration in homes and inns, reaching an audience even in rural areas and humble dwellings.[122] Pictures of 'a Grotto and Views of Italy, &c. in a Cottage at Spalding' were the inspiration for a correspondent poet in 1766. In another Old Bailey theft case (slightly later than this book's period) the defendant, a waiter at Theodosius Williams' New Post-office coffeehouse, St Martin's-le-Grand, stole from his master a substantial amount of cash and seven prints cut from the *Gentleman's Magazine*, 'stamped "Williams coffee and reading rooms" '.[123] Like fellow-thief John Bates, he understood them to have a monetary or even intrinsic aesthetic value. A series of maps of Germany published 1760–61 was intended to be detached. Instructions were provided for removing them to create, side-by-side on a table, one large map for following the progress of the war.[124] An indication of the additional reach of these images is the 20,000 sales of a map of the West Indies and North American coast, published in the January 1740 magazine but also available separately for sixpence.[125]

Despite the good survival rate of bound runs, the vast majority of all the copies of the *Gentleman's Magazine* that ever existed were, however, never destined for preservation. Correspondents were aware of this. Samuel Pegge junior pleaded with Nichols to print the final part of his father's life in December 1796 rather than in the supplement, as many who bought the magazine 'do not bind them and so do not buy the supplement'.[126] Copies were read when fresh, then joined the pages of newspapers, other periodicals and even books (Benjamin Franklin's self-penned epitaph described his body as 'Like the Cover of an old Book, Its Contents torn out') to be reused at least once before their final destruction.[127] Scrap paper had a monetary value. It was among the items scavenged from the streets by the indigent Israel Potter in the early 1790s.[128] In the 1785 Preface Nichols had to apologize to readers for a delay in issuing reprints due to 'The Perfidy of knavish Servants, who stole, and sold for Waste Paper, what will cost much Time and Expence to prepare again for the Public'.[129]

Wrappers and pages were therefore kept for recycling.[130] Bookbinders would have had a large supply of discarded wrappers after making up annual volumes for customers.[131] They and others retained these for domestic use or for sale to waste paper dealers (who presumably bought Potter's gleanings and to whom Nichols' 'knavish Servants' fenced the stolen sheets). In the home they lined cake and pie tins, were twisted for kindling, placed between freshly ironed shirts and strung up as toilet paper: 'Mrs Urban' had complained that her paper-strewn home looked like a jakes.[132] Hairdressers tore paper to 'screw up curls', retailers kept old papers to wrap items such as medicines and foodstuffs, and trunk and luggage makers used them as lining. In the 1751 Preface, Cave gloated over the fate of failed competitor magazines 'their bodies consigned to the Trunkmakers'. The 1752 Supplement had a humorous 'literary Bill of Mortality' in which the fates of unsold books included 'Yellow-fever in a jakes', 'Trunkmaker' and 'Pastry-cook'.[133]

In all these settings the *Gentleman's Magazine* had a half-life of diminishing resonance and influence where its contents were still heard and seen. Lesser tradesmen, their customers, families, employees and servants – literate men, women and children below the middling sort and better-off artisans – would, like the *Idler's* fictional kitchen-maid, 'Betty Broom', have encountered it and read some of its pages before they rejoined the scrap cycle or were finally destroyed in the privy.[134] This was not the primary audience for the magazine, and it was not the audience that responded with contributions, but equally it was not entirely unaware of the values it represented.

'Mechanical readers' and 'men of learning'[135]

Education was a component of social status and gender. In particular, the classical languages were major elements in the English university, public and grammar school syllabuses. They were gentlemanly and not readily acquired by anyone taught in humbler establishments or for only a few years, that is by artisan and many middling-sort boys. Most girls, even the well-educated (Anna Seward, for example), knew little Latin and less Greek.[136]

Sometimes the *Gentleman's Magazine* content implies a highly-educated reader, at variance with a middling-sort core readership and their practical, vernacular schooling. There were Latin poems, complicated mathematical problems and earnest debates between correspondents about academic and theological matters, such as the correct translations of the Psalms from the Hebrew. Some contributors adopted classically derived pseudonyms. Compounds of the Greek 'Philo-' ('lover' or 'friend') were especially popular: 'Philalethes' ('lover of the truth') or 'Philoclerus' ('friend of the clergy'). As early as 1738 'Philo-all-souls' wrote to 'Urban' from Oxford: 'I congratulate you on your Magazine's gaining Ground in this University'.[137] The Corpus Christi Junior Combination Room copy and contributions from students indicate that some acquired the magazine-reading habit as undergraduates.[138] Scholars such as classicists Revd Charles Blomfield (1786–1857, a future Bishop of London) and Edmund Henry Barker (1788–1839), advanced their disputes in its pages.[139]

Nor was the magazine restricted to an educated Anglican audience. Dissenting ministers and students in dissenting academies were among the readers and contributors.[140] Between 1791 and 1796 there was a long correspondence on New College, Hackney, from critics of the institution and its tutors, students and subscribers.[141] Although the magazine was not especially favourable towards Roman Catholicism, Joseph Berington (1743–1827, Roman Catholic priest and religious controversialist), Abbé Mann (1735–1809, Yorkshire-born Catholic convert, natural philosopher and historian) and John Milner (1752–1826, Vicar Apostolic of the Midland District) were all correspondents between the 1780s and 1800s.[142]

Most literate people might have felt excluded from this part of the magazine's content, although they possessed some familiarity with classical themes and characters through works in translation (Pope's *Iliad* and *Odyssey* for example) and theatrical productions based on Greek tragedies.[143] The *Gentleman's Magazine* editors were fully aware of this and limited its impact. Latin poetry often came with a translation 'Render'd into plain *English*, for the sake of many of our Readers'.[144] Johnson's Lilliputian parliamentary reports retained Lord Carteret's ('Hurgo Quadrert's') grandiloquent use of Latin expressions, but these too were paraphrased into English.[145] Popular too were English versions of classical poetry, especially Horace and Anacreon.[146]

In this context the *Gentleman's Magazine*'s Latin appears less an exclusionary tactic than an inclusive, aspirational, democratizing one, aimed at the middling sort, many of whom, like 'M.E.' (M. Elstob) of Shotton, esteemed the classics as 'the basis of sound learning'.[147] At the very least it permitted the reader to pretend to classical knowledge more subtly than the library customer in 'Bath, a Poem' of 1738:

> Illiteratus Greek aloud demands,
> Who common English hardly understands.[148]

More positively, it brought this learning and literature to a wider audience, maybe even to labourers like William Temple, a weaver from Newcastle, and Paisley mechanic Hugh Simon, both praised in obituaries for self-taught mastery of classical languages.[149] The same argument holds true for other items, such as excerpts from the *Philosophical Transactions* or the 'many mathematical Biblical and Divinity Polemical Questions' which Cave's correspondent John Anstis felt 'one in 500 of your Readers dont [*sic*] understand'.[150]

Anstis thought the *London Magazine* more tempting because lighter, but he underestimated the thirst for knowledge. There were plenty of readers towards the bottom of the educational pyramid. Joseph Hunter had 'received a basic classical education' and Charles Fothergill's was geared towards business.[151] Others had far less schooling. James Bisset attended a dame-school. William Hutton, like many children from artisan backgrounds (his father was a wool-comber), had only a rudimentary formal education, attending a school in Derby between the ages of five and seven, and was largely self-taught, as was Henry Jones who read the classics while learning the brick-laying trade.[152] As noted above, the educational books advertised on the wrappers included titles targeting readers interested in self-improvement or at least the avoidance of embarrassment. In addition to the *New General English Dictionary*, there was the 49th edition of Dyche's popular *Guide to the English Tongue*, 'corrected for the use of schools'. Its promise to eliminate 'vicious pronunciation', especially the 'barbarous Rusticisms' referred to inside, surely appealed to the upwardly-mobile.[153]

By the final quarter of the eighteenth century a tension between academically trained and other correspondents was detectable within the magazine. This focussed on distinctions of education rather than social origin *per se*.[154] The scholarly felt that anonymity encouraged too much ill-considered correspondence. In 1777 'Veritatis Amicus' ('A Friend of Truth', but not so far as to reveal his own identity, as 'W.L.' hypocritically pointed out) expressed in pithy language his complaint that it permitted articles that were 'most *scurrilous*' attacks on the work of others, suggesting that anonymity was only 'warrantable and laudable' when the result of modesty in men of learning.[155] Ten years later Berington proposed that all correspondents sign their real names in order to deter premature, incautious rushing into print. His aim was to privilege the contributions of 'men of real science' over those of the less-learned ruck.[156]

The following month, two readers replied in support of anonymity. 'Your Occasional Correspondent' argued that it encouraged variety, with contributions from those who demanded 'neither fame nor profit'. This elevated the *Gentleman's Magazine* and its readers above the unmanly triviality of its rivals which were 'confined to the perusal of feeble amateurs, or ladies' maids'. 'D.R.' felt it promoted innovation by permitting 'men of science or literature to investigate subjects without the necessity of standing forth as the authors'.[157] The tension continued. In 1812 antiquary William Hamper (1776–1831) told Nichols that at least his friend Mr Weetman of Liverpool 'well knows what he is writing about, which is not always the case with Candidates for admission into your Pages'.[158]

'Urban' never yielded to intellectual elitism, however, but always upheld the right of all his readers to participate and debate – 'trying their strength in our "Ulysses his bow" ' – provided only that they avoided malicious or *ad hominem* attacks:

> We open with pleasure our Periodical Publications, as a free Channel, through which Gentlemen and Scholars may converse with each other on all useful or entertaining subjects, and give and get mutual Information *cognito* or *incognito*, as they please; but being determined to keep our Publication *decent* and *respectable*.[159]

In consequence, the magazine remained accessible to all literate persons, whatever their educational level. As a repository of the minimum knowledge that was required to be considered polite – politics, news, literature – it was 'a higher-order metamedium' that 'allowed readers to maintain a certain intellectual confidence'.[160]

Geography of the readership

'Bardus" poem in the 1736 Preface claimed that the *Gentleman's Magazine* was known not only throughout England, Scotland and Wales, but in 'British Colonies, and foreign Kingdoms'. The 1753 Preface referred to the many correspondents in 'remote counties'. These were no empty boasts. The magazine consistently drew readers and contributors across Britain and beyond. This characteristic distinguished it from periodical predecessors such as the *Tatler* and *Spectator*, which were more metropolitan in tone and reach.[161]

(i) Distribution

The *Gentleman's Magazine*, like many eighteenth-century publications, was advertised as sold by 'booksellers in town and country'. It could also be posted direct from the printers.[162] Book publication and sales were centred on London, but other cities and towns were expanding rapidly. There were 381 booksellers in 174 provincial urban centres by the mid-1740s, and growth in local newspaper titles produced local distribution networks.[163] A postscript to a 1740 letter to Cave from Charles Powell of Brecon, mid-Wales, reveals how these operated in relatively isolated spots: 'I take yr magazine by the person that brings the Gloucester Journal to these parts'.[164] The development of the Post Office and improvements in transport (turnpike roads and canals) meant that communication became much faster.[165] A credit-worthy provincial bookseller could expect to receive an order placed for a customer within a few days or, at the outside, a few weeks.[166]

Postal supply was suggested in an editorial reply to 'J.T.' in the Downs who complained the magazine was unobtainable at Deal, though other publications were to be found there.[167] Some correspondents used the pseudonym 'Post Paid'. They understood the postal system as a 'shared experience', using it with facility both to receive the magazine and to correspond with 'Sylvanus Urban'.[168] 'One years [*sic*] Magazines sent hither by the Post' would stimulate correspondence every alternate month from 'those authors who are 8 miles of any bookseller', Dod told Edward Cave.[169]

The magazine was readily available beyond the British mainland. W.H. Pratt of Randalstown, County Antrim, ordered it direct from the London publishers through the post.[170] Alternatively, Irish readers could buy a local reprint in Dublin stationers and other retailers. The Atlantic colonies and Caribbean islands were also served by imprints from presses in the 'Plantations'.[171] There were regular shipping services to the Americas and West Indies, and books, newspapers and periodicals were ordered and sent via merchants or friends in Britain.[172] Far from home in 1778, William Jones consulted the *Gentleman's Magazine* for 1754 in the home of Thomas Harrison, Attorney General for Jamaica, to whose sons he was tutor.[173] In the factories of the East India Company it was 'as eagerly sought after as any part of the lading of an European ship'.[174] It was also read in and received articles and letters from continental Europe. A 'late order' for 51 magazines was received from Rotterdam in 1751.[175] Abbé Mann was living in Brussels when he first took the magazine in 1784.[176] Overseas readers were still actively courted in the 1770s when it was promoted as 'an acceptable present for their friends abroad' from 'the mercantile class of Gentlemen [...] Naval Officers and Mariners.'[177]

This exploitation of provincial and overseas markets was a deliberate policy of Cave (himself provincial with insider knowledge of both the post office and local newspapers). The title page listing of provincial, Scottish, Irish and colonial papers (to the right) as well as London papers (to the left) was an overtly inclusive gesture, albeit rarely delivered in the press excerpts or news.[178] Even the title page woodcut did not shout its metropolitan origins: St John's Gate was not a traditional symbol of the capital and only became a landmark because of the *Gentleman's Magazine* rather than *vice versa*. The opposite was true of the *London Magazine* title and title page cut – an iconic view of the City, dominated by London Bridge and St Paul's Cathedral. The editorial *persona* ('Sylvanus' indicating the country and 'Urban' the town) provided a more subliminal hint of geographical inclusivity.

(ii) Geographical evidence in the magazine

Nichols gave a location for 117 of the 521 contributors named in his 'Prefatory Introduction'. With the caveat that this was biased towards his own circle of literary, antiquarian and other correspondents (13 of the 117 were based in Leicestershire for example), these ranged from the London suburbs (Isleworth, Deptford, Lambeth and Greenwich), to other major cities and towns (Durham, York, Bristol, Norwich) and newer urban centres (Liverpool, Manchester, Birmingham). Rural counties were represented (Boconnoc in Cornwall, Crediton in Devon, Nayland and Woodbridge in Suffolk), as were Wales and Scotland. Overseas there were five Irish locations and Brussels, Jamaica and Philadelphia.

The pattern was repeated in the addresses of correspondents published in the magazine itself.[179] Ram concludes that most of the poetry contributions to 1754 came from the provinces, detecting a reducing level of contributions the further one moved from London and the South-East. Stafford notes a similar bias for 1785 to 1815, with around 27 per cent of addressed contributions falling within a ten-mile radius of the capital and only four per cent from Ireland, Scotland and Wales combined. The locations of the men and women recorded in the obituaries were also geographically as well as socially broadly based, with something of an urban bias.[180]

Nevertheless, and in line with Pailler's belief that farmers were among the readership, some of the magazine's content implied a rural, or semi-rural, audience. There was extensive coverage of the nationwide cattle distemper and possible cures throughout 1746 and 1747. In January 1753, beneath a letter from 'S.L.' on the benefits of marling, was a direct editorial appeal for pieces from farmers, which did not expect them to be men of letters: 'the farmer need not be at any trouble about the stile, the bare facts in the plainest words are sufficient'.[181] The enduring popularity of the pseudonym 'Rusticus' indicates that a section of the readership proudly maintained a rural rather than urban identity.

The wrappers reveal a similar geographical spread.[182] Although many advertisements were for books published in London, these were usually, like the magazine, available 'at all the booksellers in town and country' or could be sent 'to all Parts of the Kingdom (Post free) with the greatest regularity, and on the most moderate Terms'.[183] Advertisements for subscription works provided lists of provincial retailers where interest could be registered. In 1785 orders for Revd John Hellins' *Mathematical Essays* could be placed in Oxford, Cambridge, Coventry, Birmingham, Northampton, Peterborough, Bristol, Norwich, Daventry,

Towcester, Hereford, Sherborne, York, Exeter, Salisbury and Bideford.[184] There were advertisements for works of regional interest: *A Plan of the Town of Northampton* in January 1748 or *A History of the Town and Port of Faversham* in September 1774. A few non-book advertisements were placed by provincial advertisers at a distance from the metropolis who must have expected the magazine to be read locally: a portable camera obscura stocked by A.B. John's bookshop in Plymouth; 'a gallery of paintings, painted cabinets, natural and artificial curiosities' for sale in Salisbury; an opportunity to enter the upholstery trade in Liverpool; James Russell's clinical lectures in Edinburgh.[185]

(iii) 'People in small places labour under many disadvantages'[186]

Distance from London and remoteness from a major town did not render the magazine impossible to find. What it did determine was how soon after publication and how regularly it was received, and how rapidly a reader could see a contribution turned into print.[187]

Correspondents kept Nichols informed of how easily, or not, they could obtain the magazine. The reliable, prompt publishing schedule created demanding expectations. As early as 3 April 1809, Anglican clergyman and theological writer Ralph Churton (1754–1831), moaned that the magazine had not yet arrived in Banbury.[188] Joseph Palmer (ex-Budworth, 1756–1815), who contributed articles as 'Rambler,' had not seen the magazine regularly since leaving town but was taking it in Durham.[189] In rural Devon, clergyman, poet and antiquary William Tasker (1740–1800) described himself, with some exaggeration although he was ill, as 'confined in my dreary situation at Starvation-Hall, 40 miles below Exeter, out of the verge of Literature & where even your extensive Magazine has never yet reached'.[190]

Scotland and Ireland often received it late. The December number arrived in Montrose in early March according to Thomas Christie, and in Dromore, County Down, Percy complained in March 1799 that 'The Gentleman's Magazine reaches this remote part but slowly' claiming only recently to have seen articles in the numbers for May and July 1798.[191]

Overseas readers had the longest wait. Edward Gibbon wrote to Nichols from Lausanne, Switzerland, in 1792: 'At this distance from England you will not be surprised that this morning only, by a mere accident, the Gentleman's Magazine for August 1788 should have reached my knowledge'.[192] The Atlantic crossing took anything from three weeks to three months and news from the colonies and reader correspondence with 'Urban' were subject to an inevitable time-lag.[193] In March 1735 a poem was reprinted from the *Barbados Gazette* of 23 November 1734, as an answer to an enigma in the magazine for June 1734.[194] In March 1741 a letter defending plantation slavery from 'Your constant reader' in the Leeward Islands was published. Dated 24 December 1740, it was written in response to the anti-slavery letter of 'Mercator Honestus' ('honest merchant') of July 1740.[195]

Despite these difficulties, there was transatlantic correspondence throughout the period. In 1753 Cave received a letter and manuscript book 'Suggestions for the Improvement of Practical Navigation, Geography and Astronomy' from 'H.J.', Cecil County, Maryland, who had read the magazine for at least eight years (he had contributed an article on calendar and coinage reform in 1745).[196] Nichols' list of contributors included Benjamin Franklin, Edward Long of Jamaica and Benjamin Rush of Philadelphia.[197] Post-independence, the American market remained strong. Temporary exile William Cobbett (1763–1835), writing from Philadelphia in 1797, told Nichols that with a regular supply he could sell 50 to 100 copies a month.[198]

Nor were non-metropolitan readers inhibited from contributing by the magazine's London base. Brewer considers that Anna Seward chose the magazine as an outlet because it offered an opportunity for provincial readers to achieve publication in a national medium that circumvented the London critics.[199] On the contrary, their many contributions of poetry praising local landscapes and towns, and of articles (often illustrated) on local antiquities and topography brought information about the outlying regions to the centre and out again to the nation as a whole. As a result the magazine did not diminish provincial culture or mark a shift towards regarding London and towns as the norm and the countryside as a curiosity.[200]

Distance therefore only affected the rate at which the magazine spread information, although at least one correspondent was self-conscious about this. 'Diogenes', writing in 1775 on the 'well known' literary dispute between Lord Chesterfield and Dr Johnson, remarked: 'It may be so to the residents in and near London; but we country folks know only in general that the Doctor inscribed the printed plan of his Dictionary to that Lord'.[201]

Women readers

The *Gentleman's Magazine* title gendered it as masculine. As with social status, this is relatively unexplored in the historiography. Most commentators conclude that the magazine made no deliberate concessions to a female readership, citing its serious and sober tone, the absence of gossip about the *beau monde*, little serialized fiction and lack of interest in the novel as a literary form.[202] Nichols unapologetically addressed this critique in the 1784 Preface.[203] However, we should be wary of taking at face value discourses, both eighteenth-century and current, the underlying purpose of which is to promote an essentialist view of the sexes as fundamentally different, with women's interests 'naturally' restricted to domestic or 'frivolous' matters catered for, rather than shaped by, specialist, women's publications.[204]

Empirical research demonstrates the fallacy of associating particular forms and styles of literature with women readers. Berry points to the male readership of 'ladies' issues' of the *Athenian Mercury* in the previous century. Fergus' work on eighteenth-century reading material purchased and borrowed in the Midlands challenges the alleged link between women and the novel, by showing a considerable intersection between the tastes of male and female readers, and crossing in both directions of the gender-coded boundaries of magazine titles.[205] Although from 1770 the 'winner' with her women purchasers was the *Lady's Magazine*, women were also among the identified buyers of the *Gentleman's* and the *London Magazines* at Samuel Clay's bookshops in Daventry, Rugby, Lutterworth and Warwick. Most of these women were from the professional and gentry classes, had conservative tastes, and a preference for the older titles.[206] An 1808 *Gentleman's Magazine* correspondent calling herself 'A Very Old Female Subscriber' was presumably one such.[207]

Purchaser and reader is not the same thing of course. Women readers of and contributors to the *Gentleman's Magazine* might also be concealed behind a male purchaser or correspondent as household members sharing a copy, as 'Cocceius' and his daughter Jugg did. John Elderton, a regular correspondent from Bath in the 1790s, worked with his daughter on his pieces, acknowledging her as the artist of a view of Glastonbury Tor accompanying his letter in May 1791, for example.[208]

(i) 'Our Fair Readers': the Gentleman's Magazine's ladies[209]

Contemporaries thought women a minority among the magazine's readers. Cave's 1735 correspondent Dod believed 'Readers of our sex exceed 100 to 1 of theirs', using this low figure to justify a lack of need for delicacy in the poetry pages. Yet women's own voices confirm them as established readers. The Dowager Countess of Spencer wrote to her friend Caroline Howe about a 'great deal of pleasant reading' in the magazine, enjoyed after an exhausting morning reorganizing her library at St Albans.[210] Novelist Jane Porter (1776–1850) told Nichols in 1811: 'Tho' yours be professedly a Gentleman's Mag: yet ladies find pleasure in its pages'.[211] Correspondence between Barbara Johnson and her family and friends mentioned magazine and periodical articles, including criticism of William Crowe's poem 'Lewesdon Hills' in the *Gentleman's Magazine* of February 1788.[212] A Suffolk lady copied a piece from the *Gentleman's Magazine* for February 1793 on Robert Fleming's 1701 'prophecies' of the French Wars into her commonplace book, and Frances Burney critical endorsement of *Cecilia* into hers.[213] Goodeth, second wife of Samuel Pegge junior, continued to take the magazine after her husband's death in 1800, as did Selina Moor of Northiam, Sussex.[214]

Women were equally among the correspondents, but again probably in small numbers. Mary Masters (*fl.* 1733–55) contributed poetry and letters as 'Maria' from 1737 and became a personal friend of Cave.[215] Although Nichols' 1784 Preface claimed 'we can boast of some of the first female names in Europe among our regular correspondents', he only included nine women, all prominent in the literary world, among the 521 names in the 'Prefatory Introduction'. Stafford calculated the proportion of identified female correspondents between 1785 and 1815 at a slightly higher five per cent.[216]

There were also more obscure women contributors. Stephen Howard suggests that most obituaries, regardless of the sex of the subject, were composed by men.[217] Nichols' correspondence reveals, to the contrary, that widows often authored their husbands' obituaries. In 1795 for instance, the widow of Sir John Prestwich wrote to Nichols asking for his death to be announced in the magazine (and for a copy to be sent to her via the Dublin GPO).[218] Two years after Tasker wrote from 'Starvation-Hall', his widow Eleanor sent Nichols a letter with unvarnished details of his death 'in grat agony's [*sic*] after a total suppression of urine'. She chased the matter up in March as the notice had not appeared and the obituary was finally published that month (spelling corrected).[219]

There were women among the poets. Nichols thought this section of his magazine of particular interest to 'the Sex': 'the feast provided for our fair readers'.[220] Others joined the political, literary or antiquarian debates, often, like Mary Streeter, writing under initials or pseudonyms in order to be taken more seriously. 'C.C.' of Aberdeen defended capital punishment in the *Miscellaneous Correspondence* for 1742.[221] She was, however, identified as 'Mrs' in an advertisement, where her sex was spotted by eagle-eyed correspondent R. Yate, perhaps because he thought it unusual.[222] In 1758 an anonymous lady made quite technical comments on a recent naval engagement, proposing uniform changes to reduce high rates of combat death among officers. She anticipated her letter would be thought to be by a man, 'somebody in the sea-service'.[223]

A few wrote on more personal subjects such as courtship, marriage and education. In 1739 'Prudentia Motherly' protested at slighting treatment by her husband of 40 years and his children from his first marriage, and 'a Lady' wrote with *'A Method to make* WOMEN *useful'* by training young women to respectable trades (as retailers of textiles, haberdashery, clothing accessories and food items), thereby enabling them to earn a living were they to join the dreaded ranks of the unwed.[224] The following year 'M.S.', a young lady in Norfolk, asked for advice on excessive sweating.[225] When in 1797 'Aged Matron', already introduced as a regular and enthusiastic reader, recommended 'Viator's' letter on smoking chimneys, she also offered her views on the control and education of servants.[226] In the same year 'A.B.C.' of Chertsey, Surrey, combined both public and private spheres in a letter that rambled from the antiquarian topic of monumental inscriptions to a discussion of the disadvantages of being a third wife and stepmother.[227]

Pailler, commenting only on the Cave period, believes these letters might be from men writing in a female voice.[228] While this may sometimes have been the case ('Prudentia Motherly' perhaps, or 'Sharlot Wealthy'), there are two points worth making: firstly the opposite case, women concealing themselves as men through modesty or, like Anna Seward/'Benvolio', fear of ridicule, is equally or more probable.[229] This anxiety may have been weakening towards the end of the century when Kuist detects an increase in articles submitted by women as women. He attributes this to confidence gained from reading the submissions of others in a 'chain-reaction' characteristic of the magazine's correspondence.[230] Secondly, where men wrote in a female voice, this surely still reveals something about attitudes to gender: the style and subject matter that was appropriate to each sex, for instance.

(ii) The implied female reader

Cave advertised his magazine as: 'Very proper for private Families.'[231] Evidence from the contents and wrappers confirms that, despite the title, the magazine was aimed at a domestic market that included men, women, and their lisping children eager to see the pictures. There were regular contributions of recipes for home-made medicines and of domestic tips: how to destroy bed bugs and 'Viator's' smoking chimneys.[232] Wrapper advertisements also implied the household audience of *The Economist's* budgets. Book titles included *The Modern Cook* by Vincent la Chapelle *(fl.* 1733–6). Despite elevated positions as Chief Cook to the Earl of Chesterfield and the Prince of Orange, he had a section on 'the least expensive Methods of providing for private

Families'. There were *The House-keeper's Pocket-Book, and Compleat Family Cook* and *The Family's Best Companion* with instructions on 'marking on Linen, how to pickle and preserve, to make divers sorts of wine and many excellent Plaisters and Medicines necessary in all Families'. There were Gould & Co.'s patent portable family mangles and Stephenson & Co.'s water closets.[233]

Women were direct targets of some advertisements: *The Ladies Complete Letter Writer, The Frugal Housewife: or, Complete Woman Cook,* Welch's Dancing Academy with 'ladies only' sessions on Thursday and Saturday afternoons and, addressed 'to married ladies in particular', Turner's Imperial Lotion, a remedy *inter alia* for 'sore and inflamed breasts and nipples on lying-in'.[234] Towards the end of the century at least, the advertisements did not envisage these ladies as passive and confined to the home: a 1784 course of lectures on midwifery by John Leake (1729–92, man-midwife at the Westminster Lying-in Hospital) announced 'Female Pupils allowed to attend'. In 1812 an opportunity to acquire the sole rights to a valuable medicine was described as suitable for 'a Lady or Gentleman in the Country', and arrangements for the 1814 Annual General Meeting of the Church Missionary Society at the Crown & Anchor in the Strand included 'accommodations [...] provided for such Ladies as are Members of the Society'.[235]

Women were, then, serious readers and contributors, but with two differences between them and the male readership. Firstly, all the evidence is of reading in the private home. The second and more important difference is that of social class: the artisan woman is absent from the sources. Women were not using the magazine to acquire gentility. They arrived at it already, to use Connell's terminology, complicit in the gendered world the magazine constructed.

How the *Gentleman's Magazine* was read

How and why a text was read, and the responses it produced in readers, are elusive. Historical documents 'rarely show readers at work, fashioning meaning' from them.[236] Nonetheless, studies of eighteenth-century readers reveal a great diversity of individual practices.[237] As a miscellany the *Gentleman's Magazine* was, in the words of Cave's correspondent Dod, 'a Ragoust with Difft ingredients in the sauce, so it may possibly hit the tast of several difft persons'.[238] There were therefore several ways of reading and understanding it. 'A Traveller' even knew a man who read it like 'a Hebrew book' from the back (the obituaries) to the front.[239]

Its size and format, with relatively short articles, cross-referenced to back numbers where necessary, contents page, section headings, continuous pagination and index suggest two likely reading modes identified as new by historians of the eighteenth century: 'extensive' rather than 'intensive' reading, where a wide variety of material was read, typically briefly, before moving on to something fresh, and 'desultory' reading, in which volumes, numbers and articles were read out of order, singularly or over a long time frame.[240] Of course, different reading styles were not mutually exclusive.[241] 'O.B.' of Farnborough read the magazine both extensively and intensively: 'My second reading is, of course, less rapid than the first'.[242]

'We profess an affection'[243]

Readers' responses, contributions and letters to Cave and Nichols provide greater insight. Their attention to the timing of the magazine's arrival in different locations has already been noted. The four-weekly cycle until 'thy lov'd page again salutes our eyes', was an important part of the routine of their lives.[244] In 1799 'Veritas', like 'Aged Matron', described an exciting and pleasurable ritual: 'As soon as your Magazine arrives, it is dried, the leaves cut by my servant, and presented for my inspection. I immediately run my eye over the table of contents, wishing to read the most valuable parts first'.[245] The pleasure was probably redoubled when, like Horace Walpole, a reader saw his or her name or piece in print. Some of Nichols' correspondents asked for extra copies when they were published.[246]

John Phelan, librarian to the College of Physicians in London, incorporated it into his working life, reading it 'in separate numbers through the streets of London' as 'a walking reader many years'.[247] It was a comfort to isolated or retired readers. Poet and contributor William Newton (1750–1830), another artisan autodidact or, as he put it, 'Unschooled Hand', sent Nichols a covering letter enclosing two sonnets from Tideswell in the High Peak, 'a small Town, in the most mountainous part of Derbyshire, where I reside, and where the Gentleman's Magazine gives me frequent pleasure and information'.[248]

At Clay's Midland bookshops, it was, despite the avalanche of new titles, the older periodicals, the *Gentleman's* and *London Magazines*, which led among those taken for five years or more.[249] Many correspondents used pseudonyms drawing attention to their loyalty: 'A very old subscriber', 'A Constant Reader', 'A Reader for Twenty Years'.[250] Known readers who bought it continuously over many years include

Revd David Evans, whose name appears on wrappers spanning 31 years (from February 1743, when he was 38, to the 1774 Supplement); Revd Edward Goodwin of Sheffield, a correspondent for half a century by 1809; Cornelius Cardew, rector of St Erme, Cornwall, who told Nichols that he had 'for nearly fifty years received instruction & entertainment from the perusal of the Gentleman's Magazine', and Owen Manning (1721–1801, vicar of Godalming and county historian of Surrey) who, Thomas Collinson said, had 'taken in the Gentm Magazine from the beginning of that Poplication [*sic*]'. It was not unusual to have grown up with the magazine as James Bisset and Joseph Hunter had done: both Cardew and Manning had read it from the age of ten.[251]

The magazine had therefore a familiar quality for its readers, as Hazlitt recognized. The change of wrapper colour prompted a ribbing poem from 'S.I.P.' (Samuel Jackson Pratt, 1749–1814, writer and actor) in which he claimed that, as a 'constant Reader' from 'gay fifteen', he had not at first recognized the 'stranger'.[252] Editors and readers alike anthropomorphized it. The long-running personification of the editor assisted this process (letters to the *London Magazine* were addressed simply to 'The Author'). It was 'At once a FAV'RITE and a FRIEND' and each number was 'a Life,' though from birth it had been no infant but a wise and strong man.[253] For 'B.H.' the magazine was an attractive female companion: 'agreeable Miss *Mag.*' with whom he had 'a long and pleasing dalliance' (an interesting conceit given the importance of female company to politeness).[254] It was 'my old Chrony' declared 'a kind Correspondent', and was probably Richard Polwhele's 'dapper comrade wrapped in blue'.[255] Joseph Budworth/Palmer wrote to Nichols: 'I always meet with it as with an Old friend'.[256] Berington used the metaphor of benevolent kinship: 'a parental solicitude' for the magazine properly belonged to 'Urban' but 'yet is the publick not a little interested in its concerns'.[257] In a mobile society where close family ties were proving more difficult to maintain, the magazine was sometimes the 'friend' by which personal news was delivered, as 'J.H.' versified in 1750:

> A public paper, in confusion read,
> Brings the sad tidings that my friend is – dead.[258]

And a Mr Waldron wrote to Nichols in 1811 asking that an obituary of his son **not** be inserted as he wished to withhold the news for a while from his other children in 'various parts of the country'.[259]

It was because many correspondents assumed this personal closeness amounting to a shared sense of ownership with 'Sylvanus Urban' that they felt entitled to critique editorial policy ('Those most it mads who love it most' as 'L.S.R.' put it), to correct mistakes, and to expect that their offerings would appear in print.[260] Obituaries were amended and supplemented to the extent that there was often a sub-section: 'Additions and Corrections in former Obituaries'. In January 1787 'Amicus', dissatisfied with the 'very meagre article' that had been printed, submitted a one-and-a-half page eulogy of Revd William Cawthorn Unwin, and in 1807 B. Proby wrote to Nichols from Lichfield noting an error in the obituary of his father, and insisting on a correction.[261] They were querulous if their contributions were not published promptly. B. Drake sent Cave a poem as 'Theophilus' and was so outraged that this was not printed when long Latin poems had taken up so much space that he planned to call round in person to retrieve it.[262] Cardew cited his long-standing readership when he sent an illustrated local history item. He was tenacious in chasing it up and sent a fresh manuscript 18 months later when it had still not appeared.[263] On the more positive side, many readers immediately rallied round to offer sympathy and articles to ensure the continuity of 'their' magazine after the 1808 print-works fire.[264]

'One of the most useful and entertaining Miscellanies I know'[265]

The magazine of course had its mission to entertain, Cave's *'delectare'*. There were sensational news stories in the 'Historical Chronicle', humorous extracts in the 1730s and 1740s from publications such as the *Universal Spectator*, and lighter verse. Edward Cave justified the insertion of these 'gayer pieces' of poetry on the serious, educational grounds that they were 'leading' less-literary readers 'to perceive the force and beauty of more elevated compositions'.[266]

Yet readers' reactions indicated a degree of conflict between the gay and the serious content. Edward Blithe of Wisbech thought some articles 'intolerable trash'.[267] 'M.M.M.' (Revd William Tooke) regarded reading for pleasure as a trivial pursuit: 'He that reads merely for amusement may as well be employed at push-pin'.[268] For Walter Scott the magazine was like a pawnbroker's. 'Peter Pindar' described it as:

> [...] A Pedlar's, Huckster's Shop,
> That harbours brush, and cabbage-net, and mop. [269]

What such readers valued most was 'usefulness', the opportunity the magazine provided for debate both to correct error and to lead them towards a fuller state of knowledge. Berington regarded it as 'your charge to hand down to posterity, perhaps, the seeds of great discoveries'.[270] The diffusion of this knowledge was horizontal, between readers or particular groups such as Porter's physicians, or clergymen, and vertical, up the social scale as far as Parliament. In 1748 a correspondent on the iniquities of the Poor Law removal system, 'Crispin', a shoemaker, described the magazine as a route by which men such as himself might contact 'the great and noble'.[271] Cave's Maryland correspondent 'H.J.' anticipated that his contribution on navigation would 'fall into the Hands of far greater Numbers' through publication in the *Gentleman's Magazine* than it would 'if printed alone', that it would be 'thoroughly debated [...] as it were by a dispersed council of public-spirited ingenious Gentlemen', and that it would be corrected as necessary.[272] 'A Free Briton', an attorney writing in 1751 to advocate copyhold reform, chose the *Gentleman's Magazine* as his forum because 'your books are become a channel for conveying hints to the legislature'.[273]

It was therefore generally the informative articles, Cave's *'prodesse'*, which prompted readers to join the ranks of the correspondents and to transfer information from the magazine to journals and commonplace books. These responses tended to be swift. Byrom noted a conversation about an article on Methodism in the August 1739 issue as early as 5 September, for example.[274] Reader contributions had a similarly rapid turnaround. In July 1786, 'S.P.W.' of Statfold (Samuel Pipe Wolferstan) wrote to 'Urban' while 'warm from the impression of some articles' in a magazine received only three hours previously.[275]

Commonplacing entailed the selection and reorganization of read material, often alongside the reader's own prose and verse compositions. David Allan's recent study recovers the transformational nature of the practice: shaping, as well reflecting, readers' tastes and their sense of personal and community identity.[276] Commonplacers' compilations in several respects mirrored the contents of the *Gentleman's Magazine*: poetry 'of wildly fluctuating merit', records of significant life dates and travel notes.[277] Articles were also copied from the magazine, especially practical advice that built a private encyclopedia of useful information (Robert Chaplin of Norfolk, like Benjamin Rogers, transcribed medical recipes), news items that conjured a 'wider frame of reference within which the individual's own identity could be better defined and articulated' (the Suffolk lady and Fleming's prophecies), and literary material that helped shape critical abilities and self-image ('E.D.' of Derbyshire's note on Francis Hutcheson's *A System of Moral Philosophy* cross-referenced to the magazine's review of April 1755).

Commonplacing and corresponding demanded active reading with a sense of immediacy. It gave the magazine the air of a dialogue, of 'Urban' as Socrates. It also provides a strong counter-argument to Isaac Watts' contemporary complaint in his 1741 educational textbook, *Improvement of the Mind*, that works in octavo, unlike the scholarly folio, encouraged the reader to 'hover always on the surface of things' and to Steven Zwicker's claim that the development of indexing and formatting was an aid to skipping through a text in a passive manner, in contrast to the active early modern scholarly practice of annotation. [278]

The magazine was useful because it broadened horizons. This was summed up by Thomas Carter, a Colchester schoolboy of humble origins, who devoured his schoolmaster's 'old and odd volumes': 'They helped to give me a wider and more varied view of many more things than I had previously been able to command'.[279] For autodidact readers especially, it could even be transformative, their participation in the magazine facilitated by its stress on inclusivity and moderation in argument. Several moved from reading to corresponding, and then to a career as a published author. Henry Jones' 'Poem addressed to the Earl of Chesterfield' appeared in January 1746.[280] By 1749 he was in England publishing poetry with Chesterfield as his patron.[281] Hutton recalled that by 1762 'Some of my productions crept into the Magazines'. In 1782 he published *The History of Birmingham* and from the 1790s was a regular *Gentleman's Magazine* contributor under his own name.[282] Bisset's letter on the delights of his new home town of Leamington Spa was published in 1813.[283] Hunter left the cutlery trade, trained as a Presbyterian minister, published religious works and a history of Sheffield and established himself as a records scholar.[284]

'Copious, and distinct, and systematically arranged': the *Gentleman's Magazine* as a work of reference[285]

Entomologist, naturalist and Anglican cleric William Kirby (1759–1850) used back volumes of the magazine for scientific research, apologizing to antiquary George Ashby (1724–1808) when unable to answer a query. He had been unable to consult the *Gentleman's Magazine*.[286] For men like Kirby, the usefulness of bound volumes of the magazine was enhanced by the publication of general indexes, which scholars and would-be scholars used to find past articles. These indexes selected material, discarding what the indexer considered trivial or ephemeral, and further categorized it.

Edward Kimber (1719–69) compiled the first in 1753, covering the 20 volumes to 1750.[287] It met an expressed need: one reader wrote in anticipation to say how much he 'wish'd for such a thing'.[288] Its preface, attributed to Johnson, announced that it would 'enable those who read for higher purposes than mere Amusement, to class the many Subjects which our extensive Plan has included'. The indexed content was restricted: the 'Historical Chronicle' 'to the most regular', and the births, marriages, deaths and promotions to 'every Family, that is not too obscure to raise Curiosity'. But it was more than a finding-aid. Johnson regarded the index as in itself 'as Useful as a Common-place Book for these purposes as any extant'. [289]

Updated indexes were produced in 1789 and 1821.[290] The move away from reading for 'mere Amusement' was further emphasized in 1809 when John Walker of New College, Oxford (1770–1831) published his four-volume *Selection* of articles from the magazine, an idea first mooted in 1792 by Edward Gibbon as a means of rescuing the valuable content 'at present buried in a heap of trash'.[291] Walker's preface announced that 'all matters of temporary nature are omitted'. So were articles 'written in a hasty manner' and 'of doubtful authority'.[292] In 1804 the reader-driven victory of the *Gentleman's Magazine* mission to record and inform over that to entertain was recognized by the rival *Universal Magazine*: 'As a work of general amusement it can advance few claims to general approbation; but it may advance claims to something better, – that of being a repository of numerous interesting and important facts'.[293]

'In bright order rang'd': the *Gentleman's Magazine* and collecting

Books are not just for reading. As possessions, especially when displayed, they carry meaning for owners as part of material culture: 'used to project a social identity, a civil or domestic ideal, or a religious or ethical aspect of themselves, and by which they could proclaim adherence to a social group or a particular set of values, or conversely differentiate themselves from others'.[294] Defoe had stressed the importance of a proper library for gentlemanly status.[295] In the *Gentleman's Magazine*, 'A.C.' (Alexander Chalmers, 1759–1834, biographer and literary editor) argued that collecting books was a gentlemanly pursuit, preferable to racing, bull-baiting and such sports (and with the added prospect of rising value).[296]

Elaborate, rich bindings, like those of Thackeray's John Osborne and Cave's fondly imagined Prince of Wales and Duke of Cumberland, were a symbol of gentlemanly wealth and status. Many such runs of the magazine survive in the libraries of high-status homes. The library of Audley End House, Essex, was remodelled by Robert Adam when the owner, Sir John Griffin Griffin (1719–97) returned from the Seven Years' War.[297] More professional soldier than man of letters, he had his books, including his run of the *Gentleman's Magazine*, rebound in red and gold chequered calf to complement Adam's decorative scheme. That this was largely for show is indicated by his frugal approach: on many only the spine is in livery, the boards are marbled card.

Books and associated furniture (bookcases, shelving and desks) were also increasingly found in urban middling-sort homes.[298] Cave understood the aspiration of this class of readers for volumes that would 'make a pleasing appearance in a regular library'.[299] 50 years later, the 80 volumes of the magazine advertised by Mary Flavell & Sons, bookbinders of Shoe Lane, were still aimed at cost-conscious middling-sort customers emulating the libraries of the elite: 'bound in cheap elegant Binding, and ornamented in a peculiar Style; and which, as to ornament, is a *unique* Set, as no other person is in Possession of the appropriate Figures, nor were they ever before used'.[300]

Newspaper advertisements for auctions of effects including the *Gentleman's Magazine* show the geographical and social spread of these libraries and the other publications that the readers possessed. A medical gentleman had professional texts and the *Monthly Review*.[301] Revd John Piper of Sudbury owned Blair's *Sermons*, the *Universal Magazine*, *Annual Register*, Homer's *Iliad* and various *Histories* of England. Linen draper William Notcutt of Ipswich had a range of periodicals, works on natural philosophy, and scientific equipment that included an orrery, electrical machine and telescope.[302]

Their bound *Gentleman's Magazine* volumes on the shelves of a library or more humble bookcase both signalled the appropriation of the systems of knowledge they contained and represented their gentlemanly standing and taste. The constant availability of reprints and back numbers, advertised on wrappers and title pages, reveals the strong desire of many readers to acquire such sets. It was a pleasure they expressed in writing. For 'Philargyrus' (Revd William Rider, 1723–85, historian and writer) they were both 'profitable' and 'ornamental to my study'.[303] 'D.R.' of Warwick Street happily reflected: 'I can't help looking at my twenty volumes as the most amusing and valuable set of books in my library'.[304] What became Volume V of the 1821 index (illustrations) was originally compiled by Charles St Barbe for the 'ease of reference to the Set of the Magazine in his own Library'.[305]

The demand surprised even Nichols: 'The Proprietors were aware that the FIRST VOLUME was scarce, but had no idea that the Call for it would have been so great as they have experienced'.[306] It accounts for the thriving second-hand markets in single numbers and bound runs. Nichols fielded numerous enquiries from readers about buying missing copies or volumes. John Goodford of Bath had sought an intact 1773 volume. Sir William Curtis had the magazine to 1765 and wanted to complete the run to the end of 1813. In 1819 John Upham, also of Bath, had bought a complete set to 1802 and hoped Nichols could supply 'the residue'.[307]

These back numbers could be literally profitable. In 1812 Revd Arthur Atkinson of Enham, near Andover, enquired about selling his complete set from 1731 (failing eyesight meant he could 'scarcely read any print, especially the Gentleman's Magazine'). Nichols replied that the average price of a good set might be 50 guineas and the range 35–70 guineas, recommending book auctioneers Messrs King of King Street, Covent Garden.[308] Scarce numbers also commanded a high price. In July 1810 a tart reply through the 'Index Indicatorius' explained market forces to 'A Constant Reader' who complained that a bookseller had demanded 2s 6d for one 1806 number.[309]

Conclusion

While the *Gentleman's Magazine*, with its title, luxury edition and memorializing of their family achievements, appeared addressed to the nobility and gentry, the evidence of real and implied readers is that its success was based on the targeting, capture and consolidation of a readership among the much larger middling-sort market, especially professionals and tradesmen. For many of these readers it was a long-term, routine and valued part of their cultural lives, often from adolescence. Like its predecessor 'magazines' it was 'useful' and, increasingly, serious. The knowledge it imparted was circulated among friends and commonplaced. It was preserved as a work of reference by binding and, collected and displayed, became a part of genteel material culture. The magazine also had an impact lower down the social scale, especially on ambitious, autodidact artisan men. As the thieves or the literate beggar Simon Edy and his audience demonstrate, the dividing line between an elite culture of print and a low, popular, oral culture was not a solid brick wall.

Despite its title the magazine never excluded female readers and contributors, although they were a minority. Instead, advertising, both for the magazine and on the wrappers, implies an audience of men and women reading together within the private sphere of the family. The debates and issues it covered were shaped and absorbed by women as well as men. Its female readership paralleled the social role women were thought to play as a civilizing influence that helped shape polite masculinity. There was no brick wall between the sexes either.

The *Gentleman's Magazine*, aided by communications improvements, also broke down the barrier to information that distance from London had imposed in previous centuries.[310] Its national circulation bound together readers from the metropolis, provinces and colonies, facilitating a process of debate and information that flowed in all directions. Its large readership made it a major mechanism facilitating the spread of Wahrman's culture of a homogenous 'national society'.[311] It kept provincial readers *au fait* with the London theatre, for example, through the lists of plays, reviews and the reprinting of prologues, epilogues and songs. At the same time, the presence of material from and about the regions suggests that there was still a significant place in readers' minds for Wahrman's traditional 'polymorphous communal provincial culture' that here sat proudly within 'national society', rather than forming an alternative.[312]

The penetration into the middling sort similarly had potential for the broad dissemination of ideas and the creation of a shared outlook across the boundary of rank with the social and educational elite. It was in many respects analogous to the clubs and societies that from the beginning of the century had proliferated in London and outwards into the provinces as a major form of new social institution for landed, middling and artisanal people.[313] It was read sociably, and its audience felt a sense of belonging. Unlike a club, however, it was not limited by location and 'members' required no personal introduction or patronage. It was a 'portable coffeehouse', or a mini-Republic of Letters that built 'communal values' and 'a network of obligation' relatively free of the hierarchies of birth and wealth.[314] Its readers were no longer Richard Sennett's 'strangers' who were 'increasingly like each other but didn't know it', but an 'imagined community' aware of the presence of fellow magazine readers across Britain and her colonies.[315] Through the seriality of their letters, 'the correspondents become acquainted', claimed the 1777 Preface. 'E.J.' (Revd Edward Jones) confirmed this, saying of 'R.N.' (Revd Ralph Nicholson): 'Not being personally known to him [...] I owe the pleasure of a correspondence with him to the communications he gave the publick in your Magazine'.[316]

Carlson is therefore correct in seeing it as a democratizing force. It evened out social and regional differences, undermining Langford's assertion that 'What was polite in Berkeley Square was not necessarily what was polite in Finsbury or Hammersmith, let alone in Shadwell or Wapping'.[317] Anonymity and the high value placed on civility mediated by 'Sylvanus Urban' ('Urbanus' as 'urbane' as one correspondent saw it) ensured that the merit of an argument, serious content properly treated, rather than the social standing of the writer, lent authority.[318]

The readers' construction of gentlemanly masculinity, whether shared or disputed, stable or changing, is the subject of the following three chapters. This chapter has established the magazine as playing a significant role in furthering the spread of polite culture beyond its epicentre, London, and into the middling-sort and artisan circles. In this respect it was formative, an aspirational and educative tool, equipping readers for participation in the debates of the public sphere, allowing engagement as contributors and, as a material object, proclaiming their new gentility. Becoming a published correspondent marked a further, more confident move beyond the organizing and contemplative process of commonplacing, by taking previously private musings to the public sphere and the scrutiny of others. There were also intimations of social changes that affected gentlemanly masculinity: growing anxiety over decency, a shift away from entertainment, and tension between those who saw the magazine as a strictly learned publication and those who saw it as a nursery of ideas.

4
Gentlemanly Masculinity in the *Gentleman's Magazine*, 1731 to 1756

Introduction

'*All the World cries*, There goes a GENTLEMAN: – *And, when you have said* GENTLEMAN, *you have said* EVERY THING', ran the introduction to an excerpt from the *Prompter* in the *Gentleman's Magazine* for January 1736.[1] The lines came from John Crowne's comedy, *Sir Courtly Nice*, spoken by the eponymous fop to explain as gentlemanly 'complaisance' his apparent hypocrisy in praising singers to their faces, only to criticize them later.[2]

Written and first performed in 1685, the play remained an eighteenth-century 'staple of the English stage'.[3] The *Gentleman's Magazine* listed it under 'Plays Acted at the Theatre' at Drury Lane in October 1751 and November 1753.[4] The quoted lines were well-known. In 1746 Samuel Foote used them to mimic rival comic actor Henry Woodward. But Foote did not merely ape Woodward's performance in the role. Slipping into his own voice, he replaced the final clause with 'you have said more than is true'.[5] It was a mean dig at Woodward's humble origins: he had initially followed his father's trade of tallow-chandler, whereas Foote's father was a well-to-do Cornish lawyer and magistrate.

These lines were associated, then, with an enduring understanding that gentlemanliness was conveyed by a polite appearance, manner or deportment, but that underlying traditional gentlemanliness was of greater importance: polite dress and manners might indicate foppery or disguise an unworthy gentleman or social interloper. This ambivalence continued in the substance of the *Prompter* excerpt: a fable in

which a man of genteel family thought only of his dignity and pleasure. When he seized the land of a neighbouring peasant basket-maker
to improve the hunting and fishing on his estate, the country's ruler
transported both men to a desert island. Here the 'gentleman' discovered that *'the Superiority of his Blood was imaginary'*. The basket-maker's
practical skills were of greater use. The story's origin (allegedly from a
Peruvian manuscript) and setting (the Solomon Islands) were exotic. The
moral, however, that gentlemen had to 'to give a better Reason for their
Pride, than that they were BORN, *to do No thing'*, was directed at British
men: 'some *Thousand* pretty GENTLEMEN about Town, whose Eyes are
too full of *Themselves'*.

In reprinting Sir Courtly's lines and the *Prompter* article, The *Gentleman's Magazine* engaged with the early-eighteenth-century concerns
about gentlemanly masculinity that arose from the more fluid concept
of the gentleman. If gentlemanliness was not simply a matter of lineage, but also depended upon qualities that could be acquired, then
new categories of men – in particular the merchants, other tradesmen
and professionals who formed such a significant proportion of the
Gentleman's Magazine readership – might demand that they too be
acknowledged as gentlemen. Could they be incorporated within the old
definition by birth and, if so, how? What were the qualities they had
to demonstrate? Did any possible exemplars resonate especially effectively with the readership, such that there was a discernible *Gentleman's
Magazine* ideal binding together its readers from the nobility, gentry and
middling sort?

This chapter examines how the *Gentleman's Magazine* handled these
issues of the 'new gentleman' from its launch in 1731 to the disastrous
opening months of the Seven Years' War in 1756. For most of this period
it was edited by founder Edward Cave, and from 1754 by Richard Cave
and David Henry. The 26 years were dominated at home by the Walpole
administration and the aftermath of its fall in 1742, and by military conflicts overseas (the War of the Austrian Succession, 1739–48, continual
skirmishes with the French and Spanish, especially over the Americas
and Caribbean), and at home (the Jacobite rebellion and invasion of
1745–46). They ended with the disgrace of Admiral Byng after the loss
of Minorca to the French in June 1756. News of the loss and Byng in person reached Britain in time for the July issue of the magazine in which
Byng was compared unfavourably to General Blakeney, the defender of
Fort St Phillip on Minorca. This coverage is used as a case study as a
terminal point to the chapter.

Paradigm gentlemen: club members, Sir Charles Grandison and ChristianHeroes

In January 1733, the *Gentleman's Magazine* provided readers with models of gentlemanly characters in a 'Weekly Essays' extract from the first three numbers of a new publication, the *Auditor*.[6] This was self-consciously in the didactic tradition of the Whig essay periodicals of the early century, the *Spectator* and *Tatler*, which had aimed to instruct in politeness men and women in 'all well regulated Families, that set apart an Hour in every Morning for Tea and Bread and Butter'.[7] Numbers I and II admitted the debt – 'the Example of the *Spectator*, will justify my entering into the Scenes of active Life' – and stated its own aim: to update the tradition for the follies of the current decade: 'Stagnation of Taste' and 'Want of Desire in People to improve themselves'. The title, editorial *persona* (a gentleman's son born into the Whig revolution in 1689), and stress on self-improvement in mixed company ('Mr Auditor' had an instrument that blotted out sound 'whenever the Discourse turns to Lewdness, &c.') confirmed the heritage.[8]

Number III was an account of 'Mr Auditor's' club. The club conceit was of course taken directly from the *Spectator's* club of six members, each representing a polite 'type': a traditional country gentleman 'of antient Descent' Sir Roger de Coverly, a Middle Temple lawyer, City merchant Sir Andrew Freeport, retired soldier Captain Sentry, elderly roué Will Honeycomb, and a clergyman.[9]

The *Auditor's* club, immediately republished to the wider audience of the *Gentleman's Magazine*, had four members, each of whom was also an archetypal gentleman. 'Sir Charles Freeman' was of gentry stock (son of the late Sir Robert) and a retired army officer. University-educated, he had served in Marlborough's army before retiring to his estate after the Peace of Utrecht (1713). Maturity and military experience qualified him 'to be a perfect Judge of Men'. He was 'In his Conversation [...] open and unconfined; in his Behaviour free and disengaged' with 'the Courage and Impartiality of *Manly* in the *Plain-Dealer*, without his Spleen or Bitterness'.[10]

The second man, 'Frank Easy' was a '*Woman's Man*', a polite gentleman-about-town, proficient in dancing and music, with a smattering of understanding of art. He was no foppish caricature, however, but like Freeman was restrained: 'His Dress is rich, but not tawdry; and his Conversation *light*, yet agreeable enough'. Even his amours were presented as conducted with 'Sentiments of probity and Good-nature' (though in fact little more than *ex post facto* settlements on women he had seduced).

Next was an Italian polymath. He brought continental learning and reminded readers both of the superiority of English Protestantism to Roman Catholicism (he had left his native country because of his 'Aversion to Bigotry and Superstition') and of the need to avoid a national characteristic of excessive self-admiration ('that Prevention and Redundancy of Zeal, so natural to an *Englishman*, in Favour of ourselves'). He therefore performed on home soil some of the educational functions of the Grand Tour. Since the late seventeenth century, this had developed as a masculine rite of passage 'requisite to [. . .] accomplish a gentleman', intended to confer polished manners, fluency in French and Italian, and an understanding of the customs and government of other countries.[11] The final member was scholarly 'Tom Cynick', whose taciturn mastery of that key component of traditional gentlemanly education, classical learning, was a counterpoise to 'Easy's' shallower learning and talkative style.

Each man was a model of gentlemanliness primarily by virtue of outward manifestations of character and social behaviour judged in company against other men, rather than by lineage. Only 'Freeman' was overtly a man of property and birth. Even in his case, however, gentlemanliness relied on something more: an active role in public life as a soldier, and a considered character. They were therefore templates of the new, polite masculinity that could be acquired through the appropriate education by the magazine's less socially exalted readers. 'Easy's' politeness – sociability and skill in conversation tempered by the learning of the 'Italian' and of 'Cynick' – was presented in a positive light, but it was 'Freeman' who, as his name implied, was the exemplar of the gentlemanly qualities that might be followed: rooted in the traditions of family descent and land, but confirmed by social performance.

In 1736 the magazine provided a real-life parallel to 'Freeman' in an anonymous poem addressed to the late Sir William Fytch:

> Kind the Companion, and sincere the Friend,
> With sweet good nature temper'd what he spoke.
> His Wit was pleasing, not severe the Joke;
> Fix'd in his Morals, in his Conduct nice [. . .][12]

The model was also followed in the deaths notices. Longer entries celebrated lineage. Sir William Hardres' status derived from family residence at Hardres Court, Kent, a seat held 'since *William* the conqueror', for example.[13] However, the notices increasingly added detail of polite personal attributes. Sir George Fleming, Bishop of Carlisle, died in July 1747. Of gentry birth (the fifth son of Sir Daniel Fleming of Rydal Hall, Westmoreland), through the accidents of death he inherited the baronetcy in 1736. His death notice referred the reader to his 'character', a three-page eulogy, in the first half of the magazine among the readers' letters. In his career 'in each Step, his Merit preceded his Promotion'. His private virtues included 'affability', 'Tenderness and Affection in the nearer Relations of Life' and moderation: 'Reason constantly maintain'd its proper Sway over his Passions'. He was benevolent and hospitable within the bounds of prudent financial management, and the centre of family and household life: to 'his Children the best Father, his Servants the best Master, the Poor their best benefactor, and Numbers of Men the best Friend'.[14] In July 1753 Sir John Stuart of Allanbank was memorialized in similar terms:

> In him the virtues of private life, candour, moderation, and humanity, were amiable and eminent. –He was happy in friendship, and in all the charities. –From integrity of heart, and simplicity of manners, he knew no inward reproach, nor blame from the world.[15]

The resonance of this paradigm of the polite gentleman was demonstrated by the swift and very positive response the *Gentleman's Magazine* gave to Samuel Richardson's novel of a self-consciously virtuous man, *Sir Charles Grandison*, also in 1753.[16] It greeted the first four volumes enthusiastically in an unusually lengthy comment under 'Books publish'd in November' (a half-column at a date when this section was little more than a list of titles). The public would not be disappointed with this exhibition of 'the character and actions of a man of true honour' whose 'every natural and accidental advantage, is improved by virtue and piety; that these polish elegance, heighten dignity and produce universal love, esteem and veneration'.[17] Grandison also resonated with women. In January 1754 Johnson's friend and companion Anna Williams (1706–83) addressed a magazine poem to Richardson on his new work. Whereas the 'idle novels' of the 'degen'rate age' had elevated to fame such unsuitable characters as prostitutes, *Grandison*, she said, offered softer female beauties and, above all, Sir Charles himself in whom:

> The firm and kind, the daring and polite,
> To form one character, in one unite.[18]

By April 1755, correspondent 'Oxoniensis', in a letter describing the town of Stamford, Lincolnshire, was already using the name as commendatory short-hand. A nobleman in the district 'who by his polite and condescending behaviour had deservedly gained the affection of all the inhabitants in it', was 'The Sir Charles Grandison of the age'.[19]

Richardson had already published conduct books aimed at the middling sort.[20] As all these examples indicate, the hero Grandison was tantamount to a conduct book model of the polite gentleman, whose steadfast piety, virtue and sympathetic benevolence won others over to his way of thinking. Like the *Prompter*'s 'Sir Charles Freeman' and many subjects of the Deaths columns, he was a man of property. After a Tour of Italy he had returned home and committed himself to Grandison Hall as a site of polite company, order and restraint. He resisted the constant temptation to seduce the women who fell in love with him. Although prepared to exercise manly force in a just cause (rescuing Harriet Byron from Sir Hargrave Pollexfen on Hounslow Heath, for instance), he abhorred harm to others, refusing Pollexfen's and others' challenges to duel. Instead he deployed negotiation, love and consideration for the feelings of others, especially his sisters and Italian betrothed Clementina, to persuade rather than compel deference. In all these respects he represented a break with the old aristocratic notion of personal honour and a contrast with the unreformed generation of his father, the libertine Sir Thomas.[21]

Grandison has also been compared to Richard Steele's earlier model, *The Christian Hero*.[22] In this work, published in 1701 and running to 20 editions over the century, Steele replaced pagan Romans, such as Caesar and Cato, with a template fit for modern behaviour.[23] Like Grandison, his Christian Hero acted not in the erroneous pursuit of personal ambition or pleasure (the 'changeable Heat of mere Courage and Blood') but on 'firm motives of Duty, Valour and Constancy of Soul' based on inner virtue and reason. He was a man of action, but action tempered by a pious virtue.[24]

The *Gentleman's Magazine* set 'The Christian Hero' as the theme for its fifth poetry competition announced at the end of 1735. The prize was a gold medal said to be worth £40 with a real 'Christian Hero' on either face: James Oglethorpe (1696–1785), army officer and benevolent reformist founder of the new American colony of Georgia, and Archbishop Tillotson (1630–94), whose collected sermons were popular texts throughout the eighteenth century.[25] They were advertised on the magazine's wrappers and, perhaps with their less-educated magazine readers in mind, David Henry and Richard Cave published an abridged version, *Twenty Discourses*, 'adapted to the meanest capacities'. Tillotson's themes were Grandisonian *avant la lettre,* piety in public and private, and self-restraint: 'governing his passions and *bridling* his tongue'.[26] Oglethorpe also enjoyed a lasting reputation with readers. A correspondent submitted a *Life* in 1785, for instance.[27]

Steele's tract may have inspired Cave's choice of theme (one entry addressed him in its opening lines).[28] Equally it may have been prompted by George Lillo's tragedy of the same name, recently played at Drury Lane. Lillo's hero, Scanderbeg, like the basket-maker fable, accounted deeds rather than birth the measure of a man:

> Superior Birth, unmerited Success,
> The Name of Prince, of Conqueror and King,
> Are Gifts of Fortune and of little Worth.
> They may be, and too often are, possest
> By sordid Souls, who know no Joy but Wealth [...]
> Our Actions form our Characters [...][29]

In either case it worked. There were 24 competition entries, eight of them published between June and September 1736. The middling-sort pen-cutter Moses Browne inevitably took the prize. Numbers III, IV and V, were printed in the sampled month of July. Long and studded with biblical footnotes, they reflected readers' assumptions about the Hero's attributes. He endured conflict couched in the language of warfare: 'taking up arms', 'battle after battle', 'to live and die', 'this glorious strife'.[30] But his was a conflict of the mind or spirit. Their Hero resisted the temptations of this earthly world (amours, ambition and avarice in Poem V), resigning himself to its pains in order to achieve ultimate bliss in heaven. A successful 'warrior' in this fight had the general good as his guiding principle manifested in benevolent actions and self-improvement.[31]

The entries endorsed a notion of superior Christian virtue that paved the way for its reception of Grandison. Qualities of piety, benevolence and resignation were of course achievable and commendable in women. Indeed, when the competition was first announced the prize medal was to have a portrait of one such, Lady Elizabeth Hastings (1682–1739). Tillotson was a safely dead replacement when she objected to the use of her image without prior permission.[32] However, the poems implicitly gendered the virtue as male through their active, martial spirit and the feminization of temptation as a seductress.

Adapting the paradigm: reader 'types'

Between 1731 and 1756 readers were, therefore, presented with model and real versions of the polite gentleman motivated by an active Christianity. He demonstrated his status through a combination of propertied standing, learning, restraint, piety and benevolence. He played a role in the public world of men both as, for example, a soldier or churchman, and as a member of a club of like-minded gentlemen. It was here that his gentlemanliness was judged, against that of other men. *Gentleman's Magazine* readers who shared Grandison's and 'Freeman's' status would have seen themselves reflected in this paradigm and acknowledged in the announcements.

However, as Chapter 3 shows, the magazine's core readership did not come from this elite, propertied world but from the professional and trading middling sort (as did Grandison's creator, Richardson). They lacked lineage, estates and education and were unlikely to afford a Grand Tour and the worldly experience this brought. For them Grandison truly was a fiction, yet by reading the magazine they were surely buying into a belief that they too were or might become gentlemen like him.[33]

'Sylvanus Urban' was well aware of this. Two prefaces from the period listed types of 'gentlemen' who came from a broader range of backgrounds, yet would find something useful and to their taste in his miscellany. In 1740 these were the 'Scholar', 'Soldier' and 'Politician' (not so different from the *Auditor*'s club) but with two additional middling-sort characters. Their potentially contested right to inclusion was indicated by the need for complimentary explanatory epithets: the 'industrious Merchant' and the 'honest Shopkeeper'.[34]

In 1755, 22 years on from the *Auditor* piece and two years after Edward Cave's death, the Preface consisted of the seven letters from imagined reader-correspondents on the future direction of the magazine (see Chapter 2). Again there was an overlap with the *Auditor*'s gentlemen, but also something new. 'Jack Dactyl' was close to 'Frank Easy', speaking the language of the young buck-about-town ('d – n it', 'what the devil') and demanding modern literature. 'The Italian' and 'Cynick' were paralleled by 'Mr Sylvester Polyglot', 'Mr Jonathan Vertu' and 'Mr Jacob Lemma', favouring scholarly articles on, variously, philology, natural history, antiquity, mathematics, mechanics and astronomy. 'Mr Rus', his Latin name implying an educated country gentleman living, like 'Freeman', a retired life on his estates, wanted biographies as examples for the living, and to be informed of books worth ordering from London. They were, however, joined by a professional, 'Dr Pulse', for whom the magazine was a useful conduit for medical information, and a man of commerce, 'Mr Tradewell'. 'Tradewell' brought a moral, middling-sort politeness to the circle. He claimed to speak for 'all sober and sensible men' and (perhaps with 'Easy' and 'Dactyl' in his sights) derided the poetry as 'frothy merryment' produced by 'some amorous and idle coxcomb' to 'tickle the fancy of idle and voluptuous youth'. His preference was the most political: 'a serious account of publick affairs'.

The *Gentleman's Magazine* and the polite 'new gentlemen'

A course of education

This section examines the *Gentleman's Magazine* response to its middling-sort, 'Pulse' and 'Tradewell' readers' desire for inclusion in its wider world of the idealized polite gentleman. Although, like the basket-maker fable and Scanderbeg, such readers questioned the primacy of land and birth without accompanying moral worth, their new gentlemanliness did not fundamentally disturb the fabric of the hierarchical society with the traditional gentleman at its pinnacle.

Indeed, a high proportion of the magazine content in this period continued to report and support, both directly and indirectly, the gendered concerns of lineage, land and patronage within which Grandison and Freeman were positioned as gentlemen. There was extensive coverage of the all-male preserves of politics and religion (with an emphasis on support for the established church, primarily against the challenge posed by dissent) in the press extracts, the original 'Debates in Parliament' and the news section, the 'Historical Chronicle', with its reports on diplomacy, the court and the business worlds of the South Sea and East India Companies and the Bank.[35]

The regular back-half columns depicted a similar world.[36] Births were dominated by the upper ranks of society: nobles, baronets, gentry, Members of Parliament, bishops. They were couched in terms of the lineage family, of the male line of descent. The sample shows a bias towards announcing the birth of sons (139) rather than daughters (95). 36 were of the birth of 'a son and heir', a privileged position available only to males.[37] The bias corroborates Trumbach's finding from his study of 30 noble families that 'the only successful termination to a great lady's labor' was the birth of a son, and of a corresponding disappointment often felt over the birth of daughters.[38] This very special delight at the birth of a son was encapsulated in a *Gentleman's Magazine* poem by 'W. C – e' (William Coke) in 'On the Birth of a Male-Infant':

> That bless'd thy father with a better store
> Than all his wishes met before![39]

Marriage announcements also reflected elite concerns. They were business-like in their brevity. The bride was named, underscoring the uniting of two persons and families, but often (38 per cent of sampled entries) so too was the amount of the marriage settlement. An egregious example was that of Hon. Mr Verney, son of Lord Fermanagh, to Miss Nichols of Clapham 'with 30,000 l. down, and 1,000 l. at the Birth of every Child'.[40] The sometimes eye-watering sums confirmed Lady Mary Wortley Montagu's dim view of elite marriage as legal prostitution:

> This Nuptial Sale, this *Auction* of their Love.[41]

Promotions (or 'Preferments') were divided into civil (the army, navy, court and royal household, colonial administration, law and diplomatic posts) and ecclesiastical (Church of England) offices, with occasional additional lists of, for example, the sheriffs of the counties and newly elected Members of Parliament.[42] Sourcing from the official government paper, the *London Gazette*, and monthly repetition reinforced the importance of these public institutions that underpinned the social hierarchy.[43] Many appointees were members of lineage families: Lord Robert Manners as Gentleman Usher to the King in 1735; Charles Compton Esq., brother to the Earl of Northampton, Envoy Extraordinary to the King of Portugal in 1742 and Rt Hon. George Doddington Esq., Treasurer of the Navy in 1756.[44] This too was a male sphere: only 14 promotions were of women, of whom 13 were court or royal appointments. The exception was Christina Roccati, 'a celebrated Italian *virtuosa* – doctress in philosophy at the university of Bologna'. The point of her inclusion was the extreme novelty of her achievement in a world where what counted was advancement in fields that were male prerogatives.[45]

All this material confirmed the central importance of the public world of elite men to readers from this station and below alike. But the same reportage can also be read, like the classical content, as an educational tool for men aspiring to gentlemanly status. If, therefore, the magazine represented and supported an apparently fixed and stable social hierarchy, it also fulfilled a didactic role. It provided a window into the lives of the elite and the potted knowledge that would assist those not born to greatness to pass for polite, as a 'Lemma', 'Polyglot' or 'Vertu'. To those remote, literally or metaphorically, from the Cities of London and Westminster, it extended, albeit at one remove, the opportunity to:

> Frequent Coffee houses, and all Places of public Resort, where Men are to be seen and practiced, go to the shops of Mechanics as well as the Clubs of the Learned, Courts of Justice and particularly the Houses of Parliament, in order to learn something of the Laws and Interests of [their] Country,

advised in 1745, by David Fordyce as a means of acquiring polish and public spiritedness.[46]

This was also true of the gendered knowledge of other countries gained by wealthy, well-connected gentlemen on the Grand Tour.[47] Richard Hurd used Locke's voice to suggest this 'a paltry thing', to be acquired without leaving Britain's shores: 'My next advice is [...] that he stay at home: read *Europe* in the mirror of his own country [...] and for the rest take up with the best information he can get from the books and narratives of the best voyagers'.[48] Impecunity forced this approach upon Samuel Johnson. To his regret, his only travel outside the British Isles was a brief trip to Paris in 1775, and he had to use his extensive reading to conjure up the foreign settings of his biographies and fictions.[49]

Britain was the focus of the magazine in this period. News from overseas looked chiefly to her Atlantic colonies or was dominated by reports, adversarial in tone, of conflict with Spain and France. However, the number of articles which mimicked the beneficial effects of travel and contact with men such as the *Prompter*'s 'Italian', slowly increased, backed by reader contributions. The magazine published, in English, the papers of European academies and institutions. In January 1749 three continuous pages were taken up with the 'Memoirs of the Royal Academy of Sciences in Sweden', followed by a paper on cattle murrain read at the Royal Academy of Sciences at Paris.[50] In 1741 two of Johnson's 'lives' brought European scholars to readers' attention: Philip Barretier (Johan Philip Baratier), recently deceased German polymath, and Dr Louis Morin, seventeenth-century French physician and scientist.[51] In January 1753 'D.L.' supplied 'An Account of the Baths of Naples, Pozzuoli (or Puteoli) and Baia' again translated (from Italian) to 'follow your Account of Vesuvius'; 'West.Hall.' (Westley Hall, 1711–76, brother-in-law of John Wesley) addressed a poem proposing a 'Universal History of experimental Knowledge' to Frederick the Great of Prussia, and the news opened with a 'Foreign History' section which took the reader through affairs of state and commerce in Persia, Russia, Denmark, Germany, Italy, Spain and France.[52]

The 'new gentlemen'

Factual coverage of public life was valued by *Gentleman's Magazine* readers, as the large print runs, urgent reprints of the mid-1740s and expansion in active reader engagement in the form of correspondence spilling over into the *Miscellaneous Correspondence* indicated. The take-off in reader engagement coincided with the years when the magazine was most renowned for the 'Debates in Parliament' and peaked during the 1745 rebellion.[53] Despite this, the magazine's correspondents (perhaps 600–700 in this period, most writing only once or twice) did not generally comment either on affairs of state or the politics covered in the press excerpts and news.[54] The exception was where these touched on trade and taxation, topics probably dear to the heart of 'Mr Tradewell'. For example 'For the benefit of the country batchelors' was an amusing, anonymous call for a reduction in tea duty as from a middling-sort provincial society coming, pertinently, in a general election year.[55] Readers were more typically moved to write by theology and religion, scientific developments, including the weather and astrology and their own experiments, mathematics, medicine and health and, to a more limited extent, literature, history and geography. These are, of course, indicative of the subject matter they both enjoyed and considered appropriate in a periodical with 'gentleman' in its title. They matched the editors' identification of the 'Scholar', 'Polyglot', 'Vertu', 'Lemma' and 'Pulse' as reader 'types'.

This section considers how readers' letters and poems, juxtaposed with editorial material, promoted a vision of the new gentlemanliness that allowed middling-sort readers to be more than imitators: the equals of those with the bloodline and the estates. It was effected by asserting the overriding importance of inner character demonstrated by success, politeness and good works. Such gentlemanliness was, as was recognized elsewhere in eighteenth-century writing, potentially universal and so achievable across boundaries of class and race. Francis Hutcheson's *System of Moral Philosophy*, reviewed in the *Gentleman's Magazine* in April 1755, and noted by commonplacer 'E.D.', was praised as 'proof that this sense of moral excellence and of honour is universal'.[56]

The magazine often depicted plebeian men as counter-examples to its gentlemen. They were impolite: possessing physical rather than mental powers and with a tendency to irrational outbursts of violence that underscored their ungentlemanliness. They were villains in alarming news reports of incomprehensibly vile crimes: two cases of wife-murder on one page in January 1732, one by beating and throwing the pregnant woman out of a window and the other by imprisonment and starvation, or the gruesome killing of Customs man Galley and informer Chater by smugglers in 1749. Collectively they were the riotous 'mob': weavers and labourers in Spitalfields in 1736 or English soldiers and local butchers at Ghent in 1742.[57] Their births, marriages and deaths were recorded only when extraordinary (extreme old age, again reinforcing physicality, such as 105-year-old Robert Bristow of Stamford who was deaf but retained his other senses to the end) or 'amusing' (the wife of 'one Kirkeen' of Dublin, who 'immediately put her in a Coffin, had it nailed up and buryed her the next Day' as she had twice previously come back to life).[58]

However, the universal nature of 'moral excellence, and of honour' meant that, in theory, with the appropriate education anyone could become a gentleman, even plebeian men. In 'A Pastoral Dialogue' an anonymous poet imagined polite gentlemanly qualities extending down the social scale to Roger, a shepherd. According to his sweetheart and her friend, he added to plebeian physical manliness and rough with the gentility of the Christian Hero. He was pious in public and private, benevolent to those less fortunate than himself:

> Yet kind he was, for once a month he came,
> And left a shilling with our *Meg* that's lame,

and so gentle that he tended sick animals and wept at the cruelty of rural sports, which were routinely criticized by the magazine's readers as unchristian and 'unmanly':

> Cudgel at shrovetide-cock he never flung;
> And once I saw him at the baiting bull,
> With heart just bursting, and with eyes brimful.[59]

Gentlemanliness might also extend to non-white men, including former slaves. In January 1735 the *Gentleman's Magazine* reprinted a *Prompter* article purporting to be a speech by 'Moses Bon Sàam', Maroon leader of a Jamaican slave revolt.[60] Bon Sàam was dignified, speaking not Creole *patois* but the oratorical language of an educated British gentleman and politician. He envisaged a future black Caribbean civilization with which the British would be compelled to trade on equal terms because the differences between them were of 'Education and Accident' rather than 'Genius'. 'Mercator Honestus' picked up this theme in his contro-versial 1740 letter that provoked the Caribbean response discussed in Chapter 3: 'I don't doubt the Blacks are more civilized than they are generally represented, and it is very certain, that with some pain, they might become much more so'.[61]

This universality was, however, not articulated politically. The *Gentle-man's Magazine* excerpted opposition press articles criticizing Walpole's administration for corruption, but far from being calls for broaden-ing the suffrage or access to Parliament, these merely demanded a change in the elite personnel of government and were in any case bal-anced by excerpts from pro-government papers. Towards the end of the period there were signs of change. Surely political intent lay behind the 1751 call from one of the new professional breed of gentlemen, 'A Free Briton', for the abolition of copyhold with the added inciden-tal benefit of an enlarged franchise.[62] He followed two earlier letters from 'An Attorney', also proposing law reforms, themselves in response to letters on encouraging British iron manufacture.[63] All critiqued the customary management of gentlemen's estates and called for the pro-fessionalization of land management and transfers, and the abolition of entails ('rather mischievous to the people in general') to make land more marketable, promote commerce and add lesser property holders to the county electorate. However, rather than overthrowing the system, these letters still proposed an alliance of the meritocratic commercial and professional classes with the elite in the economic interests of the nation.

Promotions lists assisted to some extent in this redefinition of the boundaries of gentlemanliness. They included some non-elite sources of authority, such as provincial mayoralties, the newer manifestations of de-centralized government, such as the Customs and Excise and the Post Office, and professional appointments within the two English and the Scottish universities, schools and the legal and medical professions.[64] The election as mayor of St Albans of Mr Nichols, brewer and maltster was recorded in July 1732; the appointment of Mr Sharp as excise col-lector in January 1749 and the admission of six men to the College of Physicians in July 1752. There were also separate lists of 'Ecclesiastical Promotions' within the Church of England, an institution embedded both within the constitution and, through the dioceses and parishes, in more local networks of authority, with careers increasingly open to educated men of middling background.

The noble Lord Chesterfield considered these professions appropriate for the sons of men in his circle. The law was the most prestigious: 'the truly independent profession' for 'one of quick, lively and distinguishing parts', the army or navy suitable for 'a boy of warm constitution, strong animal spirits, and a cold genius', and the Church least dignified, fit for 'a good, dull and decent boy' and, significantly, only one rung above trade for 'an acute thinking, and laborious one'.[65] But all also created growing opportunities for middling-sort participation as entry increasingly came to depend on professional merit. This equation between gentlemanly status and an occupation which required mental capital was made by Joseph Emin in the mid-1750s when he abandoned working as a grocer's porter and gained a place at the bottom end of professional life as a writer in an attorney's office. He described this as 'genteel success'. His former colleagues recognized it too, taunting him with 'the little Armenian porter is turned a gentleman'.[66] In these professions and the notices, therefore, men from noble families and 'Pulses' and 'Tradewells' from less privileged backgrounds who had risen by merit, rubbed shoulders metaphorically, if not literally. They were allied by their shared interests in stability, although the latter were often still indebted to the patronage of the former for advancement. Diarist Revd George Woodward for example owed his clerical positions to the Duke of Grafton and Bishop of Salisbury and attended assiduously to business with them.[67]

Middling-sort men were also beginning to infiltrate the magazine's lists of the married and the dead.[68] Between 1750 and 1756, 34 per cent of sampled grooms were described by a middling-sort professional or commercial occupation, compared to only 23 per cent in the 1730s. To army officers, clergymen, lawyers, physicians, surgeons and merchants were added a haberdasher, ironmonger, booksellers, apothecaries, a brewer, distiller and an organ builder. The deceased were even more democratic: around half the sample was defined by a similar range of occupations, often accompanied by the epithet 'eminent'. This was applied to merchants, doctors, attorneys, dissenting ministers and Quaker preachers, even a toyman (Mr Peter Dubeck), writing master (Mr Charles Snell), sugar-baker (Mr Colebland Anamet), hosier (Mr Holford), painter of horses (Mr Seymoor) and stationer (Mr Thomas Brewer).[69] Similar terms that became standard were 'noted', 'celebrated', 'known' and 'well-known'. Reputation might come from being obviously in the public eye (actors or authors for example), or learned: Mr Williams the 'celebrated tragedian' of the Theatre Royal Drury Lane, the 'well-known' Mr John Dennis, literary critic from a trading family, and James

Dawkins Esq., MP, son of a Jamaican sugar planter, and author of an antiquarian work on Palmyra. Others had demonstrated unique inventiveness: Mr John Senex, bookseller and 'celebrated' globe-maker and Mr Zachariah Williams, an experimental philosopher 'known' for his work on magnetism and the longitude problem.[70]

Success was also measured in money. Some five per cent of sampled male deaths were accompanied by an estimate of reputed assets or income. More still were described as 'very rich' or 'of a large estate'. Some of the wealthy were landed gentlemen, several were merchants, but others were professionals and tradesmen across the nation who had made fortunes in the course of their careers. Isaac Finch of Watford died aged 104 and, having 'followed the Trade of a Leatherseller 80 Years', had amassed £15,000. Abingdon attorney Mr Boot was worth £20,000 on his death in 1734 and Thomas Sharp, gold and silver orris-weaver (lace-maker) of Little Moorfields, £40,000. In 1751 West Country conveyancer, Richard Hillier, Esq., left £3,000 a year and £40,000 in the funds.[71]

Success, eminence and worth through work were not only middling-sort but were represented as distinctly masculine, even though in reality many women also worked.[72] Deceased women were in the minority (less than 15 per cent of the sample), usually described either by their relationship to men as daughters, mothers, wives and widows, or for their exceptional standing either as members of the nobility, very elderly or very wealthy, the fortune typically derived from fathers or husbands. Only five deceased women in the 26-year sample were described as having an occupation and the only woman who earned a longer obituary (recording her amiability, solid judgment, polite manners, sense of honour and charity) was the aristocratic Lady Elizabeth Hastings who had objected to the use of her portrait on the poetry prize medal.[73]

The importance of working for success was reinforced by the magazine's promotion of the industrious over the slothful life. It was industry that won material self-advancement and personal independence. This was the moral both of 'Anonymus' account of the disappointment of 'The Death-Waiter', a young man who mistakenly thought he could idle until he inherited, and of 'The Ant's Philosophy', a poetic fable.[74] The *Gentleman's Magazine* approach was part of a wider cultural phenomenon by which industry was represented as patriotically furthering British commerce. Contemporary didactic and economic writing, novels and plays portrayed men achieving independent standing by merit and making a valuable contribution to national wealth.[75] Mr Thorowgood in Lillo's best-known play, *The London Merchant*, declared: 'As the name of merchant never degrades the gentleman, so by no means does it exclude him'. He added that an upright character (quite unlike Sir Courtly Nice) was the determinant: 'only take heed not to purchase the character of complaisant at the expense of your sincerity'.[76] Samuel Richardson's *Apprentice's Vade Mecum*, excerpted in the magazine, expressed the same view. Industry, diligence and punctuality gained a tradesman 'the name of a *generous* and *Gentleman-like* Man, epithets in no sort incompatible with Trade and Business', and benefitted 'this great Trading Kingdom'.[77]

Independence, whether through birth or commercial success, was not in itself sufficient to guarantee gentlemanliness, however. Wealth, as featured in the deaths notices, contributed to status, but articles and correspondence revealed that what mattered most was not so much the quantum or means of accumulation, as how it was spent. This worked both to elevate and sink a gentleman. While a successful tradesman might rise to gentlemanly status, so too could a man, even if well-born, lose his status by obsessive hoarding or uncontrolled spending. Meanness and rapacity were ungentlemanly, aspects of 'the sordid philosophy' and associated with anti-social and impolite behaviour according to 'P.S.'. 'Wealth, not Poverty's the Test that's given' and miserliness and avarice were to be avoided, warned an anonymous poem, 'A Character'. Another anonymous poet painted an unattractive picture of 'the Stingy Beau, in London' whose kitchen and dining-room remained immaculate because he was too tight to entertain.[78] And there was something distasteful about the nameless leather-cutter in Barnaby Street who died 'old and seemingly in want' but had 1,100 guineas under the floorboards.[79] The true gentleman was generous and hospitable, like Sir George Fleming, and benevolent, as charitable bequests recorded in obituaries suggested. Captain Stephens, for example, left £1,000 to a poor cobbler of Southwark; Thomas Emerson, sugar-baker, £12,000 to the Foundling Hospital among other large legacies, and George Jennings Esq. of Shropshire a more modest £50 each to the London and St George's Hospitals.[80]

Equally he must beware spending on the 'wrong' things. These were excessive display, especially finery in dress, gambling, lechery and drink, all of which led to loss of financial and bodily self-control. Vicious gentlemen were also a danger to the economic and social fabric of society. Vice rendered them unfit to govern and their example was emulated lower down the social scale, warned articles from the *Universal Spectator* and *Common Sense* on adultery and the keeping of mistresses, and from *Common Sense* on degeneracy caused by luxury.[81] The anonymous poem 'Drunkenness: a Satire' pointed to the evils of lack of restraint in a number of imaginary well-to-do characters. It damaged their reason, reputation, finances and health. 'Reform your manners', commanded line seven.[82]

Luxury in dress was a fault in both men and women. Where men were concerned, this was not so much an indication of foppery or effeminacy as of 'modern *Pride*' or '*want* of *sense* or [...] *Thought*'.[83] Hitchcock describes how 'more than perhaps at any time before or since, clothes made the man or woman in eighteenth-century London. Lace and frills, velvets and brocades marked out the very rich from their humbler contemporaries'.[84] It was also a national concern. Outward appearance, especially neatness and cleanliness, was an important clue to gentility.[85] Nevertheless, display could distract from the wearer's true underlying character and worth, as a 1733 article advised: 'A *smart Coat, powder'd Wigg,* and *laced Linnen,* may give a Man Preference in the Street, but the *Man* of *Mode* should be inform'd that these Ornaments will be a Prejudice to him if not supported by real Merit'.[86] The *Gentleman's Magazine* therefore fretted over mixed signals: shop-boys who looked like gentlemen and young gentlemen who looked like servants.[87] A fashion for dressing down – as servants, jockeys or '*Wrap-Rascals*' in '*Rug* and *Duffel* Coats' – was attributed to the loss of authority that came with the loss of a fortune.[88]

The potentially ruinous consequences of luxury and the confusion over status it bred were exposed in the magazine's report of the fraud trial of William Stroud in January 1752.[89] Stroud, although 'formerly a man of fortune', was an impostor, and, as Natalie Zemon Davis notes, 'Each age remakes its impostor tales to some extent to stress its own concerns'.[90] Stroud cheated tradesmen of hundreds of pounds, 'personating various characters and names' ('a gentleman attended with livery servants', nobleman's steward, doctor and clergymen) to obtain credit. He bought all the expensive accoutrements of a gentleman: velvet clothes trimmed with gold lace, jewels, a watch, accessories, a chaise and carved furniture. The *Gentleman's Magazine* used Stroud to point a middling-sort moral about frugality. His disgrace was to have used the appearance of gentility 'in order to support his extravagancies'.[91]

The magazine regarded young gentlemen as particularly prone to rakish vice. They were 'Coffee-House Savages' who disturbed 'Sober Citizens' with their 'Ribaldry and Horse-Laughs, singing, swearing and damning themselves, and cursing the Waiters, and blaspheming all that's sacred'.[92] So too did Revd George Woodward. He commented disapprovingly in 1753 on a 'young Hertfordshire squire, who seems to be setting out into the world with no very good grace' led by 'his own fiery inclinations'.[93] The correct discipline could, however, ensure this was merely a passing phase. As one 'Christian Hero' poem explained, it was possible:

> T'erase the weeds which over-run the soil,
> And plant the vertues with incessant toil.[94]

This was the aim of the restrictions on dress, curfews and sanctions for riotous behaviour imposed by new undergraduate regulations at Cambridge University and reported by 'Academicus'.[95]

The magazine's most pointed critiques of debauchery and gambling and the indebtedness they incurred represented these as vices originating with the landed classes. It therefore differed from the focus of the middling-sort Societies for the Reformation of Manners, still active in the 1730s. Their zeal was directed at sexual morality, order and religious observance rather than private character or social comportment, and many of their targets were plebeian.[96] In the 1740s, a precursor to the more political content of some readers' letters, readers were presented with two real-life noble anti-heroes beyond the excuse of youth who fell far short of what would become the Grandisonian ideal.

The first was Irish peer Arthur Annesley, fourth Baron Altham. From January to November 1744 the magazine printed a series of lengthy transcripts of Mr James Annesley's Dublin suit against the Earl of Anglesey over the disputed Anglesey title and estates. This hinged upon James' true identity: legitimate but abandoned son of Altham and his second wife Mary, or illegitimate son by kitchen-maid and wet-nurse Joan 'Juggy' Landy. Witnesses both for prosecution and defence depicted Altham as dissipated, debauched, violent and despotic. They agreed for example that he had attacked one Tom Paliser, allegedly his wife's lover, with his sword, cutting off his ear, and that in a fit of temper he had smashed in the fireplace china saucers, decorated with 'indecent Figures' disliked by Lady Altham. It was, then, morally fitting that he died 'miserably poor'.[97]

The second exemplar was octogenarian Simon Fraser, Lord Lovat, the Jacobite leader executed on 9 April 1747 for his role in the 1745 rebellion. The *Gentleman's Magazine* gave extensive coverage to his capture, imprisonment, trial and execution. In July 1747 it printed a whole page 'Character of Lord Lovat', taken from the *Memoirs of his Life*.[98] The author explained that his subject's physical robustness, bravery, 'some learning, great parts and abilities', politeness and affability all masked an inner ungentlemanly character. His politeness concealed 'flattery and dissimulation'. He was 'sordidly avaricious'. Guilty of 'violence, rapes, cruelty, revenge, treachery, and every infamous practice', he was 'in short [...] a cruel master, an imperious husband, a tyrannical parent, a treacherous friend, and an arbitrary chief'. It was this bad character that had informed his very aristocratic treachery.

Comparison with the *London Magazine's* coverage of the Lovat affair suggests that the *Gentleman's Magazine* and its readers were especially interested in the issue of bad character. 'Character' had already been rehearsed in April in the introduction to the account of the execution, which omitted details in the *London Magazine* of Lovat's 'sober and regular Way of Living'. Although the reporting of the rebellion's aftermath through 1746 and 1747 in the two publications was almost identical, the *London Magazine* did not publish the 'Character' or extracts from this or other *Memoirs*. Its execution narrative was more sensational in tone: a lengthy description of the collapse of a crowded viewing scaffold and the suffering of the victims, and an engraving of the death scene with the axe at its height prior to the fatal blow and, centre stage and ghoulishly labelled, the 'cloth to receive the head'. The *Gentleman's Magazine* tucked a shorter version of the scaffold accident in the 'Historical Chronicle' with a list of the more eminent male dead and, in March, offered a sombre engraving of an empty 'Westminsterhall, as prepared for the Tryal'.[99]

The limits of the 'polite' paradigm

The model of the hard-working, rational, pious and restrained polite gentleman was therefore woven throughout the *Gentleman's Magazine*. It was not, however, accepted uncritically by either editors or readers. There were challenges to its apparent stability, universality and confidence. Magazine correspondence provides evidence of its fragility, resistance, unresolved internal contradictions and anxieties that undermined the certainty even of those who did subscribe to it.

(i) Fragility

Middling-sort success was precarious.[100] Samuel Richardson acknowledged that not all lineage gentlemen were ready to accept the man of business among them, but might, like Chesterfield or Foote, cast 'little Aspersions'.[101] The propriety of their ambitions was sometimes mocked, even within the magazine. In July 1755 an article excerpted from the *Connoisseur* lamented that 'When an obscure grocer or tallow-chandler dies at his lodgings at *Islington*, the news-papers are stuffed with the same parade of his virtues and good qualities, as when a duke goes out of the world'.[102] In the death notices 'obscure' social origins might therefore be concealed behind the catch-all 'Esquire', accounting for around half of all entries. Thomas Martin Esq., of Saffron Walden was a small-town draper and William Forster Esq., alderman of Durham, a merchant. The magazine obituarized John Barber Esq., Edward Cave's erstwhile employer, as an alderman, former Lord Mayor and president of St Bartholomew's Hospital rather than as a printer whose father was a journeyman barber-surgeon. An acquired title could also camouflage modest beginnings. Sir Gilbert Heathcote, Alderman of Bridge Ward Without and Member of Parliament for St Germain's, Cornwall, warranted a half-column listing his political achievements, vast wealth and charitable bequests. There was no mention of his roots as the merchant son of a Chesterfield ironmonger and mine investor.[103]

Working for self-advancement was also stressful. The young Dudley Ryder had worried that he might cut 'a very mean figure in the law'.[104] It gave physician Richard Kay nightmares.[105] Deaths in the magazine included men for whom it all proved too much. That of Mr Burroughs at his father's house in Golden Square in January 1732 'was occasion'd, 'tis said, by the Loss he sustain'd in the Charitable Corporation'. In some unspecified way, maybe suicide, Burroughs died because he was unable to face failure, whether of his investments, his reputation or both was unspoken.[106] The death of Mr Stephens, surgeon to the Prince of Wales, was a result of his professional endeavours: 'Occasion'd by his Fatigue in sitting up to attend Mr *Spence*, one of whose Legs he cut off'.[107]

Moreover, cheek-by-jowl with the honour and prestige of the promotions, was another regular magazine feature: the bankrupts. Also reprinted from the *London Gazette*, this was effectively a public roll call of a specifically male failure.[108] 831 bankrupts were named in the sampled magazines for this period: 286 in the 1730s, 249 in the 1740s and 296 in 1750–56.[109] Only 16 were women.[110] The re-publication of bankruptcy information was useful to *Gentleman's Magazine* readers who were themselves engaged in trade. It also served as a moral reminder of the awful consequences of excessive risk-taking, as the 1746 Preface preached:

> When private woes expos'd to fame
> I see, and read the Bankrupt's name,
> Alarmed at fortune's ebb and flow,
> I lift my thoughts from all below.

The shame was compounded by the heading of the lists 'B-K-S' or 'B–KR-Ts', as though the word and fate were too foul to mention. For the loss was not only of money but of personal credit and status. The bankrupts, stripped in their misfortune of the 'Mr' or even 'Esq.' they might previously have commanded, were defined by place of residence and middling-sort occupation alone.[111] Only one was given any sort of title (Sir Thomas Bury, merchant of Exeter in July 1733). Apart from four bankers and a money scrivener, they were from the retail, food and drink, manufacturing and dealing trades (including brokers). The devastating impact of bankruptcy presumably lay behind the faked death and ignominious flight of one failure, Andrew Pringle, merchant of Fan Court, Fenchurch Street, whose '*hat, wig and cane were found bloody on* Tower hill, *on the* 14th, *but he was seen next day near* Dover'.[112]

(ii) Resistance: the impolite

Politeness was regarded by contemporaries, as well by historians, as an urban phenomenon. However, despite the growth in the eighteenth century of Britain's towns and cities and their amenities (assemblies, clubs, walks, theatres) the vast majority of the population, remained rural.[113] The *Gentleman's Magazine* had always assumed that farmers might be readers and had encouraged the idea that the two 'halves' of the nation could be united through the conceit of 'Sylvanus Urban'. Nevertheless opposition to the politeness that 'Urbanus-as-urbane' signified came from the country, from 'Mr Rus'. It proposed an alternative, old-fashioned English gentleman whose simplicity and bluntness denoted a sincerity that contrasted with the superficiality of town manners. This was of course an ancient device, as old as Aesop's town and country mice. The 1735 anonymous poem 'The Contented Peasant' was in this genre. On the same page was 'W. B – d's' 'November. A Pastoral Elegy' which, like much of the readers' poetry, assumed a rural setting for verses on the seasons and love in particular.[114]

The town/country motif was also used to critique polite society. In January 1744, 'The Farmer's Blunder', a poem by 'Retrop Bajalus', recounted the disastrous supper of a tenant at his landlord's London house.[115] It ridiculed the farmer for his crude manners in polite company and carried the moral that men should not be placed above their station. But its portrait of polite metropolitan society was also far from flattering. Sympathy ultimately lay with the farmer as his dinner companions openly mocked him. He had the last laugh when, his chair pulled from under him as a jape, he fell to the floor dragging table-cloth and feast with him and bespattering their fine clothes.

In 1746 the pseudonymous 'Will. Downright', described himself proudly as 'an old unpolish'd country gentleman [...] but lately come to town'. 'Downright' added patriotism to the superior qualities of such a man, expressing horror at the Frenchification of fashionable life at a time of war.[116] 'Lear' of K – by S – n introduced a generational element, suggesting that the fashion for urban politeness and the pursuit of money led children to neglect the traditional respect owed to parents. His son, whom he had established at the Bar and lent money for a venture, now excluded him from smart dinners and banished him to Westmoreland, sneering, 'you have generally lived in your own little house in a remote county. *Your* notions, *your* customs, *your* hours, and *your* manner of living are so very different from those which now prevail in town'.[117]

There was also resistance in the magazine's 'Swiftean underside' of material that transgressed the delicacy expected in polite company or a polite magazine.[118] Among poetry celebrating love, nature, patriotism and divine power were less inhibited, bawdy verses. These were occasioning some criticism by 1734. An enigma beginning:

> I am an Implement that's common,
> Much occupy'd by man and woman

piled *double entendre* on *double entendre* to hint at 'a penis' (the correct answer was 'a pen'), prompting accusations of immodesty.[119] The correct answer, submitted in rhyme, castigated the author for making female readers blush, like Cave's correspondent Thomas Dod, using the gendered argument that this was inappropriate material for ladies' eyes.[120]

This was not the only example of continued relish among the genteel for crude or cruel rhymes and jokes. Other subjects for riddles included the stays identified by Daughter Jugg and a chamber pot used by the queen and fine ladies who missed their aim and stained their white stockings. There was scatological humour about farts (by 'Sir Puffly Blast') and boils on the 'a – e'. There was sexual innuendo. In 'The Poetick Couple', dedicated to a clergyman and his wife, Richie and Pattie began an innocent game of crambo on the theme of 'enjoyment' but 'stripp'd and soon finish'd the poem in bed'. In 'On Tobacco' a lawyer's wife found her disappointing post-honeymoon love-life revived when she tolerated his smoking habit and 'He had his pipe, and she had her's [*sic*]'. There was guffawing over others' mishaps. In lines reminiscent of exciseman John Cannon's and his male friends' delight at an accident that exposed a young woman's genitals, 'Winter. A Pastoral Ballad' had a 'sweet country maiden' slipping on the ice and revealing 'All the charms that her modesty hides' to an audience of laughing rustics.[121] The 'pen/penis' had occasioned complaint, but this had not stemmed the flow. Impolite and 'low' material continued to sit alongside the magazine's serious and educational items, but, as the dates of the examples used demonstrate, was less prevalent by the 1750s.

(iii) Contradictions: the soldier

The gentlemen's clubs of the *Spectator, Auditor* and 1740 *Gentleman's Magazine* Preface all included an army officer. Entrants in the poetry competition addressed the subject of the 'Christian Hero' in military spirit. By the 1755 Preface, he had disappeared, despite the intervening war, 1745 rebellion and growth in army numbers.[122]

On the face of it, the army or navy officer was the most masculine gentlemanly type: a public, independent, courageous, disciplined, vigilant hero. He was crucial to national strength, protecting not only the state but the vital commercial endeavours of its merchants. As a group they united traditional gentlemen, like 'Sir Charles Freeman,' and new gentlemen, through a slow and patchy process of professionalization.[123] Recruitment was relatively open and in the navy qualification entailed examination. The army and navy were therefore significant routes into gentlemanliness for middling-sort men, the very acquisition of a commission proof of status. As Nicholas Rodger says of naval officers: 'Though their social backgrounds varied widely [they were] always regarded as gentlemen and expected to behave as such'.[124]

The magazine recognized the officer's role positively in some excerpted articles, such as 'On heroism', and in the official sourcing and leading position of army and navy appointments in its promotions lists.[125] Yet the homosocial roughness inherent in military life was often incompatible with the urbanity, mixed company, mildness and restraint expected of the gentleman. Sir Charles Grandison, after all, eschewed force other than *in extremis* as self-defence.

The problem was magnified once Britain was at war in the 1740s and 1750s. Although soldiers sometime took politeness on their travels (gentlemen of the army and navy in Bombay performed Nicholas Rowe's *The Fair Penitent* on Easter Monday 1756), the magazine found it hard to avoid the violence inherent in their profession. It was the very stuff of the 'Historical Chronicle'.[126] A particularly bloody example was the account of a fight between a privateer and Dutch merchantman bound for Spain in January 1742: 'We ply'd our Cutlasses against their yellow Buffs till we made them of another Colour'.[127] Unlike private soldiers and ratings who were merely counted in numbers, the magazine obituarized officers whose battle records were literally written on their bodies. Long-serving Colonel James Cunningham had suffered 'several dangerous Wounds; particularly at the battle of *Hockstett*, where he was shot thro' the Body; and at the siege of *Air'*. Captain Hughs who died at Hertford in 1736 had served for 48 years and 'at the Battle of *Schellemberg*, was shot thro' the Cheek, at *Namur* thro' the Wrist, and wounded in the Head'.[128]

The 'soldier problem' was potentially resolved in the republican concept of the militia: defensive, and led by propertied gentlemen.[129] In the 1730s and 1740s, the *Gentleman's Magazine* reprinted articles and covered parliamentary debates on the virtues of a militia and the dangers posed by a standing or mercenary army, regarded by its opponents as burdensomely expensive and, being outside the landed interest, potentially subversive of the constitution.[130] A pamphlet putting the case for a militia reflecting the social hierarchy was summarized in January 1745 in a five-page letter from 'J.S.' annotated by the editor. Landed gentlemen were to compose 'the superior militia,' with those of 'superior fortunes' forming the cavalry. They would be both patriotic and enhance their gendered politeness: 'Military exercise [is] more manly and graceful than country sports and horse-races'.[131]

The magazine and its readers did consider it possible for the regular officer similarly to combine bravery with merit and polite gentlemanliness. Johnson's 'Life of Sir Francis Drake', serialized in 1740 and 1741, provided a historical example of a man of modest beginnings (the son of a clergyman apprenticed to the master of a small trading vessel) rising through professional skill and bravery, who never lost sight of the need for restraint and who 'never made War with a Spirit of Cruelty or Revenge, or carried Hostilities further than was necessary for his own Advantage or Defence'.[132] Two poems in July 1748 commemorated polite soldiers fallen at Hispaniola and Carthagena respectively. 'Captain C –' was 'bold yet gentle, courteous tho' sincere' and Lord Aubrey Beauclerk 'brave, active, undismay'd' yet also 'With manners, how sincere, polite with ease'.[133]

Still, this refinement of manners sometimes sat uneasily with the military ideal and there was more than the usual anxiety over the effect of excess in dress and manners where officers were concerned. 'An Essay on Fashions', excerpted from *Fog's Journal*, warned of the adverse impact on the political and military classes, asking: 'Do such nice young Gentlemen who dress and play with their Bodies, as with puppets, promise their native country either refined and active Statesmen, or hardy and intrepid Soldiers?'[134] 'Phil. Cockade', a vain, foppish and cowardly officer, was mocked in a 'letter' from Flanders to 'Captain Herculus Vinegar', editor of the *Champion* (Henry Fielding), excerpted in 1743. Cockade loved only the civil, social advancement that officer status conferred:

> […] It reads well in the Gazette, is a pretty Adjunct in Conversation, it authorizes a Man to overlook an old Acquaintance, to take place of an Equal, entrench a little upon a Superior, and give oneself a thousand smart Airs beside-But the grinning Honour to be met with in the Field, I have as little Passion for, as Sir John Falstaff himself.

Even though it was a time of war, Cockade continued, 'I studied my Dress, Air, Face &c. assum'd a Look of Importance to awe the Burghers'.[135]

There was, too, the risk of unheroic failure exposed in reports of armed conflict. A tradesman's professional reputation was lost in bankruptcy. An officer's melted away through foppish cowardice. The *Gentleman's Magazine* counterposed the actions of a brave and a cowardly officer in a 1745 news story. In an engagement with French man-of-war the *Mercury*, Captain Brett of the *Lion* was wounded in the arm and foot and bruised black and blue by flying timber 'yet he moved up and down upon the deck all the time, and was cover'd with blood and brains'. His Captain of Marines, on the other hand, was found by the ship's chaplain cowering 'between two trusses of hay, but refusing to fight', for which he had to walk the main deck followed by a soldier saying 'Here's the fellow that wou'd not fight'.[136] Such mockery respected neither rank nor death. In 1747 an anonymous rhyming epitaph ridiculed Admiral Lestock, who died of the gout six months after his acquittal at a court martial on a charge of not engaging with the French at Toulon in 1744:

> Averse to strike a blow in fight;
> Inaction was his chief delight.
> He quiet lies, as off *Toulon*.[137]

If the army or navy officer was particularly at risk of overdoing politeness, he was also prone to forget polite self-control altogether. In the full heat of the War of the Austrian Succession, an anonymous reader-poet complained about the 'shocking Profaneness of our Marines'.[138] In disputes officers often displayed not the reason of a Grandison but the rash and violent reactions of the ungentlemanly plebeian. The 'Historical Chronicle' for July 1748 reported two such cases in which gentlemen were, atypically, criminals. In the first, Henry Williams of the navy and Thomas Jenkins, an artillery officer, riotously and with a hired mob (suggesting inappropriate mixing with the lower orders) broke into a lady's house to 'get possession of her person and fortune' on the pretence she was Williams' wife. The second reported the trial of Mr George Tymewell, secretary to Commodore Mitchell of the navy for the murder in a duel of Captain Gregory of the *Folkestone*.[139] Tymewell was acquitted but convicted of a misdemeanour, sentenced to two years in the Marshalsea and banned from serving in the navy. This was one of several news reports of duelling, not always fatal, involving army and navy officers over the period and accords with artilleryman James Wood's numerous diary entries of army duels.[140] The magazine, like Grandison, abhorred this violence. It was incompatible with gentlemanly restraint.[141] The text of the magazine therefore suggested that as a gentleman the officer was ambiguous and not easily reconciled with its essentially civilian polite paradigm.

(iv) Anxieties: women

Female company was essential to acquiring politeness. We have seen how women as fellow-readers and correspondents performed this function within the *Gentleman's Magazine*. One poet, 'Gamble', described the beneficial effect of his personal 'Fair Reformer':

> My charming monitor, I own,
> Since your reproof, I'm better grown.

He now avoided his club and, instead of tippling and joking, soberly took tea and attended church twice on Sundays.[142]

Yet women have hardly featured in this account of gentlemanliness. The worlds presented here of clubs, promotions, financial success and failure, and the military were strictly male. Establishing oneself as a gentleman depended very much on a combination of the approbation of male peers and a distancing from men who did not meet gentlemanly standards. Women have been little more than a presence 'between the lines': the targets of 'Easy's' and 'Dactyl's' conversation and amorous intrigues, the butts of ribald male laughter, and alongside men in articles and debates on luxury and fashion. This section examines in more detail the relationship the magazine and its male readers had with women and how this informed their sense of themselves as gentlemen.

The *Gentleman's Magazine* excerpted from controversial or satirical papers such as *Common Sense* and the *Universal Spectator* articles that were 'diatribes against women'.[143] In July 1732, for example, 'Female Extravagancies' attacked women who inverted the social order by behaving like men: striding around the room whistling, talking laddishly, even making the first move in courtship.[144] By contrast, readers' articles and letters, which Hunter estimates at three-quarters of the material on women, were neither fundamentally hostile nor misogynistic.

However, women remained subordinate to men in the magazine's assessment. Poem III in the 'Christian Hero' competition admitted women were capable of piety and benevolence but regarded their victories in the Christian battle as inferior to those of male heroes, paraphrasing Proverbs 31:

> There's many daughters worthy deeds have done,
> But thou, in thine, excel'st them ev'ry one.[145]

Women could even be brave. July 1750 opened with 'Some account of Hannah Snell, the female soldier'.[146] Hannah had spent four years as a man, for three of which, her imposture undiscovered, she served and saw active service abroad in a regiment of marines, only disclosing her secret once paid off on her return to England. The article (a condensed version of her *Life and Adventures* published in June) represented her as possessing gentlemanly qualities: rescuing a girl from the unwanted attention of her sergeant, 'signalizing' herself at the attempt on Mauritius, fighting courageously and taking a wound at Pondicherry. But the account also compromized her achievements, with its running thread of salacious interest in her cross-dressing, close female friendships, her semi-naked punishments by flogging, and enforced bed-sharing with men in Portsmouth lodgings.[147]

Men's correspondence revealed that their relationships with allegedly subordinate women were similarly not straightforward. They needed the esteem of other men, but achieving this required them to court women's company to establish themselves as polite, as independent heads of households, as husbands and fathers.[148] Marriage was therefore extremely important. It was, an excerpt from the *Northampton Mercury* declared in 1732, 'a State which most persons one time or other are desirous of entering into'. It was expected that a couple would derive happiness from compatibility: 'When good Nature, Respect, and Equality of Tempers meet, this State is an inexhaustible course of Felicity'.[149] The Lockean social contract demanded this consensual approach to marriage, as only feelings of mutual love could produce willing female subordination.[150] Men remained socially and culturally superior but this depended at least in part upon a Grandisonian ability to use personal, persuasive charm on eligible women.

Women may not have defined men, but they did pose a significant threat to their sense of self-controlled, independent masculinity since they could refuse to be charmed. All too often men struggled with refusal. They struggled in courtship because women for once had the upper hand until their consent was given. Charlotte Lennox advised women to use this temporary power to their advantage in her poem 'The Art of Coquetry', printed in the magazine for November 1750.[151] And men struggled in marriage because the ideal of the consenting, yet submissive, wife did not always work out in practice. The *Gentleman's Magazine* did not offer direct advice on these issues in the manner of the *Athenian Mercury* of the previous century, but courtship and marriage were tackled in excerpts from periodicals such as the *Universal Spectator* and in readers' poems which revealed something of Michael Roper's psychic and emotional aspects of masculinity.[152]

Men often used poetry to communicate with their beloved in real life.[153] Readers submitted similar verses on the travails of love and courtship to the *Gentleman's Magazine* in this period, addressing it to named, thinly disguised or idealized women, the latter often in the pastoral genre of a 'Damon,' 'Colin' or 'Strephon' to a 'Celia' 'Daphne' or 'Chloe'. Stuffed full of clichés they had a common theme – a man's love at first sight for a lady who cruelly ignored or rejected his approaches – which betrayed an underlying anxiety about the impact of women on masculine rationality and strength. The problem with love was that it sapped male independence: 'Nature ne'er meant me for a woman's slave', complained 'Amasius' (Dr John Swan) to 'Celia'.[154]

A single issue of the magazine from the middle of the chapter period illustrates this well. In July 1743 there were five pages of poetry containing 22 poems of varying length (from a page to four lines), all anonymous or pseudonymous, though eight are attributed to known authors.[155] It was the height of the European war and the month in which the Battle of Dettingen was reported. A single poem, 'Stanzas from Albion's Triumph. An Ode', commemorated Dettingen. Another, 'The Progress of Charity' marked the plan for a County Hospital in Northampton. No fewer than seven were by a man observing and falling in love with a woman. 'Damon' was 'caught' by the singing of Miss Boyse of Canterbury; another was pierced by Cupid's dart on seeing 'Miss – d'; 'Celadon' was possessed by the panting white bosom of 'Delia' and in a second poem feared she would be swayed by coaches and equipages or beaux dressed in lace; 'M***' (another 'Damon') shrank from showing 'Clarissa' his love and told 'Miss S – H –' that she needed no artifice of toilette to pierce a lover's heart; 'Tim Worthy' was never as happy as when resting on 'Miss A – B –'s' breast, whose mind surpassed even her beauty. All these poets were physically and mentally weakened by their unacknowledged love: they smarted, despaired, were wounded, enthralled and slain.

To men's anxiety over unrequited love was added fear that women did not always respect their character as true gentlemen. Delicacy and politeness worked very well for fictional heroes like Grandison, but sometimes the ladies seemed to prefer a dashing to a plain and sober man, rather as Clarissa Harlowe and many of Richardson's female readers were attracted to the rakish Lovelace. Modesty in a man was disagreeable to ladies, warned a letter taken from the (*Universal*) *Spectator* in July 1742. Accompanying the letter was a poem in which a lady tripped, and, far from being embarrassed by revealing 'all her Limbs and Beauties bare', actually preferred the man who took advantage of her situation.[156] As 'Song for an Amazon' put it:

> Rough and hardy, bold and free,
> Be the man that's made for me.[157]

Thus, in a 1736 poem, 'Parson Lovemore to Miss Manage', a lovelorn clergyman rued unfair competition from Captain Fido whose 'brockade,/Embroid'ry, ruffles and cockade' were superficially seductive compared to the parson's 'more decent' plain garb.[158] In 'Written upon not being Admitted', 'Fl.' asked Sylvia whom in her 'nice perverseness' she most admired, running through a list of gentlemen:

> The man of title, or the man of land,
> The booby Baron, or the looby Squire?
> The lace-bedaubed Hero, blustering fierce and big;
> Or the soft Couns'lor, mantled o'er with wig?

before putting in a plaintive plea for himself: 'A love-sick youth [...] the man of truth'.[159] Towards the end of the period 'A.B', a country curate, endured a rebuff when, via the magazine, he issued a modest poetic invitation to tea to 'Miss L –'. Her reply the following month was blunt: 'A visit, Sir! I can't endure it'. He was only rescued from public humiliation by 'L.', claiming to be the real invitee who had been delighted by his 'amusing chat'.[160] Was the misogyny in poems gloating over the unattractiveness of older women male revenge for this power women exerted in their youth? Another of the 22 poems in July 1743 reflected on the folly of young Nan who had rejected a clergyman's love token. Old, ugly and toothless she could not be so fussy. In 1745 George Ogle's (1704–76) 'Aurelia' derided a woman who, fascinating enough by candlelight, in the cold light of day displayed the signs of 'with'ring age'.[161]

Once married, the gentleman was on surer ground, because, as excerpted *Prompter* essay 'On Wives' stated, '*Man* claims Superiority over the Fairer Sex'. However, even a married man faced the possibility of discord. The *Prompter* continued: 'And the Woman that will contest that Point, lays a Foundation for future Misery in the married State'.[162] It was primarily the task of wives rather than husbands to ensure this harmony, advised the poem 'Matrimonial Advice, an Epistle from Senex to his Niece': Their 'gentle Manners must the Heart retain.'[163]

Some *Gentleman's Magazine* poets celebrated successful marriages that were enduring, loving and companionable. 'Bristoliensis' sent a letter and verses in 1745 commemorating 'Mr M – dd – x' and his wife. The perfect genteel couple, he an instructor in 'dancing and polite behaviour', she an educator of young ladies, they were married for 60 years without 'the least word, nor contradiction'. Fittingly they died within hours of one another. 'Indianus' of Dartmouth wished 'Rev'd Mr L – thbr-dg-' well on his marriage and suggested that mutual love in marriage was both a refuge after the heat of youth's passion and ambition, and a bulwark against life's sorrows. 'A.A.' of Southwark sent two Latin poems on the death of 'Chloe' written in 1744 by 'T.D.' and 'J.D.', which were printed with English translations. 'T.D.', the widower (an unidentified Northumberland clergyman), lamented the loss of his wife and her 'tender dalliance, connubial play' in dramatic, sincere lines.[164]

But male attitudes in which wives and marriage were 'the bane' of men's friendships, survived.[165] Male friendship, according to the *Gentleman's Magazine*, was the purest form of love. It relied upon 'uncovering one's Heart [...] without Difficulty or Fear' and entailed 'thorough Confidence'. The 'Good-breeding and Respect' that were 'necessary' in marriage were 'indispensable' between friends.[166] In 'The Proof of Friendship', a story from the *Universal Spectator*, two gentlemen, Octavius and Leobellus, were as 'one Will, or two Bodies actuated by one soul', their differences resolved by reason and justice alone. Leobellus was even prepared even to lay down his life for his friend.[167]

'Gamble' may have sacrificed the pleasures of his club for his 'Fair Reformer', but some magazine poems continued to honour the pleasure of exclusively male company. Smoking was often a motif for male escape from domestic life. In 'On Tobacco', for example, the husband had taken to sneaking out of the house to shoot snipe and smoke with a friend. In the 'The Pig: A Tale', husbands, 'met to laugh their spleen away' over a drink, set each other a challenge: to prove they were 'sovereign lord' in their own homes by sending messages to their wives to boil a roasting pig, as they had invited friends to supper. All the wives refused bar one, who agreed to spoil the pig provided she did not share a meal which would give her a lifelong nickname (for bad cookery). The stated moral was that wives were most obedient when unprovoked, which at least put some of the onus for harmony on men. Unstated was the risk that a wife might humiliatingly invert the proper hierarchical relationship between spouses.[168]

Far less humorous outcomes to marital disagreement, reminiscent of Kirkeen of Dublin, were depicted in four comic poems in July 1736 and January 1738. An anonymous epigram on marriage suggested that weddings should be compulsorily held in Lent as they were a matter of mortification and repentance. In the second a husband chose bleeding over purging for a sick wife as it carried a greater risk of death. Domestic violence was the subject of 'Q.Z.'s' Latin poem (with translation), in which a drunken tailor insulted and beat his scolding wife, dunked her in the well and was attacked in return, and of four lines by 'Agamon' ('the unwed') in which it was a woman's turn to drub her husband.[169]

These examples cannot simply be explained away as attacks on the impolite plebeian man who might find himself the subject of a crime report. Men from the polite professions were also shown in unhappy, failing relationships. The country curate of an eponymous poem faced 'the well known power of an English wife' whose 'wit unrein'd promotes eternal strife'. Unlike 'Mr and Mrs M – dd – x', old age and poverty aggravated matters: 'Still worse and worse her lashing tongue he feels'.[170] Nor was it restricted to the early years of the chapter period. Within a rumbling poetical and prose 'contest' between *alumni* of Winchester and Westminster schools was a poem by 'Wiccamicus', 'The Temple of Hymen', that appeared in March 1751. Couples entered the temple optimistically, but men soon learned that marriage was a bed of woes, of cuckoldry and nagging, especially for those who married for beauty and wealth. Happier the contented bachelor![171]

Admiral Byng and General Blakeney: a case study

A case study of the *Gentleman's Magazine* coverage of the Admiral Byng affair of 1756–57 concludes this chapter. Calculatedly contrasting portrayals of Byng and Blakeney illuminate further the versions of gentlemanly masculinity seen in the magazine to this date.

On 6 April 1756, at the start of the Seven Years' War, 52-year-old Admiral John Byng, who had served in the navy since the age of 14, set sail from Spithead with ten ships under his command. His mission was to stand ready at Gibraltar to deliver reinforcements to the Fort St Phillip garrison under veteran General William Blakeney, which guarded the port of Mahon, a crucial naval base on the island of Minorca (a British possession since 1708). In May French forces landed on the island and laid siege to the fort. A council of war at Gibraltar decided that sending further troops was a pointless sacrifice. Byng therefore sailed to Minorca with 13 ships of the line but no reinforcements. He encountered 12 French naval ships on 20 May. Byng's tactics and British signalling were confused, his flagship ended up behind the line and, while the van engaged, the rear did not. The French eventually withdrew and Byng claimed victory but did not press on to Fort St Phillip or establish contact with the garrison, instead returning to Gibraltar after holding a further council of war. On 28 June Blakeney was forced to surrender, though on honourable terms.

News of the capitulation in this, Britain's first serious European action since the declaration of war, reached London in mid-July. There was outrage at all levels of society: among politicians, in the press, in letters to ministers and on the streets.[172] When Byng arrived back at Spithead on 26 July he was arrested, taken to Greenwich and confined pending a court martial. This opened at Portsmouth in December and on 27 January 1757 found Byng guilty of failing to 'do his utmost' (the term of the 12th Article of War) in the naval engagement and in abandoning Blakeney. He received the death sentence mandatory under the 12th Article.[173] After two months of wrangling over the sentence, the blindfolded Byng was executed by firing squad on board the *Monarque* in Portsmouth harbour on 14 March 1757.

The *Gentleman's Magazine* took an intense interest in the story. In April it reported Byng's departure.[174] In May it covered the siege, still confident that Byng's arrival and a naval engagement would determine Minorca's fate in Britain's favour.[175] In June the mood changed: it published Byng's post-engagement letter to the Admiralty, followed by observations from an anonymous sea-officer who criticized Byng for a dilatory start to the mission compounded by excessive caution.[176] By July, the fiasco dominated the entire magazine. 14 pages (around a quarter of the total) concerned Minorca, Byng and Blakeney.[177]

Byng, a younger son of George Byng, 1st Viscount Torrington (1663–1733), was an archetypal gentleman-by-birth. He had benefitted from the ties of the lineage family and the patronage system. Unsurprisingly, his to-date untarnished public career had already featured in the *Gentleman's Magazine*. He was one of the signatories to an honourable paper of apology to Lord Chief Justice Sir John Willes in 1746; the recipient as Commander of the British Squadron in the Mediterranean of a letter of instruction from the Duke of Newcastle after the signing of the Peace of Aix-la-Chapelle in 1748; re-elected Member of Parliament for the Admiralty seat of Rochester in 1754, and in a 'New List of Admirals' in 1756.[178]

By July 1756, however, coverage was distinctly unflattering. The naval engagement had become a 'mock fight'. Holding back in the rear and strategic withdrawal to Gibraltar was 'running away', cowardice that led to ridicule from other nations. His unapologetic letter to the Admiralty was inglorious, breaking the code of gentlemanly honour to which he had subscribed in 1746: 'nothing is more becoming to the gentleman, than to acknowledge himself to be in the wrong, as soon as he is sensible that he is so'.[179] 'Mock articles', purportedly composed by sailors at the Lion & Anchor in Wapping, found Byng guilty and proposed punishment beneath his rank on the gang-way (as the *Lion*'s Captain of Marines had received). Byng's Admiralty letter was satirized in rhyme, suggesting that Byng, a well-known collector of fine china, had been more interested in the feminized social rituals of polite society than fighting:

> And now being tea-time, we thought it was the time,
> To talk over what we had done;
> So we put on the kettle, our tempers to settle [...]

and had priorities other than the damage to *HMS Intrepid*:

> Moreover, ' twas plain, three ships in the van,
> Had their glasses and china all broke;
> *And this gave the balance* [...][180]

Extravagance and indulgence in enervating foreign luxuries were implied in a 'Historical Chronicle' report of his delaying the journey to Minorca by putting into Malaga to 'take in his wines', and in a poem lamenting that modern officers were no longer satisfied with the ale and beef that had nourished Drake and Howard. They preferred champagne, 'ragoos', 'nerve-impairing tea' or gin.

The *Gentleman's Magazine* continued to report the story in each number to April 1757, following its vaunted approach of presenting the arguments on each side of the political debate over the correct attribution of blame for Minorca: Byng or an Administration that had equipped him inadequately.[181] In September letters from Gibraltar criticized Byng, but in October two pamphlets defending him were excerpted. The account of the court martial was printed without comment.[182] Robert Spector calls this style 'a conglomeration of contemporary opinion' less 'heated' than the politicized essay journals.[183]

However, the magazine departed from neutrality in its insistence on the contrasting characters of the two gentleman-protagonists. The *Gentleman's* Byng was avaricious, cowardly, over-proud of his social position and foppish. He was too fond of the 'touch of gold', afraid of the smell of gunpowder, had complained that his top-floor accommodation in Greenwich Hospital (up 170 stairs) was unfit for the son of a peer, Member of Parliament and Vice-Admiral. When a crowd hanged and burnt his effigy on Tower Hill it was 'richly dress'd'.[184]

Its Blakeney was distinguished as a rugged hero who had risen outside the world of noble patronage. An editorial footnote to the poem 'On General Blakeney's conduct in Minorca', by 'W.O.' of Mars[h]field, pointed out that he had gained a regiment 'merely by merit, without parliamentary interest'. To 'W.O.' and other poets he was 'Eager to conquer, or resign'd to die', 'that *Hibernian* brave' (he was from Limerick, his father a country gentleman), intrepid, dauntless, experienced, reflective, zealous and more. An engraving showed him looking rather younger than his 84 years.[185] In August the magazine printed a two-page 'Life'.[186] He was courageous from his youth and a man's man. Far from fussing over his dignity like Byng, as an officer he had 'always lived at quarters; [...] and was seldom absent from his corps'. His meritocratic rise was reiterated. He was as polite as 'Frank Easy', enjoying dancing and spending his first evening back on English soil at an assembly playing cards and tripping two minuets with a young lady. He obeyed the rules of the gentleman in his expenditure: 'he is generous without profusion, and though he despises money, does not throw it away', and was benevolent to his brothers. He was a good listener and his conversation was serious ('chiefly historical') rather than idle tea-table chat. He had never issued a challenge to a duel. His only possible fault seemed to be a convivial fondness for punch. Unlike Byng's, his arrival home (at Portsmouth on 17 November) met with huge public rejoicing. Bells rang, there were illuminations and bonfires, and (manly, English) free beer all round.[187]

This insistence on character marks a point of departure from the *London Magazine's* otherwise similar reporting. As with Lord Lovat, the

London was less concerned with character and more sensational, printing an engraving of the execution frozen at the point of firing and
death.[188] The *Gentleman's Magazine* used Minorca, Byng and Blakeney to
comment on two types of gentlemanliness: the true gentlemanliness of
Blakeney in which restrained politeness was combined with masculine
professionalism and merit, and the failed gentlemanliness of the noble
Byng, debilitated by aristocratic patronage and luxury. The difference
between success and failure in male worlds was starkly delineated. Apart
from the single mention of Blakeney's dancing partner, women played
no part in the construction of either Byng's or Blakeney's masculinity.
(In fact both were bachelors and the magazine was silent on the subject
of Byng's mistress, widow Mrs Susannah Hickson, with whom he lived
from 1751 until her death in 1755.)[189] That the *Gentleman's Magazine*
was consciously creating archetypes is revealed by the more damning
private verdicts on Blakeney of a serving soldier, James Wolfe, and the
ever-gossipy Horace Walpole. For Wolfe he had lost St Phillips 'by igno-
rance and dotage'. Walpole told Sir Horace Mann that at the time of the
siege he had been 'bedrid'.[190]

The archetypes accorded with the increasing attention paid in the
magazine to the virtuous and professional man judged by his male peers.
The role of merit and application in forming gentlemanliness was underlined in a letter from 'an honest tar before the mast'. He believed that
effort would have saved Minorca and that victory would have put it 'in
our power to finish the war and make ourselves gentlemen'.[191] A letter
from regular correspondent 'P. Gemsege' (Pegge) continued the theme.
He asked readers to consider:

> What it is that makes the gentleman of the army or the navy objects
> of our esteem. It is not their birth, or their being meerly [*sic*] and
> simply gentlemen, for the Hon. Mr Anybody, that sits at home and
> does nothing, ranks equally with them in that respect.

For Pegge, what counted was 'acquired desert', being 'raised by a train of
good services to his country'.[192] The author of 'Reasons of the Miscon-
duct and Miscarriages of the Navy' felt that the parliamentary interest of
'men of large property, and in eminent stations' in appointing their relatives to naval commands was in Britain's interest for the standard reason
that their land gave them a true stake in the nation. Notwithstanding,
he demanded that they too 'take notice of extraordinary merit, wherever 'tis found, that the meanest may see, if they excel, they will surely
be rewarded'.[193]

Conclusion

Between 1731 and 1756 the *Gentleman's Magazine* was a vehicle for debate about the qualities of the polite gentleman. Initially these debates were presented through the didactic 'clubs' and model gentlemen familiar from the *Spectator*. By the 1740s, real-life gentlemen and anti-gentlemen were replacing fictional 'types', although Richardson's exemplary fictional gentleman, Sir Charles Grandison, was an important later template. However, from the magazine's launch polite gentlemanliness was also threaded throughout the magazine's articles, reader correspondence and poetry on a wide range of subjects.

Both fictional and real gentlemen were valued for Christian piety in action, restraint and benevolence, always within the constraints of the ordered hierarchical society where landed, lineage families represented the uppermost layer. There were, though, increasing opportunities for middling-sort assertions of gentlemanliness via a process of self-improvement. The magazine's educational articles contributed to this directly. Indirectly the magazine facilitated their advance by promoting masculine 'merit' through commercial and professional success. Success demonstrated industry rewarded, and was configured as patriotic. Failure was its opposite. The verdicts on Byng and Blakeney made this point. It was not an entirely secular concept, but an aspect of the prevalent Christian belief in divine providence. In this way the businessman could be the Christian Hero, his worldly achievements evidence of God's favour. By the 1740s, there was emerging a critique of the vices of the nobility and the development by the new gentlemen of a moral code and associated social performance derived from sobriety, seriousness and the ' "domestick order" and prudential morality' that Hunt identifies as key values of the professional and trading middling sort.[194]

Gentlemanly success was judged by and against other men, both gentlemen and non-polite plebeians. Women were chiefly represented as ideally supportive, but potentially disruptive, accessories to male standing. They weakened a man in love, and in marriage might threaten his independence by refusing a subordinate role, humiliating him in the eyes of his male peers. This was not a new gender panic, but a continuation of the anxieties generated by early modern masculinity that depended upon male independence through the control of women. Displayed in 1716 by the young, unmarried Dudley Ryder and his cousin Billio who 'agreed that the sorrows and cares and burdens to which it [marriage] exposes a man don't seem to be sufficiently balanced by the joys and pleasures once can expect from it', it still influenced

52-year-old bachelor and magazine-reader Henry Purefoy in 1749 when he re-ordered a copy of *The Disadvantages of the Married State* [. . .] *Preferable to that of Marriage* from his bookseller who had in error sent *A Serious Proposal for Promoting Marriage*.[195]

There were also indications, however, that this polite gentleman was not a template that was easily applied to real life. Success was always fragile and contingent, with failure lurking around the corner. There were too pre-existing masculinities, especially 'provincial rusticity and old world manners' and the rougher culture of the soldier, with which this new style of gentlemanliness was not readily reconciled.[196]

5
Gentlemanly Masculinity in the *Gentleman's Magazine*, 1757 to 1789

Introduction

The fall of Minorca was just one example of British weakness as war spread around the globe. North American territory was lost to the French. French ally the Nawab of Bengal stormed Fort William in Calcutta and a large number of British prisoners of war perished in the notorious 'Black Hole'. Battles fought in continental Europe as Prussia's ally resulted in defeat or stalemate. The governments of Newcastle and Pitt fell in turn and their coalition faced a potential French invasion. There was a mood of national self-examination: did military losses indicate that Britain had lost its way, was no longer favoured by God?

Anglican clergyman and author John Brown (1715–66) certainly thought so. In his popular polemical work of 1757, *An Estimate of the Manners and Principles of the Times*, written immediately after Minorca, he placed the blame squarely with British men of the ruling class. For 20 years they had wallowed in 'a *vain, luxurious,* and *selfish* EFFEMINACY' while females had 'advanced into Boldness' such that the two sexes were indistinguishable. Military courage, said Brown, was not always natural and so men needed to replace soft child-rearing, frivolous reading and devotion to fashion with a training 'infused by an early and continued Discipline'.[1] The *Gentleman's Magazine* was quick to excerpt the *Estimate* in April 1757, alongside coverage of Byng's trial and execution, ending with an editorial prompt to read the original and hope that reader numbers 'will not be few'.[2]

By the end of that same year, however, the tide of war was moving in Britain's favour on all fronts. At war's end in 1763, the Treaty of Paris gave Britain an empire by conquest. In India the French recovered their ports on condition they destroyed the fortifications, ending their military presence on the sub-continent. In North America, Britain acquired most of New France (Canada) which, together with Florida from Spain, gave control of all land east of the Mississippi. Minorca, the island at the eye of the storm of dissatisfaction in 1756, also returned to British control.

Brown's *Estimate* is regarded by some historians as evidence of a 'gender panic', and the outcome of the Seven Years' War as marking a change in Britons' perception of both nation and gender. Men rather than women had won the war and the resulting empire produced new categories of 'others', colonials, indigenous peoples and the enslaved, against whom gentlemen could compute their manliness and politeness.[3] These others were defined by race and religion and, often, by the 'stage' of civilization they had reached relative to the British.

At home many commercial middling-sort men saw their trading interests both supported by pro-war parties and enhanced by the peace treaty.[4] There had been the opportunity for rapid social rise through service in the forces as officers and other professionals (commissaries, surgeons and chaplains). It was the war that had 'catapulted' Elizabeth Marsh's male relatives into the ranks of the gentlemanly, for example.[5] Post-war, there were also new career openings overseas in government and private trading companies, especially the East India Company.

There were negative outcomes too. Benefits were not evenly spread, and the high cost had to be recouped via taxation. The war, as Conway puts it, 'accelerated, rather than caused, movement both up and down the social hierarchy', deepening tensions between gentleman and gentleman, and between gentlemen and the rest.[6] Paradoxically then, the commercial and professional middling sort in particular were both newly self-confident and increasingly apprehensive.

Their political confidence was demonstrated in displays of public opinion during the war and in a revived interest in political affairs. 'We are all *Politicians* now', announced *Gentleman's Magazine* correspondent Pegge in 1758.[7] German Count Kielmansegge, in England for George III's coronation, remarked that once the ice was broken between strangers in a coach 'a political discussion is sure to follow'.[8] It was war that brought Pitt the Elder to the fore as a politician who appealed directly to this class of men, turning his initially insulting soubriquet 'the Great Commoner' on its head as a compliment.[9]

Political flexing of muscle by men 'out-of-doors', under the slogan of liberty and typically directed at an allegedly corrupt governing class, continued after 1763. The disturbances in the late 1760s around John Wilkes (despite his education and pretensions, no gentleman by birth) and the Middlesex election, and the rise of London's middling-sort debating societies with politics on their agenda were examples of the phenomenon.[10] So too was American colonists' growing dissatisfaction with their status: taxed heavily by the mother country to pay for the war but without Commons representation. A magazine obituary of 1786 described one such new 'activist', the late Caleb Jeacocke: 'the celebrated baker who disputed so much at the Robin Hood Society, where he presided'.[11]

Through the magazine, readers were made aware of the new global potential for British ambition. In January 1767 'An Exhortation to Gentlemen of small Fortunes' encouraged settlement in newly acquired East Florida where an 'estate' (a slave plantation) could be had for as little as £1,000.[12] Marriage notices also presented an empire of possibility for transplanted young British men in parallel genteel societies they created overseas.[13] There had always been the occasional announcement where groom, bride or wealth was located outside the British Isles in, for example, the Caribbean or America. In the 1770s and 1780s sample their numbers rose to eight and 14 respectively, with a further 14 grooms involved in East India Company business. Three Indian weddings opened the July 1788 marriages, for instance.[14] Sometimes, as in the instance of Lt William Sandiford to Miss Ramsay, daughter of the Governor, in Bombay, the bride's family was also embedded in genteel British Indian society.[15] Articles, news reports and promotions all signalled a gentleman's world of expanding horizons.[16]

At the same time, there were distinct signs of middling-sort uneasiness over social mobility and change. A poem in the 1769 Preface referred to 'foes at home', and there was continued interest in news stories of impostors, men whose outward appearance belied their inner lack of gentlemanliness: the well-dressed rapist or genteelly-turned-out robber. Reporting of the forgery trial of twins Daniel and Robert Perreau contrasted Daniel's expensive 'genteel life in Pall-mall' with his brother's more modest lifestyle.[17] It was equally vital, warned 'Pro Clero' (David Wells), that a real gentleman looked the part and could be distinguished from 'a common mechanic'. He for one had failed to recognize an inappropriately dressed bishop.[18]

The specifically male, middling-sort risk of failure was still represented in the bankrupts lists, a steady feature of the back half of the magazine to the late 1780s.[19] Indeed there was a rise in the number of names listed: from 145 in 1757–9 (an average of 48 a year) to 720 (72) in the 1770s and 652 (65) in the 1780s. In January 1786 a list for the whole of 1785 ran to a solid two-and-a-half pages. The impression given to readers was of the potentially unstable post-war Britain Conway describes, in which it was hard for many men to make their way (including a small but rising number of professional men), but consequently the more impressive when they did.[20]

Nor was the British imperial world a sanctuary. Notices of deaths abroad and on the high seas of British soldiers and civilians, men and women, rose in parallel with overseas marriages. Anxiety such as Brown's over luxury, extravagance and corruption was now linked to new wealth as the empire visibly came home. There were covetable exotic products, and rich financiers, Indian 'nabobs' and planters from the Caribbean slave economies who used money to stake a claim to gentlemanliness in Britain. This was debated in literature and theatre. Foote's *Commissary*, a comedy of 1765 reviewed in the magazine, satirized the *nouveaux riches* and their pretensions. Zachary Fungus, his landlady gleefully reported, had 'brought home from the wars a whole cart-load of money'. He now devoted time and cash to acquiring appropriate gentlemanly skills to match: dancing, fencing, riding and public speaking.[21] In Richard Cumberland's *West Indian* of 1771, by contrast, it was London that teemed with venality and coldness and the *parvenu* planter who was the spontaneous and sincere 'natural gentleman'.[22]

This chapter explores how the *Gentleman's Magazine* and its readers addressed gentlemanly masculinity within this new context. It identifies two emerging versions: a politicized, outspoken independent 'public' gentleman who challenged elite mores, and a private, family gentleman of sensibility. These masculinities were sometimes difficult to reconcile with one another. The military gentleman too remained problematic. He was inevitably conspicuous in decades dominated by actual and impending war (correspondent Pegge anticipated in 1758 'we are always to be at war with *France*').[23] The chapter covers not only the Seven Years' War, but the American Revolutionary War and the outbreak of the French Revolution. In July 1789 this was reported and welcomed in the magazine on the grounds that the *ancien régime* of the old enemy had broken down completely and 'the English constitution had all the appearance of being then established'.[24] The chapter concludes with a case study of the magazine's long-running interest in prison reformer John Howard as the idolized representative of a new national gentlemanliness that was peaceable but bore favourable comparison with heroic military manliness.

Gentlemanly continuities

As Chapter 2 demonstrates, the magazine in this period (which saw the closure in 1785 of chief rival, the *London Magazine*) remained recognizable to those who had known its first 26 years. The back half was relatively unchanged but the front half contained markedly fewer press excerpts and was now dominated by readers' letters on subjects broadly as in 1731–56: theology, science, topography, history and literature. Christianity still infused all sections of the magazine. From 1778, John Nichols' influence was seen in the growing antiquarian correspondence and in the additional space devoted to, and the style of, obituaries. Their proliferation was due, of course, to readers' shared interest in these subjects. The immediate overall impression was therefore of a continuity of gentlemanly interests.

As press excerpts withered away, so too did the idealized gentlemen of the fictional clubs. In their place, editorial material and reader contributions supplied examples of good and failed gentlemen, real and imagined. The magazine's fundamental version of masculine politeness survived: a gentleman was still substantially defined by merit and its earthly reward, success, derived from 'complaisance', piety, restraint and industry. In July 1761 for example, 'A.M.' of Royston sent a character taken from a memorial to recently deceased Bishop Sherlock of London, whose 'own actions will be his highest praise'. Sherlock was judicious, pleasing, instructive, cheerful, pious, benevolent and lived as 'a perfect pattern of Decorum'. In the same number an anonymous reader replied to a letter on the good clergyman with examples of the opposite: ministers who indulged in cruel country sports, gambling, drinking and a domineering manner over their servants.[25]

This importance of inner character driving outward actions persisted and strengthened. In 1770 the prolific Pegge lamented want of character in many men. Character pushed a man into 'aiming at excellency in some way [...] to distinguish himself above the herd'. It was reminiscent of the 12th Article of War that had proved Byng's undoing: that a man 'do his utmost'. Pegge concluded with a list of great characters from history. All were men and the gendering of 'character' was heightened by the use of a quotation from Pope to head the letter: 'Most Women have no Character at all'.[26] In the obituaries, women, despite now representing an increased 19 per cent of the sample, 'possessed relatively little individual identity'. They too lacked character.[27]

The magazine continued to promote commercial and professional work as fields where this melding of mental capital, effort, character and providential success formed the new gentleman. 'Lysander's' 1776 poem, 'On my birth-day', expressed the hope that he would in the coming year become a wiser, more serious and pious man, but also that he would work harder:

> And mind my business, and my pen,
> And be an early riser.[28]

'M.O.N.', writing in July 1787, praised commerce and industry for their contribution to the nation and warned against retiring too early from business since excess leisure dulled mental acuity and produced a quarrelsome temper. In the same month, success in work and business received the royal *imprimatur* when the 'Historical Chronicle' reported at length the visit of the king, queen and their entourage to Whitbread's Chiswell Street brewery.[29]

If the ethos of the industrious gentleman represented continuity, there was a step-change in scale as readers adopted the identity enthusiastically in marriage and death notices. (Births, by contrast, remained distinctly elite.) It was a change that satirists had noticed. 'Every man believes himself important to the publick', pronounced Samuel Johnson in an *Idler* piece on obituaries in July 1758.[30]

By the 1780s, over 40 per cent of the sampled 610 marriages provided a groom's occupation. There were professionals – military officers, ministers, physicians – but alongside them were 59 men of trade, from merchants, bankers and stockbrokers to dealers in wine, oysters and timber, an innkeeper and a coffeehouse man, brewers, haberdashers and booksellers. The 1783 announcement of the marriage between two provincial, self-made business families revealed a new confidence in celebrating commercial success in this national magazine:

> Lately at Hackney, Tho. Walker, esq; (son of the late Sam. W. esq; near Rotherham, eminent for having established the very extensive iron works there) to Miss Need, dau. of Sam. N, esq; late of Nottingham, a proprietor of the curious cotton mills near Nottingham.[31]

The change was even more marked in the deaths columns. To be sure, there was still a place for members of the nobility and gentry whose distinction was expressed in lineage and land: Rt Hon. Marmaduke, Lord Langdale, 'succeeded in the Title and Estate by his only Son', or Sir Thomas Alston, Bart, of Odell, Bedfordshire 'succeeded in title and his estate by his brother, now Sir Rowland Alston'.[32] However, by the 1780s the proportion of men whose death notice mentioned occupational standing had risen to over 700 of the sampled 1,248 male deaths for the decade. Over half were professional men: 102 army and navy officers, 144 clergy of the Church of England, 53 lawyers, 35 doctors and surgeons and 25 schoolmasters and academics. Others were involved in the administration of government departments and the colonies. Again this was allied to growth in the number of men from the commercial and financial sectors: over 90 merchants, bankers, 'businessmen', employees of the South Seas and East India Companies and as many again who were retailers, dealers, manufacturers, writers and artists of every hue. There were apothecaries and turpentine merchants, linen drapers and fishmongers, hatters and goldsmiths, coffeehouse and innkeepers and cheesemongers.

They were most definitely Hunt's middling sort engaged in 'the translating of work into money'. They were also urban rather than rural: there were only 11 farmers and one grazier in the sample. The pleasure these families took in associating with the elite, both in work and finally when obituarized, is hinted at in the death notice of Mr George Hawkins, a bookseller in Fleet Street and at Tunbridge Wells during the season, who was 'much respected by the nobility and gentry who frequented his shop'.[33]

The longer obituaries were now used to celebrate the lives not just of the nobility and gentry, but of these middling-sort men who formed the magazine's core readership, and their values. They too were now exemplars of the good gentleman rewarded. The key terms of 1731–56 marking success, skill and merit – 'celebrated', 'ingenious', 'eminent' – remained important, but what was new was the inclusion of detailed accounts of the deceased as proudly self-made and independent. For the families of men such as Sir Daniel Wray (1701–83) there was no shame in the world knowing that his father had started out as a Smithfield soap-boiler.[34] These biographies therefore built a new, public 'narrative identity' that was the very opposite of the traditional gentleman's lineage, because it began with the gentleman himself.[35] It is worth quoting almost in full the 1785 tribute to Mr Richard Atkinson (1738–85), director of the East India Company, who was specifically billed as an exemplar of the growing numbers of such men whose standing was literally all their own work:

[…] One of the many instances of good sense and persevering industry, well-directed, in a commercial country, like England, rising from the bottom of society to the summit of affluence. Mr

A. when he came from the North was a mere adventurer, unsustained by any inheritance, by few family friends of any power, and by no acquisitions which education imparts, but common penmanship and arithmetic. Thus circumstanced, he came to London, and, passing through different 'compting houses, and experiments in trade, accumulated that prodigious wealth of which he died possessed.[36]

The narrative of industry was also applied to professional men. The elevation of lawyer and judge Sir George Nares (1716–86), for example, did not come by patronage: 'without any powerful friends he raised himself by his own diligence and merits; in the duties of his office he was active and indefatigable'.[37] He was, it was implied, truly independent.

New wealth was therefore good, the public reward for effort. Obituaries, however, cited the monetary worth of the deceased less frequently than in earlier decades. Instead, what was increasingly blazoned was Raven's 'bourgeois ideal of gentlemanliness, based on ideas of responsibility and service'.[38] Picking up the idea of 'Character', from the 1780s they commended qualities of morality, devotion to family, feeling benevolence and engagement in public life (as militia officers, aldermen, mayors or justices) for elite and new gentlemen alike.

The January 1785 magazine illustrates the impact of the repetition of this catalogue of virtue. A large number of obituaries referred to these qualities, often wrapped up together in one individual.[39] Langhorne Burton Esq. had 'a high character' as an impartial magistrate and was remembered for his 'liberality to the poor'. Revd John Allen, Vice Principal of Magdalen College, Oxford, was not an exceptional academic but he was 'very convivial' and 'his moral character was unimpeached'. Captain Rickard, a packet-boat commander drowned at New York, had 'numerous moral and social virtues'. Clergyman and author Thomas Hartley was 'in his conversation and deportment [...] humble and devout, abounding in love; of charitable sentiments towards others'. Charles Thompson, retired Russia merchant of Mansfield, left bequests to clubs and the poor there, Nottingham General Hospital, and his indigent relations. Barrister Edward Wynne's knowledge of polite literature was 'only exceeded by his charity and benevolence'. Dr John Pearce also loved polite literature, a pursuit which 'endeared him as a husband, a father, a friend and a man'. Mr Richard Hillis spent 40 years 'industriously pursuing business' and performing too many 'benevolent and generous actions' to recall but one: the rescue of a friend from bankruptcy. Mr Nevil Fether, formerly an eminent sword-cutler, had devoted his retirement to 'acts of beneficence and charity' such that 'the necessitous' would lament his passing. Beeston Long Esq.'s 'well-spent life' endeared him to 'the world and to his family'. He had dispensed charity liberally, was a hospital governor and 'united the various and more amiable offices of a parent, a Christian, and a citizen of the world!' These were, of course, self-serving eulogies. The enslaved on the Longs' West Indian estates (the location merely hinted at in a reference to a subscription for sufferers in a recent hurricane) surely had not been consulted about his benevolence or amiability.

As before, it was improper spending which editors and contributors regarded as ungentlemanly. Failure was still explained by undue extravagance on luxuries, often of French origin. In 1787 'A Plain Englishman's' pseudonym alluded to the plainness (rather than show) that denoted the gentleman, and his letter extended it to the debasement of the English language by imported French words and phrases.[40] Raven detects in novels of the period a tendency to gender tasteless extravagance as female, attributed to the desire by wives and families of businessmen to 'follow the fashion'.[41] The *Gentleman's Magazine* did on occasion disapprove of female luxury. As 'J.N.', Nichols himself contributed a 1773 letter decrying provincial wives with tastes above their station.[42] In an anonymous poem of 1779, 'Celia' made a fool of her husband in her pursuit of 'jewels and gew-gaws' and 'endless visits'.[43] However, its stream of real-life stories, of which the Perreaus' was just one, constituted a moral warning to men rather than women of the risk to their standing, and even life, of inappropriate excess.[44] It was a 'moral panic', but it was a panic about the vulgarity of masculine display rather than feminization.[45]

Anxiety about extravagant wealth was especially evident in criticism of 'speculation in the stocks', closer to the noble vice of gambling than to trade, and of the corrupting influence of India.[46] 'Gaming in Change-alley' allegedly caused the downfall of banker Alexander Fordyce (1729–89), which in turn sparked a wider financial crash.[47] He had, the magazine explained, started well in approved meritocratic fashion: using natural ability, education and enterprise to work his way up from Aberdeen hosier to partner in a City bank. It was ostentation, especially the acquisition of 'a large estate' and a 'most elegant villa' where he built a family chapel with, notably, the 'aim at surpassing Commissaries and Nabobs in grandeur and magnificence', that undid him, leading him to betray his partners and flee in an ungentlemanlike fashion.[48] 'The last solemn Declaration' of condemned forger and 'Macaroni Parson', Dr Dodd (1729–77), printed under July 1777's review section, conveyed the same moral message: 'Vanity and pleasure, into which I plunged, required expence disproportionate to my income [and] urged me to temporary fraud'.[49]

Together with this emphasis on plainness, there was in the magazine's tone a detectable move towards the seriousness and restraint favoured by 'Mr Tradewell'. There were fewer riddles, no wife-beating jokes. Ribald content continued its decline. In the sample only two poems were in this genre: Robert Lloyd's comic 'The New-River Head: A Tale', which concluded by punishing a peasant woman with a non-stop stream of *al fresco* urination, and anti-Semitic lines by 'Z' about a Jewish man vomiting copiously during a memorial concert for Handel at the Pantheon.[50]

The risqué still had enthusiasts at all levels of society.[51] Lloyd (1733–64) dedicated his poem to Wilkes, editor of the far more obscene 'Essay on Woman', in whose rakish circle Lloyd moved.[52] 'Z's' verses had already been 'handed about at Bath and the Hot-well with some approbation'. In 1771, correspondent 'Impartialis' commended William Jackson's *The Beauties of Nature Displayed* after criticism in the *Monthly Review*. 'Impartialis' approved Jackson's by now old-fashioned view of marriage as 'aloes wrapped in honey'. What he did not mention, but presumably knew, was that the back half of this cod-philosophical work harboured equally old-fashioned humour in 'Poems on Various Occasions'. The 'occasions' included bee-stung breasts, a country wench pissing loud as a mill wheel, 'Chloe's' exposure on falling from her horse, and a mouse that a lucky gentleman pulled from under his lady's petticoat.[53]

This material therefore had its discrete and discreet place, but that was emphatically not in the pages of this family-orientated miscellany.[54] 'To the Author of these Stanzas it is not necessary to assign the Reason why the others were omitted' ran the editorial footnote to 'Oxonienis" 1759 poem, 'On seeing Miss B-ts-y N-ch-les', in which the poet spied the eponymous 'lovely maid' strolling by the Isis where 'nymphs and swains promiscuous stray'. Readers could only imagine what happened in the banned verses.[55] A 1788 editorial note to the poetry pages warned that 'our prurient and priapic correspondent at *Cambridge*' would not see his work printed, for 'Decency has hitherto been the established characteristic of the Gentleman's Magazine'.[56] This poet's inspiration was Edward Gibbon's notes on Mohammed and Moseilama in the newly-published fifth volume of *Decline and Fall of the Roman Empire*. Excerpts had opened the June magazine on the basis that they were 'learned' as well as 'entertaining' (reflecting the magazine's motto).[57] 'Urban' was guilty, however, under this pretext, of some prurience himself. His selection included pederasty, naked orgies and sexually voracious women. July's indignant editorial note perhaps contained an element of self-reproach. The ponderously styled 'Quod Verum Atque Decens Curo Atque Rogo' ('Truth and decency are my concerns ', slightly misquoted from Horace) agreed. These were 'filthy extracts from a silly book' that corrupted the pages of the magazine and the minds of its fair readers.[58]

It was therefore a gendered issue, just as it had been for Cave's 1735 correspondent Thomas Dod. The difference was that by the late 1780s the discourse of gentlemanly concern over women readers' heightened sensitivity to sexual material had prevailed. The *Gentleman's Magazine* regarded criticism and censorship of such items as progressive. Its 1783 account of William Cook's comedy *The Capricious Lady*, adapted from Beaumont's and Fletcher's *Scornful Lady* of 1614, noted that the original contained 'many indelicacies which [...] would ill-suit with the manners of the present time'.[59] However, the extent to which this was discourse rather than reality is demonstrated in an early-nineteenth-century diary entry by Revd William Jones. He expressed distaste over old women, who would have been brought up in this period, 'who will twist something of indelicacy, -not to say *smut*, out of almost anything that may be uttered!'[60]

'He's manly yet tender, he's fond & yet wise'[61]

The protective family man

Farewell, 'Frank Easy' and his amours! The magazine's gentleman now eagerly adopted the role of guardian of woman, differentiated by her alleged frailty.[62] Woman was fine china, 'vessels so pure and so refin'd', to man's 'strong earthen vessel of clay', according to an anonymous poem 'To a Lady'.[63] Male violence towards women was relegated to the crime reports where it was disapproved as plebeian. Gentlemen respected and protected women in public and in the family and home. Women were no longer the troublesome sex, but were reconfigured as possessing only the 'soft virtues'.[64] In obituaries they were chiefly described for their relationship to and the comforts they brought to men, often as good wives and mothers. Mrs Elderton, who died in January 1789, was 'an affectionate wife, a tender parent, and an uniform promoter of happiness in others', for example.[65]

A 1776 news story of an elderly Leicestershire woman persecuted as a witch captures all the polite gentlemanly attributes favoured by the magazine: knowledge, restraint and the protection of the weak, especially women. The enlightened implied reader understood the woman was ill ('seized with an uncommon disorder' and 'could scarce crawl'), whereas her tormentors were irrational ('took it into their heads') in believing in witches. They were inferior, a 'mob', and cruel: forcing her to be bled by threat of violence and ducking her in the pond. She had to be 'rescued from their hands by the humanity of the neighbouring gentlemen'.[66]

The woman's husband and soldier son were active among her persecutors. They had, to gentlemanly eyes, failed to observe one of the most important of male duties: to preside over a loving, private, domestic world as head of a family, Dr Primrose's 'little republic to which I gave laws'.[67] The *Gentleman's Magazine* had from the start advertised itself as 'Very proper for private Families', and wrapper advertising implied a family readership. It had strongly supported the ideal of the Grandisonian gentleman as a kindly domestic governor. A feature of the magazine from the Seven Years' War onwards was a more insistent and positive focus in both editorial and reader-supplied material on marriage and the family with none of the earlier ambiguity of feeling over loss of male freedom, William Jackson's 'aloes wrapped in honey'.

War-time patriotism had promoted procreation within marriage to provide manpower (numbers and quality) to compete militarily and commercially with the much more populous (*c.* 20 million) enemy, France. In the magazine, 'Publicola's' letter of 1762 as well as proposing taxes on a now hackneyed list of corrupting luxuries (dogs, horse-racing, wigs, swords in civil society, theatres and assemblies) stated 'the encouraging of matrimony is a piece of good policy, inasmuch as the number of useful subjects is the riches and strength of a nation'. It could be encouraged by a levy on old bachelors and exemption from militia service for fathers of three or more children.[68]

The emphasis on marriage, its role as the foundation-stone of social stability more important now than population, continued in peacetime. The sentimental family was, as Sarah Pearsall explains of British families separated by the Atlantic, 'one way of coping with the dislocations of the eighteenth century'.[69] In January 1763 an anonymous correspondent suggested settling veterans on wasteland small-holdings, a benefit being procreation in the national interest.[70] By July 1772 the author of *Considerations on the Causes of the Present Stagnation of Matrimony* (noted under the 'Catalogue of new Publications') regarded 'the promotion of matrimony' as 'a grand object to every nation' but after inveighing against the usual suspects (luxury, vice and debauchery) proposed that marriage was strongest when based on 'the free principle of choice and inclination'.[71]

A dramatic decline in the inclusion of settlement figures in the Marriages column coincided with this preference for conjugal affection.[72] That is not to say that settlements no longer existed. Indeed, in January 1766 the magazine carried the marriage announcement of Captain Powlett of the 5th Regiment of Foot to Mrs Poore of Plymouth ten pages on from an anonymous poem 'On Mrs Poor [*sic*], at P – th' which played on her name and the proverbial allure of 'ten thousand pounds [. . .] sure to have ten thousand charms'.[73] 'On a Lady of Fortune', another anonymous poem in July 1772, covered similar ground, mocking a suitor's propensity to admire his lady's £15,000 as much as her person.[74] Rather, it was no longer proper to highlight financial aspects of marriage in such a public manner.

Articles depicting love, marriage and fatherhood as emotionally fulfilling for men also increased, Conjugal bliss replaced male friendship as the key human relationship.[75] The affectionate nuclear family with the 'tender father' at its beating heart was found throughout the magazine. There were still some traditional poems from lovers rendered powerless. William Brooke's 1764 'Instructions to *M*. Soffani, of Covent Garden [i.e. Zoffany], for drawing a lady's picture here' ran through the gamut of clichés: Celia, roses and lilies, slavery, lightning, darts, pain.[76] This was now balanced by more poems celebrating enduring mutual love in a long and contented marriage, such as 'Sonnet by a Husband', happy as he reclined on his wife's bosom to think how:

> The tender love, the melting kiss,
> Ev'n years have not destroy'd,

and 'To Mrs – with a Ring', a sixteenth anniversary gift from a husband renewing his vows who, far from scorning the effect of ageing as George Ogle had in 1745, praised the 'riper virtues' that 'the wife has added to the bride'.[77]

Poets also took up the father's cause. In a translation of a fragment by fifth-century-BC Greek poet Simonides, a weeping widow recalled her husband as a loving, involved father:

> Whose knee so oft you climb'd in frolick play;
> Or wanton springing high in air he toss'd,
> Or prompted mild your tongue's first rude essay.[78]

'Rustic Simplicity, or, Happy Peasantry' by 'W.O.' of Marshfield depicted an improbably self-sufficient and robust poor family sustained by 'mutual loves, and mutual cares' because:

> The dear domestic joys of life
> Are worth a thousand others;
> A tender husband, prudent wife,
> Kind sisters, and good brothers.[79]

The magazine promoted the works of Swiss painter and poet Salomon Gessner, whose popular appeal derived from 'sentiments and virtues [that] corresponded to middle class ideals'.[80] A February 1776 review praised William Hooper MD's translation of Gessner's *New Idyls* [*sic*] as 'a laudable design, namely, that of exhibiting the *benevolent affections* in the most natural and amiable light'.[81] One of its pastoral stories, *Mirtilus and Chloe*, was printed in July 1776.[82] Menalcas, the sick father of little Mirtilus and Chloe, whom he had been wont to caress and take on his knee, reaped the benefit of this gentle love when his children's prayers and sacrifices were answered. He was restored to health and success, to live 'surrounded by prosperity, to see his children's children'. An engraving of Gessner's painting in which the family, recovering father at the centre, embraced for joy, accompanied the tale. It was a popular image: a footnote attributed its poor quality to the large number of copies having worn the plate.

The Gessner extract suggested that the happy, sentimental family was a timeless European phenomenon. Other magazine articles and letters saw the post-war loving, faithful marriage and respect for women as peculiarly British. A learned Italian was a member of the 1733 *Auditor's* club. Now the magazine reported on the immorality of the Italian practice of *cicisbeismo*, whereby a married woman, with her husband's tacit approval, took a gallant lover.[83] In the magazine a review of *Letters on the French Nation* contrasted French and British mores and 'W.A.' of Oxford told of a French uxoricide where a man married without love and took a mistress.[84] Frenchman De La Rochefoucauld thought it in fact a notable characteristic of the Englishmen he met on his visit in 1784: 'Three marriages out of four are based on affection' and 'They spend their leisure hours with their wives and children'.[85]

Through the magazine British men depicted themselves as the loving heads of their households. In 1760 an anonymous reader supplied an approving account of the large, industrious, plain-living family of a poor clergyman, visited while 'with a child upon his knee eating breakfast'.[86] Forger Robert Perreau's defence made much of his 'maintaining, in a decent sort, a worthy wife and three promising children'.[87] 'J.A.' of Cannon Street mourned his child whose smiles and lisps had 'kindled rapture at each pleasing gaze'.[88] In the 1787 Preface, 'E.B.G.'s 'Ode to Affection' lamented his dead daughter, Maria, recalling 'How oft upon the parent knee/Meek Innocency play'd'.

In obituaries 'tender' had already been used to describe men's personal relationships. It was now extended to more individuals and repeated formulaically: the deceased was an affectionate husband, a tender, even indulgent, parent, a kind and generous master. There were vignettes of him as an engaged family man. Revd Wharton was a real-life model clergyman. His clerical income never rose above £30 a year in 50 years of ministry, yet he brought up 11 children to maturity on this miserable stipend.[89] Innkeeper Mr Dancy 'suddenly dropped down dead' while strolling with his four-year-old son.[90] A 1789 obituary took the reader into Mr Kennedy's bustling Islington home. One of his daughters was 'fetching some hot water for her father to shave himself', bumped into her ten-year-old sister in a doorway, spilling the water which scalded and killed the sister.[91]

The idealized British domestic, 'tender husband and father' acquired such resonance that he was used to rehabilitate George III. During the 1760s, satirical prints and articles routinely portrayed the king as a 'blind and ductile child' at the mercy of events and counsellors, especially Lord Bute.[92] In July 1775, ten years ahead of the turning point in royal iconography Colley identifies, a *Gentleman's Magazine* article (already published in May's *London Magazine*) recreated him as the paradigm husband and father, a stable national focus for middling-sort patriotism during an era of internal and external conflict.[93]

The article described the summer routine of the king, queen and their ten children at Kew Palace. It relied on a relaxed informality in stark contrast to hierarchical court etiquette. The royal couple, who 'place[d] their felicity [...] in social and domestic gratification', resembled nothing so much as virtuous and industrious bourgeois. Rising at six, they spent two happy hours together before breakfasting with their five older children. During the day he read while she 'worked' (presumably at decorative needlework). As a family they enjoyed exercise in the fresh air together and were abstemious, partaking of a 'light diet' and the king scarcely drinking. Their expenditure on clothing was restrained. They paid their tradesmen promptly. The sovereign, as 'the father of his family', had grown up (he was 37) and his 'Private conduct [...] as exemplary as it is amiable' demonstrated his moral integrity as an adult man able to assume the role of father of the nation.

The benevolent affections

Affectionate relationships entailed the demonstration of emotional connection, or sympathy, through correctly refined feelings. This in turn denoted superiority to unimproved men of lower social class or, in the imperial context, 'savages', adjudged as led by instinct rather than reason. 'Sensibility', the acknowledgement and expression of feeling, was therefore a badge both of gentlemanliness and of British cultural superiority.[94] It marked a change from the early decades of the century when the young Dudley Ryder avoided public grief on his grandmother's death and felt shame at weeping in private over love.[95] By 1752 Roger, the polite shepherd, cried over bull-baiting. By 1767 William Hutton was devastated, reduced to 'daily tears', at the death of his son.[96]

The grief of bereavement was now present in obituaries. Men were by turns both lamenting and lamented (by family, friends and the poor). Thomas Blackburne MD was 'beloved, honoured and lamented', perhaps in part because he was only 33; the death of the female paragon Mrs Elderton (see above) would 'claim a tear' from relatives and friends who would 'sincerely lament her'.[97] The family, friends and death-bed were sometimes conjured by mention of the painful, lingering, bravely borne final illness.[98]

This all implied a feeling audience of magazine readers, who might themselves be moved to weep in sympathy. Their sensibility was stirred in July 1782 by an unusually middling-sort birth announcement: of a son to Mrs Woodmason of Leadenhall Street.[99] They were reminded that her 'recent calamity is fresh in every feeling heart': a disastrous fire in January at the Woodmasons' home and place of business (James Woodmason was a printer and publisher and at the time out, having gone 'to see the company in the ball-room at St James's') that killed all seven of their children.[100] The tragedy had already inspired an act of gentlemanly benevolence, reported in March under 'Civil Promotions': 'Mr Woodmason, whose house in Leaden-hall-street was lately burnt, with his seven children, is appointed stationer to the royal household, owing to the humane interference of E. Talbot'.[101] The October 1783 magazine pursued the story, printing the epitaph on Bartolozzi's memorial plaque in St Peter upon Cornhill, erected as the 'spontaneous Tribute of the Feelings of his Mind' of 'a sympathising Friend' of 'the sorrowing Parents'. Each child was named and with a date of birth, and the inscription invoked a 'Scene of Distress beyond the Powers of Language, perhaps of Imagination!'[102]

Heartfelt feeling was thought to prompt gentlemanly benevolence like Talbot's. The magazine and its readers strongly supported humane and charitable responses not only to the frailty of women and children but to the suffering of unfortunate men, and even of dumb animals. The 'manual' was Henry Mackenzie's 1771 *Man of Feeling*, its plot a series of tear-inducing encounters with assorted human miseries by gentlemanly hero, Harley.[103] Despite general popularity, this novel did not resonate directly with *Gentleman's Magazine* readers as *Grandison* had done.[104] Its theme, however, did. A review of John Langhorne's *Country Justice* in September 1774 praised this poem, which similarly deployed poignant scenes to inspire charity, for offering 'excellent advice'. Even before this, from the 1760s, correspondents made abundant use of the concept of manly tears to show their sensibility and encourage the acts of benevolence that were a hallmark of the gentleman.[105]

In 1768 'L.', in 'An Address to the Electors of Great Britain', directed to 'Gentlemen and Fellow Citizens', appealed to sensibility in his call for the abolition of corrupting, expensive government places and a corresponding reduction in taxation on necessities. They 'must have a heart of flint, not to be moved with the piercing cries of the poor for daily bread'.[106] 'Man: a Poem' by 'Philo-Benevol.' of Elvet, Durham, evoked the 'sympathizing heart' and 'kind fraternal part' that could 'make the sorrows of mankind their own', listing triggers to benevolence: 'tender infant's tears', 'declining years', 'friendless orphant's cries' and 'mournful widow's sighs'.[107] 'W.J.' greeted the death of his friend, Mr C. Howard, proctor, with an 'elegiac impromptu' in which, unlike Dudley Ryder, he positively revelled in uncontrollable crying:

> I bid my tears, but bid in vain, to cease;
> Like hidden springs oppress'd, they bubbling rise,
> And fall incessant from my streaming eyes.[108]

John Coakley Lettsom (1744–1815, Quaker physician, philanthropist and regular contributor) took the magazine reader on a harrowing 'Morning Walk in the Metropolis' in the cold of December 1779. It led through a 'dark passage' in Little Greenwich (a court off Aldersgate Street) and up the stairs to a meanly furnished 'little chamber'. This was home to a day-labourer, prevented from working by illness, and his sick family, a wife and four children. Lettsom dwelt on visible signs of suffering: the husband thin and weak, the mother's lips and gums putrid and black, in her side an open sore, the children semi-naked and crying for want of water. It was a scene calculated to 'excite in our hearts that kind of compassion, and obtain that aid from us, which we should look for, were such afflictions suffered to overtake us'. He was pleased to tell his audience that his solution was simple, fast and successful. He paid for medical help and a nurse, and organized parish relief which resulted in the family's 'total deliverance'. In return he received 'gratitude and thankfulness'.[109] This sort of response was 'a pleasure [...] superior to all the gratifications of sense and passion', as another letter-writer of 1786 put it.[110]

Care for the poor and sick was of course a long-standing and essential Christian duty. Charity and benevolence were the subject of several of Hugh Blair's popular sermons of the 1770s, praised in the magazine's review as 'excellent discourses' (and later situated alongside the magazine in John Osborne's bookcases).[111] However, the existence of the needy and suffering was also crucial to gentlemanliness as understood in the magazine. Feeling benevolence had a self-serving element as 'L.'s' tax-cutting message and Lettsom's psychic reward indicated. It demonstrated the refined sensibility of the individual donor and indicated his participation in the gentlemanly economies of charity and reform which made inequality acceptable. It juxtaposed new gentlemen with the aristocracy and gentry in subscription lists and at annual dinners, underpinning a sense of shared superiority over charity's objects.[112]

Richard Cumberland remarked of his patron's, Lord George Sackville's, handouts to his tenants, 'these sixpences were not indiscriminately bestowed'.[113] Gentlemanly superiority derived in part from this power of discrimination, of deciding whether victims were 'innocent', and hence deserving of relief, or the undeserving authors of their own misfortunes.[114] The magazine and its correspondents supported a widening range of benevolent concerns for the former. The annual anxiety over cock-throwing continued. It was extended to other animals and even the 'manly sports' of 'hunting, shooting, fishing, and horse-racing'.[115] Readers sent in 'soup-kitchen' recipes and championed institutions for the 'industrious poor', the mentally ill and the sick.[116] They called for the reform of imprisonment for debt and enthusiastically supported the Royal Humane Society's work on resuscitation.[117] In 1775 'D.H.' (Gough) expressed horror that a lion recently presented to the king had been captured by a soldier at the expense of the lives of two African 'innocent savages'.[118] Even duelling was framed in this way, as inhumane for the 'domestic misery' it caused.[119] The most deserving of all were often men in their own image who had fallen on the hard times at which the bankruptcy lists and Lettsom hinted. For example a 'proposed home for the industrious poor' was aimed at the children of 'officers of the army or navy, of gentlemen, merchants, and tradesmen, who are left without fortunes'.[120]

The loss of the *Halsewell*: a case study in family and feeling

These emerging gendered themes in the magazine, man as the protector of weaker woman, the devoted father, the gentlemanly ownership of sensibility and benevolence, lay at the centre of a tragic true story of 1786. On 6 January outward-bound East Indiaman the *Halsewell* ran aground during a furious winter storm and was wrecked off the Isle of Purbeck, Dorset. It remains one of the worst-ever shipping disasters on that part of the British coast. Some 170 sailors, soldiers and passengers, including the commander, Captain Pierce, his two daughters, two nieces and three other 'beautiful young ladies', drowned as the ship went down or were dashed to pieces against the rocks in attempting to reach the shore. 74 men survived a freezing, wet night and scaled the almost-vertical cliffs to safety.

The next day the Second Mate, Mr Henry Meriton, arrived at India House in London with the 'melancholy news', which immediately captured the popular imagination. Within 15 days Meriton and Third Mate Mr John Rogers published their account of the wreck.[121] January's *Gentleman's Magazine* gave three-and-a-half pages to a review of their book and a further page to the calamity in the 'Historical Chronicle'.[122] Both articles drew on accounts by men who expected to be regarded as gentlemen. They illustrate how their understanding of this social identity was framed in gendered and class terms and presented in the language of sentiment and sensibility.

The news report dwelt on the scene in the cuddy (a cabin to the rear under the round-house) as Pierce, the helpless ladies 'clinging round him for protection', realized escape was impossible: 'addressing himself to his daughters, and enfolding them in his arms, he said, Then, my dear children, we will perish together'. The reviewer commended the emotions the book both portrayed and produced. It was 'one of the most affecting Narratives that is to be met with in any language', it excited pity and it was impossible to read the last tender scene without sharing Pierce's grief. Excerpts replayed the moment of the fatherly embrace, feeling and self-sacrifice, with Pierce 'struggling to suppress the parental tear which then burst into his eyes'. Readers responded. 'M' captured the scene in verse, ending with 'Brave Pierce' who 'Locks his daughters in his arms, and dies'. Three years after the event 'L.M.' proposed 'the daughter's [sic] wretched fate' in the 'parent-arms' to Sir Joshua Reynolds as a 'proper subject for a picture'.[123]

The magazine's account also set gentlemen against others. The ship's officers made calm efforts to rescue the passengers. They manned the pumps and consoled the 'unfortunate ladies' without regard for personal danger. The ordinary seamen on the other hand were lazy and unconcerned: they 'skulked in their hammocks' until the very last moment, and when they did appear on deck were uselessly hysterical, indulging in 'frantic exclamations'.

The *Gentleman's Magazine* selectivity went further, however. Its stress was on the genteel victims, whereas the book mentioned both these 'respectable passengers' and others, including three black women and two soldiers' wives, and listed all survivors by name.[124] The magazine's reviewer also added a local clergyman's account of the rescue of survivors caught at the bottom of the cliff which, again, contrasted gentlemen and others. He and a Mr Garland were men 'of sufficient authority to encourage or direct' the rescuers, many of whom were 'quarriers', and (a detail not mentioned in the book) had to be restrained from excessive drinking on the job. Garland 'allowed the survivors to gather at his house, he was their benevolent friend'. A letter from Christchurch also quoted by the reviewer made a similar point. The 'savage shore-walkers' (a description recalling peoples met in voyages of discovery) stripped the corpses washed up on the beaches while 'the gentlemen of the neighbourhood' were once more the white knights.

Gentlemen, class and politics: noble vices, independent virtues

In January 1761 the *Gentleman's Magazine* summarized the newly published 'A letter from Miss F – d to a Person of Distinction', giving it national publicity well beyond its dramatic first-day sale of 500 copies.[125] The pamphlet recounted the mistreatment of Ann Ford (1737–1824, writer, musician and later second wife of correspondent Philip Thicknesse) at the hands of an unnamed married lord (in fact William Villiers, 3rd Earl of Jersey). He had professed interest in her music as a precursor to attempted seduction, offering her £800 a year to be his mistress. Unsupported by her father, who welcomed Villiers' scheme, Ford pluckily undertook a concert to which Lord and Lady Villiers refused the five guinea subscription. The magazine printed Villiers' anonymous reply in February, possibly in the interest of its boasted impartiality (or maybe because the story was mildly titillating). He denied Ford's allegations and self-servingly used gentlemanly benevolence as the excuse for his initial 'friendship'.[126]

The airing of Ford's complaint was one instance of the magazine's continued negative coverage of the masculine vice of the nobility and political classes: their lack of moral restraint. Other cases included the fatal tavern-duel in January 1765 between 'Lord B-r-n' (William, 5th Baron Byron) and his cousin Mr Chaworth after a well-oiled dinner-table dispute over the game on their neighbouring Nottinghamshire estates.[127] In May the magazine followed up the brief news story with a three-page narrative of the duel. Although exonerating Byron as having acted in self-defence, it finished with a reproof over his lack of self-control: 'His lordship [...] may wish that he had, in that situation, disabled him only; but in the heat of duelling who can always be collected?'[128] In the same month, the poem 'Isabella: or, The Morning', set at the Duchess of Manchester's *levée*, and featuring identifiable visiting beaux, satirized elite social life. To the more broadly drawn readership of the *Gentleman's Magazine* these gentlemen must have appeared idle, dilettante, amoral and effeminate as they lounged in married female company.[129]

Some correspondents still expressed hope for the moral improvement of the unruly plebian by inculcating the bourgeois values of 'honesty, sobriety, and virtue', for 'they must become good men before they can become good citizens'.[130] This was, however, now less significant and less strident than calls for the reform of the upper echelons. This politicization of middling-sort values was a new feature in the magazine's representation of gentlemanliness.

'The Modern Lucretia'

In the late 1760s, the magazine's criticism of the elite from a middling-sort vantage point sharpened. Anna Clark shows how the eighteenth-century press used sexual scandals at very specific moments to debate both the boundaries between public and private masculine morality and the places (Parliament or 'out-of-doors') in which this debate could take place.[131] Just such a moment came in 1768 in the stressful post-war period: a sensational *cause célèbre*, the capital trial of Frederick Calvert, Lord Baltimore (1732–71), for the rape of Sarah Woodcock, a London milliner. The *Gentleman's Magazine* response to this case reveals its newly class-driven approach to noble vices, gender and sensibility and its divergence from the *London Magazine*.

Baltimore's wealthy family were hereditary proprietors of the American colony of Maryland. He was a renowned libertine. A childless marriage to a daughter of the Duke of Bridgewater had ended in separation, but he had a number of illegitimate children. He had recently published an account of his travels to Turkey, the tone of which was aristocratic, amply peppered with quotations from the Latin poets and Dryden. Nonetheless, among the *literati* the tour was primarily a byword for debauchery. Even the young James Boswell considered his lifestyle a moral warning: he had lived at Constantinople 'as a Turk, with his seraglio around him'.[132] Pitted against Baltimore was a shop-girl from a respectable, industrious, chapel-going family on the unfashionable side of town. It was a thrilling clash of class, culture and sex.

The scandal broke among metropolitan society and in the press, including the *Gentleman's Magazine*, in January 1768 when a Mrs Harvey was arrested and committed to Newgate for having lured Sarah from the family shop in King Street, Tower Hill, to Baltimore's London house in Southampton Row. Here she 'was kept some time, and afterwards conveyed in to the country against her consent' until her 'parents and friends' tracked her down, obtained her release by appearing before Lord Mansfield, and launched the rape prosecution.[133] Baltimore's trial (as a commoner, since the barony was Irish) took place on Saturday 26 March at Kingston assizes, near his country seat of Woodcote Park, Epsom, where the alleged offence occurred. It lasted from 7 am to 3 am the next day, an astonishing length for a trial at the time.[134] The jury, agreeing with the defence that Sarah had stayed too willingly and cheerfully at Woodcote, acquitted Baltimore (and his accomplices, Harvey and a Dr and Mrs Griffinburg). He left England in disgrace and died three years later in Naples.

Public interest in the Baltimore affair spawned column inches of text and images for months. Joseph Gurney took shorthand notes at the trial and immediately published the proceedings in London, Edinburgh and Ireland.[135] Fleet Street bookseller John Williams offered a 1s 6d print of a fetching, flirtatious 'Miss W-, The Modern Lucretia'.[136] It was impossible to avoid taking sides. The *Public Advertiser* declared the acquittal honourable and based on 'the clearest Evidence', but for the *North Briton* it came 'to the surprised indignation of most people'.[137] Papers, periodicals and pamphlets all selected elements of the story and styles of reportage to depict the protagonists, Baltimore and Woodcock, in the light of either the values of elite society, or those of the new gentleman. The *Gentleman's Magazine* was firmly in the latter camp, using the Baltimore case to present women as weak and in need of male protection, and to contrast unfavourably the morals of the nobility with those of the middling sort.

This was clear from the outset. In the same January number as the news of Harvey's arrest, its reviewer, 'X' (Hawkesworth), was scathing about a sixpenny pamphlet, *An Apology for Lord Baltimore*, for suggesting that lack of force was an extenuating circumstance in seduction. 'It is presumed', 'X' thundered, introducing the notion of the protective father of an affectionate family, 'that if he [the pamphleteer] has daughters, he will not be very solicitous to preserve them from the soft arts of a fine gentleman'.[138] On the same page he prudishly dismissed the *Memoirs of the Seraglio of the Bashaw of Merryland*, purportedly by a 'discarded Sultana', as 'silly' and not, as might be expected, a 'secret history of Lord Baltimore'. In fact it was exactly that, a scurrilous romp by former mistress Sophia Watson. Even without knowledge of the precise contents, the title alone alerted readers that here was a rake whose behaviour was incompatible with the magazine's decency policy. 'Merryland' alluded to Baltimore's American interests but was also a well-established euphemism in contemporary 'botanical pornography' for female genitalia.[139] 'Seraglio' was a knowing reference to Baltimore's Turkish exploits and a reminder of the corrupting, feminizing effect of the Orient.

The trial dominated the April number. Eight pages, almost a sixth of the magazine, were devoted to a review by 'X' of Gurney's *Trial*.[140] Six pages paraphrased Gurney's record of Sarah's testimony, telling the story sympathetically from her point of view. Her account (and so the review) owed much to well-known novels such as Richardson's *Pamela* and *Clarissa*, even *Fanny Hill*, for 'plot': the milliner's shop and rakish lord, procuress and 'housekeeper' accomplices, abduction in a carriage with the glasses drawn up, captivity and mysterious 'draughts'.[141] Like a sentimental novel, her performance 'drew tears from many of the audience'.[142]

But Baltimore had misread the situation when he dallied in her shop, engaging Sarah in chat and inviting her to the play.[143] She was no Fanny Hill, but an innocent woman who lived a decent, religious family life, and was most properly engaged to a Mr Davis. Once kidnapped, she was distressed and weak, like the virtuous Clarissa unable to eat or drink, and made tearful appeals based on family-feeling. She reminded Baltimore of her 'tender attachment' to her fiancé, and asked, 'If he himself had been a father? [...] Surely you cannot but consider what my father must feel at the loss of a child whom he tenderly loves'. She resisted all temptation. Baltimore, on the other hand, lacked private morality. Atheistic, he abused his wealth on trinkets and bribery, spoke in French and was unmoved by a woman in distress. On the sixth night of her captivity he used violence to take his pleasure, 'forcing himself between her, [he] pressed her with all his weight, held her lips together that she might not cry out'. He raped her again the next morning.

What the *Gentleman's Magazine* omitted from Gurney's *Trial* was equally telling. Sarah represented herself to Baltimore as the mainstay of the millinery shop: 'we were engaged in business, and they could not carry on the business without me'. Nor was she an ingénue. At the trial she dissimulated over her age, initially claiming 27, but under questioning nudging upwards to 30 on her next birthday.[144] The magazine's Sarah Woodcock was helpless. The reality seems rather different. She was mature, independent and brave: willing to prosecute her social superior, able to endure a gruelling four and a half hours of examination and a further two of cross-examination (during which she was 'consistent steady and sensible'), and undergoing internal examination by a man-midwife made public in 'the severe arena' of the court when he testified to the 'marks of great force' on her body.[145]

The magazine's reviewer reflected in his conclusion that Baltimore's defence of lack of force rested on a fallacy and over-relied on evidence from his own servants and dependants. He expressed sympathy for Sarah's subsequent dilemma as a ruined woman. The magazine's final verdict on Baltimore was harsh. His body was returned to England in December 1771 and in January lay in state in Exeter Exchange, Strand, before removal to Epsom for burial. Once the funeral party left, the room was plundered by what the 'Historical Chronicle' termed 'the populace'. Their sacrilege was, surprisingly, reported without criticism, their irreverence justified by Baltimore's actions: 'His Lordship had injured his character in his life by seduction'.[146]

Comparison with the *London Magazine* reveals quite how distinctive was the *Gentleman's Magazine* approach. The *Gentleman's* used the affair to highlight a middling-sort, bourgeois view of gentlemanliness and gender founded on male restraint and female dependency. The *London* upheld both a traditional view of women as sexually conniving, and a respect for rank regardless of behaviour. The *Gentleman's* showed considerable regard for 'the publick' and their opinions. The *London* followed 'The Town', the fashionable West End set, to whom much of the often savage criticism of Sarah was addressed, and suggested that any intelligent observer doubted Sarah's story. Both reviewed *Modern Chastity, or the Agreeable Rape*, a poem purportedly by a 16-year-old gentleman, which came out before the trial and described Sarah variously as 'this middle-aged lady', a Methodist hypocrite, and whore. The *London* thought Sarah's story 'not a little doubted by the intelligent part of the public'. The *Gentleman's* damned the close links between such authors and 'the town'.[147]

The *London's* reporting went on to mitigate negative representations of Baltimore's libertine lifestyle by refocussing on the 'mob' threat to Baltimore from Woodcock supporters. In March it reviewed *A Letter on the Behaviour of the Populace*, a pamphlet account, not mentioned in the *Gentleman's*, of a pre-trial attack on Baltimore's London house, in which his 'faithful servant' was fatally assaulted and 14-year-old daughter collapsed and died of fear 'for a father she tenderly loved'. Its reviewer accused the 'lower orders of mankind' of being 'always extremely happy, when they have the least opportunity of censuring their superiors'.[148] Gurney's *Trial* filled five pages in April, but two of those were devoted to defence arguments and Sarah's evidence was presented as straightforward reportage regularly punctuated by 'according to her', 'Miss Woodcock tells us', 'Miss Woodcock informs the world', and so forth. The effect distanced its readers emotionally and cast further doubt on her story.[149] An uncritical Calvert genealogy and portrait of Baltimore opened its June number and in September it reported Sarah's marriage to Davis, implying that she and her circle had emerged unscathed. Neither of these two items appeared in the *Gentleman's*. Baltimore's death was reported in October 1771, his character and past unspoken, and there was no report of the January disturbances in the Strand.[150]

Although there was never again quite such a dramatic opportunity to contrast noble vices with bourgeois virtues, the *Gentleman's Magazine* steadily maintained an approach to gentlemanliness that demanded private morality of those in public life, and attacked the nobility for failings in this regard. In 1769 Henrietta, wife of Lord Grosvenor, and the Duke of Cumberland, brother to the uxorious king, had openly embarked on an affair. Grosvenor had his servants burst in upon the pair in a room of a St Albans inn, discovering them *in flagrante delicto*, and in July 1770 launched a £100,000 criminal conversation suit against Cumberland. The jury awarded him £10,000.[151] A trial account filled five pages of the July *Gentleman's Magazine* and a further four in October reviewed the published trial. It confirmed to readers that moral shortcomings extended as high as the royal family (and provided the bare breasts, unbuttoned breeches and tumbled bedsheets now absent from the poetry pages).[152]

In 1774 the hostile review of Chesterfield's *Letters to his Son*, in addition to criticizing the hypocrisy that might lie behind politeness, added the class element found in the Baltimore rape case. The reviewer accused

Chesterfield of deploring only debauchery that was brutal and vulgar, which allowed latitude for libertinism and the mistreatment of women, whereas 'had he been in a middling station of life, virtue would have appeared more essential'.[153] Correspondent 'Mentes' agreed and feared emulation: 'Noblemen instruct their children to prefer outward show to intrinsic worth', a 'disposition which descends to most ranks of life'.[154] 12 years after Baltimore's trial and nine after his death, the magazine passed a similarly damning verdict on Augustus Hervey (1724–79, third Earl of Bristol, naval commander and politician). His public success was forever tainted by his libertinism and reckless marriage to notorious bigamist Miss Chudleigh:

> As a naval commander [...] the late Earl [...] displayed [...] on all occasions, that activity and true British spirit which characterise the Herveys; but though, "in a professional line", as he termed it, this eulogium is his due, we can extend it no farther; his moral character, his matrimonial transactions &c. excite our pity and contempt.[155]

Independent virtues

Where the *London Magazine* used the Baltimore case to represent a 'mob' of the lower orders prone to making unjustified attacks on their betters, the *Gentleman's* found a 'populace' horrified at aristocratic corruption. In formal politics, too, the late 1760s marked a turning point. 1768 was the year when 'riotous outrage was, to use a modern phrase, organized'.[156] In both January and July 1768, alongside its class-based critique of the Baltimore case, the *Gentleman's Magazine* covered the disturbances arising from Wilkes' Middlesex election contest and the deepening conflict with the American colonists. Its watchwords were liberty and public opinion. Although less prominent in the magazine's pages, the Irish campaign for independence for its (Protestant) parliament was also presented as a patriotic call for restoration of 'constitutional rights' and liberties.[157]

   This rising interest in politics and political activism was evident in the magazine from the conclusion of the Seven Years' War. In addition to regular coverage of 'American Affairs' or 'Letters from America' with frequent pleas for a peaceful reconciliation, it reinstated regular summaries under separate headings of the 'political papers', prompted by the journalistic polemics of Wilkes and his circle in the *Monitor* and the *North Briton*.[158] Between 1769 and 1772 the magazine reprinted Junius' letters to the *Public Advertiser,* exposing political corruption in both public and private life, especially of the Prime Minister, the Duke of Grafton. In 1770 parliamentary reporting was re-established, initially tentatively as 'debates in an Old Etonian club', but eventually settling down as genuine reporting with speakers only slightly disguised by their initials.[159]

There was also an upsurge in manifestations of middling-sort public opinion from men who saw themselves as independent of the corruption of places and pensions. The evidence came both in news stories and from readers themselves. In 1769, for example, the magazine reported a 'great concourse of people' as far away as Plymouth celebrating the election of two Wilkites (John Sawbridge and James Townshend) as Sheriffs of London. They rang the church bells and on being dispersed by the mayor took control of the ship *Barrington* and renamed it *Liberty*, holding a bonfire of its panels depicting Secretary at War Lord Barrington, a Wilkite foe. The action was 'conducted by an eminent attorney', just the sort of provincial new gentleman who read the *Gentleman's Magazine*.[160] The magazine attacked anti-Wilkite Sir Richard Perrot, who had presented a loyal petition from Flintshire to the king, representing him as privately flawed: a deceitful seducer and possible impostor, and so no gentleman. It remained silent, however, on the non-aristocratic Wilkes' libertinism, duelling and indebtedness. Like the magazine, he stood outside the world of patronage.[161]

Middling-sort concerns over liberty, tax and rights were similarly addressed and disseminated in reporting of the Society for Constitutional Information, most of whose members were 'educated middle-class reformers', and in coverage of the campaign against Pitt's Shop Tax between 1785 and its repeal in 1789. It hailed the 149 Members of Parliament voting unsuccessfully for repeal in 1787 as 'unconnected with any aristocratical interest'.[162] Nichols did use the term 'mob' in his description of the Gordon Riots in 1780, but here the popular action was against the very institutions – private property and trade – that were the foundation of the English liberty it approved, and the vigilant 'gentlemen' of the militia and volunteers (including Wilkes before the Bank of England) acted as its defenders.[163]

Although for some the anarchy of the Gordon Riots led to disaffection with Wilkite politics, there was long-term Wilkite support among the magazine's readership, in London and beyond.[164] The wrapper from the 1787 Supplement advertised a new single-volume edition of *The Speeches of Mr Wilkes in the House of Commons*, 'collected from news-papers and oral tradition', promoted for its truth and Wilkes' attachment to public duty and the people. Two obituaries ten years apart publicized bequests made to Wilkes. In 1764 Mr Henry Walton, 'a considerable farmer' in Devon, left £5,000 'as an acknowledgement to him, who bravely defended the constitutional liberties of his country, and checked the dangerous progress of arbitrary power'. In 1774 Robert Baldy Esq. of Northumberland Street left him £100, 'a mark of my regard and attention to the cause for which he has been so unjustly and wickedly persecuted by a most abandoned and profligate Administration for these ten years past'.[165]

Readers from the 1760s to 1780s responded to all these events with letters to 'Urban' on political issues, framed in the language of liberties and rights and revealing a general mistrust of the political class, a phenomenon only just evident in the 1750s. In January 1763 'Attal.' promoted a plan for a society in support of liberty, a project discussed in the magazine's pages since the previous January by 'J.S.', 'Humanus' of Devon and himself.[166] Correspondents saw the rebellious American colonists in Wilkite terms. They had 'the right of Englishmen to give their money with their own consent' and had been betrayed by the arbitrary imposition of the Stamp Act.[167] Once war was declared, 'A Friend of the King and Constitution' urged Britain to 'treat with the Americans as brethren; to make concessions to them', 'Philander' of High Wycombe defended Congress on the basis of the inalienable natural rights of man, and 'The King and People's Friend' blamed George III's courtly advisors for the ruinous state of affairs.[168]

Some readers criticized the Game Laws. To 'W.' they were 'tyrannical oppressions' by lords, infringing the property and rights of less powerful neighbours. Over the page, an attack on 'Rt. Hon. L – W – ' (Lord Weymouth) alleged he was 'so devoted to the sports of the chase' that he had neglected legal business, allowing a pardoned man to be hanged.[169] An anonymous correspondent of 1780 demanded greater involvement in public affairs from those of 'high rank'. They should neither abandon the countryside for the follies of the town, nor retreat there from the world. His solution was for the heir to an estate to be educated in a profession. This would 'rouse him to action, and [...] make him at once a happy and respectable member of society' – presumably how the magazine's readers saw themselves.[170]

Some correspondents were reformers. In 1782 'R.J.' outlined proposals for financial and moral reform of the universities, cathedrals and corporation estates, and tithes, inviting further debate on these issues. In 1788 'Philander' advocated the 'natural rights' of the poor as well as the rich, repeating the story of the castaway prince and basketmaker, and stressing their contribution to the economy and equal sense of 'the charities of father, son, and husband'. Others identified directly with the middling sort. 'P.Q.R.'s' poem addressed to his wealthy friend 'Rufus' compared him to 'us more middling, walking, honest folks'. 'B.J.' was concerned at the impact of 30 years of inflation which made it hard for 'people in a middling station to maintain their families in decency and credit'. 'Inspector' worried that interest rates would fall below five per cent, hurting not landowners but 'proprietors of the public funds, private traders, merchants, and manufacturers'.[171]

The implication of these articles and letters was clear: gentlemen by merit as well as by birth should as a matter of right and duty be actively and patriotically involved as 'independent men' in the affairs of the nation. To do so was manly. As 'C.L.' (Capel Lofft, 1751–1824, radical editor and writer) said of Thomas Brand Hollis, his fellow member of the Society for Constitutional Information, in a poem printed in January1787, it required a mind:

> Enkindled with the generous love of truth,
> Of freedom, of our country, of mankind!
> This is true taste; – which manly thou hast lov'd.[172]

The soldier as a hero of sensibility

The masculinity described above was civilian, but the figure of the soldier was present in the magazine throughout the chapter period. Fictional template 'Sir Charles Freeman' was abandoned, but the exigencies of war provided plenty of examples of the genuine thing. Army and navy appointments remained prominent among the promotions and the news supplied flesh-and-blood modern British heroes whose deeds compensated for the Byng fiasco. The 1775 article on the royal family's summer praised the king for his personal courage and understanding of 'martial manoeuvres'. Although he never led troops in battle, military knowledge was still important in establishing his fitness to govern.

However, the realities of war revealed its sickening impoliteness. A grisly obituary account of the battle of Bucker Muhl of 1762 recorded British deaths so fast and furious that 'the soldiers piled up the dead bodies of their slain comrades, and sheltered themselves behind them, as behind a parapet'. Thomas Twistleton, Viscount Saye and Sele, ended up standing unawares on his brother John's corpse.[173] The professional soldier's masculinity therefore remained both complex and ambiguous. Too refined and polite and he might be labelled effeminate. Too eager for the fight and he was potentially no gentleman but irrational (like duellist Lord Byron) or a brute.

The fear of a weakened military seen in Fielding's 'Phil. Cockade' and Brown's *Estimate* was pursued in 1758 by 'T. Row' (Pegge): 'Our present race of officers seem to know little more, than how to dress for a ball, and to gallant the ladies, which are the very last things they should be employed in'.[174] It continued after the peace. A comic poem of 1769, 'On seeing Capt. A – at Mrs Cornely's drest fantastically', accused British soldiers of growing lazy 'with luxury, plenty, and ease', spending more on dancing at balls and hair powder than on cannon balls and gunpowder.[175] During the American War the reviewer reprinted observations on the (mis)conduct of British officers there. General Howe, for example, had been 'at New York in the lap of ease; or rather amusing himself in the lap of a Mrs L – g' and at Philadelphia had 'found another Desdemona'.[176] 'Old Blunderbuss' of Oxford railed that 'Commissions are squandered upon men whose field of action is a drawing-room; whilst the sturdy soldier, who fought the battles of his country, is rewarded with disappointment and neglect'.[177]

In victory the Americans were everything the defeated British, who had been 'regaling themselves at concerts and assemblies', were not.[178] Ironically America's triumph validated the magazine's vision of the independent British man. 'Memoirs of Major-General Greene, in the American Service' underlined the superior masculinity of American officers. Greene was an almost perfect example of a new gentleman: from a respectable trading family, married with four children, of 'open and manly countenance' and 'pleasing aspect'. As a commander he deployed skill, exertions, bravery and humanity in the defence of (colonial) liberties.[179] Cobbett's discovery in 1797 of a large American market for the magazine and the fulsome obituary in January 1800 of 'illustrious' George Washington's 'well-spent life' showed a continuing mutual respect.[180]

Greene's defence of colonial liberties had its patriotic counterpart at home: the militia officer dedicated to national defence. The Militia Act of 1757 created the 'new militia', embodied during the Seven Years' and American Wars.[181] It provided an opportunity for the many subaltern officers of modest origins to dress and live as gentlemen, enjoying travel and a round of assemblies, dinners and balls. They might even move, without buying a commission, into the officer ranks of the regular army.[182] Militia experience was therefore gentrifying, broadened opportunities for active engagement in public service and provided a psychological boost to men's sense of their masculinity.[183] Edward Gibbon, a Hampshire officer from 1759 to 1762, summed it up in his journal. He was already a member of the gentry, but still relished the uniform 'as well appointed as the Guards', the competition with other battalions in drill and exercises and the sense of superiority to the 'set of fellows all whose behaviour was low'. It gave him 'knowledge [...] of mankind in general, and of my own country in particular', and 'indelible lessons of action and experience'.[184] Wilkes was so fond of the symbolism of the 'warrior citizen' that he continued to sport his scarlet regimentals long after he ceased service in the Buckinghamshire militia.[185]

Support for the militia and other volunteer defence forces, 'understood as the true repositories of the nation's masculine martial independence' and as protectors of the nation, home and family, was now stronger in the *Gentleman's Magazine*.[186] Self-confessed armchair politician, 'honest citizen and an impartial bystander' Pegge, saw the militia rather than regular army as best-fitted to thwart a French invasion.[187] A 1759 epigram mocked the gentlemen of Middlesex for not implementing the Act more rapidly, a letter-writer of 1760 thought the militia offered an opportunity for gentlemen officers to reform the morals of men under their command, and in 1762 a list of the officers of all 51 militia battalions celebrated these gentlemen.[188]

It was, however, in its treatment of the men and battles of the regular army that the magazine attempted the rehabilitation of the soldier, by framing his actions not as aggression, but in terms of the public and private virtues valued in civilian life: successful action in public and in private, family, benevolence and feeling. Victory over the French on the Plains of Abraham, Quebec, on 13 September 1759 produced a hero in these terms: 32-year-old General James Wolfe. 'Urban' commended Wolfe's letter to Pitt ahead of the encounter for 'manly fortitude', and news of the battle and his death appeared in the October magazine. Readers responded immediately with poems in November, when his funeral at Greenwich was reported in the 'Historical Chronicle'.[189] He remained newsworthy in both sampled numbers for 1760 which contained Wolfe's eve-of-battle speech to his troops and a further battle narrative.[190]

In reality Wolfe's was not the only important role in the battle: 'People like Wolfe are seldom in control of their "heroism", which is constructed by others out of filaments of their lives and refashioned into different narratives over the course of time'.[191] This is what the *Gentleman's Magazine* did in adopting and commodifying him as a him as a model hero. In 1764 a description of Gaspé Bay was illustrated with a plate of 'the house on the beach in which Genl. Wolf resided in 1759', rendering it a place of almost holy significance. In 1773 a poetic epitaph by 'R.B.' of H – used the old language of the Christian Hero, and facing the title page of the annual volume for 1789 was an engraving of Roubiliac's proposed monument.[192] Roubiliac did not win the commission, but like many other artists, including Benjamin West in his 1770 *The Death of General Wolfe*, portrayed Wolfe in contemporary rather than classical dress to signal the modernity of his heroism.[193] This later mythology around Wolfe emphasized his advancement through professional skill rather than political contacts, his sexual restraint and his benevolence, expressed as concern for his men 'in the character of a military parent' and as the bearer of civilization to a country peopled by 'savages' (native Americans).[194] His sometimes harsh approach to discipline and youthful falling-out with his parents and subsequent period of dissipation in 1750 and 1751 were deleted from the hagiographic record.[195]

The theme of the meritorious, benevolent, feeling gentleman officer became a culturally dominant one. In 1765 Edward Penny painted the aristocratic Marquis of Granby giving alms to a begging veteran and his family. Uniformed and mounted, he was military and superior yet peaceable and benevolent. Reminiscing in the 1770s, upwardly mobile Edward Ives, a man of obscure origins who had served as a naval surgeon in India, used sentimental language to describe losses there: 'Every humane bosom must needs commiserate the death of so many gallant *British* youth'. He described Admiral Watson moved by the weeping grandson of Angria the pirate: 'He found himself under a necessity of turning from the innocent youth for a while to prevent the falling of those tears, which stood ready to gush from his eyes'.[196] Ensign John Gabriel Stedman's journal recorded his efforts to raise money for the poor and victims of accidents and recalled unembarrassed crying over an abused 12-year-old boy.[197]

The *Gentleman's Magazine* joined the trend. 'An Old Officer's' pamphlet printed in July 1760 advocated fair treatment of the men: '*Never beat your Soldiers*, it is unmanly'.[198] An anonymous poem of 1763 commemorated Captain Gordon of the man-of-war *Bideford*, who died in a wreck on the Happisburgh Sands, Norfolk, as possessed of 'merit too little known' coupled with gentleness in manners, strictness in morals and alacrity in performing good deeds.[199] Benevolence as the 'civilizing mission' was implied in the description of barbaric behaviour faced by Captain Clive in India: 'In violation of the most sacred oaths' a surrendered prisoner was decapitated, his head tied to a camel and carried five times round the city walls. In these conditions, Clive could claim to be 'restoring tranquillity in the province'.[200]

Nowhere were military merit and benevolence more felicitously combined than in naval explorer Captain James Cook (1728–79), who took the magazine by storm. It had epitomized the narratives of his round-the-world voyage of 1768–71 and southern exploration of 1772–5, but it was his violent death in Hawaii in February 1779 during the third voyage that prompted outpourings of praise.[201] An account of his life in the 'Historical Chronicle' for January 1780 singled out his meritocratic rise through the ranks from humble beginnings, 'spirit of enterprise' and patriotic public duty, and 'domestick happiness' based on 'mutual affection'. He was no aggressor but 'always studied to benefit the savages whom he visited'.[202]

Like Wolfe's, Cook's celebrity and significance increased with the years. A letter and illustration of the Royal Society's newly struck commemorative medal, opened the July 1784 number.[203] The medal depicted Cook, as Wolfe had been, in uniform to symbolize modernity. On the reverse, Britannia stretched her right arm over the globe to represent his patriotic achievements. The next year, a further three-page 'sketch' of his life and character was taken from James King's three-volume work. This, too, commended Cook for his self-taught, meritocratic rise, unremitting pursuit of his goals, and benevolence, especially 'tender compassion for the Savages'. Cook's manly reputation, memorialized in paintings, poems, plays and biographies, came to embody 'Englishness itself'.[204] His private virtue, plainness, humanity and peaceable scientific aims facilitated a blurring of the boundaries between military and civilian gentlemanliness during the controversial American War. The antithesis of a fop, rake or libertine, he redeemed the reputation British officers had established there.

However, although 'War' was masculine it was destructive. 'Humanity' or peace was feminine and good, according to the magazine's day-labourer poet William Hamilton.[205] The role of the soldier in the empire remained difficult for the magazine to reconcile with its essentially civilian version of polite gentlemanliness, as traditional homosocial military manners survived alongside the 'soldier of feeling'. Stedman for example recorded routine, communal drunkenness and whoring as well as weeping.

The 'Historical Chronicle', like military diaries, carried plenty of accounts of duels between army and navy officers. A reprinted letter from the 'American Plenipotentiaries' (signed *inter alios* by Franklin) accused the British command of mistreating prisoners and encouraging their local 'Indian savage' allies to 'drink the blood and feast upon the body' of their enemy.[206] Ten years later (Warren Hastings' impeachment for corruption as Governor of Bengal having just opened) the magazine filled three pages with a report of an East India Company attempt to vindicate allegations of cruelty, looting and mistreatment of women by General Mathews' forces. The officers' defence was once more the civilizing mission: they had not abandoned 'the feelings of humanity', their action was 'just and meritorious' because they were protecting the region from greater harm inflicted by Tippoo Saib (Tipu Sultan).[207]

Even the virtuous Cook had not always been passive where native people were concerned, as the *Gentleman's Magazine* itself revealed. Its 1774 account of the round-the-world voyage included details of skirmishes in which a number of islanders armed only with spears were shot dead in circumstances of misunderstanding.[208] And as Gananath Obeyesekere points out, Cook's 'domestick happiness' was something of a figment as he spent remarkably little time at home with his wife and children.[209]

An officer was a gentleman, but his life story usually required careful editing to fit the polite ideal.

John Howard: a case study

The *Gentleman's Magazine* was fond of commemorating benevolent men. Merchant-philanthropist Jonas Hanway's death was greeted by verse, and the Westminster Abbey memorial to this 'citizen of the world', 'friend and father of the poor' was described at length, for example.[210] Nothing, however, matched its enthusiasm for prison reformer John Howard (*c.* 1726–90). He was the subject during his lifetime of both editorial and reader praise as an ideally benevolent and humane gentleman. This case study of the *Gentleman's Magazine* coverage and its readers' calls for recognition of his public work in visiting prisons and reporting conditions pulls together the themes of this chapter and reveals the difficulties they posed in practice.

Like Admiral Byng, Howard had featured in the *Gentleman's Magazine* prior to his surge to national fame: as the author of a memoir on a new variety of potato and at his appointment as Sheriff of Bedfordshire.[211] But unlike Byng, he was not a member of the landed elite. He came from just the sort of industrious middling-sort family that fitted the magazine paradigm of upwardly mobile meritocracy. His father, a dissenter of Clapton, Hackney, was successful enough as an upholsterer and carpet warehouseman in Long Lane, Smithfield to purchase and retire to a small estate at Cardington, Bedfordshire. In his teens John was apprenticed to a City wholesale grocer, but on inheriting a substantial sum at

his father's death in 1742 he left the commercial world, toured France
and Italy and led the life of a 'gentleman of ample fortune'.[212]

He was not idle, however. It was work, uncovering and publishing
conditions in gaols, that brought Howard success and celebrity status. The magazine enthusiastically adopted the man and his cause as
emblems of the benevolence crucial to the moral standing of a gentleman. It gave a very positive four-page review to his *New State of Prisons* in
1777, commending Howard's massive research undertaking as humane,
patriotic and public-spirited. It highlighted the suffering of prisoners to
evoke sentimental pity in the reader. It stressed the sheer scale of his
travels across Britain and Europe and the element of personal danger
(from infection) to which it exposed him. The review lent his work the
air of hardship of a military campaign, putting Howard on the same
pedestal as soldier-heroes. Indeed, the final paragraph compared him to
Marlborough, Amherst, Hawke and Captain Cook.[213]

In May 1786 'Anglus' (Revd John Warner, 1736–1800), who 'did all
but worship him' after briefly encountering Howard in Italy, wrote
proposing a subscription, raised through the good offices of the *Gentleman's Magazine*, for the erection of a statue.[214] Warner too focused on
the sentimental appeal of Howard's campaign – prisoners subject to sorrows, suffering and horrors – and on Howard's intrepid, hardy character.
He also introduced an element of class, criticizing the nobility for inac-
tion, asking 'Before this glorious man arose, what had ever been done
for mankind by *all the blood of all the Howards*?' An editorial footnote
warmly welcomed the scheme. Howard himself, still abroad when this
was broached, rejected the honour.[215]

Despite this (or maybe because of it: Howard's modesty, like Cook's
plainness, implying gentlemanly restraint) there was an immediate and
steady stream of donations and letters and poems endorsing the scheme
over the next two years.[216] In July 1786 six letters from fans and subscribers filled three pages.[217] Among them was 'Polyxena' (Thicknesse),
who had met many 'great men', but regarded a personal visit from
Howard as 'the greatest honour I have received, during a long and
chequered life'. He praised the benevolence, modesty, humility, and
philanthropy of 'the doer' and enclosed a draft for one guinea.

The one guinea entry level for subscriptions was low enough to be
inclusive. Howard and his cause proved attractive to a wide range of
magazine readers. A letter to Nichols referred to 365 guineas lodged at
Bland's Bank in Birchin Lane, London, being 'a London Tradesman's one
year's profit'.[218] A poem in July 1788, 'To John Howard, Esq. F.R.S.', came
from J. Swanwick of Philadelphia, an English-born American politician

involved in the prison reform movement there. Swanwick admired Howard as a man of 'character' and used the same language of sentiment ('the shiv'ring wretch', for example) that had produced such a positive response in Britain.[219] The political re-working of the ranking of gentlemen and others was evident not only in Warner's comment on the Howards, but also in the list 'A Subscriber' appended to his letter and donation: a 'Scale of Beings, or of Merit', all explicitly or implicitly male:

> GOD
> Friend to Nature
> Tyrannicide
> Man of Honour
> Honest Man
> PLAIN LABOURER
> Knave Secular
> Saint
> Statesman
> Hero
> DEVIL.[220]

He placed 'god-like' Howard in the second category. The universal 'natural gentleman' was now the most elevated man, and the corrupt or warlike statesman and hero below the honourable and honest man of whatever background or profession, only a little better than the devil. The list represented graphically the new mistrust of the political class as a whole.

Howard died in Russia in January 1790, just beyond the period of this chapter. His apotheosis for his public actions as an indefatigable and benevolent man, and the deployment of conceits of heart-rending suffering relieved was dramatically unpicked by the magazine's obituarist. Howard's public life was recorded in glowing terms but he failed the domestic test. He had initially sent his only son Jack to a ladies' boarding school, had devoted money inherited from his sister to his prison work 'without making any provision for his son', and, far from dispensing 'the milk of human kindness' at home as a tender and affectionate father, his 'paternal severity' had caused Jack's lunacy. This would come as no surprise, remarked the obituarist, to 'those who knew the singularity of Mr H's ideas and temper'.[221] These unflattering details of Howard's life were unique to the *Gentleman's Magazine*. Other papers and periodicals only published them subsequently, and typically cast doubt on them.[222]

An instant response from readers unwilling to see their hero traduced shows how they wrestled with the difficulty of combining public and private virtues. 'Philo Veritatis' of Bedford felt that Jack's attendance at a boarding school exonerated Howard from responsibility. He challenged the modern notion that the public should meddle with 'the *private* concerns of families'. Howard's friend, 'W.F.' of Plymouth, admitted he was 'in some respects eccentric', but thought it improbable that one who 'manifested such extreme sensibility' could be severe to an only child. Dr John Aikin of Yarmouth, Howard's friend, literary executor and biographer, refuted a charge 'of a nature so heinous, that it cannot fail [...] greatly to injure his character in the estimation of the world'. While Howard believed in 'implicit obedience', he had never struck his son, had made perfectly sensible educational arrangements and was entitled to use his sister's money as he chose. 'A.B.' sought to undermine the whole obituary by questioning these and other assertions including his father's trade, his insolent treatment of a French captain when taken prisoner by a privateer in 1756, and his backing by the 'sectaries'' interest when standing for Bedford in the 1774 general election. 'Jack Prancer' moved to restore his reputation by once again proposing a memorial as a tribute to his public work, his 'active virtues'.[223]

In August the magazine published more positive material: a letter from 'Hibernicus' of Dublin enclosing original correspondence from Howard and a 'pencilled likeness' made without the subject's knowledge (reproduced on the facing page), and some provisions of his will. In addition to traditionally paternalistic bequests to the poor, tenants and current and former servants, he left the bulk of his estate to Jack. On the same page was a letter from Samuel Palmer (1741–1813), an Independent minister who had published a funeral sermon in Howard's memory, again attempting to lay to rest doubts about his private life. He recounted an anecdote about a minister's bearding Howard over the alleged confinement of his son 'for some trivial offence'. Howard had been able to prove this without foundation.[224] In 1793 Howard's rehabilitation was further advanced by an illustrated letter from 'M. Green' (Nichols) on his recently demolished Clapton birthplace, reminiscent of the treatment of Wolfe's Gaspé Bay house.[225]

The interest in Howard during his life and after his death is strong evidence of the increasing adoption by the *Gentleman's Magazine* of the feeling, benevolent, reformist gentleman-hero who came from outside the established political class. He single-mindedly 'did his utmost' in civilian public life but was also required to demonstrate an affectionate and cosy private domestic life. It was a lasting model for some readers.

Mr Robinson of Huddersfield was described in his obituary of 1814 as 'like Howard, most happy when doing good'.[226]

The magazine's policy of honesty in biographical obituaries had, however, laid bare the difficulty in practice of combining public and private virtues. Women might have been rendered unthreatening, but the continued rumours of Howard's excessive parental strictness revealed again the simmering inter-generational conflict that had upset 'Lear' in 1755. Inherent in the nature of the new gentlemanly masculinity was tension between driven, self-disciplined fathers and young adult sons.[227] The reputation of fathers depended on tender control within the family, but as they moved into adulthood, their sons of necessity needed to escape this control and establish the independence which gave them, in turn, gentlemanly status. Some were not enamoured of the hard work involved.

This was a conflict identified as particularly middling-sort by Hunt and evident both within and outside the confines of the *Gentleman's Magazine*.[228] In 1760 Samuel Johnson's *Idler* portrayed the troubled relationship between a fictional trader proud of the business his frugality and industry had created and his son, seduced from behind the counter by the glamorous, and apparently easier, gentlemanly life of two armyofficer friends.[229] David Garrick feared the consequences of disobedient children so much that he never regretted his childlessness.[230] Such struggles were woven into the relationship between Smithfield linen draper William Mawhood and his sons William and Charles. His diary recorded battles throughout the 1780s over spending, drinking, sex and career choices. As in the *Idler*, army life appeared much more exciting than the toil of shop-keeping.[231] Not even the monarch escaped this friction. The 'Historical Chronicle' of July 1786 recorded his dispute with the Prince of Wales over the latter's £250,000 debts. The stern 'motives of the father' in refusing to assist and the 'honourable principles of the son' as the prince allegedly submitted and retrenched were approved by the *Gentleman's Magazine*.[232]

Conclusion

The *Gentleman's Magazine* of 1757–89 displayed continuity with the previous 26 years in format and content. However, the rising tide of readersubmitted material reveals a change in the concept of gentlemanly masculinities that developed against a background of empire but was primarily played out at home, in both senses of the word: Britain and the family. The gentleman was still expected to be polite, benevolent and above all soberly devoted to work and public success, but there was greater stress on allying these qualities to virtue in private life, expressed as demonstrative tenderness in family life and towards the deserving poor. This was more overtly linked to bourgeois, middling-sort values than before, lying behind the removal of indecent content from the magazine, for example. This shift is detectable from the 1760s and 1750s, but most marked from 1768 and the Baltimore affair.

Extravagance was sometimes depicted as a female fault, but the luxury debate in the magazine was more directed to upholding the positive masculine values of work, restraint and sobriety. Gentlemanliness was therefore measured, as before, primarily against other men: unfeeling plebeians, but more especially libertine and imprudent nobility and men corrupted by Eastern luxury.

This criticism of elite lifestyles was much stronger than in 1731–56, or in the rival *London Magazine*. It was politicized by using the concept of the universal rights of British men who had merit, were polite and restrained but also independent: financially, as the married head of a virtuous family, and as possessors of integrity. The masculine value of independence informed readers' belief in the importance of engagement in public life, persuaded many that there was justice in the American colonists' grievances and prompted the welcoming of the French Revolution.

A key word was 'character'. This was closely related to 'manly', 'plain', and ideas of striving and merit. From 1768 and throughout the American war and loss of the colonies these middling-sort virtues were used in a class-conscious way to press a case for reform. Reform did not entail overthrowing the political or social order, but rather recognition by the political class of middling-sort values and public opinion and an end to corruption. Indeed, as Retford points out, some aristocrats took up the cause of merit. Emily Lennox, for example, promoted her second husband, former tutor to her children by the Earl of Kildare, as a man of 'sense'. Her sister Louisa, wife of wealthy Irish landowner Thomas Connolly, claimed that 'merit is *the* thing to admire' and reported with 'anthropological fervour' her visits to middling-sort households.[233]

Women were now 'tamed' by the rhetoric of feeling and benevolence which confirmed gentlemanly men in their superior, independent, protective position. Plebeian others were those who rejected the bourgeois morality of work and decency and so were 'undeserving'. No consistent use of race to define 'others' is evident, but new ethnic groups encountered in the contact zones of empire were often understood as 'savages', another group on whom benevolence could be practised in the

interests of civilization. The most difficult dependant group to accommodate within the new gentlemanliness was young adult sons seeking
their own gentlemanly independence.

This leaves the figure of the soldier. The reception of Brown's *Estimate* in the *Gentleman's Magazine* can be read as a continuation of the
middling-sort concern seen in Fielding's 'Phil. Cockade' of 1743 over
luxury and the unprofessionalism of Britain's ruling class, and the military in particular. There was now further unfavourable comparison with
the officers of the American Revolutionary Army. While war and militant nationalism provided examples of heroic British officers who 'did
their utmost' in patriotic service to the nation, their work remained
hard to reconcile with the essentially pacific gentlemanly virtues of
benevolence and tenderness. Although attempting to justify the brutality inherent in imperial conquest and discovery as the civilizing mission,
magazine reports of atrocities implicitly recognized this.

For this reason the civilian Howard was a more satisfactory exemplar.
However, even in his case maintenance of the gentlemanly narrative
required the economy with the truth, especially where private life was
concerned, which had distinguished the magazine's treatment of other
heroes, such as Wilkes, Wolfe and Cook. It was an economy with which
its readers colluded.

6
Gentlemanly Masculinity in the *Gentleman's Magazine*, 1790 to 1815

Introduction

The final chapter begins in the heady early days of the French Revolution, covers the long years of the French Wars, and ends in July 1815, a month after the decisive Battle of Waterloo. The *Gentleman's Magazine* in the 'Historical Chronicle', special news sections and excerpts from the *Gazette* gave regular coverage to revolutionary affairs across the Channel and, from 1793, to Britain's renewed world-wide military engagements. At war's end in June 1815, Wellington's dispatch from Waterloo filled ten pages, seven of them a doleful list of killed, wounded and missing officers.[1] Private soldiers were accorded only a summary total (5,087 unnamed rank-and-file on 18 June, for example) at the end. The effect was to highlight and personalize the selfless sacrifice of so many gallant gentlemen. Palpable relief on home soil was evident in correspondent M. (Mason jun.) Chamberlin's poem, 'On the Victories of the Duke of Wellington', the final line of which looked to a new age, 'When *Wars* and *Tumults* shall no more prevail'.[2]

The triumphant mood continued into July, the final sampled issue of the magazine. There were further extracts from Wellington's dispatches and more patriotic poetry from readers. William Thomas Fitzgerald Esq. (1759–1829, a regular contributor noted, like many of the magazine's poets, for 'enthusiasm more pronounced than his talent') praised Wellington and three high-ranking officers (the Duke of Brunswick, Sir Thomas Picton and Sir William Ponsonby) who 'join'd in death THE GALLANT and THE GREAT'. Other poets extended their praise to Pitt, Captain Broke and Vice-Admiral Alexander Cochrane, two naval officers who had served against America. The poem to Broke was composed for a public dinner in his honour at Ipswich. Publication in the magazine therefore united officers from the frontline, a grateful home front and the wider nation.[3] Waterloo was also literally at the forefront of the magazine in the 1815 Preface, composed at the end of the year but, in the binding process, inserted at its beginning.

Victory at Waterloo therefore took its place in the pages of the *Gentleman's Magazine* as the culmination of 22 almost-uninterrupted years of war. War had both filled a substantial proportion of the news sections of the magazine and thrown up not only the aristocratic Wellington as a template of the military hero, but also the more middling-sort Admiral Nelson. This chapter therefore reopens the problematic relationship between polite, civilian gentlemanly masculinity and the potentially unruly masculinity of the soldier. The readers' relationship with Nelson, captured through representation in news stories, letters, poetry and other forms of commemoration, is used to demonstrate their ongoing interest in restraint, sensibility and domestic propriety as key qualities of the gentlemanly hero.

It was not 'total war', however. French-born American Louis Simond commented on a curious phenomenon during his visit to war-time England: that although there was an expectation of 'dreadful crisis', yet Britons went about their business unconcerned.[4] Indeed, despite the war conditions, most of the magazine's content continued as before, especially that supplied by the readers. Even in July 1815 their letters did not respond to Waterloo. They were more interested in matters rather closer to home. These included Unitarianism, the state of the Church of England, local, family and other history, the closure of Ranelagh Gardens, monumental inscriptions, a cure for deafness (a brown-paper cap under a flannel night-cap) and a charity scheme to clothe the poor in the 'left-off apparel' of the well-to-do.[5]

This truly was Peter Pindar's huckster's shop, with its brush, cabbage-net, and mop. It also suggests a return to the ideal of a retired gentleman, a reworking of the 'Mr Rus' of 1755, withdrawn from worldly affairs, from the hurly-burly of independent politics and mid-century activism. 'Our Repository seems to have been sought by Men of deep Reflection and exalted Talents, as a Shelter beneath which they might repose in literary Ease from the Tumults of the World around them', as the 1796 Preface put it. Immediately post-Waterloo, July 1815 in fact opened not with news from the front but with a series of 'Rural Inscriptions' from 'J.C.' (Joseph Cockfield, of Upton, Essex), the first of which, by J. Bamfylde (John, 1754–96), was 'For a Cottage' where a neat and fragrant garden 'far from noise in courtly land so rife' provided 'a safe retreat and peaceful'.[6]

'The horrible phantom of democracy': Priestley, Burke and Paine[7]

Nonetheless, contrary to Simond's impression and Stafford's claim that the late-century *Gentleman's Magazine* conveyed a 'comfortable impression' of British society, hidden within July 1815's 'huckster's shop' were pointers to domestic political fears of 'dreadful crisis' that went to the heart of readers' vision of gentlemanliness.[8] 'A Priest of the Established Church' wrote to challenge Unitarianism, citing *Letters to Dr. Priestley* of 1789. Theologian and natural philosopher Priestley (1733–1804) was the subject of much correspondence during the early 1790s, for his religious views rather than his scientific discoveries. His critics in the magazine became more strident after the July 1791 Birmingham Riots.[9] Despite the destruction of property, this conservative backlash against dissent and disruption of the social order perhaps gave them confidence that there was underlying support for their case.[10] For them, Priestley was inextricably connected with French revolutionary ideas and so with Thomas Paine (1737–1809), author of the profoundly unsettling *Rights of Man* published that same spring.

In the 1791 Preface 'R.G.' (Gough) portrayed Edmund Burke (1730–97) as the solid defender of the British mixed constitution under attack from these two men:

> Priestley and Payne belabour Burke [...]
> The rights of men and heresy
> *Felo de se* alike, must die.

This preface marked a turning point. It was an alarmed reaction to *Rights of Man*, to which Gough gave a hostile four-page review in August, a month after Priestley's home and Birmingham had burned, and after a dinner celebrating the storming of the Bastille, to boot.[11] The greater seriousness in the magazine and the tension over who was entitled to speak noted in Chapter 3 took a political turn.

Priestley was at least still given the magazine's polite, gentlemanly treatment. The July 1791 coverage of the riots included letters from him and from one of his supporters (William Russell), denying the more lurid accounts of events and their involvement in them. Paine, on the other hand, became for editor and readers alike the undisputed bogey-man of the 1790s. Examples of their revulsion, which gathered pace following the publication from 1794 of his critique of organized religion, *The Age of Reason*, abound in the sampled numbers alone. In 1792 a review of 'An Heroic Epistle to Thomas Paine' criticized the satirical poem for mildness towards its target. 'T.B.' of Chester's poem 'The Ghost and the Doctor' linked Priestley and Paine as the 'rebel brood' who loved 'civil strife'. An anonymous poet declared *Age of Reason*, 'deistic trash and treason' and its author impudent and 'mad-brain'd'. 'C.', a young reader ('just entered on the grand theatre of the world'), was appalled at the 'grossness and audacity' of the same work. Ten pages on, 'M.N.' commended and excerpted Lord Erskine's speech in prosecution (on behalf of the Proclamation Society) of *Age of Reason's* publisher, Thomas Williams.[12]

Obituaries marked men associated with Paine as dangerous: John Martin, Williams' defence attorney, had 'figured away for some years in all the scandalous transactions of our seditious societies'. Executed Irish nationalists, Henry and John Sheares, had been 'constantly in the company of Thomas Paine' in revolutionary France.[13] In contrast, Revd John Towers (*c.*1747–1804), independent minister and school-master to pupils whom he made fit 'for the middle class of society', was commended for having 'attacked [...] with great success' Paine's publications.[14] When Paine himself died in 1809 he was memorialized as 'the *notorious*' whose death was 'admonitory': he had aimed at a legacy of confusion, but British rather than French liberty was the victor.[15]

And yet there was a degree of contrariness in this furious criticism of Paine the man. His life-story was in most respects a *Gentleman's Magazine* dream, his world view similar to that of many readers: 'bourgeois economic individualism', recognizing 'only [...] inequalities that are personally earned, and therefore [...] deserved'.[16] Perseverance and industry overcame early handicaps for this son of a provincial stay-maker. Largely self-taught, he loved coffeehouse and club debates. His picaresque early career included periods at sea, stay-making, as a school-master and in the excise, experience of the colonies and eventual reinvention as a man of letters (including a stint from 1775 as editor of a new American journal, the *Pennsylvania Magazine*, a miscellany with content similar to the *Gentleman's Magazine*). He was later involved in a project to construct new bridges, a subject that often featured in the magazine as symbolic of commercial progress.[17] This was ordinarily enough to be accounted a new gentleman, was the very stuff of the obituary column and should have resonated positively with readers.

The undiluted loathing of Paine is important because it marks a move towards the ideological which had a profound impact on the magazine's vision of the social order and, within this, of gentlemanliness. In *Rights of Man*, Paine rejected the self-improving middling-sort complicity in the 'mixed constitution' led by reformed members of the ruling class as favoured by Burke and so many readers and correspondents. He decoupled achievement from private morality, championing 'measures and not men'.[18] He attacked the very foundations of the hierarchical, monarchical political and social system, by asserting that entitlement to political status attached to each individual, 'as if there was not a natural distinction of ranks', as the horrified Gough put it.[19] It was an 'age of Revolutions' (a phrase tellingly picked out in Gough's review) and Paine's aim was republican 'Government by representation' (which, it should be noted, did not include women).[20] For Gough (the most propertied of the magazine's team), but not for all commentators (the Terror had not begun and in 1791 many still thought the French Revolution marked the adoption across the Channel of the glories of the British constitution), the champion of this natural distinction and its totem, the landed gentleman, was Edmund Burke, against whose *Reflections on the French Revolution* Paine directed his polemic. *Reflections* crystallized a gendered vision of an allegedly rational 'austere and masculine morality' which underpinned society (and was implicitly contrasted with French dissolution and feminine weakness).[21]

The perils of 'confusion' in the social order were emphasized by the magazine's reporting of the Terror.[22] December 1792 featured an engraving of 'the people in tumult with the Head of Princess Lamballe', decapitated and displayed on a pole. January 1793 contained a 'Particular account of the Murder of Louis XVI'. In death the French king was no longer the foreign despot but, like George III, a family man of sensibility who 'exhibited on this sad occasion all the tenderness of a Husband, a Father, and a Brother'.[23] Obituaries from France hammered home the horror. Political author M. Breboin had fled Paris 'in a female garb' and died in Lyons, the Duc de Biron, 25-year-old Armand-Louis Philip Custine and German nobleman Nicholas Luckner were all guillotined in January 1794 and as late as 1799 physician Peter Isaac Poissonnier was marked out as having been imprisoned, with his family, under Robespierre.[24]

In the context of events in France, it was easy to share Burke's interpretation of bread riots, mutinies, treason trials and Luddism in Britain as presaging the imminent collapse not only of order but of the institutions of the state. In *Reflections* the Gordon riots were for Burke, as for others, fresh in the memory. In consequence, the atmosphere at home throughout the chapter period was febrile and unstable. The choice seemed to be revolution or reaction. Post-*Rights of Man* it was no longer possible to avoid entanglement in a partisan politics which was increasingly inflected with class.[25] One member of the elite, John Byng (1742–1813, 5th Viscount Torrington and nephew of the executed admiral), captured the mood in his diary for 1794: 'One part of the nation worrying for wealth: another for a reform of Parliament: All running to and fro like mad dogs'.[26]

In the *Gentleman's Magazine*, earlier editorial positions were swiftly reversed. It was no longer neutral, but held an 'undisguised opinion'.[27] Gough's 1791 Preface declared: 'all Men are not equal in their natural or acquired Advantages'. Its pages rarely used 'democracy' to describe the reform aspirations of those below the gentlemanly class, but when they did do so it was pejorative.[28] In France it was like a disease, a 'rage'. Anglican curate 'Clericus' attributed a suicide to its poisonous principles. 'B.T.' used it to cast aspersions on Junius, the once-favoured opposition writer now thought likely to be of 'low birth', 'capable of little feeling', 'a violent Jacobin'.[29]

Returning to July 1815 then, the 'huckster's shop' of readers' letters can be reinterpreted as profoundly political and fearful. Anxiety over Ranelagh Gardens and clothing the poor arose from the desire to control the lower orders, and reduce the incidence of unrest spurred on by the French example and the economic hardships war created. 'Ruricola' wanted at least some part of the gardens to remain open to public recreation for the benefit of the morals and health of the lower classes whose 'youths ought to be trained to manhood by manly exercises'. Such purposeful activity was a means of preventing the decay of the nation itself. 'B.S***' similarly saw his proposed clothing bank as a way of ensuring the decency of the poor, thus making them ready for education or work. Their children might otherwise develop minds 'vitiated by running about the streets'. The Church of England was expected to provide an institutional bulwark against unrest, and there were calls for it to be reformed, the better to meet this challenge. A frequent plea in the magazine was for ministers 'on the ground', compulsorily resident in their parishes.[30]

The period has been called 'the Age of Reform'.[31] In 1811, correspondent 'A Friend of Manners, Not of Men' presented a list of 'moderate' reforms aimed at preserving the 'Happy Order of Things'.[32] For him and others, the reform mood extended beyond the franchise to encompass not only other institutions such as the church, law, and universities, but also the moral rearmament message of the Evangelical movement.

Reform was often conservative rather than radical in intent. It was, for example, the thrust of Revd Thomas Gisborne's advice in *An Enquiry into the Duties of Men* that the 'upper and middle classes' in both public and private life should comport themselves as Christians in the interests of the public good.[33] This message was a natural 'fit' with the industry, domestic probity and religious orthodoxy already advocated in the *Gentleman's Magazine*. 'A.P.', for example, regarded it as patriotic for each man to attend to 'the reform of what is in himself amiss'.[34] It is important therefore to see readers' suggestions for benevolent change as a vital part of this wider reform movement but not from egalitarian motives. It was a means of pacifying the lower orders who might otherwise be drawn to radical causes, as Revd Dr Vernon, Bishop of Carlisle was reported as preaching at the Radcliffe Infirmary, Oxford in July 1791 – 'politicks [...] from the pulpit' that the magazine approved.[35]

The middling-sort, independent critique of a ruling class in need of reform seen in the magazine of 1757–89 was now replaced by a more reactionary alliance with that ruling class, focussed on the alleged menace from below. Correspondents were generally agreed that this would be through setting a leading example to the labouring classes. 'Tresmegistus' hoped the 'higher orders', in which he included professionals, would unite to produce an official 'history of the world' to persuade the 'inferior orders' of the importance of national religious and political institutions.[36] Two book reviews in 1804 were for 'well-principled' pamphlets directed at showing the 'labouring Part of the Community' how to 'study to be quiet, and mind their own business'.[37] An 1813 wrapper advertisement from the Religious Tract Society promoted a scheme to inculcate the work habit in beggars. 'The Benevolent Public' would offer them tickets rather than money, which entitled them to receive in exchange 12 'entertaining penny tracts with cuts, and thus to commence a profitable trade'.[38]

The magazine threw up two seemingly incompatible versions of the gentleman who would produce this result. On the one hand, there was the self-made gentleman who believed in market forces, work and strict morals.[39] On the other, there was a backlash against his values represented by a restored faith in the old-fashioned English country gentleman. These two cultures are explored below and their clash over Sunday schools for the poor used as a case study of this split in the ranks.

'A nation of heroes'

From being a nation of shopkeepers we became a nation of heroes. All professions were neglected for the profession of arms.[40]

Colley describes 'an ostentatious cult of heroism and state service [that] served as an important propaganda function for the British elite'.[41] Understandably, the magazine lionized gallant, brave soldiers during a long war which carried the threat of invasion and national extinction. Their fame, however, typically relied on deeds, not polite words. The magazine reported Vice-Admiral Waldegrave saying just this on receipt of the Freedom of the City in 1798. 'Oratory is not a British Naval Officer's forte', he added.[42] 'Biographical Memoirs' of General Sir John Moore, the fallen hero of Corunna, emphasized similar unsentimental qualities. He was 'a man exclusively devoted to the military profession. He was a complete soldier, and a strict disciplinarian'.[43] Although an anonymous 'Non-commissioned Officer of the Fifty-first Regiment' was sentimental enough to call to 'Ye Sons of Britannia' to 'With me drop a tear' for Moore, it was Moore's actions that he sang in a poem sent to the magazine:

And tell to thy children thy deeds and thy name.[44]

'The domestic army'[45]

As in previous wars, there was the opportunity for men at home both to claim a little of this military glory without putting themselves in the line of fire, and to acquire or enhance their genteel status by serving as officers in the militia (embodied from 1792), or in the volunteers and yeomanry (some 118,000 enlisted men by 1801). Their committee members, like magazine readers and the obituaries, ranged from attorneys, bankers and apothecaries to booksellers, tanners and butchers.[46] In the new political climate these forces also served as a party of 'order', dominated by a middling-sort culture: 'Householders who have an interest in the Defence of their Property' according to a Devon committee.[47]

Many magazine obituaries from the period referred to service in the militia, volunteers or yeomanry, either alongside a civilian occupation or as a primary identity, and to funerals conducted with military honours. Individuals undoubtedly valued highly the standing these public masculine roles lent them. For example, Mr Creedy, of Langford, Somerset had spent 40 years in the militia and was 'indefatigable in disciplining'. In the same issue, an officer in the 21st Light Dragoons of the regular army, Captain James Calder, was buried with considerable pomp involving the Woodbridge Volunteers as well as his regiment. The entry was immediately preceded by that for Mr James Vickers, a 20-year-old carpenter from Merton, Surrey who died of a lung haemorrhage and was, as a member of the local volunteer corps, also buried with military honours.[48]

For the *Gentleman's Magazine* and its correspondents these defence forces were very much a means of happily uniting, under the watchful eyes of gentlemen, a society that was potentially fractured by revolutionary ideas. 'Rambler' (Budworth/Palmer) sent a letter as from a militiaman at Waterdown Camp near Tunbridge Wells. His account was of a cheerful and busy life. Hardships were dismissed with comedy and officers praised for their sense of duty and paternal concern for their men.[49] In July 1796 'A Loyalist' enclosed chaplain Revd Dr Ford's speech to the Melton Mowbray Volunteers at the presentation of their colours. Ford emphasized the divine institution of the 'military character as well as the civil' and the patriotic nature of service. The ceremony was reported under the news as a polite social event, starring the local gentry and with 'a crouded and brilliant assembly in the evening'. But it was also represented as harmoniously inclusive. Women were active supporters. Mrs Caldecott, the lieutenant's wife, had worked the colours and joined the parade with 12 other ladies 'dressed in white, with light blue ribbands (the uniform of the day)'.[50] Nor were the lower orders disruptive, although the comment that the day passed 'without the smallest sign of disaffection, interruption, or irregularity', suggested that insubordination or opposition had been a distinct possibility. July 1800 devoted four pages to an even grander review, of the Hertfordshire Volunteers by the king at Hatfield Park. This was a lavish, aristocratic occasion funded by the Marquis of Salisbury. But it too incorporated all levels of society. Local labourers and innkeepers worked on the camp, 1,482 private volunteers sat down to dinner and women again paraded in virginal white. It was a contented, hierarchical pyramid.[51]

This was a traditional, paternalistic vision, as 'Rambler' acknowledged. Richard Cumberland agreed. In retirement, aged 60, he drew considerable satisfaction from service as Major Commandant of the men of the Tunbridge Wells yeomanry cavalry, a pleasure he compared to fatherhood: 'as a father loves his children, so do I love them'.[52] There was not universal applause for the volunteer service, however, as Cumberland also recognized.[53] Magazine correspondent 'Southern Faunist' expressed the old view that the volunteers and yeomanry corrupted proper masculinity, encouraging the sons of 'gentlemen' farmers to foppish posing, 'flourishing their broadswords, and exhibiting their neatly-buskined [sic] posteriors to the admiration of the misses their sisters, or neighbours', when they should instead be working the land.[54]

Officers and gentlemen

Officers of the regular army were similarly subject to criticism as well as praise. Readers remained concerned that military gentlemen, with their emphasis on action rather than complaisant conversation, did not always meet polite standards. Mutual distrust between military and civilian gentlemen is evident in Byng's diaries and Gisborne's *Enquiry*. Byng was frequently nostalgic for the tough, homosocial life on campaign, testy about family matters and critical of the refinement of polite urban dwellers. Gisborne, as a civilian, was keen to educate such men out of the bad habits of the life military: duelling, bragging, a roving disposition.[55]

Despite their admitted bravery, army and navy officers were, then, still problematic figures in the essentially civilian *Gentleman's Magazine*. There were continued reports of duels between officers who allowed impolite 'animosity' to get the better of them.[56] During the short-lived truce under the Treaty of Amiens 'M.' translated Juvenal's 16th Satire for fellow-readers. This painted an unflattering picture of unruly soldiers causing mayhem among the home civilian population – violence, theft and plunder – safe in the knowledge that the courts martial protected them from giving redress.[57] It was all close to the conclusion drawn in real life by Revd Edward Mangin after five unhappy months as a naval chaplain in 1812. He found most of his officer mess-mates uncongenial company. He admired their professional competence and sense of duty, but loathed their repulsive manners and ill tempers. He gave greatest praise to Captain Thomas Inches of the Marines who resembled his friends ashore, 'the polite, the learned and the effeminate'. Effeminacy was manifestly no insult. Inches was an 'affectionate husband', 'the fond father of a large family' and possessed 'a liberal, tender heart'.[58]

Admiral Lord Nelson

A 'liberal tender heart' was crucial to the reputation of the supreme hero of the wars, Horatio Nelson, whose fame both preceded and outlived his death. Magazine readers had learned of his public deeds from the mid-1790s, when the news featured dispatches from his Mediterranean cruises. Interest exploded from 1798 following his victory at the Battle of the Nile and ennobling as Baron Nelson of the Nile. In January 1799 his coat of arms and a facsimile of his left-handed signature faced page 29, and an account of action by his squadron running up to this battle stressed in its conclusion Nelson's private virtue of piety. In the same number a lengthy and dramatic poem, 'The Battle of the Nile' by J. Wood of Christ's Hospital, portrayed Nelson as a hero of sensibility. Although stern and bent on glory, he regarded his men 'with guardian care' and knew when to exercise mercy and compassion even over the defeated enemy:

The Briton melts with pity for the Foe,
And, though the arm was rais'd, arrests th'impending blow.[59]

Nelson's portrait was displayed at the July 1800 review of volunteers at Hatfield Park, and an obituary in January 1800 indicated his early adoption as a role model by those in the magazine's orbit. Revd Peter Joliffe of Poole had named his deceased youngest son, born on the day of the Battle of the Nile, Nelson.[60]

As with Wilkes, Wolfe, Cook and Howard, however, these *Gentleman's Magazine* accounts suppressed information that did not readily fit its image of a polite gentleman-hero. Nelson's irregular private life – his affair with low-born, married celebrity Emma Hamilton and dizzy social round in Italy in a *ménage à trois* with Emma and her aristocratic husband, Sir William – though common knowledge, went unmentioned.[61] Nelson was publicly fêted on his return to England in the winter of 1800. The magazine reported a glittering reception thrown for him in December by William Beckford at Fonthill. He was again presented as a man of sensibility, who 'with the brilliant qualities of a hero [...]] unites a feeling and generous heart'. *En route* to the event he had been moved by the sight of veterans and indulged in liberal charitable giving. The Hamiltons were honoured guests. Emma appeared, 'most classically graceful', in various tableaux, such as Agrippina clutching the urn containing the ashes of her dead husband Germanicus.[62] It was unexplained, though in fact it was a reprise of her 'Attitudes' for which Hamilton's parties in Naples in the 1780s and 1790s were famous.[63] That she was heavily pregnant by Nelson, now separated from his wife, was also unspoken.[64]

Again it was death that led readers' effusions to their apogee. News of the Battle of Trafalgar, fought on 21 October 1805, reached England in early November. It made a deep impact across the nation. It was noted by several diarists and memoirists. Joseph Farington, for example, read it in a newspaper on 7 November and, being in Norfolk, made an immediate pilgrimage to Burnham Thorpe and looked up Nelson's family in the parish registers.[65] The response in November's magazine was equally immediate. There were 19 poems on the subject from the well-known (Cumberland) to the obscure and anonymous ('S.B.' of Shrewsbury), and only three on other subjects. An editorial footnote indicated that many more had been received.[66] The frontispiece to the annual volume was a sketch of a proposed memorial building and the preface quoted his famous words 'Let every Englishman do his duty to his country'.

Details of Nelson's state funeral filled eight magazine pages in January 1806.[67] At a time of internal as well as external strife, the two-day spectacle of naval, military, royal, ecclesiastical and civil precedence and power, splendid with heraldry and dress uniforms, was another opportunity to present traditional social hierarchy and the military as uniting the nation. Lord Nelson's coronet, coat of arms and six 'bannerolls of the family lineage' located him towards the summit of this hierarchy. Nelson was the grammar-school-educated son of a Norfolk rector who had risen largely by merit.[68] They therefore also implied its permeability for men of ability, a permeability that justified inequality.

The account highlighted too the ceremonial roles for ordinary seamen of the *Victory* and the Greenwich Pensioners, for Nelson's servants and his physicians, and for a public that provided a huge but well-behaved street audience. Like the militia reviews, it was the very picture of the harmonious 'great chain of being', of the vital national and gendered links between the gentlemanly, masculine ruling classes, women and those lower down the social order. The obituaries for the same month show a gendered response. Among the funeral crowd was a Mrs Bayne 'so affected by the scene that she fell into hysterics and died in a few minutes'. More restrained was Mr Houghton, a shoemaker in the Butter Market, Bury St Edmunds, for whom Nelson provided a manly and stoic ideal. Having cut a finger while chopping wood, he refused a dressing, telling his wife 'what is this wound compared to Lord Nelson's?', before dying of an apoplectic fit.[69]

This model of military gentlemanliness was followed in the magazine's obituaries of other army and navy officers. Fewer and fewer were the descriptions of wounds borne. More and more were they narratives of manly courage in service joined to a sensitive and polite character. Lt Col. James Malcolm, who fell aged 28 at the storming of Morne Chabot, St Lucia, earned a whole page. Like a Marlborough or Wolfe, he 'possessed talents as an officer' in tactics and man-management and displayed 'the most heroic bravery' allied to 'unbounded generosity' and a 'feeling heart'. Lt John Squire of the Royal Engineers not only had 'all the qualities of a good Soldier; vigilance, activity, enterprise, industry and the most cheerful and exemplary patience under every species of hardship' but 'the virtues of his heart and his conduct in private life secured him the warm attachment of all with whom he was connected'. The death at the siege of Burgos of Captain White of the 12th Portuguese Regiment was attributed to this combination of bravery and benevolence. He was shot while stooping to help a wounded comrade, 'an act of the most laudable kindness'.[70]

In 1810 the magazine returned posthumously to Nelson and his reputation. In 1809 Revd James Stanier Clarke published a monumental two-volume, quarto, illustrated *Life* of Nelson. Revd William Vincent (1739–1815, Dean of Westminster) reviewed it for the magazine over nine pages in December and in January 1811.[71] Vincent, an ardent Tory supporter of the social order, admitted 'a partiality' for the book's subject whom 'we honour almost to idolatry'. In his first instalment he was delighted with passages on Nelson's bravery, dwelling not so much on martial matters as on his 'extraordinary attention to the commercial interest of his country' (Vincent was a merchant's son) in the Caribbean in the 1780s. In the second instalment he turned on Clarke. While admitting that 'No human being is perfect', Vincent struggled to deal with episodes that reflected less favourably on his hero's moral character as a gentleman: his marital shortcomings, involvement in Italian political intrigues, the unseemly execution of Neapolitan naval officer Caraccioli, and irritability of temper. As with Howard, so with Nelson: it was extremely difficult for any one man to combine in his person the requisite public and private gentlemanly qualities. This was especially so when the gentleman's profession was war.

Civilian gentlemen

The nation of shopkeepers

Despite the war-time conditions and adulation of Nelson, the magazine's preference for the civilian gentleman-hero remained strong. In January 1790, before war broke out, 'Edit' (Nichols) introduced memoirs of physician Dr Benjamin Moseley (1742–1819) with the reflection that 'The actions of individuals, however splendid, which have been unconnected with the welfare of others, have little in them worthy remembering'. Moseley's distinction lay in the application of professional knowledge to the public good.[72] Even after the outbreak of war, Zachariah Cozens, a regular correspondent as 'T. Mot, F.S.M.' (the Master of the Free School, Margate), in a retrospective of the century just past, listed by name as 'eminent men' Locke, Johnson, Handel, Wren, Chambers, Reynolds, Hanway and Howard. Unnamed 'patriotic statesmen' and 'intrepid and successful warriors' were to be 'blended with these' – almost an afterthought.[73] A year later poet 'I.P.' took a similar line. Forswearing verses on:

> Pride and the pomp of heroes, and the deeds
> Of high ambition and superior fame,

his aim was to:

> To unobtrusive worth a structure raise;
> Commend the gentle, -elevate the good;
> And give to peaceful aims a juster praise.[74]

Masculine success in civilian life, achieved through merit in a profession or commerce, and measured against other men, became an ever more dominant version of gentlemanly masculinity that was present throughout the magazine. Those engaged in trade and commerce were depicted as pulling together alongside other professionals in the war effort as 'a nation of farmers, merchants, men of independent fortunes, and of advantageous occupations, men of science, and men of law, and even ministers of religion'.[75] William Hutton (who presented his own life as a journey via industry to prosperity) reminded readers in the 1803 Preface of the proverb 'trade makes the man'. In 1809 'C. Duillius' wrote from Cambridge: 'It has ever been a part of your plan to allow admission to the claims of true Merit, from whatever quarter they come'.[76] Seven years previously another Cambridge man, 'A Cantab.' (Revd Weeden Butler jun.), had written to promote just such a case of merit, that of John Dawson, an 'almost self-taught' mathematician of humble origins.[77]

Self-improvement was now an end in itself for a generation of readers grown to maturity in the spirit of independence after the Seven Years' War. It was justified as part of an imperial project that was infused with gender, class and race. For 'Southern Faunist', 'the general object of a man in a civilized country is to rise above the station he is born in'. His letter made it plain that gipsies, whom he compared to Bedouins and Arabs, were incapable of sharing the British outlook on industry and ambition. 'Nauticus' identified a national 'laudable wish to enable the son to outdo the father'. He proposed capitalizing on this characteristic by opening an inexpensive school for boys that would 'rear up our sons to profitable members of the empire'.[78]

Autodidact scholars like Hutton were correspondents and others, like Mr Custance, a carpenter who had become an expert on microscopy, or William Temple, the Newcastle weaver who had taught himself Arabic, Greek, and Latin among other languages, were obituarized.[79] Narratives of industrious self-made gentlemen were now commonplace in the deaths columns. Of these, the most enduringly famous from the sample was Josiah Wedgwood, who died in January 1795. A whole page, compiled from at least two correspondents' accounts, hymned his commercial success. He had started with 'little or no property from his father' and was 'the maker of his own fortune'. The establishment of the manufactory was 'owing to his indefatigable labours'. He had been involved in public improvement works such as turnpikes and canals and was 'a kind master and generous benefactor' whose 'purse was always open to the calls of charity'. Unlike Howard, he had not neglected his private life, where his virtues endeared him to relations, friends and neighbours.[80] Even in this number of the magazine Wedgwood was not the only self-made man. Banbury attorney Richard Bignell had qualified as a lawyer by the application of talent and the taking of opportunities and had in consequence amassed a fortune. From James Brasbridge we further know that Bignell was a charity-school boy and that his marriage to the partner's daughter, far from assisting his progress from clerk, had led to his being sacked and having to set up for himself.[81]

There are too many similar obituaries over these 26 years to list them all, but a few examples illustrate the range of occupations to which this model of upward social mobility was applied, and the remorselessness of the repetition of rags-to-riches stories. Mr Thomas Preston came to London from Staffordshire aged 17 to drive a distiller's cart, rising to become 'the first ale-brewer of the age'. Of bricklayer John Bell it was said that 'Few men, in his line, ever acquired so large a property': some 500 tenanted houses. Robert Edmonds made a £60,000 fortune as a market-gardener, relying on 'watchful industry' (although some said a £20,000 lottery prize had helped). Sir James Sanderson started life in York, the grammar-school-educated son of a widowed mother who ran her late husband's grocer's shop. He worked his way up in the hop merchant business in London and by the time of his death had served as Lord Mayor, Member of Parliament and on the boards of various charities. His rise had been sealed by a knighthood (1786) and baronetcy (1794). Thomas Evans died a retired 'eminent' bookseller but had commenced his working life with 'very little to boast of in point of origin', as a porter. Hitchin miller James Whittingstall stood out as, 'Amongst the variety of instances which the present War has produced of persons raised from obscure situations to the acquisition of immense wealth [...] a very striking example.'[82]

The key virtues associated with all these successful men were industry, integrity, self-restraint, temperance, frugality and decency, but it was industry in particular that was noted in obituaries as the source of dead men's achievements. The same qualities were promoted elsewhere in the magazine. Marriage was now enlisted as a spur to much-valued masculine industry and the link between heterosexual married life and male public worth became ever closer. Contributing to a debate about collegiate celibacy, even the traditionalist 'Benedict in a Bustle' of Shadwell agreed with reformer 'O.C.D.D.' that marriage was a benefit: 'among men who are engaged in active life [...] those who are married are the most diligent.' 'O.C.D.D.' had gone further to describe how this operated psychologically on the husband: 'a bachelor and an idler are little less than synonymous terms. The hopes of raising a name, and of establishing a family in affluence and independence, make every labour light, and sooth every fatigue, even of the most disagreeable employment'.[83]

The middling-sort ethic of work, thrift and family was promoted in sets of rules amounting to conduct guides. Three years before he contributed the proverbs to the 1803 Preface, Hutton had submitted 'Twelve True Old Golden Rules'. Idleness and drunkenness were vices to be avoided. A comfortable family life was the goal: 'He who does not make his family comfortable, will himself never be happy any where; and he who is not happy at home, will never be happy any where'.[84] In 1808 the book reviews included the second edition of *Men and Manners*, a collection of maxims by Alexander Hunter MD (1729–1809), published to raise funds for the York Dispensary (the sale and purchase therefore acts of benevolence). The reviewer criticized some of Hunter's *sententiae* for 'savouring too much of the School of Chesterfield', but his prudent bourgeois advice was approvingly excerpted: 'Never be without a will', 'Idleness travels very leisurely, and Poverty soon overtakes her', 'The shortest way to the church-yard is to pass through the dram-shop'.[85] Professions such as medicine were not for the vain, fashionable, over-refined or lazy, warned another review, in 1813, of William Chamberlaine's *Tirocinium Medicum,* which emphasized the importance of application to study and work in making the physician or apothecary.[86]

The moral code behind Hunter's book and the *Tirocinium* chimed with readers. Gambling and self-indulgence were as disapproved as ever and frugality promoted, in letters on dissipation in country life and the universities for example.[87] 'Temperance', a man from the same mould as Briggs in Burney's *Cecilia*, advocated six household rules to avoid wasting bread in a time of scarcity, including no eating it until stale and less appetizing, no toast, rolls, muffins or French bread, and hawk-eyed watching of servants' consumption.[88]

The overriding impression here is that of an audience of 'Tradewells' and 'Pulses', to use the 1755 stereotypes. These men were newly-genteel but not in the least embarrassed by their origins or values. They saw a world pregnant with opportunity, given only the will to succeed and dynamism. Those who failed had simply not worked and saved hard enough. These entrepreneurial new gentlemen seemed to be everywhere. John Marshall, for instance, a prosperous Leeds flax-spinner, remarked, 'By pursuing any one object with steadiness or perseverance either as a profession or a trade, a man with common abilities will almost always succeed'.[89] Brasbridge too believed that 'honesty, frugality, and industry, will invariably in the long run be rewarded'. He regarded himself not as 'a common shopkeeper, but as a gentleman and a man of honour', and admiringly told stories of other self-made men.[90] The magazine commended Lackington's *Memoirs* (which opened with a frontispiece portrait of the author inscribed 'Who, a few years since, began Business with five Pounds, now sells one Hundred Thousand Volumes Annually') for showing, 'Diligence progressively rewarded, and rising, by its exertions, from distress to opulence'.[91]

A successful 'Tradewell' or 'Pulse' still had to demonstrate the old Grandisonian virtues of politeness, sensibility and benevolence, though – sometimes a difficult feat for a new gentleman. Gisborne thought manufacturers all-too-often inclined, through lack of a liberal education and the suddenness of their rise to wealth, to excessive displays of opulence.[92] Blair's *Sermons* repeatedly counselled modesty, moderation and integrity.[93] One reason for the magazine obituarist's approval of miller James Whittingstall's family was that the *paterfamilias*, Henry, had retained 'very modest and unassuming manners [...] he was a stranger to that overbearing disposition so frequently and so justly complained of in illiterate persons accidentally raised from low stations in life'.[94]

James Lackington, whose own book collection included 'odd magazines, &c.' had, like so many *Gentleman's Magazine* readers, used reading 'to raise himself socially to the rank of gentleman and make a fortune [...]'.[95] The pursuit of 'peaceful Science' as a member of the *Gentleman's Magazine* circle of readers and correspondents continued to be one means of achieving this polite ideal, of adding a touch of 1755's 'Polyglot', 'Vertu' or 'Lemma' to one's business credentials.[96] The magazine also offered readers examples of both pitfalls to avoid and paths to tread. The potential hypocritical gap between public success and private virtue was laid bare, for example, in Southey's poem, 'The Alderman's Funeral', printed in 1812. It was a savage attack on a Bristol merchant, worth half a million pounds, buried with massive pomp and lauded in the papers 'for industry and honourable wealth', but irredeemably hard of heart. For him 'Love had no place, nor natural charity'.[97]

It could have been a warning aimed specifically at the magazine's readers, men like Revd John-Cole Galloway who 'frequently expressed a wish to be well-spoken of in this Obituary'.[98] Galloway was relatively lucky, merely described as 'tolerable' in Classical literature and 'out of his depth' as a justice. Other obituaries deployed lack of proper complaisance and self-restraint as a warning to men on the rise. Joseph Payne's merit as a lawyer went unrewarded because he was given to excessive conviviality and levity which breached the rules of decorum at the Bar. Fellow lawyer, Thomas Lowten, had 'an understanding truly masculine' marred by 'the harsher traits in his character': 'a stern sever-ity of temper' which rendered him more feared than loved. Pastry cook Richard Wood was worth £60,000 but his greed and 'penuriousness' proved fatal. Accustomed to eat at friends' to save expense, he literally gorged himself to death. Joseph Gulston provided a truly terrible lesson, dying aged only 22 of drink, after a life of vice and debauchery that exhausted the family coffers.[99]

There were also pointers to positive behaviour. William Beloe (1758–1817, writer and translator) explained in July 1814 that the gentleman's demeanour should be 'manly and dignified' and not descend to rude-ness or ferocity.[100] 'Manly', a term which surfaced in the magazine described in Chapter 5, was increasingly deployed to mean an admired straightforwardness and directness of manner, speech or deportment. It was applied variously by readers to a preference for poetry that exhib-ited 'simplicity, manliness and classicality', to a call for political 'manly courage', and by Hues Carter LLB to a friend on the occasion of his mar-riage: 'Your manly honour, constancy, and love'.[101] An 1800 obituary used it in a sense that approached Tosh's late-nineteenth-century British stiff upper lip: 'silent, reserved and unshaken by waves of emotion [...] the most extreme form of manliness as self-control'.[102] Charles Nevison Howard, Viscount Andover, died a horribly lingering death after a shooting accident, yet uttered no words of 'unmanly complaint'.[103]

According to the 1804 Preface, the *Gentleman's Magazine* itself pos-sessed 'manly freedom' as it scanned the worlds of politics, guided youth and protected tender females. On occasion, correspondents abused this freedom, bringing opprobrium on their heads. Artifice and impositions were 'unmanly'.[104] When argument (over repair work at Westminster Abbey) between 'Architect' (John Carter, 1748–1817, draughtsman and antiquary, Gothic enthusiast and a regular architectural correspon-dent under this pseudonym) and 'Amateur' (Revd Vincent again) descended to the personal, 'A.G.' of Newcastle complained: 'I expect more politeness from them' and 'it reflects dishonour on him [i.e. Vincent] as a gentleman'.[105]

The magazine's politeness now entailed an ever stricter view of decency that accorded with the views of Evangelicals. It was a gentleman's duty to uphold public standards. Propriety now definitely stemmed the flow of racy poetry. One example that hit the cutting-room floor is catalogued by Peoples:

> What dapper youth on Sofa now,
> Thee, Mary Ann, embraces?
> To whose enraptur'd sight dost thou
> Stark naked shew thy graces?[106]

Correspondent 'I.S.' of Dover supported prosecutions by the 'Society for the Reformation of Manners' of two vendors of obscene prints and pamphlets. He expressed horror at their exhibition in 'diabolical shops surrounded with youths of all ages (and I am sorry to add) of both sexes'.[107] The private home too required careful surveillance to protect its womenfolk, according to W. Chamberlaine (perhaps the author of *Tirocinium Medicum*). In January 1805 he warned readers, ahead of St Valentine's Day, of the importance of censoring any 'amorous billets' that arrived in the post for their daughters. These could be vehicles for the 'grossest ribaldry'. The previous year he had snatched them from his young ladies' hands and thrown them on the fire before they could corrupt the household morals.[108] This was the same year in which Farington reported both the fury of Bishop Porteous of London, a keen supporter of moral reformation, at the naked woman illustrating the frontispiece of Hoppner's *Oriental Tales*, wholly unsuitable for the eyes of Mrs Porteous, and Mr Annesley's concern that Ruben's naked *Ganymede* was an unfit picture for a lady's apartment.[109] The following year, 1806, 'A.B.' contributed a letter from another father concerned at reputation and decorum, begging his daughter not to follow the fashion for 'naked' dresses.[110]

Marriage and family remained, however, more than 'Benedict in a Bustle's' aid to middling-sort industry or sites of patriarchal control. Open affection for wives was still an important indicator of polite manly feeling and sensibility. Poems to beloved partners continued. 'On the anniversary of my Marriage', by a Leicestershire reader, declared that Lucy was 'My Joy! my Transport! and my Pride!' In similar vein was 'To Mrs Bishop with a Pocket-looking-glass'. In this poem, written to accompany a wedding anniversary gift, Revd Samuel Bishop, headmaster of Merchant Taylors' School, London, described his wife Molly as the confidante to whom he could reveal his secret soul. Bishop's friend, Revd Thomas Clare, published his poetry after his death in 1796. Volume II included several of these anniversary poems. One reader who had seen this emulated Bishop: 'To my Wife on her Birth-day'. He could not offer Julia the same gems and 'pretty toys' but brought 'a constant true heart'.[111]

Love of and engagement with one's children remained a positive pleasure too. 'Benevolus' letter of 1799 on a friend's illness and cure mentioned his 'affectionate wife' and 'little lovely family'. 'L.B.M.' reported a holiday visit with 'my young folks' to London. 'T.L.' of Snelston, Derbyshire recalled the past year as co-parent with his dear wife in 'On New Year's Day':

> How often nurs'd our little boy,
> Wip'd off his tears, and hush'd his sigh;
> Assay'd his sorrows to beguile,
> And hung in raptures o'er his angel's smile.

When 'M. Green' (Nichols) supplied an extract from Richard Cumberland's *Memoir* of his grandfather, the great classical scholar of Trinity College, Cambridge, Dr Richard Bentley, he chose the passage refuting rumours of Howard-like sternness. Here Cumberland reminisced over Bentley's willingness to break off from work to read picture-books to him and his sister or join their 'childish sports and sallies'.[112] The importance to readers of fatherly tenderness was underlined by their warm response to the lines in Homer's *Iliad* where the Trojan warrior Hector, the soldier's soldier, took leave of his wife and baby son before departing for battle. The child was terrified of Hector's shining helmet with its horsehair crest, and so this most manly of men removed it before kissing and dandling his son. The January 1808 issue contained three letters in reply to one in September 1807 on Pope's English translation of this passage.[113]

The family was, then, central to the British gentleman's sense of self. It was stressed as such by Evangelicals.[114] The universality of family feeling was, however, like equality in nature, now sometimes denied. Feeling was a British and Christian preserve in 'East India News' for January 1795. Tipu Sultan, it was reported, when his sons were restored after being held hostage, 'instead of advancing to embrace his children, contented himself with placing a cold hand on the neck of each'.[115]

The 'Beauty of Buttermere' and the 'Keswick Impostor': a case study

As Dabhoiwala notes, by the late century men were increasingly regarded as naturally prone to aggressive assaults on female purity.[116]

However, the contemporary challenge to acceptance of this norm was greater than he acknowledges. Gentlemanly protection of women within the sheltering family actually strengthened as a theme in the *Gentleman's Magazine* of this period. In July 1798 it published Thomas Lister's poem 'The Prostitute', in which the fallen woman was the pitiful, angel-faced, virginal victim of 'the foul seducer ravening'.[117] Horror at violence, physical and verbal, towards genteel women lay behind interest in the 'Monster' attacks in 1790, the magazine devoting three pages to the trial of Renwick Williams in the July number.[118] When 'A Wanderer' (Thicknesse) wanted to injure the Wesleys' reputations, he turned to anecdotes and insinuations about their sexual conduct, rather than doctrinal or church matters.[119] For the middling-sort correspondent the sexual impulse was one that a gentleman must tame.

The magazine, its readers, and the wider reading public, were therefore captivated by the failure of gentlemanliness involved in the seduction of the famous 'Beauty of Buttermere' by impostor John Hatfield in 1802. Hatfield (*c.* 1758–1803), a long-time fraudster, had recently absconded from Tiverton, Devon, leaving behind a trail of debts, a pregnant wife and a child. By July he had arrived in Keswick where, using 'specious manners and gentlemanlike demeanour', he enjoyed an active social life and obtained substantial credit as the Honourable Colonel Alexander Augustus Hope, MP, brother to the Earl of Linlithgow. (The real Col. Hope was conveniently absent on the continent.) Here, after various escapades, including a failed engagement to an heiress, he met and bigamously married the 'Beauty', Mary Robinson, daughter of the landlord of the Fish Inn, Buttermere.[120] Coleridge, now living in the Lake District, brought their story to national attention when he reported the 'Romantic Marriage' in the *Morning Post* for 11 October. He covered the story as it unfolded. On 22 October Hatfield's imposture was discovered and subsequent flight reported. By 8 November it was the 'Fraudulent Marriage'. For months it remained a leading story in national and local papers.

Both marriage and imposture headed the *Gentleman's Magazine* marriages column for November.[121] Here the addition of back-references highlighted an added piquancy for its readers. For, years earlier, the magazine had played a significant part in bringing Mary celebrity status as the epitome of beautiful, shy, pure, rural British womanhood. She first came to their attention aged 14, as 'Sally' in Budworth/Palmer's *A Fortnight's Ramble to the Lakes*, reviewed and excerpted in 1792. Budworth encouraged future travellers to seek her out. In 1800 he reported a repeat revisit to Buttermere and the Fish made in 1797/8. His advice had been taken. Adoring graffiti (in gentlemanly Latin, Greek and French as well as English) adorned the inn's walls. Budworth further observed Mary over three voyeuristic pages. Before he left he warned her, prophetically it transpired, to be on her guard against strangers with 'bad intentions'.[122]

Readers were, nonetheless, outraged by Hatfield's betrayal of female innocence. 'Indignant' sent in a compendium of Hatfield's sins. He was a travesty of new gentlemanliness: guilty, in addition to desertion of wife and family, seduction and bigamy, of financial swindling and dishonesty, bankruptcy, boastfulness and an insincerity that might have reminded readers of Lord Chesterfield. There were also three poems lamenting Mary's 'fate'. All saw Mary as the tragic, blameless victim of the artful villain's 'black deceit'.[123]

The story featured in the wider press throughout the following year as Hatfield was captured in Wales, taken to London for questioning, and tried for forgery, convicted and executed in Carlisle in September 1803. It was 'the novel of real life', published indeed as *Augustus and Mary* [...] *a Domestic Tale*.[124] It inspired articles, songs, prints, a play and the inevitable pamphlet account of the trial and inclusion in the *Newgate Calendar*.[125] Mary's portrait even hung at the Royal Academy.[126]

Public opinion was firmly on her side, which the *Morning Post*, under 'Fashionable World' , declared unusual 'for one in her rank of life'. A subscription was raised for her, to which the Duke of Roxburgh contributed £10 (and 'Rambler' two guineas).[127] There was also considerable interest in Hatfield and his gentlemanliness. His interrogation at Bow Street was 'the theme of our young lads in the streets' and attended by '*men of fashion*', the Duke of Cumberland and 'many of the Nobility'. Here, and at the thronged trial and execution, Hatfield was by all accounts a gentleman to the eye and ear of the observer of any class: composed, knowledgeable, neat in dress, genteel in manners. He evidently had something of the charmer about him. He was 'attentive in the extreme to females' and at the trial 'the ladies were not the least numerous or the least curious'.[128] The only suspect thing about him had been the lack of a servant at Keswick.[129]

The *Gentleman's Magazine* coverage can be distinguished in several respects from this broader and sensationalized popular response. Its version of events, as with the Baltimore case 34 years before, increased the apparent helplessness and passivity of the female victim and so the dastardliness of her deceiver. For the magazine and its readers Mary was commodified, initially as a tourist attraction for the benefit of the male gaze and then as a type: the wronged innocent woman. Her story was adapted by presenting her as irrationally lured into a union above her station by the blandishments of a fake. The aim was to uphold gentlemanly standards.

The magazine characteristically omitted detail unhelpful to its purpose. Firstly, Coleridge had ungallantly suggested from the outset that Mary was not beautiful 'in the strict sense of the word', but 'rather gap-toothed, and somewhat pock-marked'.[130] (It seems she was buxomly sexy rather than pretty, as Gillray's print confirms.) This passage was repeated elsewhere, in *Kirby's Wonderful Museum* for example, but not in the magazine (although in his 1800 piece Budworth had pronounced her 'far from a perfect beauty', he had praised her 'heavenly countenance'). Also suppressed was Mary's statement that she had acted out of a desire to better herself and her family (as men expected to do).[131] Finally, by suspending coverage between the arrest and its final word on the affair, Hatfield's execution, it did not have to engage with his apparently genuinely gentlemanly deportment and defence, Mary's pregnancy ('very far advanced' by December 1802), and the birth of a still-born son in early June 1803. Nor did it note Mary's refusal to prosecute for bigamy.[132]

The magazine therefore 'froze' the affair in December 1802 as a straightforward contest between good and bad, with Hatfield yet another reminder of the potential unreliability of surface appearance for both literal and metaphorical gentlemanly credit, and of the importance of underlying character. There was no chivalrous defender in this story, but the industrious and self-controlled gentleman-reader could adopt the role and sit in judgement (indeed he might well be a lawyer, juryman or magistrate).[133] Hatfield's wickedness reinforced his superior approach to proper work, honesty, sincerity, compassion and chastity.[134] This last was an enduring concern. In 1810, correspondent 'C.P.' still favoured new legislation to punish the seducers of 'female innocence'.[135]

Women, like new gentlemen, formed a rising proportion of the magazine's obituaries in this period: 33 per cent of the sample for 1790–1815, in line with Kuist's recognition of greater female representation in the magazine.[136] However, the treatment of the story of Hatfield and Mary belies any suggestion that their increased presence reflected an alteration in the balance of power between either the classes or the sexes. Unlike Thomas Dunckerley, who gained a £100 *per annum* pension from George III by claiming to be a previously undiscovered illegitimate brother, Hatfield's fatal mistake as a *parvenu* impostor was to personate a real traditional gentleman whose friends used their superior power and connections to unmask and pursue him.[137] Budworth's promotion of Mary hinted at the abusive male pursuit of lower-class women, a double standard acceptable even among genteel readers of the magazine. Charles Fothergill, for example, unashamedly recorded casual sex with working girls – maids at inns and chance encounters in the open countryside – as he travelled about England in the same period.[138] Still, despite the attempts to depict Mary as 'a betrayed, sheltered peasant girl', her agency and personality in choosing to 'marry up' and stand by Hatfield were not completely obscured.[139] One reader, 'Severianus', who had looked up the magazine's back-references, spotted this, commenting that Mary was not entirely unaware of the impact of her charms.[140]

The 'Old English Gentleman'

Mary's story also fed a growing conservative conviction that the manners of upstarts from the burgeoning towns (where rural-born Hatfield had developed his tricks) were disturbing and corrupting the peace and stability of an essentially rural Old England, represented here by the Robinsons. Rural innocence was a theme of Mudford's simplified, novelized version and, in the pages of the magazine, 'R.M.R.'s' poem saw the affair in this light:

> As some rude Townsman passes by,
> And plucks the flow'r to all so dear [...][141]

Wordsworth put it to similar use in 1805 in Book VII of the *Prelude*. Mary, 'artless Daughter of the Hills' deceived by the 'Spoiler', Hatfield, was contrasted with London women 'to open shame Abandoned'.[142]

The magazine's 1801 Preface also captured this growing dissatisfaction at modern commercial society with its 'avarice of a few great capitalists, which has taught monopoly to every salesman and shopkeeper, the wholesale trader compelling the retailer to extortion'. Factors and cattle breeders, enclosure and suburban building were the co-accused. 'Constant Reader', Samuel Jackson Pratt agreed in his 1802 poem 'The Poor, or, Bread', advertised on the January wrapper (though he pitied too, the middling sort oppressed by high rates).[143] Some felt that the self-made man's pursuit of money over leisure ruled him out as a gentleman. Revd William Jones, whose Hertfordshire parishes made him a near-neighbour of the Whittingstalls, commented on James' death that, 'Everything that the W – ll's touched seemed to change into gold;

but their eager desire of getting *more & more* allowed them time & inclination to enjoy but very little of their plenteous earnings'.[144]

Retreat

Magazine-reader Jones (see Chapter 3) often found work and family, twin props of gentlemanly masculinity, stressful. He valued his leisure in a room of his own: 'I am undisturbed, I have my cheerful little fire, my books & in short every comfort which I can reasonably desire. I read, I reflect, I write, & endeavour to enjoy, as far as I can, that blessed leisure & absence of care'.[145] The work ethic was demanding and, while commercial and professional success was certainly praised as a route to gentlemanliness, obituaries more than ever suggested that achieving it could take the highest personal toll. Mr Christopher Patch, a paper maker, died, it was said, having 'sunk under the weight' of worry about an excise case against him. On the other side of the fence, James Albon applied an 'unwearied application' to his duties as an exciseman to the extent that it 'prevented him from engaging in domestic happiness'. Alexander Brander Esq. was worn out by the cares of civic office as a Common Councilman and sheriff of London and Middlesex.[146]

The bankruptcy lists had now vanished from the back half. No reason was given but maybe failure was no longer even regarded as an option: 'We [...] desire to have as little to do as possible with any thing that relates to *Bankrupts*, or *Bankruptcy*', replied the editor to 'Lycurgus' through the 'Index Indicatorius.'[147] Suicides, however, were frequently attributed to business losses: Joseph Keen died in 1790, 'literally of a broken heart' after being falsely accused of embezzlement; in 1793 Thomas Day Esq. was unable to bear his very public descent from 'amazingly rich' oilman to being gazetted; Mr Salter drowned himself in 1798 after investing heavily in property at St Chad's Well, Gray's Inn Lane, then being refused a tea-garden licence.[148] The only other comparably cited cause was humiliation in love.[149]

Happy indeed then the man who contrived to make a sufficient fortune to retire from the stresses of town and commerce. This was represented in obituaries as the pinnacle of ambition for the self-made man, a man like Gillery Pigott, 'Formerly in the haberdashery line, in Cheapside', who had 'relinquished all the emoluments of a full trade' and 'attached himself to the pleasures of a retired life' in a small house he had built on the edge of Windsor Forest.[150]

The deep longing for escape was reflected in the new fashion for genteel 'cottages', though these were the comfortable homes of the prosperous rather than the often inadequate shelters of the rural poor.[151]

It was evident in the inscription from July 1815 cited at the start of this chapter and also in family announcements from 1800.[152] It was a fashion that John Wilkes was known to have followed. A 'Biographical Memoir' in January 1798, the month after his death, referred to his visits to 'Sandham [Sandown] Cottage' on the Isle of Wight, which he called his 'villakin'.[153]

The longing was repeated in readers' enthusiasm for the study and conservation of the past – antiquarianism, genealogy, fossils – and in their poetry which mimicked a Horatian yearning for the peace that the countryside seemed to represent. 'I.P.', who had rejected 'pride and the pomp' of martial heroes, addressed his lines to his friend, retired Major Rooke (a regular magazine correspondent) of Mansfield Woodhouse:

> To yonder little hermitage confined,
> His trees, his books, his studies, all his care,
> There dwells he – to Philosophy resign'd.

Rooke's home was no tiny cell, however, but the substantial Woodhouse Place where he pursued the antiquarian and natural history interests so popular in the pages of the magazine.[154] The anonymous author of 'Epistle to Mr [Bennet] Langton' (1736–1801, friend of Samuel Johnson) sought to share rural happiness with him:

> Retir'd from all the vanities of life,
> The world's weak clamour, and the tongue of strife'.[155]

William Hutton used the device in 'A Day' in 1803. He walked from his 'cot' to Birmingham and back home where his daughter Catherine and

> [...] garden, converse, book, or pen,
> Tea, supper, music, please till ten

awaited him. It was 'A little heaven of my making'.[156] Like Rooke's, Hutton's 'cot' (Bennett's Hill, Saltley, rebuilt after destruction in the 1791 riots) was in fact elegant and spacious.[157] In the 1780s he had felt no need to downplay this, but had commissioned his portrait standing proudly before it, favourite dog at his feet and framed by the classical props of pillar and drapes, in a gentlemanly pose that instead announced the social distance he had travelled from humble beginnings.[158] John Dovaston loved his 'little boxen bower', the subject of his poem in 1812. This was both a scholarly retreat where, far from 'the paths of Power', he read the classics, and a social space where he entertained friends.[159]

This idea of retreat and retirement had existed in previous periods of the magazine's existence, of course. The preceding two chapters identify anxiety over new money well before 'The Alderman's Funeral'. It was a major theme of Cowper's *Task* of 1785. What was new was both a heightened urgency and a politicization of the concept. It was now more firmly linked to a conservative belief that old traditional ways were disappearing, to the nation's disadvantage. It was post-1793 conservatism that prompted Lackington's return to the West Country. Criticism of upper-class morals was now the preserve of Radicals, such as Charles Pigott (d.1794) who defined 'aristocrat' as 'a fool, or scoundrel, generally both; a monster of rapacity, and an enemy to mankind'.[160] From the 1790s the magazine reasserted the traditional relationship between nobility and people as its coverage of Nelson's funeral and militia reviews showed. The Hatfield House royal review was followed by a three-page report of the Duke of Bedford's huge sheep-shearing celebration at Woburn.[161]

The moral villains of the mid-century, noblemen like Lord Baltimore or the Duke of Cumberland, were now replaced by middling-sort men who were disruptive of the social order: Renwick Williams, the Wesleys and John Hatfield.[162] It was this class that now needed to reform. Many correspondents thought social disorder was a result of its failure to lead, to set the right example to the lower orders. Personal wealth had been pursued at the expense of the old reciprocal vertical ties that bound the different ranks of society together.[163]

'C.P.' had made a connection between the abomination of seduction, the commercialization of society and the Metropolis.[164] 'The Projector', a monthly essay series in the magazine self-consciously reminiscent of the *Spectator* and *Tatler*, looked back nostalgically to 'improvements that are very old, [rather] than those that are very new'.[165] Some of its targets were long-standing – fops, French manners, novels – but it also struck closer to the core readership, reminding them of standing jokes about professionals, the clergy, lawyers, physicians and tradesmen, and attacking the money-making ethic of those who 'cannot conceive how any man can fail from any other reason than idleness'.[166] 'Cacafogo' (meaning braggadocio) of Widcomb mocked the upward mobility that some admired. Attorneys were all 'solicitors' and even a humble 'botcher' (cobbler or tailor) was now a '*raccomodeur*' with letters after his name.[167] Master of Moulton Grammar School, Lincolnshire, Samuel Elsdale (1779/80–1827) submitted a poem 'Death, Judgement, Heaven, and Hell' in 1811. Alongside time-honoured sinners (murderers, atheists, fornicators and drunkards) he catalogued modern-day offenders: farmers of the work-house, greedy physicians, negligent churchwardens, lazy and venal schoolmasters, hard-hearted overseers, dishonest tradesmen.[168] 'Southern Faunist' lamented the decline of the yeoman and the rise of large farmers driven by market-forces and fashion-obsessed wives and daughters, a popular theme for satirical prints.[169] 'A.F.A.' mourned the 'violent changes which have taken place in the internal structure and combination of ranks in old England within the present reign'. The 'glut of Commerce', paper currency, 'stock-jobbers, loan-jobbers, contractors and enormous sudden wealth' had led to the near-extinction of 'the race of Country Gentlemen' who had been a 'useful link in society' and 'contributed widely to the happiness of others' through their benevolent paternalism.[170]

Some readers, therefore, hankered after a society re-rooted in land rather than commerce. This was encapsulated in *The Old English Gentleman*, Cornish correspondent Richard Polwhele's 1797 poem. 'L.U.B.' had read it (and made some of the rather pedantic comments, on the colour of mead, for which the magazine was renowned).[171] Polwhele's hero, Sir Humphrey Andarton, was a model 'primitive esquire' presiding over a harmonious world upheld by traditional masculine values (including ogling the village girls in church). He resided at Andarton Grove all year round and personally undertook all his customary responsibilities: as a magistrate, supervisor of his estate, landlord and stalwart of the Church of England. His sole visit to London was a loyalist one, to swear allegiance as High Sheriff of Cornwall on the accession of George III. Only the fashionable female extravagance of his daughter, urban, Frenchified and corrupted by her association with a Creole friend, threatened the bucolic, prelapsarian idyll. At the very end of the poem disaster was averted by the supreme blessing of the lineage family: the birth of a son and heir.[172]

Actual or assumed status as a rural landowner was more important than before. Use of the designation 'gentleman' rose in the sampled obituaries. There were 12 'gentlemen' in 1790–9, 15 in 1800–9, and 29 in the six years 1810–15. Of only five was it admitted that they were retired tradesmen or professionals (a draper, hosier, grocer, steward and tax inspector). There were also biographical notes which applauded the traditional 'country gentleman' Polwhele depicted: resident, engaged and benevolent.

As Richard Edgeworth advised, however, 'more enlargement of mind' was expected of him than in the days of Addison's 'tory *Freeholder*'.[173] 'A.C.' (see Chapter 3) preferred book-collecting to country sports.

These were therefore no fox-hunting Squire Westerns, but met readers' humane expectations.[174] Denys Rolle Esq., 'supposed to be the greatest land-owner in Devonshire', not only 'never raised the rent of an old tenant' but 'used to get up early in the morning as any of the peasants, and, cloathed like them, with a bag of provisions and his spade on his shoulder, go out for the day, and work as hard as any day-labourer on his estate'. He was an active campaigner against cruelty to animals.[175] Sir Joseph Andrews was described as 'very happily combining the manners and dignity of the old country gentleman with great attention to the public institutions in London'.[176] Sir Wilfred Lawson, 'lived in the old British style upon his estates, giving employment to numbers of industrious men, in the various improvements which he planned and executed'.[177]

Politicized nostalgia was also seen in readers' choice of pseudonyms and the formal and informal institutions they supported (and Paine attacked). One correspondent styled himself 'A Lover of the old Order of Things'. He was concerned at the neglect of 'the monumental records in the families of our Nobility'.[178] 'Oswald', who enjoyed the magazine because its correspondents were men who revered the nation's institutions, defended the fellows of the English universities who had been described as 'old women' in a piece in December.[179] For 'An Englishman', toleration of dissent had led to a diminution of respect for the established church, but it was not too late for 'the Friends of social order' to 'check the evils'.[180]

The Sunday school debate

One battleground over which the two cultures clashed in the pages of the magazine was Sunday schools, identified in Chapter 5 as a site of gentlemanly benevolence towards the deserving poor. In the light of Paine's works (especially *Age of Reason*), and the regicide and Terror across the Channel, the movement presented for some a new and dangerous face.[181] John Byng felt that it was a better world when labourers were illiterate, could not access 'Amours' or 'Paine's Pamphlets', and were taught what to believe by their superiors and the clergy.[182] In the year of the Spithead and Nore mutinies, Farington recorded naval officer Sir Alan Gardner's belief that Sunday schools were responsible for over-educating sailors who now read opposition newspapers sent out to ships and corresponded back to dry land.[183]

The conflict in the magazine was between those advocating hard grind to reform and control the poor, and those believing in the efficacy of the moral example set by the established Church and ruling class. For each the nation itself was at stake. The lengthy and often vituperative debate began in October 1797 with a letter from 'Eusebius' (Revd Joseph Robertson, 1726–1802). He doubted the value of this misguided form of charity. One day's instruction could not counter what he saw as the ingrained wickedness of the labouring classes on the other six. And a little reading led all-too-often to misplaced ambition and the spirit of rebellion. The only restraint on their behaviour was fear of the gallows. They should instead be taught the bourgeois value of industry which would keep them in their useful place.[184] There were two angry replies the following month from regular correspondents ('T. Mot, F.S.M.' and Revd Edward Goodwin of Sheffield), both of whom reasserted the moral improvement from above wrought by 'the labour of love' that was Sunday schools.[185]

In January 1798 there were four letters, including a lengthy response from 'Eusebius'.[186] 'Hanslopiensis' tried to link benevolence and industry. Sunday teaching did not interfere with the work of the poor and was an antidote to the baleful alternative of the alehouse. So did a Lancashire reader who chose the cumbersome loyalist pseudonym, 'A Friend to the Established Church, and a well-Wisher to all Mankind; though an Enemy to every Thing that looks like Mischief or Rebellion'. He wanted Sunday schools devoted to Anglican religion rather than worldly matters, such as learning to read, which could be relegated to Saturday afternoon. 'Clericus' in addition drew attention to the support of the upper classes: the bishops, Dowager Lady Spencer and the ubiquitous late Denys Rolle.

'Eusebius' was unrepentant. Sunday schools were the secret subversive weapon of the Reforming Societies, whose aim was teaching the lower orders to read their own publications promising liberty and equality. He alleged that 400 copies of Paine's *Age of Reason* had been distributed free on one York market day alone to 'ordinary farmers, servants, and labourers'. Only the inculcation of industry could ameliorate their condition and that of Britain. At this point the editor indicated that there were more letters unpublished and that he now regarded the matter as now closed. It remained, however, unresolved.

Conclusion

The *Gentleman's Magazine* of 1790–1815 was not dominated by the militarized society and hardening of boundaries between a male public and female private sphere that some historians identify. Its strongly civilian emphasis (even the volunteer defence forces were regarded with mixed feelings) and nostalgic reworking of the ideal of the rural gentleman is an important corrective to Colley's placing of militarism at the heart of Britishness. The character of a military hero like Nelson still had to be forced into the civilian, polite mould.

What constituted civilian gentlemanliness was, however, more fiercely contested. The vehemence of the self-made men disturbed traditionalists. These 'new gentlemen', demonstrably proud of their lowly origins, also undermine Cain's and Hopkins' case for the dominance of 'gentlemanly capitalism' where the dirty evidence of wealth formation was well-concealed.[187]

At the same time there was change as the crucial social boundary became that between all those who had some claim to gentlemanly status and the lower orders as objects of surveillance and discipline. 1791 was the key year, marked by the publication of Burke's *Reflections* and Paine's *Rights of Man* and, in the magazine, by Gough's reviews and Preface. This drove the new gentlemen away from asserting their own independence as they had done from the 1760s. They and the once-lambasted ruling classes were instead drawn by 'The Great Fear' into a closer and mutually protective alliance to protect a social order that they necessarily portrayed as harmonious and uniting.[188] It was, less benignly, a climate of opinion that allowed Pitt's 'Reign of Terror' to erode what had been vaunted liberties.

Gentlemanly masculinity was, therefore, still a matter of comparisons between men. Women were, as before, a prop in the gentlemanly worlds of power, prestige and feeling, depicted as both supporting it and protected by it, but in no way commensurate as agents with men, even where there was evidence to the contrary. Within the shifting gentlemanly alliance there was, however, a tension between those in the commercial and professional sectors who saw money, work and discipline as the way to protect the *status quo* and those who looked to a renewal of the Grandisonian ideal grounded in the benevolent rural landowner.

The need to take sides in a politicized nation came at a price for the magazine in terms of readership as new publications catered to those who wished to engage in 'a state of literary warfare'.[189] There were the radically inclined publications noted in the Introduction. On the opposing wing, a number of the magazine's correspondents became contributors to the more combative *British Critic* (Beloe) and the *Anti-Jacobin Review* (Isaac D'Israeli, William Thomas Fitzgerald, Mavor and Polwhele).[190] As editor and readers chose to 'wield the pen, and shed the ink' and mount an assault on Paine the man, his ideas and followers, the magazine was no longer a 'ragoust' to 'hit the tast of several difft persons' but developed a distinctively conservative stance, whether that of the upright bourgeois or of the country squire was undecided.[191] In the process it became more serious but equally less restrained and polite. One disenchanted reader was 'A Protestant Dissenter' of Coventry. In 1808 he complained that ungentlemanly 'narrow-minded or bigoted invectives' now 'sometimes obtruded' themselves into the magazine.[192] It had become the magazine that Hazlitt described.

Conclusion

Engagement in depth with the *Gentleman's Magazine*, the most influential periodical of the eighteenth century which in so many ways epitomized it – decorative and useful, commercial, polite and open to all with a thirst for knowledge and debate, yet at the same time hypocritical, nit-picking and sanctimonious – increases our understanding of the cultural and social dynamics of gender and class in the period. Over 21,000 sampled family announcements take the magazine beyond the realm of representation, since they were placed by real individuals positioning themselves within the paradigm of gentlemanly masculinity. Readers by the thousand eagerly awaited then routinely devoured each monthly number. It was a cherished and integral part of their lives and one with which they could actively engage as correspondents. In this respect the magazine was an element of a public sphere that was, given literacy, genuinely open to all and within which bourgeois values and aims were furthered.

Analysis of the readership establishes it as a key medium through which middling-sort and ambitious artisan men first acquired politeness and then, through their contributions as authors, poets and obituarists, asserted their newly gentlemanly status. As they wrote about what concerned them they reached out, both horizontally to one another and, they believed, up to the elite ruling class. The magazine therefore assisted in creating a masculine, middling-sort self-awareness, and of making this class count nationally as 'public opinion'. It achieved this through being simultaneously rooted in the private sphere of the home and the social unit of the family, as its female readers, reader contributions (especially poetry) and advertising show. An idealized affection and harmony became one of the ways in which the new gentlemanly virtue was conveyed, alongside the middling-sort values of industry and respectability.

The long time-frame studied reveals the process by which this social and cultural change came about. Gentlemanly masculinity was promised in the title. Initially the message was a Whiggish, didactic one, as befitted a periodical which unashamedly targeted ambitious readers well below the nobility and gentry. There were 'club member' gentleman-stereotypes and press excerpts that followed the precedents set by the *Spectator* and *Tatler*, by conduct literature and by the improving novel, *Sir Charles Grandison*. For aspirational men of the professional and trading middling sort and for artisans, this politeness and the emphasis on personal qualities held out the prospect of a universal and accessible gentlemanliness. The magazine provided them with a window into the world of the landed elite and an easily-digested Enlightenment education that helped them to 'talk the talk'.

The gentleman of the early magazine was measured against other men and close to that described by both Carter and Maurer: polite, pious, active, temperate and benevolent: a Christian Hero. It was a construct that appeared to pose no threat to the families at the pinnacle of the established, gendered social hierarchy of land and lineage: the magazine's ideal model gentleman was landed and Grandison's real-life counterparts dominated the Births, Marriages and Deaths. However even in the 1730s there were substantial hints that this construct was neither secure nor universally adopted. Women's agency could disrupt masculine authority. They were still Foyster's rather spirited and lusty creatures, cruel in courtship and well-capable of doling out a marital battering. There were, too, alternative masculinities lurking below the surface: the unreformed, the hot-headed soldier, the unrepentant libertine, the old-fashioned country squire.

As reader contributions took off in the 1740s and 1750s, they reshaped the magazine's construction of gentlemanliness. Sharp-elbowed correspondents advanced their own model founded on the concept of public 'merit' earned through occupational success, itself the result of ability and effort, and private probity – literal and moral creditworthiness. By the 1760s a hallmark of this probity was benevolent treatment, guided by sensibility, of the weak, whether women, servants, children, 'savages' or even dumb animals. Taken together, the public and private masculine virtues comprised for readers 'character', later 'manly character'. And, as Pope and Pegge believed and obituaries confirmed, character was denied altogether to women.

'Mr Tradewell' and 'Dr Pulse' were included in the magazine's 1755 Preface. There were also rising numbers of actual 'Pulses' and 'Tradewells' commemorated in the Deaths notices alongside those from established lineage families. By the 1750s the 'new gentlemanliness' showed tentative signs of becoming a counter-hegemonic masculinity from below. This was seen in the critique of the masculine vices of the elite. Lords Annesley and Lovat were fallen gentlemen, because hasty-tempered and abusive towards women. Admiral Byng was revealed as unprofessional because he footled like a fop when he should have toiled like a Trojan.

The first real turning point in the *Gentleman's Magazine* was 1768, slightly later than that of the established historiography and without evidence of gender panic, of a reassessment of masculinity *versus* femininity, of biology entering the discourse. Instead it marked the moment when the new gentlemen as 'public opinion' confronted the ruling class with their reformed standards of gentlemanliness. In the public sphere these informed readers' attitude to the Baltimore rape case, Wilkes and the American colonists. Professional readers called for reform of the corrupt old order of patronage and places, for changes to property law, to taxation, to the universities and the Church of England. In the private sphere, the new gentlemen deployed moral probity and sensibility to 'tame' women. Marriage replaced the privileging of male friendship. The family headed by the protective husband and father and bound together by love, was honoured in poetry and commended in stories of gentlemanly rescue of damsels in distress, whether from physical harm or the horrors of indecency. In obituaries and poems women were subordinated as nurturing mothers, dutiful daughters and dear conjugal partners, all alike in their softer virtues.

By contrast, the 1780s obituaries celebrated the self-made man, his individualism and his character. Modest origins like those of Daniel Wray or Richard Atkinson were now regular cause for pride. Professions, charities and causes shaped a masculine public standing that placed these new gentlemen alongside or even above their traditional superiors. Readers increasingly defined themselves in these terms, as 'P.Q.R.'s' 'middling, walking, honest folks' for example. Their gentlemanly exemplars, unlike their fictional predecessors, were like them: middling-sort, enterprizing, benevolent and respectable: Captain Cook, John Howard, Admiral Nelson. With a fervour that contradicts Jonathan Clark's argument for a continuity of establishment loyalism, the new gentlemen were no longer subordinate.[1] They seemed to be setting the pace and, as Retford notes, many aristocrats chose to adapt and follow 'public opinion'. Even the monarch was presented as a diligent bourgeois.

'Character' was a hard taskmaster, however. It was easy to fall short of its principles as a seducer, libertine, reckless gambler, drunk or extravagant spendthrift. The *Gentleman's Magazine* gentleman-by-merit was a demanding and fragile construct. Work, family and temperance required constant competition against other men and strict self-surveillance. There was a heavy toll in disappointment, humiliation or even death. For the public gentleman, ruin was an ever-present threat as bankrupts and suicides warned. In private, governing the 'little republic' was not always straightforward. Navigating between the two was stressful (reader Revd William Jones preferred the solitude of his study) or even impossible, as many fathers of sons seeking their own independence discovered (among them John Howard).

This was especially true of the army or navy officer who had figured as a gentleman-template in the magazine's early years. He was increasingly professional – a 'Good Thing' that effectively met the criticisms most famously made in Brown's *Estimate* – but still prone to alarming outbursts of impolite behaviour. Officers led much of their lives outside the civilizing bosom of the family. Violence was their occupation, their manners could be coarse, and their ill-tempered disputes settled by the potentially fatal physical resort to the duel. Despite Britain's almost constant state of war or war-readiness throughout the 84 years of this study, the magazine and its readers persisted in holding soldiers to account by essentially civilian masculine standards. Cook and Nelson, for example, were heroes celebrated in its pages for their deeds, but with goriness deleted: their image still had to conform to expectations of benevolent, moral conduct.

At times this was so difficult to achieve that 'contort' might be a better word than 'conform'. Military violence could be explained away as the civilizing mission, and the ribald side of life in which readers had participated so joyously in the 1730s and 1740s, smuggled in under the guise of reportage, but the *Gentleman's Magazine* had to leave much more unspoken in order to maintain the illusion of gentlemanly self-control. Women were not as helpless as its coverage suggested. Reading both other publications and between the lines of the magazine itself, both Sarah Woodcock and Mary Robinson, for example, were independent agents. Double standards abounded and even its male heroes were not as virtuous as its accounts implied. The magazine chose not to mention Wilkes' libertinism, Cook's temper and absence from his wife and family. Nelson's irregular private life and Howard's lack of parental tenderness were only publicized posthumously. There was as much hypocrisy in many new gentlemen's lives as in Lord Chesterfield's *Letters*.

An external blow was dealt to this oppositional political middling-sort masculinity in the 1790s, marking a second turning point again slightly later than the historiography that focuses on the loss of America. It was not so much the French Revolution as such that prompted the change, as alarm at its mounting anarchy and bloodshed, and fear of similar disorder in Britain. The year was 1791 and the event the publication of Paine's polemic, *Rights of Man*, which envisaged reform that was a challenge to the entire political and social system, rather than a realignment. The prospect of a society where distinctions of rank counted for little or nothing disturbed lineage and new gentlemen alike. Without the promise of social differentiation what was there to strive for? There is plenty of evidence in editorials, articles, poems and obituaries of their fear, undermining Stafford's case for the magazine's representation of a calm and stable society.

The once proudly neutral *Gentleman's Magazine* now took a party line in favour of the *status quo*. For, the magazine and its gentlemanliness may have been democratizing, but they were not egalitarian. Circulation dropped as the more militant on each side of the debate drifted away. Those left agreed that all gentlemen should, for mutual self-preservation, join a conservative alliance against a perceived threat from the lower orders. In adversity the developing middling-sort political awareness of the mid-eighteenth century collapsed back into complicity with a regrouped ruling elite who had never wholly accepted their rise in the first place: Emily Lennox' tutor husband had not fitted entirely comfortably into smart Dublin drawing-rooms and Louisa's account of slumming it at a Matlock inn was tinged with snobbish humour.[2]

Readers now advanced two competing visions of the gentleman. Some retreated to a nostalgic rural past and the communitarian ideal of the 'old English gentleman', a modernized benevolent rural squire whose attention to his tenants and the poor would dampen any desire for revolution. In the opposite corner stood the meritocrats: gentlemen, if not actually created by the magazine, certainly endorsed and advanced, by both editors and readers. They maintained that market forces – the carrot of self-advancement through industry and the stick of punishment for the idle or unruly – were the solution. These entrepreneurial readers took their own success, triumphantly recorded in their obituaries, as evidence of moral superiority. By the same token the unsuccessful had *ipso facto* not worked hard enough.

This second version of gentlemanly masculinity, the respectable, meritocratic middle-class businessman or professional emerging in the mid-century, predates and explains the early nineteenth-century gendered class formation and masculinity identified by Davidoff and Hall and by Tosh by some 50 years or more. Post-Waterloo it became more potent when it was again advanced with political purpose: by 'Liberal Tories', Chartists and others to campaign for universal male suffrage, and by those who sought to introduce competitive examinations for the Civil Service. Merit was later decoupled from masculinity and deployed in unforeseen ways, by proto-feminists seeking entry to the male professions, for example.[3]

However, in the period covered by this book, despite evidence in the *Gentleman's Magazine* of a developing middling-sort political ideology of masculine merit after the Seven Years' War, the new gentlemen was, under pressure, co-opted by the elite. It was an uneasy alliance, however. Magazine correspondence between the two camps became increasingly vituperative, or impolite, as the Sunday school debate and attacks on the new gentlemen, 'sprung, like mushrooms, from the lowest stations', or 'upstarts who have chosen to distinguish themselves by that title' ['Esq.'] revealed.[4] Traces of this conflict remain in conservative thought today.

Appendix 1: Births, Marriages and Deaths

Table 1 Births, marriages and deaths, 1731–56

Year	Births	Sons	Daughters	Marriages	Settlements	Deaths	Male deaths	Total
1731	0	0	0	18	2	70	60	88
1732	3	3	0	23	12	105	87	131
1733	2	2	0	25	12	146	124	173
1734	12	4	7	23	6	122	110	157
1735	10	4	6	42	20	99	80	151
1736	6	2	4	44	27	138	123	188
1737	7	5	1	28	9	64	55	99
1738	12	8	4	26	13	45	44	83
1739	10	6	4	23	12	63	51	96
Subtotal	62	34	26	252	113	852	734	1166
1740	12	9	3	18	9	75	67	105
1741	7	6	4	19	7	49	40	75
1742	6	3	6	19	7	51	41	76
1743	6	4	2	23	11	82	65	111
1744	9	6	2	15	8	40	34	64
1745	4	3	1	28	15	54	51	86
1746	10	6	4	13	6	34	28	57
1747	12	4	6	25	11	49	46	86
1748	4	3	3	27	7	61	53	92
1749	9	9	1	31	7	70	65	110
Subtotal	79	53	32	218	88	565	490	862

Table 1 (Continued)

Year	Births	Sons	Daughters	Marriages	Settlements	Deaths	Male deaths	Total
1750	11	7	4	20	4	83	67	114
1751	16	9	10	20	10	71	61	107
1752	8	6	4	24	10	72	59	104
1753	9	6	3	27	9	62	56	98
1754	12	8	4	24	4	62	50	98
1755	13	7	6	30	4	85	71	128
1756	13	9	6	30	6	52	43	95
Subtotal	82	52	37	175	47	487	407	744
TOTAL	223	139	95	645	248	1904	1631	2772

Table 2 Births, marriages and deaths, 1757–89

Year	Births	Sons	Daughters	Marriages	Settlements	Deaths	Male deaths	Total
1757	7	4	3	37	11	74	66	118
1758	16	7	9	59	7	115	94	190
1759	10	5	5	33	5	126	93	169
Subtotal	**33**	**16**	**17**	**129**	**23**	**315**	**253**	**477**
1760	13	11	2	42	2	96	80	151
1761	10	5	6	36	3	112	87	158
1762	13	7	7	34	3	115	98	162
1763	11	6	7	41	1	144	122	196
1764	9	7	3	45	6	156	133	210
1765	4	2	2	28	2	106	89	138
1766	15	10	5	46	6	164	142	225
1767	6	5	2	46	1	170	140	222
1768	20	8	12	60	1	179	162	259
1769	10	7	5	49	2	130	109	189
Subtotal	**111**	**68**	**51**	**427**	**27**	**1372**	**1162**	**1910**
1770	12	6	5	60	2	148	132	220
1771	15	6	9	52	1	145	129	212
1772	14	6	7	72	2	163	150	249
1773	12	4	8	48	0	128	117	188
1774	10	5	5	25	2	105	87	140
1775	14	9	5	31	0	73	67	118
1776	4	1	3	34	0	87	78	125
1777	8	5	3	32	0	102	84	142
1778	6	5	1	34	1	108	92	148
1779	4	2	2	17	1	43	35	64
Subtotal	**99**	**49**	**48**	**405**	**9**	**1102**	**971**	**1606**

Table 2 (Continued)

Year	Births	Sons	Daughters	Marriages	Settlements	Deaths	Male deaths	Total
1780	10	6	4	30	0	72	60	112
1781	5	4	1	27	1	224	174	256
1782	7	4	3	41	1	155	125	203
1783	14	9	6	44	0	147	117	205
1784	6	1	5	51	0	137	111	194
1785	7	3	4	57	0	148	104	212
1786	8	5	3	42	0	167	115	217
1787	21	9	12	74	1	172	125	267
1788	8	4	4	137	1	262	175	407
1789	16	10	6	107	0	211	142	334
Subtotal	**102**	**55**	**48**	**610**	**4**	**1695**	**1248**	**2407**
TOTAL	**345**	**188**	**164**	**1571**	**63**	**4484**	**3634**	**6400**

Table 3 Births, marriages and deaths, 1789–1815

Year	Births	Sons	Daughters	Marriages	Settlements	Deaths	Male deaths	Total
1790	12	9	5	156	0	288	184	456
1791	26	13	13	152	1	296	202	474
1792	34	18	16	98	0	213	142	345
1793	31	21	10	111	0	274	190	416
1794	38	17	23	98	2	208	136	344
1795	27	18	8	87	0	213	163	327
1796	28	12	15	128	0	275	198	431
1797	26	17	11	91	0	228	147	345
1798	37	20	20	153	0	329	227	519
1799	37	26	13	80	0	368	254	485
Subtotal	**296**	**171**	**134**	**1154**	**3**	**2692**	**1843**	**4142**
1800	34	19	14	83	0	458	301	575
1801	89	44	50	104	1	321	213	514
1802	79	42	40	101	0	353	231	533
1803	88	47	45	168	0	425	298	681
1804	93	50	42	118	0	393	260	604
1805	55	32	23	64	0	404	282	523
1806	50	29	20	49	0	292	190	391
1807	65	35	33	55	1	326	199	446
1808	61	37	23	61	0	340	222	462
1809	52	30	28	52	0	334	223	438
Subtotal	**666**	**365**	**318**	**855**	**2**	**3646**	**2419**	**5167**

Table 3 (Continued)

Year	Births	Sons	Daughters	Marriages	Settlements	Deaths	Male deaths	Total
1810	30	15	18	39	1	379	248	448
1811	26	14	13	49	2	439	269	514
1812	16	9	9	35	0	229	153	280
1813	33	17	15	43	0	528	312	604
1814	31	19	12	44	0	632	438	707
1815	22	13	9	58	0	469	313	549
Subtotal	**158**	**87**	**76**	**268**	**3**	**2676**	**1733**	**3102**
TOTAL	**1120**	**536**	**452**	**2277**	**8**	**9014**	**5995**	**12411**

Note: Births of sons and daughters do not add up to the total births due to multiple births and those where no sex is given.

Appendix 2: Magazine Titles before 1731

(i) **Early English Books Online, 'EEBO'** (http://eebo.chadwyck.com /home, accessed 7.2.2011)

Methodology: a search by title keyword 'magazine' produced 96 hits in 88 records. The works below use the word 'magazine' to refer metaphorically to the book itself. The publication date given with the title is the earliest found. Later editions are noted beneath and are taken from COPAC (http://copac.ac.uk/, accessed 7.2.2011).

1. Robert Ward, *Anima'dversions of Warre; Or, A Militarie Magazine of the Truest Rules, and Ablest Instructions, for the Managing of Warre* (London, 1639).
2. Anon., *A Magazine of Scandall: Or, a Heape of Wickednesse of Two Infamous Ministers, Consorts, One Named Thomas Fowkes of Earl Soham in Suffolk, Convicted by Law for Killing a Man, and the Other Named John Lowes of Brandeston, who Hath Beene Arraigned for Witchcraft, and Convicted by Law for a Common Barrettor* (London, 1642).
3. William Bird, *The Magazine of Honour: Or, A Treatise of the Severall Degrees of the Nobility of this Kingdome with their Rights and Priviledges* (London, 1642).
4. Anon., *The Christian Souldiers Magazine of Spirituall Weapons* (London, 1644).
5. Samuel Sturmy, *The Mariners Magazine: Or Sturmy's Mathematical and Practical Arts* (London, 1679).
   Note: a 4th edition revised, corrected and enlarged by John Colson was published in 1700.
6. William Hunt, *The Gaugers Magazine* (London, 1687).

7. W. Y-Worth, *A New Treatise of Artificial Wine: Or, A Bacchean Magazine* (London, 1690).
8. W. Y-Worth, *The Britannian Magazine: Or, A New Art of Making Above Twenty Sorts of English Wines* (London, 1694).
    Note: a 3rd edition was published in 1700.
9. Edward Hatton, *The Merchant's Magazine: Or, The Trades-man's Treasury* (London, 1695).
    Note: a 12th edition was published in 1799.

(ii) English Short Title Catalogue (http://estc.bl.uk/, accessed 7.2.2011)

Methodology: as above, with publication date to 1730, produced 130 hits. Listed below are works not found in EEBO.

1. George Wilson, *Gaza Chimica: Or, A Magazine, or Store-house of Choice Chymical Medicines, Faithfully Prepared, in my Laboratory, at the Sign of Hermes Trismegistus in Bow-Lane, neer Bow-Church, in Cheapside, London* (London, 1672).
    Note: single-sheet catalogue.
2. John Smith, gent., *Profit and Pleasure United: Or, The Husbandman's Magazene, Being a Most Exact Treatise of Horses, Mares, Colts, Bulls, Oxen, Cows, Calves, Sheep, Swine, Goats, and All Other Domestick Cattle, Serviceable, Profitable, or Usefull to Man: ... Together with Easie and Plain Rules and Methods for Improving Arrable and Pasture-lands, and the Like: Improving Most Sorts of Grain to the Best Advantage, and What Is Necessary to be Observed in Sowing and Harvesting: The Management, Improvement and Preservation of Fruit-trees, Plants and Flowers: The Manner of Ordering Flax, Hemp, Saffron and Licrish: With Directions for the Increasing and Preserving of Bees, and Many Other Things of the Like Nature. To which Is Added the Art of Angling, Hunting, Hawking, and the Noble Recreation [sic] of Ringing and Making Fireworks. The Whole Elustrated with Copper Cuts* (London, 1684).
    Note: a further London edition was published in 1704 and a reprint in Boston, New England in 1718.
3. J.H., *The Magazine of War: Or, General Adjutant. In Three Parts. The First Contains the Whole Exercise of Horse, Foot and Dragoons, ... The Second of Fortification, ... The Third of Gunnery* (London, 1701).
4. John Seddon, *The Penman's Magazine: Or, A New Copy-book, of the English, French and Italian Hands, after the Best Mode; Adorn'd with about an Hundred New and Open Figures and Fancies, Never before Publish'd: After the Originals of the Late Incomparable Mr John Seddon.*

Perform'd by George Shelley Writing-master, at the Hand and Pen in Warwick-Lane, London. Supervised and Published by Thomas Read, Clerk of St Giles's in the Fields, Formerly a Scholar to the Said Mr Seddon (London, 1705).

5. Richard Hayes, *The Negociator's Magazine: Or, The Exchanges Anatomiz'd. In Two Parts. Part I. Of the Foreign Banks and Agio's; the Different Species and Denominations of their Money; the Usances and Times of their Marts or Fairs; and the Current Prices of the Exchanges for the Principal Places of Traffick in Europe; together with Great Variety of Examples in Reducing of Exchanges. Part II. Concise and Plain Instructions Relating to Bills of Exchange, Shewing, What Exchange Is; Divers Ways of Negociating; Several Forms of Bills; What Method to Take in Cases of Protests, Countermands, Letters of Credit, Securities, and Assignments in the Most Difficult and Common Occurrences of Trade. With a Large Table to the Whole* (London, 1719).

   Note: an 11th edition revised by Benjamin Webb was published in London in 1777.

6. D. Pratt, *Wits Secretary: Or, The Lovers Magazine, an Accurate and Most Compleat Academy of Wit and Mirth* (London, 1720).

7. Anon., *The Souls Magazine of Scripture Truths, Digested into an Historical Dialogue, to Inform the Ignorant, Reform the Wicked, Awake the Drowsey, and Revive Christianity by Faith and Obedience* (London, 1722).

8. Anon., *The Compleat Academy of Complements: Or, Lover's Magazine, Shewing the Whole Art of Courtship, Containing Divers Examples of Choice and Select Forms of Courtship* (London, 1729).

   Note: this was printed by and for J. Willis and T. Pettet, and Daniel Pratt and may therefore be the same work as (6.). As the only listed copy is held by the Houghton Library, Harvard University, it has not been possible to check.

9. Edward Oakley, *The Magazine of Architecture, Perspective, & Sculpture: In Five Parts* (Westminster, 1730).

   Note: a further edition was published in 1731.

Notes

Introduction

1. William Hazlitt, 'The St James's Chronicle–The Morning Chronicle [...] &c. &c.', *Edinburgh Review, or Critical Journal*, 38 (May 1823), pp. 349–78 (pp. 369–70).
2. For publishing history and historiography, see Chapter 2.
3. *GM*, 1738, title page, verso.
4. Hazlitt, 'The St James's Chronicle', p. 370.
5. Letter to Grosvenor Charles Bedford, 23.4.1804 (Revd Charles Cuthbert Southey, ed., *The Life and Correspondence of Robert Southey*, 6 vols (London, 1849–50), II, pp. 281–2).
6. See e.g. poem, *GM*, 7.1812, pp. 61–2.
7. Entry for 1.6.1828 (Sir Walter Scott, *The Journal of Sir Walter Scott, from the Original Manuscripts at Abbotsford*, 2 vols (Edinburgh, 1891), II, p. 198), quoted in James M. Kuist, 'The Gentleman's Magazine, 1754–1800: A Study of its Development as a Vehicle for the Discussion of Literature' (unpublished PhD thesis, Duke University, 1965), p. 106, where Scott's flattering comments to the editor, John Bowyer Nichols, are also recorded.
8. Charles Henry Timperley, *A Dictionary of Printers and Printing* (London, 1839), fn., p. 832. See *ODNB* for supposed super-centenarian Parr (1483–1635).
9. William Makepeace Thackeray, *Vanity Fair*, ed. J.I.M. Stewart (Harmondsworth, 1968), p. 278.
10. Kathryn Shevelow, *Women and Print Culture: The Construction of Femininity in the Early Periodical* (London, 1989).
11. For the limitations of cultural history see Dror Wahrman, 'Change and the Corporeal in Seventeenth- and Eighteenth-Century Gender History: or, Can Cultural History be Rigorous?', *Gender & History*, 20 (2008), pp. 584–602; for similar issues in gender history Penelope J. Corfield, 'History and the Challenge of Gender History', *Rethinking History*, 1(1997), pp. 241–58; Karen Harvey and Alex Shepard, 'What Have Historians Done with Masculinity? Reflections on Five Centuries of British History, circa 1550–1950', *Journal of British Studies*, 44 (2005), pp. 274–80 and Michael Roper, 'Slipping Out of View: Subjectivity and Emotion in Gender History', *History Workshop Journal*, 59 (2005), pp. 57–72.
12. Samuel Johnson, *A Dictionary of the English Language: In which the Words are Deduced from their Originals, and Illustrated in their Different Significations by Examples from the Best Writers: To which are Prefixed, a History of the Language, and an English Grammar* (London, 1755).
13. Penelope J. Corfield, 'Class by Name and Number in Eighteenth-Century Britain', *History*, 72 (1987), pp. 38–61, *Power and the Professions in Britain, 1700–1850* (London, 1995) and 'The Rivals: Landed and Other Gentlemen', in *Land and Society in Britain, 1700–1914*, ed. Negley Harte and Roland Quinault (Manchester, 1996), pp. 1–33; Henry R. French, *The Middle Sort*

of People in Provincial England 1600–1750 (Oxford, 2007); Margaret R. Hunt, *The Middling Sort: Commerce, Gender, and the Family in England, 1680–1780* (Berkeley, CA, 1996); Paul Langford, *A Polite and Commercial People: England 1727–83* (Oxford, 1998, 1st published 1989).

14. Shawn L. Maurer, *Proposing Men: Dialectics of Gender and Class in the Eighteenth-Century Periodical* (Stanford, CA, 1998), p. 3.
15. For the British Enlightenment see Roy Porter, *Enlightenment: Britain and the Creation of the Modern World* (London, 2000).
16. Leonore Davidoff and Catherine Hall, *Family Fortunes: Men and Women of the English Middle Class, 1780–1850* (London, revised edition 2002, 1st published 1987).
17. See Appendix 1.
18. William Stafford reviews a shorter time-span in 'Gentlemanly Masculinities as Represented by the Late Georgian *Gentleman's Magazine*', *History*, 93 (2008), pp. 47–68; and 'Representations of the Social Order in *The Gentleman's Magazine*, 1785-1815', *Eighteenth-Century Life*, 33 (2009), pp. 64–91.
19. Benedict Anderson, *Imagined Communities. Reflections on the Origin and Spread of Nationalism* (revised edition, 1991, 1st published London, 1983).

1   Gentlemanly Masculinity

1. Naomi Tadmor, *Family and Friends in Eighteenth-Century England: Household, Kinship, and Patronage* (Cambridge, 2001), pp. 73–102.
2. Joan Wallach Scott, *Gender and the Politics of History* (revised edition 1999, 1st published New York, 1988), p. 115.
3. See Appendix 1.
4. Joshua Scodel, *The English Poetic Epitaph: Commemoration and Conflict from Jonson to Wordsworth* (Ithaca, NY, 1991), p. 2.
5. See for example Joan Wallach Scott, 'Gender: A Useful Category of Historical Analysis', *American Historical Review*, 91 (1986), pp. 1053–75 (p. 1067) and John H. Arnold and Sean Brady, eds., *What Is Masculinity? Historical Dynamics from Antiquity to the Contemporary World* (Basingstoke, 2011), p. 1.
6. See Pierre Bourdieu, *Masculine Domination*, trans. Richard Nice (Cambridge, 2001, 1st published Paris, 1998), p. 9; Stefan Dudink, Karen Hagemann, and John Tosh, eds., *Masculinities in Politics and War: Gendering Modern History* (Manchester, 2004), 'Introduction', pp. 3–21 (pp. 3, 6); Michael S. Kimmel, *The History of Men: Essays in the History of American and British Masculinities* (New York, 2005), pp. 3–15, and Hilda L. Smith, *All Men and Both Sexes: Gender, Politics, and the False Universal in England, 1640–1832* (University Park, PA, 2002).
7. Raewyn Connell, *Masculinities* (2nd edition, Cambridge, 2005, 1st published 1995).
8. For critiques see Matthew McCormack, 'Men, "the Public" and Political History', in Matthew McCormack, ed., *Public Men: Masculinity and Politics in Modern Britain* (Basingstoke, 2007), pp. 13–32 (p. 17). Connell answers some of the criticism in R.W. Connell and James W. Messerschmidt, 'Hegemonic Masculinity. Rethinking the Concept', *Gender & Society*, 19 (2005), pp. 829–59.

9. Michael Roper and John Tosh, eds., *Manful Assertions: Masculinities in Britain since 1800* (London, 1991), p. 14. See also Antony Rowland, Emma Liggins and Eriks Uskalis, eds., *Signs of Masculinity: Men in Literature 1700 to the Present* (Amsterdam, 1998), pp. 3–36.

10. See Anna Clark, *The Struggle for the Breeches: Gender and the Making of the British Working Class* (London, 1995) and Matthew McCormack, ' "Married Men and the Fathers of Families": Fatherhood and Franchise Reform in Britain', in *Gender and Fatherhood in the Nineteenth Century*, ed. Trev Lynn Broughton and Helen Rogers (Basingstoke, 2007), pp. 43–54.

11. For the development of the conservative mindset see Don Herzog, *Poisoning the Minds of the Lower Orders* (Princeton, 1998).

12. Revd Charles Cuthbert Southey, ed., *The Life and Correspondence of Robert Southey*, 6 vols (London, 1849–50), II, pp. 281–2 and James M. Kuist, 'The *Gentleman's Magazine*, 1754–1800: A Study of its Development as a Vehicle for the Discussion of Literature' (unpublished PhD thesis, Duke University, 1965), p. 106.

13. Roy Porter, *English Society in the Eighteenth Century* (revised edition 1990, 1st published London, 1982), pp. 55, 66.

14. For accounts of early-modern masculinity see Elizabeth A. Foyster, *Manhood in Early Modern England Honour, Sex and Marriage* (London, 1999) and Alex Shepard, *Meanings of Manhood in Early Modern England* (Oxford, 2003).

15. John Locke, *Some Thoughts Concerning Education* (London, 1693).

16. For example, *GM*, 1.1800, pp. 3–4.

17. Anthony Fletcher, *Gender, Sex and Subordination in England, 1500–1800* (Yale, 1995).

18. For the rise of towns, commerce and consumption, see Peter Borsay, *The English Urban Renaissance: Culture and Society in the Provincial Town 1660–1770* (Oxford, 1989); John Brewer and Roy Porter, eds., *Consumption and the World of Goods* (London, 1993); Penelope J. Corfield, *The Impact of English Towns, 1700–1800* (Oxford, 1982); Paul Langford, *A Polite and Commercial People: England, 1727–83* (Oxford, 1998, 1st published 1989); Neil McKendrick, John Brewer, and J.H. Plumb, *The Birth of a Consumer Society: The Commercialization of Eighteenth-Century England* (London, 1983, 1st published 1982).

19. See Robert Shoemaker, 'Reforming Male Manners: Public Insult and the Decline of Violence in London, 1660–1740', in *English Masculinities 1660–1800*, ed. Tim Hitchcock and Michèle Cohen (London, 1999), pp. 133–50 (p. 138).

20. Philip Carter, *Men and the Emergence of Polite Society, Britain, 1660–1800* (Harlow, 2001).

21. Lawrence Klein, 'Politeness and the Interpretation of the British Eighteenth Century', *Historical Journal*, 45 (2002), pp. 869–98.

22. For parallel impoliteness see Helen Berry, 'Rethinking Politeness in Eighteenth-Century England: Moll King's Coffee House and the Significance of "Flash Talk": The Alexander Prize Lecture', *Transactions of the Royal Historical Society*, 6th series, XI (2001), pp. 65–81 (p. 68); Simon Dickie, *Cruelty and Laughter: Forgotten Comic Literature and the Unsentimental Eighteenth Century* (Chicago, 2011); Vic Gatrell, *City of Laughter: Sex and Satire in Eighteenth-Century London* (London, 2006).

23. George Colman and David Garrick, *The Clandestine Marriage* (London, 1765) and Frances Burney, *Evelina: or, The History of a Young Lady's Entrance into the World*, ed. Edward A. Bloom (Oxford, 2002, 1st published London, 1778).

24. John Brown, *An Estimate of the Manners and Principles of the Times* (2nd edition, London, 1757), reprinted seven times in the year of publication.

25. *GM*, 4.1757, pp. 166–71.

26. *GM*, 1.1758, pp. 20–1; Matthew McCormack, 'The New Militia: War, Politics and Gender', *Gender & History*, 19 (2007), pp. 483–500.

27. Linda Colley, *Britons: Forging the Nation 1707–1837* (paperback edition 2005, 1st published Yale, 1992), p. 101 (modified as 'slow and fitful' in Stephen Conway, *War, State, and Society in Mid-Eighteenth-Century Britain and Ireland* (Oxford, 2006), p. 193).

28. Matthew McCormack, *Independent Man. Citizenship and Gender Politics in Georgian England* (Manchester, 2005), p. 2.

29. Lisa Forman Cody, *Birthing the Nation: Sex, Science, and the Conception of Eighteenth-Century Britons* (Oxford, 2005); Thomas W. Laqueur, *Making Sex: Body and Gender from the Greeks to Freud* (Harvard, 1990) and Andrew Wells, 'Masculinity and its Other in Eighteenth-Century Racial Thought', in *Masculinity and the Other: Historical Perspectives*, ed. Heather Ellis and Jessica Meyer (Newcastle, 2009), pp. 85–113.

30. Kathleen Wilson, *The Island Race: Englishness, Empire and Gender in the Eighteenth Century* (London, 2003).

31. G.J. Barker-Benfield, *The Culture of Sensibility: Sex and Society in Eighteenth-Century Britain* (Chicago, 1992).

32. *GM*, 7.1774, pp. 319–22.

33. See Boyd Hilton, *The Age of Atonement: The Influence of Evangelicalism on Social and Economic Thought, 1785–1865* (Oxford, 1986).

34. Fletcher, *Gender, Sex and Subordination* and Michael McKeon, 'Historicizing Patriarchy: The Emergence of Gender Difference in England, 1660–1760', *Eighteenth-Century Studies*, 3 (1995), pp. 295–322.

35. Joanne Bailey, *Parenting in England, 1760–1830: Emotion, Identity, and Generation* (Oxford, 2012), p. 247. On continuities see too Henry R. French and Mark Rothery, 'Hegemonic Masculinities, 1700–1900', in *What Is Masculinity? Historical Dynamics from Antiquity to the Contemporary World*, ed. John H. Arnold and Sean Brady, pp. 139–66.

36. *A Dissertation upon Credit* (London, n.d.), quoted in James Raven, *Judging New Wealth: Popular Publishing and Responses to Commerce in England 1750–1800* (Oxford, 1992), p. 163. For middling-sort moral values see Margaret R. Hunt, *The Middling Sort: Commerce, Gender, and the Family in England, 1680–1780* (Berkeley, CA, 1996).

37. Kate Retford, *The Art of Domestic Life: Family Portraiture in Eighteenth-Century England* (New Haven, CT, 2006), pp. 230–1.

38. For the military implications of empire see Colley, *Britons*; on Wilkes, McCormack, *Independent Man*, pp. 80–103, and Kathleen Wilson, *The Sense of the People: Politics, Culture and Imperialism in England, 1715–85*, pp. 206–36.

39. Arthur Burns and Joanna Innes, eds., *Rethinking the Age of Reform: Britain 1780–1850* (Cambridge, 2003), 'Introduction', pp. 1–70; Clark, *Struggle for the Breeches*.

40. Thomas Gisborne, *An Enquiry into the Duties of the Female Sex* (London, 1797), pp. 21, 22.

41. Faramerz Dabhoiwala, *The Origins of Sex: A History of the First Sexual Revolution* (London, 2012).

42. Jürgen Habermas, *The Structural Transformation of the Public Sphere: An Inquiry into a Category of Bourgeois Society*, trans. Thomas Burger and Frederick Lawrence (Cambridge, 1989).

43. John Tosh, 'The Old Adam and the New Man: Emerging Themes in the History of English Masculinities, 1750–1850', in *Manliness and Masculinities in Nineteenth-Century Britain: Essays on Gender, Family and Empire*, ed. John Tosh (Harlow, 2005), pp. 61–82 (p. 61), and Dror Wahrman, *Imagining the Middle Class: The Political Representation of Class in Britain, c.1780–1840* (Cambridge, 1995), pp. 381–400.

44. For the salience of the public/private divide see Leonore Davidoff and Catherine Hall, *Family Fortunes: Men and Women of the English Middle Class, 1780–1850* (London, revised edition 2002, first published 1987), pp. 13–35. The hidden role of women in the public sphere is also explored in Clare Midgley, *Women Against Slavery: The British Campaigns, 1780–1870* (paperback edition 1995, 1st published London, 1992) and Kathryn Gleadle, *Borderline Citizens: Women, Gender, and Political Culture in Britain, 1815–67* (Oxford, 2009).

45. John Tosh, *A Man's Place: Masculinity and the Middle-Class Home in Victorian England* (New Haven, CT, 2007, 1st published 1999).

46. Amanda Vickery, 'Golden Age to Separate Spheres? A Review of the Categories and Chronology of English Women's History', *Historical Journal*, 36 (1993), pp. 383–414; *The Gentleman's Daughter: Women's Lives in Georgian England* (Yale, 1998), and *Behind Closed Doors: At Home in Georgian England* (Yale, 2009).

47. Benjamin Heller, 'Leisure and the Use of Domestic Space in Georgian London', *Historical Journal*, 53 (2010), pp. 623–45.

48. Heather Ellis, ' "Boys, Semi-Men and Bearded Scholars": Maturity and Manliness in Early Nineteenth-Century Oxford', in Arnold and Brady, *What is Masculinity?*, pp. 263–82 (p. 263).

49. Robert Shoemaker, *Gender in English Society 1650–1850: The Emergence of Separate Spheres?* (London, 1998), p. 318.

50. Habermas, *Public Sphere*, p. 61.

2   The History of the *Gentleman's Magazine*, 1731 to 1815

1. Publishers' terms to booksellers were usually sale-or-return or a 25 per cent fixed discount, sometimes with a middleman on 25 per cent back-to-back commission, a role F. Jefferies, Ludgate Street, undertook in the *GM*'s early days, see *GM*, 1734 title page and Anthony D. Barker, 'Edward Cave, Samuel Johnson and the *Gentleman's Magazine*' (unpublished PhD thesis, University of Oxford, 1981), p. 143.

2. *GM*, 1.1731, Preface. For prices see Jeremy Black, *The English Press in the Eighteenth Cent*ury (1991 reprint, 1st published London, 1987), p. 107 and Robert D. Mayo, *The English Novel in the Magazines, 1740–1815* (Evanston, 1962), p. 159. Mayo attributes the *GM*'s success in part to this price gap,

made possible by avoiding the halfpenny stamp payable on newspaper under the 1725 Stamp Act on the grounds that it was not news, the contents having already appeared elsewhere.

3. Anon., 'Autobiography of Sylvanus Urban', *GM*, 7.1856, p. 9, fn. 11 gives publication dates for 1731 (typically around the 5th of the next month, never later than the 7th). Some content could be typeset as the month progressed and it seems that there was initially at least a deadline of the 20th for letters and poetry (*GM*, 1.1738, p. 40, editorial note).

4. Philip Gaskell, *A New Introduction to Bibliography* (Oxford, 1972),'Paper', pp. 57–77 and R. Campbell, *The London Tradesman* (facsimile reprint 1969, 1st published London, 1747), pp. 124–5 ('Paper-maker'), 258 ('Rag-men').

5. The *Craftsman* (5 articles), *London Journal* (5), *Fog's Journal* (4), *GSJ* (4), *Weekly Register* (4), *US* (5), *Free Briton* (4), *British Journal* (2), *Daily Courant* (1) and *Read's Journal* (1).

6. *Craftsman* no. 657, 10.2.1739. For English periodical forerunners to the *GM*, see C. Lennart Carlson, *The First Magazine: A History of 'The Gentleman's Magazine* (Providence, RI, 1938), pp. 29–58 and Albert Pailler, *Edward Cave et le 'Gentleman's Magazine' (1731–54)*, 2 vols (Lille, 1975), I, pp. 13–63 and 103–26. The contents also bore some resemblance to seventeenth-century almanacs, see Keith Wrightson, *English Society 1580–1680* (London, 1982), p. 197. For the history of death notices, see Nigel Starck, *Life After Death: The Art of the Obituary* (Carlton, Vic., Australia, 2006).

7. William B. Todd, 'A Bibliographical Account of the *Gentleman's Magazine*, 1731–54', *Studies in Bibliography*, 18 (1965), pp. 81–109 (p. 82). There were up to nine reprints of some numbers, sometimes involving completely fresh typesetting and so variations in pagination, etc. There is no known original imprint of the first number.

8. The Gate was the southern entrance of the demolished medieval Priory of St John. For the early history of the woodcut see Todd, 'Bibliographical Account'. For the history of the printworks at St John's Gate, see Barker, 'Edward Cave, Samuel Johnson', pp. 1–23.

9. Andrew Oliver, ed, *The Journal of Samuel Curwen, Loyalist*, 2 vols (Harvard, 1972), I, pp. 70–1.

10. *GSJ*, no. 417, 22.12.1737 (penultimate issue). Pailler provides a list of competitors at *Edward Cave et le 'Gentleman's Magazine'*, II, pp. 669–77. The *LM* was launched in conscious imitation in 1732 by a conger of metropolitan booksellers and publishers (John Wilford, Thomas Cox, John Clarke, Charles Ackers and Thomas Astley), several of whom had been involved with the *Monthly Chronicle*, a register of books hard-hit by the *GM* launch, folding in 3.1732. It posed serious competition for five decades. See Alvin Sullivan, ed., *British Literary Magazines*, 4 vols (Westport, CT, 1983), I, pp. 202–6; Donald F. McKenzie and John C. Ross, eds., *A Ledger of Charles Ackers* (London, 1968), and *ODNB* for Wilford.

11. *GM*, 1777, Preface. The design and typography of the *LM* were superior (at the expense of content). Otherwise it was arranged in very similar fashion to the *GM*. See McKenzie and Ross, *Ledger*, p. 11, and Pailler, *Edward Cave et le 'Gentleman's Magazine'*, I, pp. 127–43.

12. Vic Gatrell, *City of Laughter: Sex and Satire in Eighteenth-Century London* (London, 2006), p. 210.

13. *GM*, 3.1733, p. 153.

14. *GM*, 1760, Preface.

15. The 1753 Preface drew attention to this novelty. The *LM*'s first illustration (a diagram of an eclipse) was also in 3.1733, p. 138. It included similar illustrations (but not in colour).

16. *GM*, 10.1737, p. 626.

17. *GM*, 11.1737, pp. 692, 694.

18. For example *GM*, 1.1751, p. 37, music for 'The Sow in the Sack. A Contre Dance' including instructions for four couples; 'Rans de Vach', *GM*, 2.1812, pp. 129–31.

19. William Snape wrote two letters to John Nichols in 1809 with a scheme for improving the magazine. The first was about 'the latter half' and the second the 'miscellaneous part' i.e. the front half of letters and essays (Bodl: MS.Eng.Lett.c.365.90–1, 92–3).

20. For a history of parliamentary reporting, see Peter D.G. Thomas, 'The Beginning of Parliamentary Reporting in Newspapers, 1768–74', *English Historical Review*, 74 (1959), pp. 623–36 and Joanna Innes, 'Legislation and Public Participation: Aspects of a Changing Relationship 1760–1830' in *The British and Their Laws*, ed. David Lemmings (Woodbridge, 2005), pp. 102–32.

21. *GM*, 1.1739, pp. 3–4 (attrib. Samuel Johnson). This was part of a wider shift from the 'scopic' to the 'repository' periodical (Karen Y. Fang, *Romantic Writing and the Empire of Signs: Periodical Culture and Post-Napoleonic Authorship* (Charlottesville, 2010)).

22. The first number (1742) was twice as long and cost one shilling. The 9th number contained an index to the continuously-paginated series which could then be bound as a single volume.

23. Francis Halliday, *Miscellanea Curiosa Mathematica* (London, 1745–55). For contemporary interest in mathematics, see Benjamin Wardaugh, *Poor Robin's Prophecies: A Curious Almanac, and the Everyday Mathematics of Georgian Britain* (Oxford, 2012).

24. From 1783 each year is generally bound in two volumes, January–June and July–December.

25. *GM*, 1.1770, pp. 3–6; 1.1784, pp. 49–64; 1.1802, pp. 65–8. See also Thomas, 'Parliamentary Reporting' and Innes, 'Legislation and Public Participation'.

26. For an account see Carlson, *First Magazine*, pp. 210–23.

27. Timperley, *Dictionary*, p. 795. The *Monthly* survived until 1844, the *Critical* (sales of 3,500 in 1797) until 1817.

28. *GM*, 1.1737, p. 60; 7.1737, p. 875.

29. Jonathan Bate, 'Parodies of Shakespeare', *Journal of Popular Culture*, 19 (1985), pp. 75–90.

30. Mayo, *English Novel*, p. 163.

31. Sullivan, *British Literary Magazines*, I, pp. 202–6, 327–30, 337–40; for fiction in periodicals see Mayo, *English Novel*, for the 'Tête à Têtes', Cindy McCreery, 'Keeping up with the *Bon Ton*: The *Tête à Tête* Series in the *Town and Country Magazine*', in *Gender in Eighteenth-Century England: Roles, Representations and Responsibilities*, ed. Hannah Barker and Elaine Chalus (London, 1997), pp. 207–29.

32. *OBP*, 21 February 1733, a17330221-1 (accessed 25.3.2011).

33. For the *Athenian Mercury*, see Helen Berry, *Gender, Society and Print Culture in Late-Stuart England: The Cultural World of the Athenian Mercury* (Aldershot,

2003); for the *Tatler* and *Spectator*, Kathryn Shevelow, *Women and Print Culture: The Construction of Femininity in the Early Periodical* (London, 1989).

34. See Pailler, *Edward Cave et le 'Gentleman's Magazine'*, I, pp. 226–33.
35. Submitted as 'Benvolio' in 1786–7 and again after the publication of James Boswell, *Life of Johnson: Together with a Journal of a Tour to the Hebrides and Johnson's Diary of a Journey into North Wales*, ed. George Birkbeck Hill, revd L.F. Powell, 6 vols (Oxford, 1934, 1st published 1791), see James M. Kuist, 'The Gentleman's Magazine, 1754–1800: A Study of its Development as a Vehicle for the Discussion of Literature' (unpublished PhD thesis, Duke University, 1965), pp. 236–9, 242–4.
36. *GM*, 1.1785, p. 15; 2.1781, p. 64; 10.1786, p. 890.
37. John Nichols, 'A Prefatory Introduction Descriptive of the Rise and Progress of the Magazine' in Samuel Ayscough and John Nichols, *General Index to the Gentleman's Magazine, 1787–1818*, 5 vols (London, 1818–21), III, pp. iii–lxxx (p. lxxi) and also published separately.
38. For immigration to London, see M. Dorothy George, *London Life in the Eighteenth Century* (Harmondsworth, 1966, 1st published London, 1925), pp. 116–57.
39. *GM*, 2.1754, pp. 55–8.
40. For references, see Bibliography.
41. Birch (1705–66, historian, biographer and Secretary to the Royal Society) was Cave's Clerkenwell neighbour and a *GM* contributor and poetry contest judge. The Cave correspondence is in BL MS: Add 4297.
42. For his admission, see G.A. Solly and others, eds., *The Rugby Register* (Rugby, 1933–57), I, p. 29.
43. *GM*, 2.1754, p. 56.
44. For the eighteenth-century Post Office see Susan E. Whyman, *The Pen and the People: English Letter Writers 1660–1800* (Oxford, 2009).
45. Raikes is noted as a bookseller in *GM*, 2.1731, p. 1 (copy in George Arents Research Library, University of Syracuse, NY). Between 1731 and 1754 of some 3,500 articles in the magazine, only 25 came from the provincial and four from the overseas press. Five of the former were from the *Gloucester Journal* (Pailler, *Edward Cave et le 'Gentleman's Magazine'*, I, fn. 2, p. 79, p. 219).
46. John Nichols, *Literary Anecdotes of the Eighteenth Century*, 9 vols (London, 1812–16), V, p. 43.
47. Barker, 'Edward Cave, Samuel Johnson', pp. 74–104 (Du Halde fiasco) and 147–80 (cotton-spinning).
48. *GM*, 12.1735, pp. 734–6.
49. Announced *GM*, 6.1738, p. 283. The *LM* reported the debates under a 'Political Club' disguise from 5.1738 ('Autobiography of Sylvanus Urban', *GM*, 11.1856, pp. 538–41, 12.1856, pp. 667–77).
50. Printed with other early letters from Johnson, *GM*, 1.1785, pp. 3–7.
51. *GM*, 6.1736, p. 360.
52. *GM*, 3.1738, p. 156; 11.1738, pp. 581–3.
53. For Johnson's parliamentary debates and politics see Medford B. Evans, 'Johnson's Debates in Parliament' (unpublished PhD thesis, Yale University, 1933).

54. For example *Rambler* essays were frequently reprinted in the magazine in the 1750s. Pailler, *Edward Cave et le 'Gentleman's Magazine'*, I, pp. 287–98 contains a summary account of sources for his involvement in the magazine. Some of Johnson's correspondence with Cave is recorded in Nichols, *Anecdotes*.

55. For a Wednesday evening literary club of the 1740s meeting at the Robin Hood, Butcher Row, Temple Bar, centred around Cave and attended by many of these contributors, where some of the magazine's poetry was composed, see C. Lennart Carlson, 'Edward Cave's Literary Club, and its Project for a Literary Review', *Philological Quarterly*, 17 (1938), pp. 115–20.

56. James Beattie, *James Beattie's London Diary, 1773*, ed. Ralph S. Walker (Aberdeen, 1946), p. 44.

57. This includes the Birch correspondence; 47 letters to Cave and one from him among other miscellaneous correspondence collected by Richard Temple-Nugent-Brydges-Chandos-Grenville, 1st Duke of Buckingham and Chandos (1776–1839), in BL: Stowe 748 VI; and a 1753 letter and manuscript notebook on navigation from a magazine reader in Maryland (BL MS: Add 4392).

58. Alternatively, Cave's assistant was an unknown 'hack-in-chief' who defected to Ilive (William Roberts, 'The *Gentleman's Magazine* and its Rivals', *Athenaeum* (1889), p. 560).

59. According to the 'Autobiography of Sylvanus Urban' (*GM*, 1.1857, p. 8), this rival was first published 3.1736 and 'continued for several months, but for how long I do not know'. Roberts, 'The *Gentleman's Magazine* and its Rivals', claims that 'odd copies came into my hands as the *Gentleman's Magazine*'. Two copies survive in the Beinecke Rare Book and Manuscript Library and the library of the University of Texas (ESTC, http://estc.bl.uk/ P2081, accessed 14.10.2013). A BL copy was destroyed in a 1941 air raid.

60. *GSJ*, no. 353, 30.9.1736.

61. *GM*, 30.9.1736, p. 4. Cave counter-alleged that Ilive, often guilty of 'intolerable remissness', had been kept on out of 'pure tenderness' (*GSJ*, no. 346, 12.8.1736). Elsewhere Ilive is described as 'disordered in his mind' (H.R. Plomer, G.H. Bushnell, and E.R.M. McClintock, *A Dictionary of the Printers and Booksellers Who Were at Work in England, Scotland and Ireland from 1726 to 1775* (Oxford, 1932), p. 136).

62. *GM*, 1735, Preface, pp. iii–iv.

63. *GM*, 1.1753, p. 18; 1.1755, pp. 12–15.

64. Publication of the *Miscellaneous Correspondence* was delayed two years after its first announcement because 'some Dissertations which we mention'd in Vol. x. p. 297 were unluckily mislaid', for example (*Miscellaneous Correspondence*, I (1742), unpaginated advertisement).

65. It was surely in honour of this family jewel that in 1736 Cave's brother William named one of his sons Urban (Solly, *Rugby Register*, I, p. 66).

66. See Boswell, *Life of Johnson*, I, p. 256, fn. 1.

67. Nichols, 'Prefatory Introduction', p. lvi. For the Newbery share see Kuist, '*Gentleman's Magazine*', pp. 354–5.

68. On antiquities at Aldfriston [Alfriston], Sussex, *GM*, 9.1767, pp. 443–4.

69. Nichols, 'Prefatory Introduction', p. lvii and *ODNB*.

70. For Lister, Bond, and Nichols' entry into the business see D. Bond, *Friendship Strikingly Exhibited in a New Light: In Letters Between Messrs D. Henry and*

J. Nichols, Managing Proprietors of the Gentleman's Magazine, and D. Bond, Late Printer of that Monthly Miscellany, with an Introductory Narrative, Notes and Observations (London, 1781), a 28-page quarto pamphlet of 11 letters between the three men outlining Bond's grievances over the handling of the changeover.

71. Richard Cave's widow Sarah died *c.* 1772 or 1776 (Nichols, *Anecdotes*, V, p. 58 and 'Additions and Corrections', p. 696). Mary died in 1811 (*GM*, 6.1811, p. 684).

72. Like Ilive, he complained of staying up all night to complete the work (Bond, *Friendship*, p. 26).

73. The printing house was moved again in 3.1820 to 25 Parliament Street, Westminster.

74. Nichols was elected to the Court of Common Council for Farringdon Without in 12.1784, losing his seat in 1786 after 'violent party collision'. He was unanimously re-elected the following year (his candidacy advertised on the *GM* wrapper for 9.1787, Bodl.: JJ) and appointed Deputy of the ward by John Wilkes, its Alderman. For the Stationers' Company, he negotiated with workers during trade unrest in 1785 and served as Master in 1804. In the 1818 general election, he voted in the notoriously rowdy and radical constituency of Westminster as one of 2,204 'plumpers' who used only one of their two votes for the losing conservative candidate favoured by the leisured classes and higher professions, Sir Murray Maxwell. See entry in Stephen, Sir Leslie, ed., *Dictionary of National Biography*, 63 vols (London, 1885–1903), XLI, pp. 2–5; *Poll Book* [...] *for the City and Liberty of Westminster, June 18, to July 4, 1818* (facsimile reprint, Exeter, 1996, 1st published London, 1818), p. 189, and R.G. Thorne, *The House of Commons, 1790–1820*, 5 vols (London, 1986), II, p. 277. Henry's share in the magazine passed to his widow and remained in that family in the nineteenth century (Nichols, 'Prefatory Introduction', p. lxxii).

75. Nichols, 'Prefatory Introduction', p. lxxiii.

76. *GM* wrapper 2.1813.

77. *GM*, 7.1765, p. 335, dedicated to old school-friend and fellow Bowyer apprentice, (Revd) William Tooke (1744–1820).

78. *GM*, Preface and 9.1784, pp. 653–5.

79. *GM*, 1788, Preface.

80. *GM*, 1.1804, p. 64. For the York Minster reference I thank Robert Welham of Saffron Walden and the staff of York Minster. The obituary is at *GM*, 5.1812, pp. 492–3.

81. For example, the notice for Mr William Temple of Trowbridge included a eulogy attributed to the *Daily Gazetteer* (*GM*, 7.1736, p. 423). This started its life in the *Gloucester Journal* for 29.6.1736, and was composed by his son, also William (*ODNB*). In *GM*, 7.1809 the obituary of fat man Daniel Lambert was taken from the *Oxford Herald* and William Perfect MD from the *Stamford Mercury* (pp. 681–3, 684–5). There are many examples of reader-submitted obituaries in the Nichols correspondence at the Bodleian Library.

82. *GM*, 7.1798, p. 622.

83. *GM*, 12.1790, p. 1147, editorial note to obituary of James Bowdoin of Boston, New England.

84. Peter Pindar (pseudonym of John Wolcott), *A Benevolent Epistle to Sylvanus Urban* (London, 1790).

85. Starck, *Life After Death*, p. 117.
86. See *GM*, 7.1739, p. 384; 1.1787, pp. 89–90; 7.1788, p. 659.
87. *GM*, 1.1783, pp. 92–3.
88. For the fire, see *GM*, 2.1808, pp. 99–100.
89. James M. Kuist, *The Nichols File of the Gentleman's Magazine: Attributions of Authorship and Other Documentation in Editorial Papers at the Folger Library* (Madison, WI, 1982) catalogues this material. The Folger also holds the Nichols Manuscript Collection of almost 6,000 documents, mainly mid-nineteenth-century, examined in Penelope Peoples, 'The Folger Nichols Manuscript Collection: A Description and Analysis' (unpublished PhD thesis, University of Wisconsin-Milwaukee, 1980). Other collections of Nichols material (not all related to the *GM*) are held by the Bodleian, British and John Rylands Libraries in Britain, and Columbia and Yale in the USA. Dr Julian Pooley's work-in-progress, The Nichols Archive Project, includes the Nichols Archive Database of the family's correspondence and collected papers from John Nichols to the death of his grandson, John Gough Nichols, in 1873 (see http://www.le.ac.uk/el/resources/nichols/index.html).
90. For nineteenth-century ownership, see account by A.H. Bullen on his appointment as editor, *GM*, 2.1906, pp. 1–2 and Kuist, *Nichols File*, pp. 3–5. Kuist refers to the magazine remaining in print to 9.1922. This was merely as a four-page 'token registration issue': National Library of Scotland catalogue: http://copac.ac.uk/search?rn=2&date=1907-1922&lib=National+Library+of+Scotland&mtl=Journals+%26+other+periodicals&ti (accessed 20.3.2011).
91. For example, Black, *English Press*; John Feather, *The Provincial Book Trade in Eighteenth-Century England* (Cambridge, 1985), and James Raven, *Publishing Business in Eighteenth-Century England* (Woodbridge, 2014).
92. It is available on the British Periodicals database at http://search.proquest.com.ezproxy.lib.bbk.ac.uk/britishperiodicals/index?accountid=8629.
93. Emily Lorraine De Montluzin, *Daily Life in Georgian England as Reported in the Gentleman's Magazine* (New York, 2002). On duelling see Donna T. Andrew, 'The Code of Honour and its Critics: The Opposition to Duelling in England, 1700–1850', *Social History*, 5 (1980), pp. 409–34, on suicide Michael MacDonald and Terence R. Murphy, *Sleepless Souls: Suicide in Early Modern England* (Oxford, 1990), and on sexuality Julie Peakman, *Lascivious Bodies: A Sexual History of the Eighteenth Century* (London, 1988).
94. See for example Barker, 'Edward Cave, Samuel Johnson'; Evans, 'Johnson's Debates in Parliament'; Arthur Sherbo, *Letters to Mr Urban of the Gentleman's Magazine, 1751–1811* (New York, 1997) and *Studies in the Johnson Circle* (West Cornwall, CT, 1988).
95. Calvin Daniel Yost, *The Poetry of the Gentleman's Magazine: A Study in Eighteenth-Century Literary Taste* (Philadelphia, 1936).
96. Ibid., p. 139.
97. Kuist, '*Gentleman's Magazine*'. In addition to *The Nichols File*, Kuist's work includes ' "What, Does she still adorn this dreary scene?" Nichols' Problems with Obituary Notices in the *Gentleman's Magazine*', *Eighteenth-Century Life*, 4 (1978), pp. 76–8 and 'A Collaboration in Learning: The *Gentleman's*

Magazine and its Ingenious Contributors', *Studies in Bibliography*, 44 (1991), pp. 302–17.

98. Kuist, *'Gentleman's Magazine'*, p. 26.
99. Ibid., pp. 115, 143, 272.
100. Carlson, *First Magazine*, pp. 9–12.
101. Ibid., pp. 29–58. Baptist minister and historian Isaac Kimber (1692–1755) was *LM* editor 1732–55.
102. Carlson, *First Magazine*, pp. 57–8 and 239–42.
103. Pailler, *Edward Cave et le 'Gentleman's Magazine'* and Titia Ram, *Magnitude in Marginality: Edward Cave and the 'Gentleman's Magazine', 1731–1754*, translated from Dutch by the author (Utrecht, 1999).
104. Pailler tabulates contents in II; readership is considered in I, pp. 451–66. For the contribution to middle-class culture see I, pp. 521–30, especially p. 529.
105. Ram, *Magnitude*, pp. 60, 169.
106. Ibid., pp. vi–vii.
107. John Brewer, *The Pleasures of the Imagination: English Culture in the Eighteenth Century* (London, 1997), p. 445 (*re* contemporary condemnation of Gay's *Beggars' Opera*).
108. Jean E. Hunter, 'The Eighteenth-Century Englishwoman: According to the *Gentleman's Magazine*' in *Woman in the Eighteenth Century and Other Essays*, ed. Paul Fritz and Richard Morton (Toronto, 1976), pp. 73–88.
109. 'Laymen, Doctors and Medical Knowledge in the Eighteenth Century: The Evidence of the *Gentleman's Magazine*' in Roy Porter, ed., *Patients and Practitioners: Lay Perceptions of Medicine in Pre-industrial Society* (Cambridge, 1985), pp. 283–314; and 'Lay Medical Knowledge in the Eighteenth Century: The Evidence of the *Gentleman's Magazine*', *Medical History*, 29 (1985), pp. 138–68.
110. Porter, 'Lay Medical Knowledge', pp. 163, 164.
111. Ibid., p. 165.
112. Emily Lorraine De Montluzin, 'Quicksilver Ladies, Odes to Turds, and Three-Seater Privies: The Scatological Underside of the *Gentleman's Magazine*', *ANQ*, 21 (2008), pp. 24–35.
113. William Stafford, 'Gentlemanly Masculinities as Represented by the Late Georgian *Gentleman's Magazine*', *History*, 93 (2008), pp. 47–68 and 'Representations of the Social Order in *The Gentleman's Magazine*, 1785–1815', *Eighteenth-Century Life*, 33 (2009), pp. 64–91.
114. Stafford, 'Social Order', p. 65.
115. Ibid., p. 87.
116. Stafford, 'Gentlemanly Masculinities', pp. 67–8.

3 Readers and Contributors

1. C. Lennart Carlson, *The First Magazine: A History of the Gentleman's Magazine* (Providence, RI, 1938), p. 239.
2. Richard D. Altick, *The English Common Reader: A Social History of the Mass Reading Public, 1800–1900* (Chicago, 1957), p. 49.
3. Samuel Johnson, *The Works of Samuel Johnson LLD*, 11 vols (London, 1787), II, p. 134; James Lackington, *Memoirs of the First Forty-Five Years of the*

Life of James Lackington (London, 1791), pp. 254–5, and *The Confessions of J. Lackington in a Series of Letters to a Friend: To Which Are Added Two Letters on the Bad Consequences of Having Daughters Educated at Boarding-schools* (2nd edition, London, 1804), p. 175.

4. For a survey of methodologies, see David Cressy, *Literacy and the Social Order: Reading and Writing in Tudor and Stuart England* (Cambridge, 1980), pp. 42–61.

5. Alvin B. Kernan, *Printing Technology, Letters and Samuel Johnson* (Princeton, 1987), pp. 60–1; John Feather, *The Provincial Book Trade in Eighteenth-Century England* (Cambridge, 1985); William St Clair, *The Reading Nation in the Romantic Period* (Cambridge, 2004); Jeremy Black, *The English Press in the Eighteenth Century* (1991 reprint, 1st published London, 1987), p. 14; and G.A. Cranfield, *The Development of the Provincial Newspaper, 1700–60* (Oxford, 1962), pp. 19–21.

6. Margaret Spufford, *Small Books and Pleasant Histories: Popular Fiction and its Readership in Seventeenth-Century England* (Cambridge, 1985) and 'First Steps in Literacy: The Reading and Writing Experiences of the Humblest Seventeenth-Century Spiritual Autobiographers', in *Literacy and Historical Development*, ed. Harvey J. Graff (Carbondale, S. Illinois, 2007), pp. 207–37; Susan E. Whyman, *The Pen and the People: English Letter Writers, 1660–1800* (Oxford, 2009), e.g. pp. 96–104, study of Jedediah and Elizabeth Strutt of Derbyshire.

7. The classic work is R.S. Schofield, 'The Measurement of Literacy in Pre-Industrial England', in *Literacy in Traditional Societies*, ed. Jack Goody (Cambridge, 1968), pp. 311–25; and 'Dimensions of Illiteracy, 1750–1850', *Explorations in Economic History*, 10 (1973), pp. 437–54. In Ireland and Scotland, the trajectory was similar to that in comparable areas of England (Rab Houston, 'The Literacy Myth? Illiteracy in Scotland, 1630–1760', in Graff, *Literacy*, pp. 183–206 and Toby Barnard, 'Reading in Eighteenth-Century Ireland: Public and Private Pleasures', in *The Experience of Reading: Irish Historical Perspectives*, eds. Bernadette Cunningham and Máire Kennedy (Dublin, 1999), pp. 60–77). In colonial America, high levels of literacy were distributed more evenly than in Europe (Farley Grubb, 'Growth of Literacy in Colonial America: Longitudinal Patterns, Economic Models, and the Direction of Future Research', in *Literacy and Historical Development*, ed. Harvey J. Graff (Carbondale, S. Illinois, 2007), pp. 272–98).

8. The balance were men like Dudley Ryder's brother's tenant, John Dear, who was 'not able to write nor read and yet keeps a very exact account of his money and what he pays and receives by his memory only', William Matthews, ed., *The Diary of Dudley Ryder, 1715–16* (London, 1939), pp. 165–6. Women are generally treated as an undifferentiated group, rarely analysed by class or occupation (an interesting reflection on our own attitudes to gender).

9. John Nichols, *Literary Anecdotes of the Eighteenth Century*, 9 vols (London, 1812–16), V, p. 6 (fn.).

10. *GM*, 1748, Preface.

11. Sir John Hawkins, *The Life of Samuel Johnson, LLD*, ed. Bertram H. Davis (London, 1962, 1st published 1787), p. 57.

12. 25.4.1778, James Boswell, *Life of Johnson: Together with a Journal of a Tour to the Hebrides and Johnson's Diary of a Journey into North Wales*, ed. George Birkbeck Hill, revd L.F. Powell, 6 vols (Oxford, 1934, 1st published 1791), III, p. 322.

13. James Raven, *Judging New Wealth: Popular Publishing and Responses to Commerce in England, 1750–1800* (Oxford, 1992), pp. 35–6.

14. John Byrom, *The Private Journal and Literary Remains of John Byrom*, ed. Richard Parkinson, 4 vols (Manchester, 1854–7), III, p. 213.

15. Carlson, *First Magazine*, p. 63, fn. 6.

16. William B. Todd, 'A Bibliographical Account of the Gentleman's Magazine, 1731–54', *Studies in Bibliography*, 18 (1965), pp. 81–109', p. 85.

17. Donald F. McKenzie and John C. Ross, *A Ledger of Charles Ackers* (London, 1968), p. 11.

18. Andrew Oliver, ed., *Journal of Samuel Curwen, Loyalist*, 2 vols (Harvard, 1972), I, pp. 70–71.

19. Todd, 'Bibliographical Account', p. 81; J. Nichols, 'A Prefatory Introduction Descriptive of the Rise and Progress of the Magazine, with Anecdotes of the Projector and his Early Associates' in Samuel Ayscough and John Nichols, *General Index to the Gentleman's Magazine, 1787–1818*, 5 vols (London, 1818–21), III', p. lix and *GM* wrapper advertisement, 2.1783 (Bodl.: JJ).

20. *GM*, 2.1797, pp. 95–6 and St Clair, *Reading Nation*, p. 30.

21. Paul Romney, ed., *The Diary of Charles Fothergill 1805: An Itinerary to York, Flamborough and the North-Western Dales of Yorkshire* (Leeds, 1984), pp. 203, 222. The articles appeared in *GM*, 12.1787, p. 1059 and 7.1790, p. 617.

22. *GM*, 1.1815, pp. 4–6 referring to letter from 'J.G.', 6.1759, p. 25.

23. *Spectator*, no. 10, 12.3.1711.

24. Pailler arbitrarily settles for a readership of 30,000–40,000 (4–5 per copy) in the Cave era (Albert Pailler, *Edward Cave et le 'Gentleman's Magazine' 1731–54*, 2 vols (Lille, 1975), I, p. 459).

25. For places of reading see James Raven, Helen Small, and Naomi Tadmor, eds., *The Practice and Representation of Reading in England* (Cambridge, 1996), p. 12.

26. *GM*, 7.1761, p. 305; 7.1800, pp. 610–11; 1.1801, pp. 12–14 and 7.1802, pp. 596–7. For coffeehouse libraries, see Paul Kaufman, *Libraries and their Users: Collected Papers in Library History* (London, 1969), and James Raven, 'From Promotion to Proscription: Arrangements for Reading and Eighteenth-Century Libraries', in Raven, Small, and Tadmor, *Practice and Representation of Reading*, pp. 175–201

27. *GM*, 1.1802, pp. 39–40.

28. 'Here we never fail to be entertained, not only with the chat of the day, but with the news papers, the magazines, and every new publication' (*Lady's Magazine*, 3.10.1773, p. 443, quoted in Jan S. Fergus, *Provincial Readers in Eighteenth-Century England* (Oxford, 2006), p. 27).

29. *GM*, 12.1774, pp. 561–2.

30. Paul Kaufman, 'Readers and their Reading in Eighteenth-Century Lichfield', *The Library*, 5th series, 28 (1973), pp. 105–15 (p. 110).

31. Dissenting Academies Online, http://vls.english.qmul.ac.uk/cgi-bin/koha/opac-detail.pl?biblionumber=2167 (accessed 14.5.2012).

32. Kaufman, *Libraries and their Users*, p. 22.

33. Paul Kaufman, 'A Bookseller's Record of Eighteenth-Century Book-Clubs', *The Library*, 5th series, 15 (1960), pp. 278–87 (p. 283).
34. MSS inscription 'Jun Com Room Corpus', *GM* wrapper 8.1794 (Bodl.: JJ). Oxford is more likely than Corpus Christi Cambridge, as John Johnson, the creator of this collection, was printer to Oxford University.
35. Paul Kaufman, 'The Community Library: A Chapter in English Social History', *Transactions of the American Philosophical Society*, NS 57 (1967), pp. 1–67 (pp. 54–5).
36. *GM*, 1766 Preface.
37. NPG: D13653.
38. For group reading aloud, see Naomi Tadmor, ' "In the even my wife read to me": Women, Reading and Household Life in the Eighteenth Century', in *The Practice and Representation of Reading in England*, ed. James Raven, Helen Small, and Naomi Tadmor (Cambridge, 1996), pp. 162–7.
39. Letter, Percy to John Nichols, 19.10.1808 (John Nichols, *Illustrations of the Literary History of the Eighteenth Century*, 8 vols (London, 1817–58), VI, p. 590).
40. *GM*, 2.1797, pp. 95–6.
41. *GM*, 11.1737, p. 697 (original enigma published October, p. 628).
42. *GM*, 8.1746, p. 435.
43. Letter to Edward Cave, 25.11.1735, BL: Stowe 748, Miscellaneous Correspondence, f. 143.
44. John Baker, *The Diary of John Baker: Being Extracts therefrom, Transcribed and Edited with an Introduction and Notes by Philip C. Yorke: A Record of Life, Family History and Society, 1751–78, in England (Mostly in Sussex and London) and the Leeward Islands, and of Two Travels Abroad*, ed. Philip C. Yorke (London, 1931).
45. Bodl.: MS.Eng.Lett.b.11.16.
46. Henry Fielding, *Miscellanies*, ed. Hugh Amory, 3 vols (Oxford, 1997), III, p. 109.
47. *GM*, 9.1809, 'Index Indicatorius', p. 852.
48. Revd Samuel Pegge (Anglican minister and antiquarian, 1704–96), himself hiding behind the initials 'L.E.', *GM*, 1792, Supplement, pp. 1195–6.
49. Robert J. Griffin, ed., *The Faces of Anonymity: Anonymous and Pseudonymous Publication from the Sixteenth to the Twentieth Century* (Basingstoke, 2003), pp. 1–18.
50. G.J. Barker-Benfield, *The Culture of Sensibility: Sex and Society in Eighteenth-Century Britain* (Chicago, 1992), p.162.
51. Letter, 18.3.1799, Bodl.: MS.Eng.Lett.b.12.47.
52. James M. Kuist, *The Nichols File of the Gentleman's Magazine: Attributions of Authorship and Other Documentation in Editorial Papers at the Folger Library* (Madison, WI, 1982), p. 20.
53. *GM*, 1.1778, pp. 21–2.
54. Nichols, 'Prefatory Introduction', pp. lxxiv–lxxviii.
55. Kuist, *Nichols File*, pp. 18, 19.
56. Emily Lorraine De Montluzin, *Attributions of Authorship in the Gentleman's Magazine, 1731–1868: An Electronic Union List* http://etext.virginia.edu/bsuva/gm2/index.html, 'Introduction' (accessed 19.4.2011). There are 16,371 identifications for 1731–1820 (averaging 183 pa), the incidence

rising during the Nichols years of better record-keeping (1783–1856). The incidence is also above the annual average (at 1,297) in the first decade as authors of press excerpts are included.

57. *GM*, 12.1765, pp. 579–80; 1.1766, p. 13; 7.1766, pp. 343–4.
58. *ODNB*, citing *Letters of Anna Seward*, ed. A. Constable, 6 vols (Edinburgh, 1811), III, p. 352.
59. Helen Berry, *Gender, Society and Print Culture in Late-Stuart England: The Cultural World of the Athenian Mercury* (Aldershot, 2003), pp. 71–4.
60. 'Eusebia' wrote on the Jewish Burial Ground at Mile End, London in *GM*, 2.1795, pp. 98–9, for example. For Thicknesse/'Polyxena' see De Montluzin, *Attributions of Authorship*.
61. See Kuist, *Nichols File*, pp. 174–95.
62. An example from the many calendared in NAD is letter, 4.6.1809, from antiquary Philip Bliss (1787–1857) who had seen Nichols' *Letters on Various Subjects to and from William Nicholson* (1809) mentioned on the magazine cover (Yale University Library: Osborne Family Correspondence, Box 2, NAD 4779).
63. *GM*, 7.1799, p. 571.
64. *GM* wrapper, 2.1813 (Bodl., JJ).
65. There are 131 *GM* wrappers from 5.1740 to 1815, Supplement in the John Johnson Collection of Printed Ephemera in the Bodleian Library, Oxford. The Folger editorial volumes include wrappers for most numbers from 1783 (Kuist, *Nichols File*, pp. vii–viii) but time and cost have so far precluded their examination. There are only 9 *LM* wrappers for 1732 to 1785 in Bodl.: JJ., making comparison impossible.
66. *GM*, 7.1736 (Trinity College Library, Cambridge, RW.40.34). Todd, 'Bibliographical Account', fn. 8 mentions a copy of 6.1752 at the Boston Public Library. Enquiries there have drawn a blank.
67. Titia Ram, *Magnitude in Marginality: Edward Cave and the 'Gentleman's Magazine', 1731–54*, trans. from Dutch by the author (Utrecht, 1999), pp. 71–9 and App. B, pp. 539–605 (short title listing by wrapper but with some omissions). Ram's study covered the 39 wrappers (miscounted as 40) for 5.1740 to 12.1748 in the John Johnson Collection, ? of the total for these years (miscalculated as 45 per cent). Because of these inaccuracies, these wrappers have been re-examined. As all bar one are in Bodl., JJ they are henceforth cited by date alone.
68. William Stafford, 'Representations of the Social Order in *The Gentleman's Magazine*, 1785–1815', *Eighteenth-Century Life*, 33 (2009), pp. 64–91', p. 66 and Jon P. Klancher, *The Making of English Reading Audiences, 1790–1832* (Madison, WI, 1987), p.24.
69. Other names on Bodl., JJ wrappers are Revd David Evans of Llanerfyl, Mr?Hyman, Mr David Good or Gooch, Mr William William [*sic*] Rug. 17–, Geo. Adams, Mr Bawden and N. Clarke. 'Thornborough' is inscribed on the wrapper of the 7.1736 number held at Trinity College Library, Cambridge.
70. Trinity College Library, Cambridge, shelfmark RW.40.35.
71. W.S. Lewis, ed., *The Yale Edition of Horace Walpole's Correspondence*, 48 vols (New Haven, CT, 1937–83), index references, XLV, pp. 1064–5.
72. *GM*, 2.1732, title page (see Todd, 'Bibliographical Account', p. 84).

73. *GM*, 1.1733, p. 40. For the royal paper copies to *c.*1749, see Anthony D. Barker, 'Edward Cave, Samuel Johnson and the Gentleman's Magazine' (unpublished PhD thesis, University of Oxford, 1981), p. 37.

74. See Penelope J. Corfield, 'Class by Name and Number in Eighteenth-Century Britain', *History*, 72 (1987), pp. 38–61, for contemporary discourse.

75. Defoe, for example, praised the 'middle station' for its industry but censured inappropriate ambition for the rank of gentleman: *The Compleat English Tradesman* (2nd edition, London, 1727), pp. 60, 106.

76. See Henry R. French, 'The Search for the "Middle Sort of People" in England, 1600–1800', *Historical Journal*, 43 (2000), pp. 277–93.

77. Lorna Weatherill, *Consumer Behaviour and Material Culture in Britain, 1660–1760* (2nd edition, London, 1996, 1st published 1988), p. 98; Peter Earle, *The Making of the English Middle Class: Business, Society and Family Life in London, 1660–1730* (London, 1989), pp. 14–15; John Brewer in Neil McKendrick, John Brewer and J.H. Plumb, *Birth of a Consumer Society: The Commercialization of Eighteenth-Century England* (London, 1983, 1st published 1982), p. 197; Jonathan Barry, 'Introduction', in *The Middling Sort of People. Culture, Society and Politics in England, 1550–1800*, ed. Jonathan Barry and Christopher Brooks (Basingstoke, 1994), pp. 1–27 (p. 2) and Margaret R. Hunt, *The Middling Sort: Commerce, Gender, and the Family in England, 1680–1780* (Berkeley, CA, 1996), p. 209. For the development of the professions as 'key contributors to the growing prestige of the middle class' see Penelope J. Corfield, *Power and the Professions in Britain, 1700–1850* (London, 1995), p. 237.

78. French, 'Search for the "Middle Sort" ', pp. 286–91 and Hunt, *Middling Sort*. See also Barry and Brooks, *Middling Sort*, Jan de Vries, *The Industrious Revolution: Consumer Behavior and the Household Economy, 1650 to the Present* (Cambridge, 2008), p. 17 and H.T. Dickinson, *The Politics of the People in Eighteenth-Century Britain* (Basingstoke, 1995).

79. Penelope J. Corfield, 'The Rivals: Landed and Other Gentlemen', in *Land and Society in Britain, 1700–1914*, ed. Negley Harte and Roland Quinault (Manchester, 1996), pp. 1–33', p. 2.

80. Samuel Johnson, *A Dictionary of the English Language: In which the Words are Deduced from their Originals, and Illustrated in their Different Significations by Examples from the Best Writers: To which are Prefixed, a History of the Language, and an English Grammar* (London, 1755).

81. Corfield, 'Rivals', p. 10.

82. Daniel Defoe, *The Compleat English Gentleman*, ed. Karl D. Bülbring (London, 1890), p. 4. Unpublished before 1890, this reflects thinking on gentlemanliness, but did not circulate widely. Its overarching theme is the need to improve the education of 'born' gentlemen ('liberal' was more-or-less synonymous with 'gentlemanly' (Johnson, *Dictionary*)). For the permeability of gentlemanly status pre-eighteenth century, see Keith Wrightson, *English Society, 1580–1680* (London, 1982) pp. 17–38.

83. Linda Colley, *The Ordeal of Elizabeth Marsh: A Woman in World History* (London, 2007), p. 23.

84. *GM*, 8.1745, pp. 415–16.

85. Ram, *Magnitude*, pp. 89–90.

86. Pailler, *Edward Cave et le 'Gentleman's Magazine'*, I, pp. 460–1.

87. Examples include Benjamin Don of Bideford (1729–98), who kept a math-
    ematical school founded by his father, and corresponded frequently on
    mathematical and astronomical subjects, and 'Chirurgus', *GM*, 12.1787,
    p. 1044.
88. Stafford, 'Social Order', pp. 72–4.
89. C.D. Linnell, ed., *The Diary of Benjamin Rogers, Rector of Carlton, 1720–71*
    (Streatley, 1950); L.G. Mitchell, ed., *The Purefoy Letters 1735–53* (London,
    1973), no. 165; William Hutton, *The Life of William Hutton, FASS* (reprint
    edition, 1998, 1st published London, 1816), p. 30; *ODNB* entry for Bisset;
    Stephen M. Colclough, 'Procuring Books and Consuming Texts: The Read-
    ing Experience of a Sheffield Apprentice, 1798', *Book History*, 3 (2000),
    pp. 21–44 (p. 31), and *Diary of Charles Fothergill*.
90. Jean Paul Bignon, *The Adventures of Abdallah* (London, 1729), pp. iii–iv,
    discussed in Barker, 'Edward Cave, Samuel Johnson', p. 23.
91. *GM*, 1735, Preface, p. iv.
92. *GSJ*, no. 168, 15.3.1733, p. 1 (dating the change to late 1731). See also Todd,
    'Bibliographical Account', p. 82.
93. Johnson, *Dictionary*. Compare the entry 20 years previously in N. Bailey,
    *Dictionarium Britannicum: Or, A More Compleat Universal Etymological Dic-
    tionary than any Extant* (London, 1736): 'MAGAZINE [...] a publick store-
    house; but it is most commonly used to signify a place where all sorts of
    warlike stores are kept [...]'.
94. This is very briefly alluded to in Ram, *Magnitude*, p. 4.
95. Appendix 2, 'Magazine Titles before 1731'.
96. For the genre see Natasha Glaisyer, *The Culture of Commerce in England,
    1660–1720* (Woodbridge, 2006), pp.100–42.
97. Edward Hatton, *The Merchant's Magazine: Or, Trades Man's Treasury* (6th edi-
    tion, London, 1712). Hatton also published ready reckoners and practical
    books on arithmetic and accounting for shopkeepers and traders. Bridget
    Cherry, 'Edward Hatton's New View of London', *Architectural History*, 44
    (2001), pp. 96–105 has a brief biography (pp. 100–2).
98. For 'the modern fact', a construct of accounting gendered as male, see Mary
    Poovey, 'Accommodating Merchants: Accounting, Civility, and the Natural
    Laws of Gender', *Differences: A Journal of Feminist Studies*, 8 (1996), pp. 1–20
    and *A History of the Modern Fact: Problems of Knowledge in the Sciences of
    Wealth and Society* (Chicago, 1998).
99. *GM*, 3.1731, pp. 112, 121–2, 133–4.
100. For following stock prices, see Miles Ogborn, *Indian Ink: Script and Print in
    the Making of the English East India Company* (Chicago, 2007), pp. 157–97.
    Frances Burney, *Evelina: or, The History of a Young Lady's Entrance into the
    World*, ed. Edward A. Bloom (Oxford, 2002, 1st published London, 1778),
    p. 91 depicts it as a comically middling-sort preoccupation: Mr Branghton,
    proprietor of a silversmith's shop in Snow Hill, Holborn, declared him-
    self unaware of the published prices of opera tickets 'The price of stocks is
    enough for me to see after'. For eighteenth-century bankruptcy, see Julian
    Hoppit, *Risk and Failure in English Business 1700–1800* (Cambridge, 1987).
101. Altick, *Common Reader*, pp. 45–6.
102. The predominance of books is in part due to the use of the wrappers to
    advertise the various owners' catalogues.

103. *GM* wrapper, 5.1740.
104. *GM* wrappers, 6.1742, 6.1744, 2.1746; 11.1742, 8.1743; 6.1742, 11.1744.
105. Some non-book advertisements were also for products sold by those involved with the magazine, notably Newbery's medicines.
106. Kuist, *Nichols File*, pp. 174–95.
107. For subject categories see Kaufman, 'Community Library', pp. 11–13.
108. *GM* wrapper, 6.1765; school-books included John Coleridge's *Sententiae Excerptae*, 8.1759 and Chambaud's *Dialogues*, 10.1776; 9. 1774.
109. 10.1774, 9.1779 and 8.1807.
110. Anon., *The Economist: Shewing in a Variety of Estimates, from Fourscore Pounds a Year to upwards of 800l., How a Family May Live with Frugality, for a Little Money* (15th edition, London, 1781).
111. Hunt, *Middling Sort*, pp. 216–8.
112. John Thomas Smith, *A Book for a Rainy Day* (1845), p. 74.
113. Jonathan Rose, 'Rereading the English Common Reader: A Preface to a History of Audiences', *Journal of the History of Ideas*, 53 (1992), pp. 47–70.
114. Pailler, *Edward Cave et le 'Gentleman's Magazine'*, I, p. 462.
115. 1.1794, p. 47.
116. 'Philalethes' (Charles Leslie), *A View of the Times* (London, 1750), cited in Peter de Bolla, *The Discourse of the Sublime: Readings in History, Aesthetics and the Subject* (Oxford, 1989), p. 252.
117. Colclough, 'Procuring Books', p. 24. See also Vic Gatrell, *City of Laughter: Sex and Satire in Eighteenth-Century London* (London, 2006), p. 235 on printshop 'gawpers'.
118. Fergus, *Provincial Readers*, p. 27. In Norfolk, Parson Woodforde's papers were delivered weekly with the meat by his butcher (John Beresford, ed., *The Diary of a Country Parson: The Reverend James Woodforde*, 5 vols (Oxford, 1924–31), V, p. 171).
119. They were for 1742–4, Hutton, *Life*, pp. 30, 32–3.
120. *OBP*, trial of John Bates, t18100606–66, 6 June 1810 (accessed 31.3.2014).
121. PC1/1/17, NAD 2239.
122. For this practice, see Thomas Holcroft, *Memoirs of the Late Thomas Holcroft, Written by Himself, and Continued to the Time of his Death, from his Diary, Notes, and Other Papers*, ed. William Hazlitt (1852 reprint, 1st published London, 1816), p. 52.
123. *GM*, 1.1766, p. 47; *OBP*, trial of William Weston, t18280410–12, 10 April 1828 (accessed 31.3.2014).
124. *GM*, 7.1761, p. 296.
125. *GM*, 7.1755, pp. 296–297.
126. Letter, 1.1.1797, Society of Antiquaries MS: 447/3 ff. 448–9, NAD 8260. The 'Life' was in fact concluded in the Supplement.
127. Written in 1728, circulated in manuscript for many years, the epitaph was not used on his tombstone (*ODNB*).
128. Tim Hitchcock, *Down and Out in Eighteenth-Century London* (London, 2004), p. 53.
129. *GM*, 1785, Preface, p. vi.
130. Almost certainly the reason why only one copy of the magazine in its original wrapper survives. For uses of waste paper see: 'Adventures of a Quire of Paper', *LM*, 10.1779, pp. 450–1; quote from *Northampton Mercury*

(23.7.1722) in Black, *English Press*, p. 18; Spufford, *Small Books*, p. 49; St Clair, *Reading Nation*, pp. 26–7; *GM*, 1752, Supplement, p. 612.

131. There is no provenance for the Bodl., JJ wrappers, but the runs of manuscript names on some suggest bookbinders as the source.

132. *GM*, 1735, Preface.

133. One reason for the *GM*'s financial success under Cave was the minimization of remaindered copies sold as waste (*GM*, 1.1748, p. 8).

134. Samuel Johnson, *The Idler*, 2 vols, no. 26, (London, 1771) 14.10.1758.

135. Phrases from *GM*, 12.1777, letters from 'M.E.', p. 568 and 'Veritatis Amicus' pp. 568–9.

136. For Seward, see *ODNB*. Many educated Scots were less-versed in Classical languages than their English counterparts. James Boswell was 'chary of classical quotations and allusions in his correspondence', familiar with the major Latin authors but not fluent in Greek beyond matching a passage to the English translation ('Boswell's Small (?) Latin and Less Greek', in Arthur Sherbo, *Studies in the Johnson Circle* (West Cornwall, CT, 1998), pp. 53–68 (p. 54)).

137. *GM*, 4.1738, p. 206.

138. See 'a young collegian's' love poem 'A Pastoral Essay', *GM*, 7.1748, p. 328 and Samuel Rogers' poems contributed 11.1751 (p. 516) and 7.1752 (p. 328) while an undergraduate at Emmanuel College, Cambridge.

139. *GM*, 7.1813, pp. 14–15, letter from Blomfield ('Misomargites') criticizing Barker's publications.

140. Nichols noted contributions from Foster Webb and other students of Mr Watkins' academy in Spital-square and from students of John Eames in Moorfields. Unitarian Revd Dr William Enfield (1741–97) and Baptist Revd Dr Andrew Gifford (1700–84) were among the 521 listed correspondents, 'Prefatory Introduction', pp. lii–liii, lxxiv–lxxviii.

141. Stephen Burley, *New College, Hackney (1786–96): A Selection of Printed and Archival Sources* (Dr Williams's Centre for Dissenting Studies, 2nd revised edition 2011, 1st published 2010) at http://www.english.qmul.ac.uk/drwilliams/pubs/Burley/DWL%20Online%20Publication.pdf (accessed 24.8.2011).

142. *Miscellaneous Correspondence, Containing Essays, Dissertations, etc. on Various Subjects, Sent to the Author of the Gentleman's Magazine*, IX (London, 1748), for example, contains a letter to an MP attacking the dangers papists posed to the state. Berington's contributions included a reply to 'J.W.'s' letter on 'Principles of the Roman Catholics fully and fairly stated' (*GM*, 8.1788, p. 696). Mann's first contribution was *GM*, 6.1787, pp. 461–2. Milner corresponded as 'J.M.' and 'J.M—r' between 1788 and 1814.

143. On classical education, see Michèle Cohen, *Fashioning Masculinity: National Identity and Language in the Eighteenth Century* (London, 1996) and Anthony Fletcher, *Gender, Sex and Subordination in England, 1500–1800* (Yale, 1995), pp. 297–321. For Greek tragedy on the eighteenth-century stage see Edith Hall and Fiona Macintosh, *Greek Tragedy and the British Theatre 1660–1914* (Oxford, 2005).

144. *GM*, 7.1735, p. 384, and Carlson, *First Magazine*, pp. 145, 235–7.

145. E.g *GM*, 10.1742, p. 516.

146. Calvin Daniel Yost, *Poetry of the Gentleman's Magazine: A Study in Eighteenth-Century Literary Taste* (Philadelphia, 1936), pp. 87–107.

147. *GM*, 7.1776, pp. 301–2, reply to 'Lancastriensis' (5.1776, pp. 215–17) who advocated early teaching of the classics away from female home influences.
148. Kaufman, 'Community Library', p. 22.
149. *GM*, 7.1808, p. 659; 1.1810, p. 91.
150. Letter, BL: Stowe 748, Miscellaneous Correspondence, f. 120, n.d., from either John Anstis (1669–1744) or his son John (1708–54), both heralds.
151. *ODNB* and *Dictionary of Canadian Biography Online*, http://www.biographi.ca/009004-119.01-e.php?&id_nbr=3392&interval=15&&PHPSESSID=qqv5dv02sa0vr9ofo334eosca3 (accessed 18.5.2011).
152. *ODNB* entries.
153. *GM* wrapper 4.1774; T. Dyche, *A Guide to the English Tongue* (London, 1707), p. 103.
154. For comparable tension in scientific circles see Andrea Rusnock, 'Correspondence Networks and the Royal Society, 1700–1750', *British Journal for the History of Science*, 32 (1999), pp. 155–69 and Anne Secord, 'Corresponding Interests: Artisans and Gentlemen in Nineteenth-Century Natural History', *British Journal for the History of Science*, 27 (1994), pp. 383–408.
155. *GM*, 12.1777, pp. 568–9 and 1.1778, pp. 21–2.
156. *GM*, 12.1787, p. 1044.
157. *GM*, 1.1788, pp. 3–4.
158. Bodl.: MS.Eng.Lett.b.18.107.
159. Editorial footnote to letters from 'Your Occasional Correspondent' and 'D.R.', *GM*, 1.1788, p. 4, and editorial statement, 'Index Indicatorius', 2.1786, p. 153.
160. C. John Sommerville, *The News Revolution in England: Cultural Dynamics of Daily Information* (Oxford, 1996), pp. 156–60.
161. Feather considers this a key *GM* feature (*Provincial Book Trade*, pp. 19–21).
162. Information from title pages and advertisements in other publications, e.g. *GSJ*, no. 321, 19.2.1736.
163. Peter Borsay, *The English Urban Renaissance: Culture and Society in the Provincial Town, 1660–1770* (Oxford, 1989), p. 131, and Cranfield, *Provincial Newspaper*, pp. 190–206.
164. BL MS: Stowe 748, Miscellaneous Correspondence, f. 179.
165. For PO development, see Whyman, *Pen and the People*, pp. 46–71; for newspapers arriving with the post, William Cowper, *The Task* (facsimile edition 1973, 1st published London, 1785), Book IV, pp. 137–9; for transport, M.J. Daunton, *Progress and Poverty: An Economic and Social History of Britain 1700–1850* (Oxford, 1995), pp. 285–318.
166. St Clair, *Reading Nation*, p. 191.
167. *GM*, 1.1748, p. 8.
168. See *GM*, 12.1737, p. 755; 1.1738, p. 17 and 11.1748, p. 519; Whyman, *Pen and the People*, p. 71.
169. BL MS: Stowe 748, Miscellaneous Correspondence, f. 143.
170. Letter, 4.1.1813 (PC1/161/14/1, NAD 10491).
171. *GM*, 1741, Preface: 'We see it reprinted from several Presses in Great Britain, Ireland, and the Plantations'. For English papers in Ireland see Barnard, 'Reading in Eighteenth-Century Ireland', pp. 70–1. In Barbados, Cave may have used as agent Thomas Finlay esq., who procured subscribers there for Du Halde's *China* (Barker, 'Edward Cave, Samuel Johnson', p. 102).

172. Thomas Thistlewood (1721–86), overseer of a Jamaican slave plantation, ordered books from Henry Hewitt of Kensington (Trevor Burnard, *Mastery, Tyranny, and Desire: Thomas Thistlewood and his Slaves in the Anglo-Jamaican World* (Chapel Hill and London, 2004), p. 108). Joshua Johnson, a Maryland merchant based in London in the 1770s, wrote to a partner back home: 'If Mrs. Howard will go the expense, I can get her second-hand papers at a penny per piece and send them as opportunities offers [*sic*] or the magazines at 6d. each' (Jacob M. Price, ed., *Joshua Johnson's Letterbook, 1771–4: Letters from a Merchant in London to his Partners in Maryland* (London, 1979), p. 7).

173. William Jones, *The Diary of the Revd William Jones, 1777–1821, Curate and Vicar of Broxbourne and the Hamlet of Hoddesdon, 1781–1821*, ed. O.F. Christie (London, 1929), p. 41.

174. Letter accompanying a piece as 'some return' for the pleasure the *GM* brought, *GM*, 1.1745, p. 33.

175. *GM*, 1751, Preface (fn.).

176. Nichols, *Anecdotes*, VIII, p. 42.

177. *GM*, 1777, Preface.

178. The American and Caribbean press are found on early numbers but not all reprint editions. Less than one per cent of excerpts to 1754 were from provincial or foreign papers (Pailler, *Edward Cave et le 'Gentleman's Magazine'*, I, p. 218).

179. To confirm this point, correspondents' addresses, when given, are provided in the following chapters.

180. Ram, *Magnitude*, pp. 91–2 and Stafford, 'Social Order', pp. 67, 72. The metropolitan area accounted for approximately ten per cent of the population of England and Wales in the period (M. Dorothy George, *London Life in the Eighteenth Century* (Harmondsworth, 1966, 1st published London, 1925), p. 319).

181. *GM*, 1.1753, p. 28.

182. With the caveat that there was, unsurprisingly, almost no overseas advertising, an exception being the Humane Society of Philadelphia medal for the best dissertation on resuscitation after apparent drowning, judged by the University of Pennsylvania (*GM* wrapper, 10.1807).

183. Advertisement by Kirkman & Oney, booksellers and stationers, 79 Fleet Street (*GM* wrapper, 9.1789). Proprietary medicines could also be posted from London suppliers, for example Cooke's Elixir Vitae from Newbery's Paternoster Row shop (*GM* wrapper, 9.1774).

184. *GM* wrapper, 9.1785. Hellins (d. 1827) was another classic case of an eighteenth-century autodidact.

185. *GM*, 3.1805; 3.1818; 1811, Supplement and 9.1787.

186. Remark of 'T.C.' (physician Thomas Christie of Montrose, 1772/3–1829), *GM*, 7.1785, pp. 535–6, writing on the town's new subscription library.

187. There is some limited evidence for reprinting in the provincial press of *GM* articles, again ensuring a wider audience, see e.g articles in *York Herald*, 14.05.1803 and *Lancaster Gazette*, 12.10.1811.

188. Bodl.: MS.Eng.lett.c.354.154–5.

189. Letter, 17.7.1798 (PC1/50/101/1–2, NAD 6238).

190. Letter, 12.3.1798 (PC/1/50/8, NAD 6217).

191. Letters to Nichols from Christie, 4.3.1785, Nichols, *Anecdotes*, IX, pp. 368–9, and Percy, 29.3.1799, Nichols, *Illustrations*, VI, pp. 582–3.
192. Nichols, *Anecdotes*, VIII, p. 557.
193. Carlson, *First Magazine*, pp. 170–96.
194. *GM*, 3.1735, p. 154.
195. *GM*, 7.1740, p. 341; 3.1741, pp. 145–7.
196. BL MS: Add 4392, item 3 and 7.1745, pp. 377–9.
197. Nichols, 'Prefatory Introduction', pp. lxxiv–lxxxviii.
198. Letter, 1.8.1797 (Pierpont Morgan Library N.Y., NAD 3318).
199. John Brewer, *The Pleasures of the Imagination: English Culture in the Eighteenth Century* (London, 1997), pp. 608–10.
200. Sommerville sets discussion of the *GM* in a claimed context of a decline in provincial culture and corresponding rise of the cultural hegemony of London (*News Revolution*, pp. 156–60). See however Carl B. Estabrook, *Urbane and Rustic England: Cultural Ties and Social Spheres in the Provinces, 1660–1780* (Manchester, 1998) where empirical research on the Bristol area challenges the view that major urban centres were dominant spheres of influence before the later eighteenth century.
201. *GM*, 4.1775, pp. 168–9.
202. See for example Pailler, *Edward Cave et le 'Gentleman's Magazine'*, I, p. 461 and Robert D. Mayo, *The English Novel in the Magazines, 1740-1815* (Evanston, 1962), pp. 159–208.
203. See Chapter 2.
204. See Shawn L. Maurer, *Proposing Men: Dialectics of Gender and Class in the Eighteenth-Century Periodical* (Stanford, CA, 1998).
205. Berry, *Gender, Society and Print Culture*, p. 53; Fergus, *Provincial Readers*, pp. 41–74 and 197–235.
206. Jan S. Fergus, 'Women, Class and the Growth of Magazine Readership in the Provinces, 1746–80', *Studies in Eighteenth-Century Culture*, 16 (1986), pp. 41–56.
207. *GM*, 4.1808, p. 295.
208. *GM*, 5.1791, p. 419 and facing.
209. *GM*, 1784, Preface.
210. 30.11.1790, BL MS: Add 75637 (thanks to Martin Price for the reference).
211. Letter from Strawberry Hill, 13.12.1811 (Pierpont Morgan Library, N.Y.: R.V. Autographs Misc. English, NAD 3312).
212. Whyman, *Pen and the People*, pp. 202–3.
213. David Allan, *Commonplace Books and Reading in Georgian England* (Cambridge, 2010), pp. 107–8, 227.
214. Letters to Nichols from Goodeth Pegge, York, 6.1.1803 (Society of Antiquaries MS: 447/3, ff. 478–9, NAD 8280) and Selina Moor, 5.3.1812 (Bodl.: MS.Eng.Lett.b.19.26–7).
215. De Montluzin, *Attributions of Authorship* (accessed 24.8.2011) and *ODNB*.
216. Nichols, 'Prefatory Introduction', pp. lxxiv–lxxviii (Mrs Eliza Berkeley, Mrs Chapone, Mrs Cowley, Mrs S. Duncombe of Canterbury, Mrs Mary Knowles, Miss Anna Seward, Mrs Charlotte Smith, Miss Catherine Talbot and Mrs Thomas of Newbold); Stafford, 'Social Order', p. 67.
217. Stephen Howard, ' "A bright pattern to all her sex": Representations of Women in Periodical and Newspaper Biography', in *Gender in*

Eighteenth-Century England: Roles, Representations and Responsibilities, ed. Hannah Barker and Elaine Chalus (London, 1997), pp. 230–49.

218. Bodl.: MS.Eng.Lett.b.15.5, 9.9.1795. It appeared in *GM*, 10.1795, p. 579.

219. Bodl.: MS.Eng.Lett.b.17.134–135; *GM*, 3.1800, pp. 283–4.

220. *GM*, 1784, Preface.

221. *Miscellaneous Correspondence*, I, pp. 36–7.

222. *GM*, 3.1743, p. 168; *Miscellaneous Correspondence*, II (1743), pp. 92–4.

223. *GM*, 6.1758, p. 275.

224. *GM*, 1.1739, pp. 13–14; 10.1739, pp. 525–6.

225. *GM*, 5.1740, p. 245.

226. *GM*, 2.1797, pp. 95–6.

227. *GM*, 3.1797, pp. 181–3.

228. Pailler, *Edward Cave et le 'Gentleman's Magazine'*, I, p. 461.

229. Letter from 'Sharlot Wealthy', lamenting that men were inclined to compliment her looks rather than her brains, *GM*, 1.1731, pp. 5–6 (from *Spectator*, 12.11.1712).

230. Kuist, 'Gentleman's Magazine', p. 120 and fn. 1.

231. *GSJ*, no. 128, 15.6.1732.

232. For medical contributions, see Roy Porter, 'Lay Medical Knowledge in the Eighteenth Century: The Evidence of the *Gentleman's Magazine*', *Medical History*, 29 (1985), pp. 138–68 and Roy Porter, ed., *Patients and Practitioners: Lay Perceptions of Medicine in Pre-Industrial Society* (Cambridge, 1985); method of killing bed bugs (by painting the dismantled bed frame with an egg white and mercury mixture), *GM*, 11.1735, p. 671, smoking chimneys, 1.1797, pp. 15–16.

233. *Modern Cook*: GM wrappers, 7.1736, 11.1743, 2.1744; *House-keeper's Pocketbook*: wrappers, 2, 3, 6, 9, 10, 11.1744, 10.1748; *Family's Best Companion*: wrapper, 9.1779; mangle: wrapper, 10.1807; water closet: wrapper, 10.1812.

234. *Ladies Complete Letter Writer* (T. Lownds, Fleet Street): *GM* wrapper, 6.1765; *Frugal Housewife* (by Susannah Carter of Clerkenwell, published by Newbery): wrappers, 10. and Supplement 1774, 1.1778; Welch's Dancing Academy (120 The Strand): wrappers, 10.1778; 10, 12.1779; 2, 3, 4.1783; Turner's Imperial Lotion: wrapper, 5.1807.

235. *GM* wrappers, 9.1784, 10.1812, 4.1814.

236. Robert Darnton, *The Kiss of Lamourette: Reflections in Cultural History* (London, 1990), p. 157.

237. Ian Jackson, 'Approaches to the History of Readers and Reading in Eighteenth-Century Britain', *Historical Journal*, 47 (2004), pp. 1041–54 and Reading Experience Database, 1450–1945, http://www.open.ac.uk/Arts /RED/.

238. BL MS: Stowe 748 Miscellaneous Correspondence, f. 143.

239. *GM*, 7.1800, pp. 633–5.

240. Asa Briggs and Peter Burke, *A Social History of the Media* (2nd edition, Cambridge, 2005, 1st published 2002), p. 53. A reading revolution in which, by 1800, 'extensive' replaced 'intensive' reading (in which a limited number of chiefly religious texts were read repeatedly) is proposed by Rolf Engelsing, *Der Bürger als Leser: Lesergeschichte in Deutschland, 1500–1800* (Stuttgart, 1974). Although Engelsing's thesis is not entirely accepted by historians

(Jackson, 'History of Readers', p. 1050), Darnton describes it as 'a useful lens' (*Kiss*, p. 166). For 'desultory' reading see Fergus, *Provincial Readers*, pp. 75–117.

241. Robert DeMaria, 'Samuel Johnson and the Reading Revolution', *Eighteenth-Century Life*, 16 (1992), pp. 86–102 positions Johnson across the intensive and extensive approaches to texts.

242. *GM*, 1.1810, p. 38.

243. William Hazlitt, 'The St James's Chronicle–The Morning Chronicle–The Times–The New Times–The Courier, &c.–Cobbett's Weekly Journal–The Examiner–The Observer–The Gentleman's Magazine–The New Monthly Magazine–The London, &c. &c.', *Edinburgh Review: Or Critical Journal*, 38 (May 1823), pp. 349–78, p. 369.

244. Anonymous prefatory poem, *GM*, 7.1810.

245. *GM*, 7.1799, p. 556.

246. For example William Hamilton Reid, 12.6.1802, Bodl.: MS.Eng.Lett.b.15.201.

247. *GM*, 7.1794, pp. 591–2.

248. Letter, 23.1.1790, Bodl.: MS.Eng.Lett.b.13.96; sonnets *GM*, 1.1790, p. 74.

249. Fergus, *Provincial Readers*, fn. 37, p. 220.

250. Examples in Penelope Peoples, 'The Folger Nichols Manuscript Collection: A Description and Analysis' (unpublished PhD thesis, University of Wisconsin-Milwaukee, 1980)', pp. 290, 291, 294.

251. Letters to Nichols from Goodwin, 12.9.1809, Bodl.: MS.Eng.Lett.c.356.210, NAD 5679; Cardew, 10.1.1808 in BL MS: Add 63652 Vol. 2, f. 249 and Collinson, 9.1.1801, PC1/27/60, NAD 4757. For Cardew, b.1748, see Alexander G. Cardew, *A Memoir of the Reverend Cornelius Cardew, DD, Master of the Truro Grammar School and Rector of St Erme, Cornwall* (Truro, 1926). Goodwin died 7.1817 in his 86th year and so was an older 28 when he started taking the magazine (memorial inscription in Joseph Hunter, *Hallamshire: The History and Topography of the Parish of Sheffield* (London, 1819), p. 242).

252. *GM*, 3.1813, p. 258.

253. *GM*, Prefaces, 1764, 1765.

254. *GM*, 7.1751, p. 294.

255. *GM*, Preface, 1766; Richard Polwhele, *The Old English Gentleman: A Poem* (London, 1797), p. 87.

256. Letter, 17.7.1798 (1 PC1/50/101/1–2, NAD 6238).

257. *GM*, 12.1787, p. 1044.

258. *GM*, 1.1750, p. 39.

259. 22.4.1811, PC1/18/73, NAD 3121. Capt. Waldron, an officer in Wellington's Portuguese army, was wounded on 12.3.1811 (*GM*, 4.1811, p. 378). For the dislocation of colonial families see Sarah M.S. Pearsall, *Atlantic Families: Lives and Letters in the Later Eighteenth Century* (Oxford, 2008).

260. *GM*, Preface, 1767.

261. *GM*, 1.1787, pp. 3–5; Bodl.: MS.Eng.Lett.b.15.78, 18.3.1807; obituary *GM*, 2.1807, p. 183, revision 3.1807, p. 275.

262. Letter, 24.11.1735, BL MS: Stowe, f. 144.

263. Letters, 10.1.1808 and 16.5.1810, BL MS: Add 63652, ff. 249–58. (One of Cardew's drawings is annotated as 'bad'.)

264. Many such are in Bodl.: MS.Eng.Lett.c.372, calendared in NAD.

265. Joseph Warton (1722–1800, poet, critic and headmaster of Winchester school) to Nichols, 3.6.1782, Nichols, *Anecdotes*, VI, p. 172.
266. *GM*, 8.1734, p. 442.
267. Letter, 21.2.1737, BL MS: Stowe 748, f. 149.
268. *GM*, 7.1786, p. 547.
269. Peter Pindar (pseudonym of John Wolcott), *A Benevolent Epistle to Sylvanus Urban Alias Master John Nichols, Printer, Common-councilman of Farringdon Ward, and Censor General of Literature: Not Forgetting Master William Hayley* (London, 1790).
270. *GM*, 12.1787, p. 1044.
271. *GM*, 7.1748, p. 332.
272. BL MS: Add 4392, item 3, ff. 1–2.
273. *GM*, 1.1751, pp. 13–14.
274. Byrom, *Private Journal*, II, p. 278.
275. *GM*, 7.1786, p. 536.
276. Allan, *Commonplace Books*, pp. 3–4.
277. Ibid., pp. 159, 226–36, 237–52.
278. Isaac Watts, *The Improvement of the Mind* (London, 1801, 1st published 1741), pp. 8–9. Watts (1674–1748, independent minister, educationalist and writer) was a leading dissenter popular with some *GM* readers; Steven N. Zwicker, 'The Constitution of Opinion and the Pacification of Reading', in *Reading, Society, and Politics in Early Modern England*, ed. Kevin Sharpe and Steven N. Zwicker (Cambridge, 2003), pp. 295–316.
279. Thomas Carter, *Memoirs of a Working Man* (London, 1845), pp. 57–8. Carter, a tailor, was born in 1792. At the time of his reading the *GM* (and Wesley's *Arminian Magazine*), he was attending a small (25 pupils) school for Protestant dissenters which taught the 'three Rs'.
280. *GM*, 1.1746, p. 38.
281. *ODNB*.
282. Hutton, *Life*, p. 42 and *ODNB*.
283. As 'Hygeia', *GM*, 5.1813, pp. 407–8.
284. *ODNB*.
285. Review of 1821 *General Index* in *Literary Chronicle &Weekly Review*, 21.4.1821, pp. 243–5.
286. Undated letter, PC1/12/5, NAD 1457.
287. *A General Index to the First Twenty Volumes of the Gentleman's Magazine, in Five Parts: To which is Added, an Index to the First Volume of the Miscellaneous Correspondence* (London, 1753). Kimber, son of Isaac whom he succeeded as *LM* editor in 1755, received £20 for the *General Index* and assisted from 8.1752 to 1.1755 at £1 per month, plus £3 for each of the three annual indexes 1752 to 1754 (notebook of Edward Kimber in private collection, S.A. Kimber, 'The "Relation of a Late Expedition to St Augustine", with Biographical and Bibliographical Notes on Isaac and Edward Kimber', *Papers of the Bibliographical Society of America*, 28 (1934), pp. 81–96 (p. 91)).
288. *GM*, 1.1751, pp. 12–13, letter from 'D.H.'
289. The preface is unpaginated. For attribution to Johnson see D.F. Foxon's 'Introduction' (also unpaginated) to Edward Kimber, *The Gentleman's Magazine, 1731–51: The Lists of Books, Collected with Annual Indexes and the Index to the First Twenty Years* (facsimile reprint, London, 1966).

290. Samuel Ayscough, *General Index to Fifty-Six Volumes of the Gentleman's Magazine, 1731–86* (London, 1789) and Ayscough and Nichols, *General Index.* Ayscough (1745–1804) was a BM librarian.
291. Nichols, *Anecdotes*, VIII, p. 557.
292. John Walker, *A Selection of Curious Articles from the Gentleman's Magazine*, 4 vols (London, 1809), 'Preface', p. vi.
293. *Universal Magazine*, NS, I, 4.1804, p. 359, letter from 'D' of Cambridge reviewing periodicals. Like Hazlitt he thought the *GM*: 'verging fast towards a state of decrepitude and empty garrulity'. The scholarly value of material in the magazine was recognized in the nineteenth and twentieth centuries in collections such as G.L. Gomme, A.B. Gomme, Lady A.C. Bickley, and F.A. Milne, eds, *The Gentleman's Magazine Library: Being a Classified Collection of the Chief Contents of the Gentleman's Magazine from 1731 to 1868*, 29 vols (London, 1883–1905), 29 volumes on subjects such as archaeology, topography, architecture, literary curiosities and folklore. There are also specialist indexes to, for example marriages, biographies, obituaries, dissenting ministers, Voltaire, West Indian maps and illustrations.
294. Andrew Morrall, 'Ornament as Evidence', in *History and Material Culture: A Student's Guide to Approaching Alternative Sources*, ed. Karen Harvey (London, 2009), pp. 47–66 (p. 47). See also John Elsner and Roger Cardinal, eds, *The Cultures of Collecting* (London, 1994), pp. 1–6.
295. Defoe, *Compleat English Gentleman*, pp. 134–41.
296. *GM*, 1.1814, pp. 33–6.
297. http://www.english-heritage.org.uk/publications/audley-end-teachers-kit /AudleyEndTeachersKitHistory.pdf (accessed 1.1.2014). The library was destroyed in 1825.
298. Weatherill, *Consumer Behaviour* charts growth in ownership of luxury goods, particularly by urban households in trading and commercial occupations, using the concept of 'front-' and 'back-stage' household activities to locate possessions and their meaning, where 'front-stage' involved the presentation of the self to others. Books were among the 'new' possessions in 'front-stage' spaces such as the parlour. Estabrook, *Urbane and Rustic England*, finds bound serial publications in private houses in mid-century Bristol, often in a room labelled the 'study'. Raven notes a rise in lots of books, bookcases and other library furniture in auction catalogues from house clearances ('From Promotion to Proscription').
299. *GM*, 1749, Preface.
300. *GM* wrapper, 10.1797.
301. *MP*, 29.5.1802.
302. *Bury & Norwich Post*, 13.5.1807, 6.12.1809.
303. *GM*, 5.1745, pp. 254–5.
304. *GM*, 1.1751, p. 22.
305. Charles St Barbe, *A Complete List of the Plates and Wood-cuts in the Gentleman's Magazine* (London, 1821). For St Barbe, businessman and landowner of Lymington, Hampshire, see obituary, *GM*, 2.1826, p. 186.
306. *GM*, wrapper, 2.1783.
307. Letter, 11.12.1814, PC1/1/17, NAD 2239; letter, 31.3.1814, PC1/50/120, NAD 6258; letter, 2.12.1819, Cambridge University Library: MS Add 8200/Ni5/1, NAD 2381.

308. Letter, 16.1and reply 31.1.1812, PC/1/65/14/1–2, NAD 7641 and 7642.
309. *GM*, 7.1810, p. 60.
310. Brendan Dooley and Sabrina Baron, eds., *The Politics of Information in Early Modern Europe* (New York, 2001), p. 7.
311. Dror Wahrman, 'National Society, Communal Culture: An Argument About the Recent Historiography of Eighteenth-Century Britain', *Social History*, 17 (1992), pp. 43–72. On the spread of culture, see too Brewer, *Pleasures* and Wrightson, *English Society*.
312. Wahrman, 'National Society', p. 43.
313. See Peter Clark, *British Clubs and Societies, 1580–1800* (Oxford, 2000). Examples include the Spalding Gentlemen's Society, founded 1710 with the aim of 'Improvement in Friendship and Knowledge'. Members corresponded and wrote on very similar subjects to those in the *GM* (indeed there was some overlap in correspondents and the library contained volumes of the magazine) and also sought to avoid unpleasant dissension; see Diana Honeybone and Michael Honeybone, eds., *The Correspondence of the Spalding Gentlemen's Society, 1710–61* (Woodbridge, 2010).
314. Klancher, *English Reading Audiences*, p. 23; Anne Goldgar, *Impolite Learning: Conduct and Community in the Republic of Letters, 1680–1750* (New Haven, CT, 1995), pp. 8, 14.
315. Richard Sennett, *The Fall of Public Man* (New York, 1977), p. 49; Benedict Anderson, *Imagined Communities: Reflections on the Origin and Spread of Nationalism* (London, revised edition 1991, 1st published 1983). Uriel Heyd reaches a similar conclusion in his study of the British and American press (*Reading Newspapers: Press and Public in Eighteenth-Century Britain and America* (Oxford, 2012)).
316. *GM*, 1.1793, pp. 16–17, letter supplying anecdotes of Nicholson (rector of Dudcote, Berks., d. Liverpool, 26.12.1792).
317. Paul Langford, 'The Uses of Politeness', *Transactions of the Royal Historical Society*, 12 (2002), pp. 311–31 (p. 314).
318. 'Musophilus', *GM*, 1.1746, pp. 7–8.

4 Gentlemanly Masculinity in the *Gentleman's Magazine*, 1731 to 1756

1. *GM*, 1.1736, pp. 11–12, from no. 121, 6.1.1736 of the semi-weekly *Prompter*, price 2d, published 1734–6, editors Aaron Hill and William Popple. Often excerpted by the *GM*, it devoted around half its space to the London stage (*ODNB* for Hill, 1685–1750, and Alvin Sullivan, ed., *British Literary Magazines*, 4 vols (Westport, CT, 1983), I, pp. 280–2).
2. J. Crown(e), *Sir Courtly Nice: Or, It Cannot Be. A Comedy, as It Is Acted by His Majesties Servants* (London, 1685), Act III, p. 20: Nice to servant: 'You Clown, don't you know what belongs to a Gentleman? Complaisance is the very thing of a Gentleman, The thing that shew's [*sic*] a Gentleman. Wherever I go, all the World cryes that's a Gentleman, my life on't a Gentleman; and when y'ave said a Gentleman, you have said all'.
3. *ODNB* for Crowne (1641–1712).
4. *GM*, 10.1751, p. 478; 11.1753, p. 539.

5. In Foote's satirical review *Tea*, first performed at the Haymarket 22.4.1746 as *The Diversions of the Morning, or, A Dish of Chocolate*.
6. *GM*, 1.1733, pp. 15–19 (pagination varies between surviving volumes).
7. *Spectator*, no. 10, 12.3.1711.
8. *GM*, 1.1733, p. 16, from *Auditor*, I and II, 2d twice-weekly, the *Auditor* contained essays on 'characters' as social commentary and pseudonymous/fictitious correspondence. It was short-lived, known to have been published from 9.1-8.5.1733 and weekly in 12.1733 (COPAC: http://copac.ac.uk/search?rn=2&date=1733&ti=auditor&sort-order=ti%2C-date (accessed 8.2.2012)).
9. *Spectator*, no. 2, 2.3.1711.
10. Manly is a character in Wycherley's 1676 comedy *The Plain-Dealer*, still popular in the eighteenth century.
11. Michèle Cohen, 'The Grand Tour: Constructing the English Gentleman in Eighteenth-Century France', *History of Education*, 21 (1992), pp. 241–57 (p. 24 for quotation, from William Ramsey, *The Gentleman's Companion* (London, 1672)). See too Jeremy Black, *The British Abroad: The Grand Tour in the Eighteenth Century* (paperback edition 1997, 1st published Stroud, 1992).
12. *GM*, 7.1736, p. 418.
13. *GM*, 7.1736, p. 423.
14. *GM*, 7.1747 pp. 324–6, 343.
15. *GM*, pp. 344–5.
16. Samuel Richardson, *The History of Sir Charles Grandison*, 7 vols (London, 1753–4).
17. *GM*, 11.1753, p. 543.
18. *GM*, 1.1754, p. 40.
19. *GM*, 4.1755, pp. 162–4, the unnamed nobleman probably Brownlow Cecil, 9th Earl of Exeter, of Burghley House, Stamford, who inherited the title in 1754.
20. Samuel Richardson, *The Apprentice's Vade Mecum: Or, Young Man's Pocket-Companion* (reprint edition 1975, 1st published London, 1734) and Samuel Richardson, *Letters Written to and for Particular Friends: On the Most Important Occasions, Directing Not Only the Requisite Style and Forms to be Observed in Writing Familiar Letters, but How to Think and Act Justly and Prudently, in the Common Concerns of Human Life* (London, 1741). His 1755 anthology of the moral lessons of *Pamela*, *Clarissa* and *Grandison* in *A Collection of Sentiments* was not as enthusiastically received as the novels (*ODNB*).
21. For *Grandison* and conduct books see Sylvia Kasey Marks, *Sir Charles Grandison: The Compleat Conduct Book* (Lewisburg, 1986) and Margaret Anne Doody, 'Samuel Richardson: Fiction and Knowledge', in *The Cambridge Companion to the Eighteenth-Century Novel*, ed. John Richetti (Cambridge, 1996), pp. 90–119.
22. Marks, *Sir Charles Grandison*, pp. 26–43.
23. Richard Steele, *The Christian Hero: An Argument Proving that No Principles but those of Religion are Sufficient to make a Great Man* (London, 1701).
24. Ibid., unpaginated Preface and p. 29.
25. *GM*, 1735, Supplement, p. 778.
26. *GM* wrapper, 10.1778; John Tillotson, *Twenty Discourses on the Most Important Subjects; Carefully Abridged, from the Works of Archbishop Tillotson,*

Adapted to the Meanest Capacities, with a View to their Being Dispersed by those who are Charitably Inclined (London, 2nd edition, 1763), XX 'On Sincerity, pp. 206, 209.

27. *GM*, 7.1785, pp. 517–9.
28. *GM*, 7.1736, p. 414.
29. George Lillo, *The Christian Hero: A Tragedy, as it is Acted at the Theatre Royal in Drury Lane* (2nd edition, London, 1735), Act II, scene I, *ll*. 71–75, 79. Fifteenth-century Albanian Christian Scanderbeg liberated his people from the Muslim Ottoman Turks. The play ran for four nights before vanishing from the repertoire, remaining available as a text with two editions in 1735, a Scottish edition in 1759 and inclusion in Lillo's collected works in 1740, 1760 and 1775, see *ODNB* and COPAC (http://copac.ac.uk/ (accessed 24.9.12)).
30. *GM*, 7.1736, p. 413, *ll*. 27, 35; p. 414, *l*. 51; p. 415, *l*. 32.
31. Ibid., Poem III, p. 413, *ll*. 64–73, Poem IV, p. 414, *l*. 119.
32. See the grovelling apology in *GM*, 1.1736, p. 42. Despite this, Poem V referred to her (7.1736, p. 414, *ll*. 61–2).
33. The Grand Tour costs of the 6th Earl of Salisbury in 1730–2 were at least £3,313. More modest tourists could reckon on spending *c*. £300 *p.a.* (Black, *British Abroad*, pp. 86–109 and Cohen, 'Grand Tour', pp. 245–6). The war years of 1740–8 made a Tour difficult whatever one's depth of pocket.
34. *GM*, 1740, Preface, p. iv.
35. See Pailler's analysis of this content for the period, *Edward Cave et le 'Gentleman's Magazine', 1731–54*, 2 vols (Lille, 1975), I, pp. 239–327 on parliamentary reporting and 387–406 on news reporting, supported by tables in II, pp. 534–9.
36. For these announcements in the eighteenth-century press, see Michael Harris, *London Newspapers in the Age of Walpole: A Study of the Origins of the Modern English Press* (London, 1987), pp. 158, 171.
37. There were approximately equal numbers of male and female baptisms in the Bills of Mortality. A female could be an heiress (to property, rarely to a title) when a subsequent male heir's birth was an impossibility. A female heir chosen from among living descendants including sons was potentially disruptive, as Richardson's *Clarissa* made clear.
38. Randolph Trumbach, *The Rise of the Egalitarian Family: Aristocratic Kinship and Domestic Relations in Eighteenth-Century England* (New York, 1978), pp. 170, 243–4.
39. *GM*, 1.1739, p. 44.
40. *GM*, 7.1736, p. 423.
41. Lady Mary Wortley Montagu, 'The Answer to the Foregoing Elegy' in James Hammond, *An Elegy to a Young Lady, in the Manner of Ovid ... With an Answer* (London, 1733).
42. For example *GM*, 1.1734, pp. 51–2.
43. *GM* lists were neither exhaustive nor always explicitly sourced, although probably for the most part taken from the *London Gazette*, supplemented by other papers. Some entries in 1.1743, for instance, were marked 'G' to indicate the *Gazette* as provenance. In some numbers, such as 7.1745, p. 389, '*Gazette* Promotions' and 'From other Papers' were sub-headings.
44. *GM*, 7.1735, p. 388; 1.1742, p. 51; 1.1756, p. 43. For the nobility's use of offices, often sinecures obtained through parliamentary influence, to settle

younger sons without damaging an heir's financial interests, see Trumbach, *Egalitarian Family*, pp. 94–5.

45. *GM*, 7.1751, p. 333.
46. David Fordyce, *Dialogues Concerning Education*, 2 vols (London, 1745), II, pp. 304–5.
47. For the gendered lens of travellers see Susan Lamb, *Bringing Travel Home to England: Tourism, Gender, and Imaginative Literature in the Eighteenth Century* (Newark, DE, 2009).
48. Richard Hurd, *Dialogues on the Uses of Foreign Travel, Considered as a Part of an English Gentleman's Education: Between Lord Shaftesbury and Mr Locke* (2nd edition, London, 1764), pp. 158–9. For the benefits and moral dangers of 'the rational Design of Travelling', see *GM*, 8.1731, p. 321 (from *London Journal*). For the extension of the Tour experience beyond the elite through antiquarian writing see Rosemary Sweet, *Antiquaries: The Discovery of the Past in Eighteenth-Century Britain* (Hambledon and London, 2004), p. 36.
49. Boswell recorded him saying 'A man who has not been in Italy, is always conscious of an inferiority, from his not having seen what it is expected a man should see' (*Life of Johnson: Together with a Journal of a Tour to the Hebrides and Johnson's Diary of a Journey into North Wales*, ed. George Birkbeck Hill, revd L.F. Powell, 6 vols (Oxford, 1934, 1st published 1791), III, p. 36).
50. *GM*, 1.1749, pp. 18–20.
51. *GM*, 1.1741, p. 15 announced the 'Life of Barratier'. The 'Life of Morin', translated from Fontanelle, was in 7.1741, pp. 375–7.
52. *GM*, 1.1753, pp. 25–7, 45, 46–7.
53. Pailler, *Edward Cave et le 'Gentleman's Magazine'*, I, p. 348.
54. Figures (for 1731–54), ibid., p. 349.
55. *GM*, 1.1741, pp. 13–15.
56. *GM*, 1.1755, p. 189 and Chapter 3.
57. *GM*, 1.1732, p. 584; 1.1749, p. 28; 7.1736, p. 422; 7.1742, p. 390.
58. *GM*, 1.1731, p. 33; 7.1743, p. 389.
59. *GM*, 7.1752, p. 331. For cock-throwing see *GM*, 1.1737, pp. 6–8; 1.1750, pp. 18–19; 1.1751, p. 8; 1.1753, p. 5.
60. *GM*, 1.1735, pp. 21–3 (from *Prompter*, XVIII, 10.1.1735). The piece drew an immediate, lengthy reply from 'M', *GM*, 2.1735, pp. 91–3. See also Léon-François Hoffmann, 'An Eighteenth Century Exponent of Black Power: Moses Bon Sàam', *Caribbean Studies*, 15 (1975), pp. 149–61.
61. *GM*, 7.1740, p. 341.
62. *GM*, 1.1751, pp. 13–14 and Chapter 3.
63. *GM*, 12.1750, pp. 556–7, 581–2; iron manufacturing 8.1750, pp. 340–1; 10.1750, pp. 445–6.
64. On the burgeoning arms of government administration see John Brewer, *The Sinews of Power: War and the English State, 1683–1783* (London, 1989).
65. Letter to Solomon Dayrolles, 27.6.1756, in *The Letters of Philip Dormer Stanhope, Earl of Chesterfield*, ed. Lord Mahon, 4 vols (London, 1845), IV, pp. 188–9.
66. Joseph Emin, *The Life and Adventures of J.E., an Armenian* (London, 1792), pp. 85–6.
67. Donald Gibson, ed., *A Parson in the Vale of White Horse: George Woodward's Letters from East Hendred, 1753–61* (Gloucester, 1983).

68. Similar middling-sort self-assertion is noted by archaeologists and historians of burials, see Sarah Tarlow, *Bereavement and Commemoration: An Archaeology of Mortality* (Oxford, 1999) and Vanessa Harding, 'Research Priorities: An Historian's Perspective', in *Grave Concerns: Death and Burial in England, 1700–1850*, ed. Margaret Cox (York, 1998), pp. 205–12 (p. 212).

69. *GM*, 7.1732, p. 876; 1.1733, pp. 45, 47; 1.1741, p. 50; 7.1752, p. 336 and 1.1755, p. 42.

70. *GM*, 1.1734, pp. 34, 50; 1.1758, p. 46; 1.1741, p. 50; 7.1755, p. 333. Snell, Seymoor/Seymour, Dennis, Dawkins, Senex and Williams earned *ODNB* entries.

71. *GM*, 1.1732, p. 586; 1.1734, p. 51; 7.1747, p. 343; 7.1751, p. 332.

72. See Amy Louise Erickson, 'Married Women's Occupations in Eighteenth-Century London', *Continuity & Change*, 23 (2008), pp. 267–307; Bridget Hill, *Women, Work, and Sexual Politics in Eighteenth-Century England* (Oxford, 1989), and Margaret R. Hunt, *The Middling Sort: Commerce, Gender, and the Family in England, 1680–1780* (Berkeley, CA, 1996), pp. 125–46.

73. *GM*, 1.1735, p. 51; 1.1740, p. 36.

74. *GM*, 1.1736, p. 6; 1.1747, p. 37 (attrib. Hawkesworth).

75. Most often cited and most controversial was Bernard Mandeville's, *The Fable of the Bees: Or, Private Vices, Public Benefits* (London, 1714), which advanced the idea that the self-interest of commerce and consumption were beneficial to society. On this general point, see Matthew McCormack, *Independent Man: Citizenship and Gender Politics in Georgian England* (Manchester, 2005), pp. 14–15 and James Raven, *Judging New Wealth: Popular Publishing and Responses to Commerce in England, 1750–1800* (Oxford, 1992), pp. 83–111.

76. George Lillo, *The London Merchant: Or, The History of George Barnwell* (London, 1731), Act I, scene 1, p. 10.

77. Richardson, *Vade Mecum*, pp. vi, 26, 40 and *GM*, 1.1734, pp. 13–14.

78. *GM*, 7.1756, pp. 330–2 (from Samuel Pegge, who considered tradesmen especially prone to these vices); 1.1742, p. 48 and 1.1745, p. 45.

79. *GM*, 1.1755, p. 43.

80. *GM*, 1.1732, p. 586; 7.1746, p. 383; 1.1752, p. 44.

81. *GM*, 7.1737, pp. 433–4; 7.1738, pp. 359–60; 7.1746, pp. 363–4.

82. *GM*, 1.1756, pp. 36–7.

83. *GM*, 1.1733, p. 35.

84. Tim Hitchcock, *Down and Out in Eighteenth-Century London* (London, 2004), pp. 98–9.

85. See for example Erasmus Jones, *The Man of Manners: Or, Plebeian Polish'd, Being Plain and Familiar Rules for a Modest and Genteel Behaviour, on Most of the Ordinary Occasions of Life* (3rd edition, London, 1737), p. 14.

86. *GM*, 1.1733, pp. 35–6 (from *Applebee's Journal*, 27.1.1733).

87. *GM*, 1.1734, pp. 13–14 (from *Weekly Review*/Richardson, *Vade Mecum*); 1.1739, pp. 28–9 (from *US*).

88. *GM*, 1.1739, pp. 28–9. A 'wrap-rascal' was a great coat. For this and 'jockey style' see Aileen Ribeiro, *Dress in Eighteenth-Century Europe, 1715–89* (New Haven, CT, 2002), pp. 24, 30. The psychology of this fashion was complicated. James Boswell for example derived pleasure from sorties as a 'blackguard' when he temporarily threw off genteel constraints (Philip Carter, 'James Boswell's Manliness', in ed. Tim Hitchcock and Michèle Cohen, *English Masculinities*, pp. 111–30).

89. *GM*, 1.1752, pp. 40–1.
90. Natalie Zemon Davis, 'Remaking Impostors: From Martin Guerre to Sommersby', *Hayes Robinson Lecture Series*, 1 (1997), http://www.rhul.ac.uk /history/documents/pdf/events/hrzemon-davis.pdf (accessed 25.10.2013). Hannah Greig considers the eighteenth-century impostor in *The Beau Monde: Fashionable Society in Georgian England* (Oxford, 2013), pp. 217–28.
91. Other versions in Anon., *The Life of the Famous William Stroud: Who Was Convicted at the Last Quarter-Sessions for the City and Liberty of Westminster, Sentenced to Six Months Imprisonment in Bridewell, together with the Substance of the Speech Justice Ledlard Made, Stroud's Own Speech, and His Behaviour on that Occasion* (London, 1752) and *The Newgate Calendar: Comprising Interesting Memoirs of the Most Notorious Characters Who Have Been Convicted of Outrages on the Laws of England since the Commencement of the Eighteenth Century, with Anecdotes and Last Exclamations of Sufferers*, 4 vols (London, 1824–6).
92. *GM*, 1.1732, pp. 552–3 (from *US*).
93. *George Woodward's Letters*, p. 47.
94. *GM*, 7.1736, Poem V, p. 415, *ll.* 59–60.
95. *GM*, 7.1750, pp. 311–12.
96. Hunt, *Middling Sort*, pp. 114–24.
97. In the sampled numbers the trial was reported at *GM*, 1.1744, pp. 25–9, 7.1744, pp. 373–9. The case was eventually decided for the claimant.
98. *GM*, 7.1747, p. 339; Anon. (attrib. Duncan Forbes), *Memoirs of the Life of Lord Lovat* (London, 1746).
99. *GM*, 7.1747, facing p. 149, 4.1747, pp. 159–63; *LM*, 4.1747, pp. 155–7.
100. Craig Muldrew, *The Economy of Obligation: The Culture of Credit and Social Relations in Early Modern England* (Basingstoke, 1998), p. 318: 'The intensification of the market thus made the social order much more fragile. Poverty was something which could happen to all but the greatest, and the iconography of success was in constant danger of being pulled away'.
101. Richardson, *Vade Mecum*, p. 40.
102. *GM*, 7.1755, p. 303. The *Connoisseur* was a two penny weekly essay paper, published 31.1.1754-30.9.1756, its editors/authors ('Mr Town') playwright George Colman and Bonnell Thornton, and main theme the 'time-worn vices and foibles of London society' (Sullivan, *British Literary Magazines*, I, pp. 46–52).
103. *GM*, 7.1745, p. 388; Essex Record Office: D/ACW 29/6/1(will); 1.1756, p. 42, and Durham County Record Office: D/Br/D 1634–5 (deed); *GM*, 1.1741, p. 50 and *ODNB*; *GM*, 1.1733, p. 47 and *ODNB*. See Rosemary Sweet, *The English Town, 1680–1840* (Harlow, 1999), p. 195 for the appropriation of 'Esq.' by leading urban men to mark their success and self-confidence.
104. William Matthews, , ed., *Diary of Dudley Ryder, 1715–16* (London, 1939) p. 291.
105. W. Brockbank and F. Kenworthy, eds., *The Diary of Richard Kay, 1716–51 of Baldingstone, Near Bury, a Lancashire Doctor*, (Manchester, 1968), p. 12.
106. *GM*, 1.1732, p. 586 (not the member of the Corporation's Partnership of Five, who was alive in 9.1732, but probably a close family member; see *History of Parliament*. http://www.historyofparliamentonline.org/volume /1715-1754/member/burroughs-william-sept-1732, accessed 13.3.12). The Charitable Corporation was established in 1707 to provide loans for

the deserving poor. Following fraudulent speculative investments by its directors it collapsed in 10.1731. After petitioning by distressed shareholders, the House of Commons investigated the fraud, reporting in 1733. Bankruptcy proceedings against some directors dragged on until the 1740s (see J.M. Bulloch, 'The Charitable Corporation', *Notes and Queries*, 160 (1931), pp. 237–41). The *GM* covered the affair extensively in the 1730s, including a long list of individuals, 'Sufferers by the *Charitable Corporation*, entitled to Relief from the Lottery granted for that Purpose', 5.1734, pp. 235–7.

107. *GM*, 7.1737, p. 451. Spence's death was in the same list.
108. It was headed as *'from the* Gazette' in, for example, *GM*, 7.1746, p. 384. A random sample of the lists cross-checked with the *London Gazette* shows that the names and sequence are the same.
109. See Julian Hoppit, *Risk and Failure in English Business, 1700–1800* (Cambridge, 1987), especially contemporary preference for security over profit maximization, pp. 170–1, and on the broader economic impact of the Seven Years' War, Stephen Conway, *War, State, and Society in Mid-Eighteenth-Century Britain and Ireland* (Oxford, 2006), pp. 83–114.
110. Under the law of couverture only a single woman (*feme sole*) was a legal person. Married women were subsumed within a husband's bankruptcy. However, this does not affect the point here, that both the fact and representation of bankruptcy were gendered as male.
111. For modes of address see Anon., *Letters on the Most Common […] as Well as the Occasions in Life* (London, 1786, 1st published 1756), pp. 21–2. Template letters to 'persons in business', such as a draper and surgeon, were prefixed 'Mr'. Merchants required a greater dignity in address.
112. *GM*, 7.1750, p. 333.
113. Sweet, *English Town*, p. 7.
114. *GM*, 1.1735, p. 46. See also Calvin Yost, *Poetry of the Gentleman's Magazine: A Study in Eighteenth-Century Literary Taste* (Philadelphia, 1936), pp. 68–86.
115. *GM*, 1.1744, p. 44.
116. *GM*, 1.1746, p. 34.
117. *GM*, 1.1755, pp. 21–3.
118. Emily Lorraine De Montluzin, 'Quicksilver Ladies, Odes to Turds, and Three-Seater Privies: The Scatological Underside of the *Gentleman's Magazine*', ANQ, 21 (2008), pp. 24–35', p. 24.
119. 'A Riddle' by 'Silvius', *GM*, 6.1734, p. 328.
120. *GM*, 7.1734, p. 387.
121. *GM*, 1.1738, p. 42 (by 'O.', attrib. John Boyle, 5th Earl of Orrery); 1.1741, p. 47; 1.1744, p.46. 7.1745, p. 445; 7.1746, p. 377; 1.1751, p. 35. Crambo is a game in which players take turns to 'cap' in rhyme a line from the opposition (*Spectator*, no. 504, 8.10.1712). For the 1718 incident, written up by *GM* reader Cannon (1684–1743) in 1742, see John Money, ed., *The Chronicles of John Cannon Excise Officer and Writing Master*, 2 vols (Oxford, 2010), I, pp. 154–5.
122. Some 27,000 men in 1738, 77,000 in 1748 and 31,000 in 1755, a participation rate of approximately 1 in 15, see Conway, *War, State, and Society*, pp. 56–82.
123. For the professional officer see John Childs, *The British Army of William III, 1689–1702* (Manchester, 1987), pp. 34–83; Conway, *War, State, and Society*,

pp. 68–9, 75–6; Penelope J. Corfield, *Power and the Professions in Britain, 1700–1850* (London, 1995), pp. 25, 191; and N.A.M. Rodger, *The Wooden World: An Anatomy of the Georgian Navy* (London, 1986), pp. 252–327.

124. Ibid., p. 18.
125. *GM*, 1.1732, p. 564 (from *Applebee's Journal*).
126. Rex Whitworth, ed., *Gunner at Large: The Diary of James Wood RA, 1746–65* (London, 1988), p. 105.
127. *GM*, 1.1742, p. 45, letter from the *Poultney* in Gibraltar.
128. *GM*, 1.1734, p. 50; 7.1736, p. 424. For these contradictions inherent in the Georgian military see Kevin Linch and Matthew McCormack, eds., *Britain's Soldiers: Rethinking War and Society, 1715–1815* (Liverpool, 2014), pp. 1–2.
129. For the militia, see Ian F.W. Beckett, *The Amateur Military Tradition, 1558–1945* (Manchester, 1991).
130. For political debates leading to the Militia Act 1757, see J.R. Western, *The English Militia in the Eighteenth Century: The Story of a Political Issue, 1660–1802* (London, 1965), pp. 104–40.
131. *GM*, 1.1745, pp. 25–9.
132. *GM*, 1.1741, p. 38. The 'Life' started at 8.1740, p. 389.
133. *GM*, 7.1748, pp. 325 (anonymous) and 327 (by 'A Lady' addressed to his widow, with epitaph in Westminster Abbey composed by Dr Young, author of the popular *Night Thoughts*, printed beneath).
134. *GM*, 7.1738, pp. 377–8.
135. *GM*, 1.1743, pp. 36–7.
136. *GM*, 7.1745, p. 387. The encounter, and the 45 British men killed outright and 107 wounded, of whom a further seven died, was reported under 'Ships Taken' (p. 352).
137. *GM*, 1.1747, p. 41.
138. *GM*, 7.1743, p. 380.
139. *GM*, 7.1748, pp. 329, 330.
140. *Gunner at Large,* e.g. p. 78.
141. See *GM*, 9.1731, pp. 376 (from *US*) and 384–5 (*Fog's Journal*). See also Andrew, 'Code of Honour', p. 418 and Elizabeth Foyster, ' "Boys will be boys?" Manhood and Aggression, 1660–1800', in ed. Tim Hitchcock and Michèle Cohen, *English Masculinities*, pp. 151–66.
142. *GM*, 1.1743, p. 45.
143. Jean E. Hunter, 'Eighteenth-Century Englishwoman: According to the *Gentleman's Magazine*' in *Woman in the Eighteenth Century and Other Essays*, ed. Paul Fritz and Richard Morton (Toronto, 1976), pp. 73–88, p. 77.
144. *GM*, 7.1732, pp. 850–1 (from *US*).
145. *GM*, 7.1736, p. 413, *ll.* 126–7.
146. *GM*, 7.1750, pp. 291–3.
147. Anon., *The Female Soldier: Or, The Surprising Life and Adventures of Hannah Snell* (London, 1750). Cross-dressing, lesbianism and flagellation had recently appeared in a pornographic context in John Cleland's *Fanny Hill or Memoirs of a Woman of Pleasure* (paperback edition Harmondsworth, n.d., 1st published 1748–9) (better known as *Fanny Hill*), published 1748–9 and listed in the *GM* 'Register of Books', 2.1749, p. 96.
148. See Henry R. French and Mark Rothery, *Man's Estate: Landed Gentry Masculinities, 1660–1900* (Oxford, 2012), pp. 232–3, and Amanda Vickery, *Behind Closed Doors: At Home in Georgian England* (Yale, 2009), p. 8.

149. *GM*, 7.1732, p. 553 (article on problems inherent in a second marriage where therewere children from the first). For companionate marriage see Lawrence Stone, *The Family, Sex and Marriage in England, 1500–1800* (abridged edition, Harmondsworth, 1979, 1st published 1977) and later critiques, notably Fletcher, *Gender, Sex and Subordination*.
150. Ibid., pp. 293–5.
151. *GM*, 11.1750, p. 518.
152. Michael Roper, 'Slipping Out of View: Subjectivity and Emotion in Gender History', *History Workshop Journal*, 59 (2005), pp. 57–72'.
153. *Diary of Dudley Ryder*, pp. 74, 203, 297, 343–4, 347, 349.
154. *GM*, 1.1740, p. 32.
155. *GM*, 7.1743, pp. 376–80, attrib. Laurence Sterne, William Rider, Samuel Johnson (4), Charlotte Brereton and Samuel Boyse.
156. *GM*, 7.1742, p. 375.
157. *GM*, 1.1741, p. 45, anonymous, the sub-title *'intended to have been sung after the complaining Pastoral Ballad in* Comus' indicating as probable author Revd John Dalton (1709–63), adaptor of Milton's *Comus* for the stage.
158. *GM*, 1.1736, p. 49, part of a jocular series on courtship between 'Melissa' (Jane Brereton) and, unbeknown to her, Thomas Beach.
159. *GM*, 7.1738, p. 369.
160. *GM*, 11.1748 p. 519; 12.1748, p. 568; 1.1749, p. 40.
161. *GM*, 1.1745, p. 48.
162. *GM*, 1.1735, pp. 14–15.
163. *GM*, 7.1736, p. 418.
164. *GM*, 1.1745, p. 46; 7.1750, pp. 323, 326–7.
165. *GM*, 6.1735, p. 304 (from *Prompter*).
166. *GM*, 'An Essay on Friendship', 1.1737, p. 29 (from *Fog's Journal*).
167. *GM*, 7.1735, pp. 353–4.
168. *GM*, 7.1733, pp. 375–6, anonymous, attrib. Samuel Wesley (1690/1–1739, clergyman, poet and older brother of John and Charles), later published in his *Poems on Several Occasions* (London, 1736).
169. *GM*, 7.1736, p. 420; 1.1738, p. 43.
170. *GM*, 1.1737, pp. 52–3.
171. *GM*, 3.1751, pp. 131–2.
172. Sarah Kinkel, 'Saving Admiral Byng: Imperial Debates, Military Governance and Popular Politics at the Outbreak of the Seven Years' War', *Journal for Maritime Research*, 13 (2011), pp. 3–19 (pp. 3–4, 9).
173. The Navy Act 1749, 23GII.c.33, which also introduced the mandatory death penalty.
174. *GM*, 4.1756, p. 201.
175. *GM*, 5.1756, pp. 257–8.
176. *GM*, 6.1756, pp. 312–3.
177. *GM*, 7.1756, pp. 319–20 (account of Byng's arrival near Minorca and siege); 321 (French account), 324–6 (plan of Fort St Phillip with explanation and portrait of Blakeney), 346 (letter stating the importance of Minorca to British commerce and the loss of maritime honour at its fall), 347–8 (articles of capitulation), 351 (mock articles against Byng), 351–2 (letter from Bristol attacking Byng), 354–6 (5 anonymous poems) and 358 (report of Byng's arrival and arrest, of his brother's death after travelling to Portsmouth to

visit him, and of an Irish cargo ship's rather faster journey to and from Mahon).

178. *GM*, 11.1746, pp. 598–9; 7.1748, p. 316; 6.1754, p. 257; 6.1756, p. 272.
179. *GM*, 11.1746, p. 598.
180. Bevis Hillier, *Early English Porcelain* (London, 1992), p. 14 and Stephen Moore, ' "A Nation of Harlequins"? Politics and Masculinity in Mid-Eighteenth-Century England', *Journal of British Studies*, 49 (2010), pp. 514–39 (p. 534).
181. See editorial statement, *GM*, 12.1756, p. 572.
182. *GM*, 9.1756, p. 412; 10.1756, pp. 479–85; 1756, Supplement, pp. 599–602; 1.1757, pp. 30–2, and Robert Donald Spector, *English Literary Periodicals and the Climate of Opinion during the Seven Years' War* (The Hague, 1966), p. 25.
183. Ibid., p. 24.
184. *GM*, 8.1756, pp. 394 (from the *Monitor*, probably referring to Byng's fortune from his flag share of Italian prizes in 1747–8 with which he bought land near Barnet, Hertfordshire and built Wrotham Park), 407, 409.
185. *GM*, 7.1756, pp. 325, 356.
186. *GM*, 8.1756, pp. 390–2, from Anon., *Memoirs of the Life* (London, 1756).
187. *GM*, 11.1756, p. 545.
188. *LM*, 4.1756, facing p. 184.
189. This assessment differs from Julia Banister, 'The Court Martial of Admiral John Byng: Politeness and the Military Man in the Mid-Eighteenth Century', in Heather Ellis and Jessica Meyer, eds. *Masculinity and the Other*, pp. 236–59, where Blakeney represents an old, anti-polite model of military masculinity and Byng effeminate 'modern' masculinity. It is closer to Moore's discussion of discourse around the Byng crisis as being about the political deployment of the archetypes of the incompetent gentleman and competent tarpaulin rather than gender as such ('Nation of Harlequins').
190. Letter to Lord George Sackville, Louisbourg, 30.1.1758, in Beckles Wilson, ed., *The Life and Letters of James Wolfe* (London, 1909), p. 390 and letter, 29.11.1756, in W. S. Lewis, ed., *The Yale Edition of Horace Walpole's Correspondence*, 48 vols (New Haven, CT, 1937–83), XXI, p. 24.
191. *GM*, 9.1756, p. 412.
192. *GM*, 10.1756, p. 486.
193. *GM*, 1756, Supplement, p. 610, written 1747 after 1746 court martial of Admirals Mathews and Lestock, and revived during the Byng affair.
194. Hunt, *Middling Sort*, p. 193.
195. *Diary of Dudley Ryder*, p. 309 (30.8.1716); L.G. Mitchell, ed., *Purefoy Letters, 1735–53* (London, 1973) p. 167, no. 220.
196. Neil McKendrick, John Brewer and J.H. Plumb, *Birth of Consumer Society: The Commercialization of Eighteenth-Century England* (London, 1983, 1st published 1982), p. 269.

5   Gentlemanly Masculinity in the *Gentleman's Magazine*, 1757 to 1789

1. John Brown, *An Estimate of the Manners and Principles of the Times* (London, 1757), pp. 5, 29, 97, 117.

2. *GM*, 4.1757, pp. 166–71.
3. Kathleen Wilson, *The Island Race: Englishness, Empire and Gender in the Eighteenth Century* (London, 2003) and ed., *A New Imperial History: Culture, Identity and Modernity in Britain and the Empire 1660–1840* (Cambridge, 2004). See also Julie Flavell, *When London Was Capital of America* (New Haven, CT, 2010); Philippa Levine, ed., *Gender and Empire* (Oxford, 2004); Matthew McCormack, *The Independent Man: Citizenship and Gender Politics in Georgian England* (Manchester, 2005); Andrew Oliver ed., *Journal of Samuel Curwen, Loyalist*, 2 vols (Harvard, 1972).
4. See Linda Colley, *Britons: Forging the Nation, 1707–1837* (paperback edition 2005, 1st published Yale, 1992); Stephen Conway, *War, State, and Society in Mid-Eighteenth-Century Britain and Ireland* (Oxford, 2006); Gerald Newman, *The Rise of English Nationalism: A Cultural History, 1740–1830* (revised edition 1997, 1st published London, 1987); Wilson, *Island Race*, pp. 29–53.
5. Linda Colley, *The Ordeal of Elizabeth Marsh: A Woman in World History* (London, 2007), pp. 40, 93.
6. Conway, *War, State, and Society*, p. 115.
7. *GM*, 1.1758, p. 20, as 'T. Row'.
8. Count Frederick Kielmansegge, trans. Countess Kielmansegg, *Diary of a Journey to England in the Years 1761–2* (London, 1902), p. 255.
9. Conway, *War, State, and Society*, pp. 167–8.
10. See Donna Andrew, ed., *London Debating Societies, 1776–99* (London, 1994); Conway, *War, State, and Society*, pp. 143–69; George F.E. Rudé, *Wilkes and Liberty: A Social Study of 1763–74* (Oxford, 1962); John Sainsbury, *John Wilkes: The Lives of a Libertine* (Ashgate, 2006).
11. *GM*, 1.1786, p. 84.
12. *GM*, 1.1767, pp. 21–2 (a scheme projected by Lord Egmont).
13. See S.C. Ghosh, *The Social Condition of the British Community in Bengal, 1757–1800* (Leiden, 1970) and P.J. Marshall, 'British Society in India under the East India Company', *Modern Asian Studies*, 31(1997), pp. 89–108.
14. *GM*, 7.1788, p. 657 (clustering at the head of the lists was due to chronological arrangement and shipping timetables).
15. *GM*, 1.1789, p. 85.
16. See Conway's comments on the 1785 *GM* (*War, State, and Society*, p. 332).
17. For impostors see *GM*, 7.1768, p. 346 and 7.1773, p. 352. The Perreaus' case was reported from 3.1775, pp. 148–50 to 1.1776 (execution, pp. 44–6). See too Donna T. Andrew and Randall McGowen, *The Perreaus and Mrs Rudd: Forgery and Betrayal in Eighteenth-Century London* (Berkeley, CA, 2001).
18. *GM*, 1.1787, pp. 23–4.
19. There were no bankrupts in the 1788 and 1789 samples. Women accounted for two per cent of bankrupts and only two men were titled: 1.1759 Sir Thomas Reynell, broker of St George Hanover Square and 7.1772 Sir Richard Glyn, banker of Birchin Lane.
20. Again corroborated in Julian Hoppit, *Risk and Failure in English Business, 1700–1800* (Cambridge, 1987). See also Conway, *War, State, and Society*, pp. 115–42; and James Raven, *Judging New Wealth: Popular Publishing and Responses to Commerce in England, 1750–1800* (Oxford, 1992), pp. 187–8.

21. *GM*, 6.1765, pp. 153–4; Samuel Foote, *The Commissary: A Comedy in Three Acts* (4th edition, London, 1782), Act I, scene I. p. 17, Act II, scene I, p. 31.
22. Richard Cumberland, *The West Indian: A Comedy* (London, 1771). The Prologue and Epilogue were printed in *GM*, 2.1771, p. 87.
23. *GM*, 1.1758, pp. 20–1.
24. *GM*, 7.1789, pp. 653–61, 'Accurate Statement of the late Revolution in France' (p. 656).
25. *GM*, 7.1761, pp. 294, 325.
26. *GM*, 1.1770, p. 16 (as 'T. Row'); Alexander Pope, *Epistle II*, 'To a Lady: *Of the* **Characters** *of Women*' (1743), *l*. 2.
27. Appendix 1 and Stephen Howard, ' "A Bright Pattern to all her sex": Representations of Women in Periodical and Newspaper Biography', in *Gender in Eighteenth-Century England: Roles, Representations and Responsibilities*, ed. Hannah Barker and Elaine Chalus (London, 1997), pp. 230–49, p. 233.
28. *GM*, 1.1776, p. 38.
29. *GM*, 7.1787, pp. 580–2, 632–3.
30. *Idler*, no. 12. 1.7.1758.
31. *GM*, 1.1783, p. 92. For the Walkers ('a classic example of a family of humble origins who rose rapidly in society through the ingenuity and hard work of the first generation and whose late members gradually withdrew from trade to live as landed gentry') see *ODNB*; for Need see *ODNB* for Sir Richard Arkwright (1732–92).
32. *GM*, 1.1771, p. 47; 1.1774, p. 334.
33. *GM*, 1.1780, p. 51.
34. *GM*, 1.1774, pp. 72–3.
35. For 'narrative identity' and emplotment in biography, see Paul Ricoeur, *Time and Narrative*, trans. Kathleen McLaughlin and David Pellauer, 3 vols (Chicago, 1984–8) and Isabel Karremann and Anja Müller, eds., *Mediating Identities in Eighteenth-Century England: Public Negotiations, Literary Discourses, Topography* (Farnham, 2011), pp. 1–30 (pp. 6–8).
36. *GM*, 7.1785, pp. 570–1.
37. *GM*, 7.1787, p. 622.
38. Raven, *New Wealth*, pp. 109–10.
39. *GM*, 1.1785, pp. 75–9.
40. *GM*, 7.1787, pp. 572–3 (citing *Idler* no. 63, 30.6.1759).
41. Raven, *New Wealth*, pp. 141–2.
42. *GM*, 1.1773, pp. 15–16.
43. *GM*, 1.1779, pp. 37–8.
44. See Andrew and McGowen, *The Perreaus*, p. 23 and Randall McGowen, 'Forgers and Forgery: Severity and Social Identity in Eighteenth-Century England', in *Moral Panics, the Media and the Law in Early Modern England*, ed. David Lemmings (Basingstoke, 2009), pp. 157–75.
45. Wilson, *Island Race*, p. 25.
46. Phyllis Deutsch, 'Moral Trespass in Georgian London: Gaming, Gender, and Electoral Politics in the Age of George III', *Historical Journal*, 39 (1996), pp. 637–56.
47. Sir Richard Glyn's bankruptcy (*q.v.*) occurred during this crisis.
48. *GM*, 7.1772, pp. 310–11.
49. *GM*, 7.1777, pp. 341–2.

50. *GM*, 7.1763, pp. 354–5; 7.1784, p. 533.
51. Simon Dickie, *Cruelty and Laughter: Forgotten Comic Literature and the Unsentimental Eighteenth Century* (Chicago, 2011).
52. *ODNB*.
53. *GM*, 1.1771, pp. 16–17; W. Jackson, *The Beauties of Nature: Displayed in a Sentimental Ramble through the Luxuriant Fields, with a Retrospective View of her, to which is Added, a Choice Collection of Thoughts, Concluded with Poems on Various Occasions* (Birmingham, 1769); *Monthly Review*, 3.1770, pp. 167–73.
54. See Edward J. Bristow, *Vice and Vigilance: Purity Movements in Britain since 1700* (Dublin, 1977), pp. 32–50 on mid-century concern at obscenity in print, and Raven, *New Wealth*, pp. 138–56 for 'changing appraisals of refinement' (p. 150).
55. *GM*, 1.1759, p. 31.
56. *GM*, 7.1788, p. 640.
57. *GM*, 6.1788, pp. 475–8.
58. *GM*, 7.1788, pp. 599–600.
59. *GM*, 1.1783, pp. 31–2.
60. William Jones, *Diary of the Revd William Jones 1777–1821, Curate and Vicar of Broxbourne and the Hamlet of Hoddesdon 1781–1821*, ed. O.F. Christie (London, 1929), p. 214.
61. *GM*, 1.1768, p. 37, lines on an ideal man, from 'The Picture', 'Sung by Mrs. Weichsell at Vaux-hall. Set to Musick by Mr Samuel Howard'.
62. There is a developing literature on male domesticity and fatherhood and their importance in public and private life, although much of this concentrates on the stern Victorian paterfamilias and the nineteenth-century legal changes to women's status within marriage. See for example: Joanne Bailey, *Parenting in England, 1760–1830: Emotion, Identity, and Generation* (Oxford, 2012),; Trev Lynn Broughton and Helen Rogers, eds., *Gender and Fatherhood in the Nineteenth Century* (Basingstoke, 2007), and John Tosh, *A Man's Place: Masculinity and the Middle-Class Home in Victorian England* (New Haven, CT, 2007, 1st published 1999).
63. *GM*, 7.1771, p. 328.
64. *GM*, 1.1788, pp. 63–4, poem on death of Lady Smith.
65. *GM*, 1.1789, p. 89.
66. *GM*, 7.1776, p. 332.
67. Oliver Goldsmith, *The Vicar of Wakefield*, in *Collected Works of Oliver Goldsmith*, ed. Arthur Friedman, 5 vols (Oxford, 1966), IV, p. 33.
68. *GM*, 1.1762, pp. 21–2. The Militia Act was in fact modified in this way in 1762 (Ian F.W. Beckett, *Amateur Military Tradition, 1558–1945* (Manchester, 1991), pp. 61–89).
69. Sarah M.S. Pearsall, *Atlantic Families: Lives and Letters in the Later Eighteenth Century* (Oxford, 2008), p. 7.
70. *GM*, 1.1763, pp. 16–17.
71. *GM*, 7.1772, p. 334; Anon., *Considerations on the Causes of the Present Stagnation of Matrimony* (London, 1772), pp. 32, 68, 69.
72. Appendix 1.
73. *GM*, 1.1766, pp. 36, 46.
74. *GM*, 1.1772, p. 336.
75. On this development from *c.* 1750 see Bailey, *Parenting in England*, pp. 22–47.

76. *GM*, 7.1764, p. 343.
77. *GM*, 7.1771, p. 328; 7.1780, p. 337.
78. *GM*, 7.1766, p. 329 (the translation process was itself gendered, the original in the *Adventurer* with Latin translation was sent to the *GM* by 'a Lady' with a request for an English version, in turn supplied by 'a young gentleman').
79. *GM*, 1.1776, p. 36.
80. J.L. Hibberd, 'Salomon Gessner's Idylls as Prose Poems', *Modern Language Review*, 68 (1973), pp. 569–76 (p. 569).
81. *GM*, 2.1776, pp. 80–2.
82. *GM*, 7.1776, p. 297 and facing.
83. See review of literary dispute between Samuel Sharp, author of *Letters from Italy*, and Giuseppe Baretti, *GM*, 7.1768, pp. 334–5 and Roberto Bizzocchi, 'Cicisbei: Italian Morality and European Values in the Eighteenth Century', in *Italy's Eighteenth Century: Gender and Culture in the Age of the Grand Tour*, ed. Paula Findlen, Wendy Wassyng Roworth, and Catherine M. Sama (Stanford, 2009), pp. 35–58.
84. *GM*, 1.1772, p. 33–7; 7.1785, pp. 532–4.
85. François de la Rochefoucauld, *A Frenchman in England 1784: Being the 'Mélanges sur l'Angleterre' of François de la Rochefoucauld*, ed. Jean Marchand, trans. S.C. Roberts (Cambridge, 1933), pp. 48, 50.
86. *GM*, 7.1760, pp. 317–18.
87. *GM*, 6.1775, p. 281.
88. *GM*, 1.1777, p. 39.
89. *GM*, 1.1774, p. 46.
90. *GM*, 1.1785, p. 76.
91. *GM*, 7.1789, p. 670.
92. Linda Colley, 'The Apotheosis of George III: Loyalty, Royalty and the British Nation, 1760–1820', *Past & Present*, 102 (1984), pp. 94–129 (p. 102). See also Lisa Forman Cody, *Birthing the Nation: Sex, Science, and the Conception of Eighteenth-Century Britons* (Oxford, 2005), p. 216.
93. *GM*, 7.1775, pp. 316–7 (*LM*, 5.1775, pp. 248–9); Colley, 'Apotheosis', p. 97.
94. See G.J. Barker-Benfield, *The Culture of Sensibility: Sex and Society in Eighteenth-Century Britain* (Chicago, 1992); Philip Carter, *Men and the Emergence of Polite Society, Britain, 1660–1800* (Harlow, 2001), pp. 88–123; and Dror Wahrman, *The Making of the Modern Self: Identity and Culture in Eighteenth-Century England* (Yale, 2006).
95. William Matthews, ed., *The Diary of Dudley Ryder, 1715–16* (London, 1939), pp. 249, 339.
96. William Hutton, *The Life of William Hutton, FASS* (reprint edition, 1998, 1st published London, 1816), p. 53.
97. *GM*, 7.1782, p. 358.
98. For instance 72-year-old Mr Philip Lermitte of Stratford Green, Essex, *GM*, 7.1782, p. 359.
99. *GM*, 7.1782, p. 357.
100. See account in *Scots Magazine*, 1.1782, p. 52.
101. *GM*, 3.1782, p. 151.
102. *GM*, 10.1783, p. 871.
103. Wahrman, *Modern Self*, p. 38.

104. The only reference found is *GM*, 9.1777, p. 452, epitaph and poem to Revd Eccles, who had falsely claimed to be the author (the novel was originally anonymous). Fittingly Eccles died attempting to save a drowning youth in the river Avon, the poem was by 'An Invalid' and both tributes were suitably sentimental.
105. *GM*, 9.1774, pp. 430–1; John Langhorne, *Country Justice: A Poem by one of his Majesty's Justices of the Peace for the County of Somerset* (London, 1774–7).
106. *GM*, 1.1768, pp. 17–18.
107. *GM*, 7.1769, p. 360.
108. *GM*, 7.1771, p. 328.
109. *GM*, 1.1780, pp. 25–6.
110. *GM*, 7.1786, pp. 538–40 ('S.H.S.', commending the Royal Humane Society).
111. *GM*, 10.1777, pp. 497–8; James Finlayson, ed., *The Sermons of Hugh Blair, Complete in Four Volumes: To which Is Prefixed, a Short Account of the Life and Character of the Author*, 4 vols (London, 1815). Individual volumes were published from 1777, collected volumes after Blair's death in 1800.
112. Donna T. Andrew, *Philanthropy and Police: London Charity in the Eighteenth Century* (Princeton, 1989), pp. 74–97.
113. Richard Cumberland, *The Memoirs of Richard Cumberland*, ed. Richard J. Dircks, 2 vols (New York, 2002), II, pp. 120–1.
114. See W.M. Jacob, *Lay People and Religion in the Early Eighteenth Century* (Cambridge, 1996), pp. 93–123 and 228; Andrew, *Philanthropy and Police*, pp. 41–2.
115. *GM*, 1.1762, pp. 6–7, letter from 'A.' attributing cock-throwing to 'the lower sort of people', whereas kindness to animals was 'a sign of an excellent and amiable disposition'; 7.1777, pp. 350–1 letter from 'A Country Churchwarden' abhorring 'the blind persecution of an helpless, innocent, being', the hedgehog, by the ignorant who believed they milked cows; 1.1789, pp. 15–17, letter from 'Humanus' linking boyhood cruelty to animals to adult love of cruel sports.
116. *GM*, 1.1758, pp. 17–20; 1.1761, pp. 291–3 and 305 (letter commending the new Oxford hospital and hoping Cambridge would follow suit); 1.1763, pp. 25–6, 'A Case humbly offered to the Consideration of Parliament' to end abuse of patients in private madhouses by promoting more accountable public charity hospitals; 7.1776, pp. 302–4 letter from 'Hygeia' expressing concern at the spread of disease due *inter alia* to insanitary conditions in London's gaols and hospitals and 1.1787, pp. 73–4, copy of letter from Robert Raikes on the reforming benefits of gentleman-sponsored Sunday schools.
117. *GM*, 7.1774, p. 311 welcomed the new Insolvency Act which improved prisoners' prospects of discharge. The 1774 Preface was given entirely to the founding of the RHS. Its prizes for essays were advertised on *GM* wrappers (5, 9 and 10.1787).
118. *GM*, 7.1775, p. 326.
119. *GM*, 1.1789, pp. 14–15, letter from 'R.R.E.'.
120. *GM*, 7.1761, p. 291.
121. H. Meriton and J. Rogers, *A Circumstantial Narrative of the Loss of the Halsewell (East-Indiaman), which was Unfortunately Wrecked at Seacombe, 6th of January, 1786* (London, 1786).

122. *GM*, 1.1786, pp. 57–60, 75–6.
123. *GM*, 7.1786, p. 436; 5.1789, p. 450. There were two subscription prints from sentimental paintings of the scene (by Thomas Stothard, National Maritime Museum: ZBA4537 and James Northcote/James Gillray, NPG: D13063).
124. Meriton and Rogers, *Circumstantial Narrative*, pp. 27–8, 58–62.
125. *GM*, 1.1761, pp. 33–4.
126. *GM*, 2.1761, pp. 79–80.
127. *GM*, 1.1765, p. 45.
128. *GM*, 5.1765, pp. 227–9.
129. *GM*, 1.1765, pp. 38–9, anonymous, by Sir Charles Hanbury Williams (1708–59) written 1740, published posthumously, see Roger Lonsdale, ed., *The New Oxford Book of Eighteenth Century Verse* (paperback edition 2009, 1st published Oxford, 1984), pp. 328–31.
130. *GM*, 1.1784, pp. 18–20, letter from 'A Parish Officer'.
131. Anna Clark, *Scandal: The Sexual Politics of the British Constitution* (Princeton, 2004).
132. F. Lord Baltimore, *A Tour to the East, in the Years 1763 and 1764* (London, 1767) and Wallace Shugg, 'The Baron and the Milliner: Lord Baltimore's Rape Trial as a Mirror of Class Tensions in Mid-Georgian London', *Maryland Historical Magazine*, 83 (1988), pp. 310–30.
133. *GM*, 1.1768, p. 42 and Shugg, 'Baron and Milliner', pp. 312–13.
134. *St James' Chronicle*, 26.2.1768.
135. Joseph Gurney, *The Trial of Frederick Calvert, Esq., Baron of Baltimore, in the Kingdom of Ireland: For a Rape on the Body of Sarah Woodcock: And of Elizabeth Griffinburg, and Ann Harvey* (London, 1768).
136. BM: AN899392001.
137. *Public Advertiser*, 28.3.1768; *North Briton*, 9.12.1769 (1768 Annual) respectively. William Bingley revived the title of Wilkes' paper between 5.1768 and 5.1771.
138. In fact *A Letter to Lord B –* (London, 1768); *GM*, 1.1768, pp. 31, 42.
139. See Thomas Stretzer, *A New Description of Merryland, Containing a Topographical, Geographical and Natural History of that Country* (London, 1740) and Julie Peakman, *Mighty Lewd Books: The Development of Pornography in Eighteenth-Century England* (Basingstoke, 2003).
140. *GM*, 4.1768, pp. 180–7.
141. Woodcock was sufficiently literate to frame her evidence in these terms, reading the *Spectator* and writing to her father while in captivity.
142. *Westminster Journal & London Political Miscellany*, 2.4.1768.
143. For the contemporary view of milliners' shops as brothels, see R. Campbell, *London Tradesman* (facsimile reprint 1969, 1st published London, 1747), p. 208 and a 1782 print 'A Morning Ramble, or, The Milliners Shop', in which two beaux lounge at the counter (BM: 1935.0522.1.31).
144. Gurney, *Trial*, pp. 9, 24
145. For comment on her testimony, see *Westminster Journal*, 2.4.1768. For problems rape plaintiffs faced giving evidence, see Esther Snell, 'Trials in Print: Narratives of Rape Trials in the *Proceedings of the Old Bailey*', in *Crime, Courtrooms, and the Public Sphere in Britain, 1700–1850*, ed. David Lemmings (Farnham, 2012), pp. 23–41.
146. *GM*, 1.1772, p. 44.

147. Anon., *Modern Chastity: Or, The Agreeable Rape: A Poem, by a Young Gentleman of Sixteen in Vindication of the Right Hon. Lord B——e* (London, 1768); *LM*, 3.1768, p. 160; *GM*, 4.1768, p. 188.
148. *LM*, 3.1768, pp. 162–3. The 'mob' was associated with magistrate Sir John Fielding (see Shugg, 'Baron and Milliner').
149. *LM*, 4.1768, pp. 215–20.
150. *LM*, 6.1768, pp. 283–5; 9.1768, p. 500; 10.1771, p. 524.
151. For attitudes to adultery and criminal conversation suits, see David M. Turner, *Fashioning Adultery: Gender, Sex and Civility in England, 1660–1740* (Cambridge, 2002).
152. *GM*, 7.1770, pp. 314–8; 10.1770, pp. 470–4 (by Hawkesworth).
153. *GM*, 7.1774, pp. 319–22.
154. *GM*, 1.1778, p. 23.
155. *GM*, 1.1780, pp. 10–14.
156. James Peller Malcolm, *Anecdotes of the Manners and Customs*, 2 vols (2nd edition, London, 1810), II, p. 69.
157. See *GM*, 1.1770, pp. 11–12, letter from Dublin; 1.1783, p. 85 'State of Affairs in Ireland'.
158. For example *GM*, 7.1762, pp. 313–19. For the press in this period, see Hannah Barker, *Newspapers, Politics and English Society, 1695–1855* (Harlow, 2000), pp. 147–70.
159. See *GM*, 1770, Preface and Peter D.G. Thomas, 'The Beginning of Parliamentary Reporting in Newspapers, 1768–74', *English Historical Review*, 74 (1959), pp. 623–36'.
160. *GM*, 7.1769, p. 361. For analysis of Wilkes' supporters, see Rudé, *Wilkes and Liberty*.
161. *GM*, 1.1770, pp. 42–3; 2.1770, pp. 59–60. See also the extended attack in R-, P-, Sir, *The Life, Adventures, and Amours of Sir R- P- Who So Recently had the Honour to Present the F— Address at the English Court* (London, 1770) and *ODNB*. For the paradox of Wilkes see Sainsbury, *John Wilkes*.
162. Society for Constitutional Information, founded 1780 by Major John Cartwright (1740–1824): *GM*, 1.1787, p. 40 and *ODNB*; Shop Tax: *GM*, 7.1785, p. 564; 7.1787, pp. 599–600; 7.1789, p. 667.
163. *GM*, 7.1780, pp. 312–16. See also Ian Haywood and John Seed, eds., *The Gordon Riots: Politics, Culture and Insurrection in Late Eighteenth-Century Britain* (Cambridge, 2012), pp. 1–17, and Matthew McCormack, 'Supporting the Civil Power: Citizen Soldiers and the Gordon Riots', *London Journal*, 37 (2012), pp. 27–41 (p. 38).
164. As did Joseph Brasbridge (*The Fruits of Experience: Or, Memoir of Joseph Brasbridge Written in his 80th and 81st Years* (2nd edition, London, 1824), p. 186).
165. *GM*, 7.1764, p. 350; 1.1774, p. 46. Baldy's bequest was not mentioned in death notices in the *Lady's* and *Town and Country* magazines for 1.1774. Baldy dined with Wilkes on four occasions in the 1770s (Robin Eagles, ed., *The Diaries of John Wilkes, 1770–79* (Woodbridge, 2014)) and his portrait was captioned 'An honest man' (NPG: D588).
166. *GM*, 1.1762, p. 71; 2.1762, pp. 132–3; 4.1762, p. 156; 9.1762, p. 422; 1.1763, pp. 27–8.
167. Letters from 'A.B.' and 'F†S', *GM*, 1.1768, pp. 6–7, 11–13.

168. *GM*, 7.1776, pp. 315–16; 1.1777, p. 11–13; 7.1777, p. 312.
169. *GM*, 1.1770, pp. 7–8, 9–10 (letter from 'S – r').
170. *GM*, 7.1780, pp. 319–20.
171. *GM*, 7.1758, p. 329; 7.1782, pp. 326–7, 333; 1.1787, pp. 18–19; 1.1788, pp. 40–1.
172. *GM*, 1.1787, p. 72.
173. *GM*, 7.1788, pp. 660–1.
174. *GM*, 1.1758, pp. 20–1.
175. *GM*, 1.1769, p. 48.
176. *GM*, 7.1779, p. 357.
177. *GM*, 7.1783, p. 577.
178. *GM*, 7.1786, p 568.
179. *GM*, 7.1784, pp. 497–9.
180. *GM*, 1.1800, p. 84.
181. 30GII.c.25.
182. J.R. Western, *The English Militia in the Eighteenth Century: The Story of a Political Issue, 1660–1802* (London, 1965), pp. 303–39.
183. Matthew McCormack, 'The New Militia: War, Politics and Gender', *Gender & History*, 19 (2007b), pp. 483–500.
184. D.M. Low, ed., *Gibbon's Journal to January 28ᵗʰ, 1763* (London, 1929), pp. 143, 191, 193–4.
185. Sainsbury, *John Wilkes*, p. 64.
186. *GM*, 7.1759, pp. 323–4, 'To the Militia Men of the County of Dorset' for example; Catriona Kennedy and Matthew McCormack, eds., *Soldiering in Britain and Ireland, 1750–1850: Men of Arms* (Basingstoke, 2012), pp. 1–14 (p. 11).
187. *GM*, 1.1758, pp. 20–1.
188. *GM*, 7.1759, p. 333; 7.1760, pp. 320–1; 1.1762, p.36.
189. *GM*, 10.1759, pp. 466–74; 11.1759, pp. 539, 549.
190. *GM*, 1.1760, pp. 31–2; 7.1760, pp. 311–15.
191. Nicholas Rogers, 'Brave Wolfe: The Making of a Hero', in Kathleen Wilson, ed., *A New Imperial History: Culture, Identity and Modernity in Britain and the Empire, 1660–1840* (Cambridge, 2004), pp. 239–59 (p. 239), and Alan McNairn, *Behold the Hero: General Wolfe and the Arts in the Eighteenth Century* (Liverpool, 1997).
192. *GM*, 7.1764, facing p. 312; 1.1773, p. 39.
193. McNairn, *Behold the Hero*, pp. 129–30.
194. Letter to mother, 17.9.1751, Beckles Wilson, ed., *The Life and Letters of James Wolfe* (London, 1909), p. 153; *GM*, 10.1759, p. 472.
195. Rogers, 'Brave Wolfe', pp. 251–2 and letter to friend Capt. Rickson, 9.6.1751, Wilson, *Life and Letters*, pp. 139–49.
196. Edward Ives, *A Voyage from England to India, in the Year MDCCLIV and an Historical Narrative of the Operations of the Squadron and Army in India, under Watson and Clive, also, a Journey from Persia to England, by an Unusual Route, with an Appendix, Containing an Account of the Diseases Prevalent in Admiral Watson's Squadron, a Description of Most of the Trees, Shrubs, and Plants of India, Illustrated with a Chart, Maps, and Other Copper-plates* (London, 1773), pp. 87, 132.

197. Stanbury Thompson, ed., *The Journal of John Gabriel Stedman, 1744–97, Soldier and Author, Including an Authentic Account of his Expedition to Surinam, in 1772* (London, 1962), pp. 93–4, 396.
198. *GM*, 7.1760, pp. 303–5.
199. *GM*, 1.1763, p. 38.
200. *GM*, 7.1766, p. 305.
201. *GM*, 12.1773-3.1774; 12.1775-3.1776.
202. *GM*, 1.1780, pp. 44–5.
203. *GM*, 7.1784, p. 483.
204. Wilson, *Island Race*, pp. 54–91(p. 59).
205. *GM*, 7.1786, pp. 601–2.
206. *GM*, 1.1778, pp. 14–15.
207. *GM*, 1.1788, pp. 66–9.
208. *GM*, 1.1774, p. 19.
209. Gananath Obeyesekere, *The Apotheosis of Captain Cook: European Mythmaking in thePacific* (Princeton, 1992), p. 24.
210. *GM*, 1786, Supplement, p. 1143; 7.1788, p. 655.
211. *GM*, 3.1771, pp. 111–12; 2.1773, p. 100.
212. *GM*, 5.1786, p. 485.
213. *GM*, 9.1777, pp. 444–7.
214. *GM*, 5.1786, pp. 359–61.
215. See James Baldwin Brown, *Memoirs of the Public and Private Life of John Howard the Philanthropist* (London, 1818), pp. 482–4. Howard was famously averse to having his image taken, see Richard W. Ireland, 'Howard and the Paparazzi: Painting Penal Reform in the Eighteenth Century', *Art, Antiquity & Law*, 4 (1999), pp. 55–62 and plea by 'Graphicus', *GM*, 9.1786, p. 726.
216. It raised £1,533 13s 6d from 615 persons in *c.* 16 months, see *GM*, 3.1790, p. 278. The subscription committee was reported on the *GM* wrapper for 9.1787. The *Universal Daily Register/The Times* printed a list of subscribers (18.9.1786, p. 3).
217. *GM*, 7.1786, pp. 535–7.
218. *GM*, 2.1787, p. 102.
219. *GM*, 7.1788, p. 638. For Swanwick see *Biographical Directory of the United States Congress, 1774 to Present* (http://bioguide.congress.gov/scripts/biodisplay.pl?index=S001095, accessed 27.11.2012).
220. *GM*, 7.1786, p. 536.
221. *GM*, 3.1790, pp. 276–8. News of Howard's death came from his friend, brewer and MP Samuel Whitbread, but it is not clear whether Whitbread was involved in the obituary. Gough was also a friend of Howard and his *ODNB* entry suggests he was the author. Howard's second wife Henrietta died shortly after Jack's birth in 1765 leaving Howard, who did not remarry, a lone parent.
222. For example *General Magazine & Impartial Review*, 4.1790, p. 145.
223. *GM*, 4.1790, pp. 287–90.
224. *GM*, 8.1790, pp. 685, 713–4.
225. *GM*, 6.1793, p. 513 and facing.
226. *GM*, 7.1814, p. 91.
227. Brown's generally favourable *Memoirs* include anecdotes of ordering Jack to walk barefoot in company as a test of absolute obedience (p. 62) and of

rebellion when Howard was in Italy in 1786. Jack, 'left the uncontrolled master of his house', invited over his dissipated Cambridge friends who upset the servants and villagers and even disrupted a dissenters' meeting (pp. 484–5).

228. See also Nicola Phillips, *The Profligate Son: or, A True Story of Family Conflict, Fashionable Vice, and Financial Ruin in Regency Britain* (Oxford, 2013).
229. *Idler*, no. 5, 19.2.1760.
230. *GM*, 7.1780, p. 331.
231. E.E. Reynolds, ed., *The Mawhood Diary: Selections from the Diary Note-books of William Mawhood, Woollen-draper of London, for the Years 1764–90* (London, 1956).
232. *GM*, 7.1786, p. 616.
233. S.K. Tillyard, *Aristocrats: Caroline, Emily and Sarah Lennox, 1740–1832* (London, 1994), pp. 343, 352–3.

6 Gentlemanly Masculinity in the *Gentleman's Magazine*, 1790 to 1815

1. *GM*, 6.1815, pp. 627–36.
2. Ibid., pp. 615–16.
3. *GM*, 7.1815, pp. 62–4; *ODNB*.
4. L. Simond, *An American in Regency England: The Journal of a Tour in 1810–11*, ed. Christopher Hibbert (London, 1968), pp. 31–2.
5. *GM*, 7.1815, pp. 3–40.
6. Ibid., p. 3.
7. 'E.E.A.', letter on the French Revolution, *GM*, 7.1795, pp. 551–2.
8. William Stafford, 'Representations of the Social Order in *The Gentleman's Magazine*, 1785–1815', *Eighteenth-Century Life*, 33 (2009), pp. 64–91, p. 87.
9. *GM*, 7.1791, pp. 596–600.
10. Arthur Sheps, 'Sedition, Vice and Atheism: The Limits of Toleration and the Orthodox Attack on Rational Religion in Late Eighteenth-Century England', in *Orthodoxy and Heresy in Eighteenth-Century Society: Essays from the De Bartolo Conference*, ed. Regina Hewitt and Pat Rogers (Lewisburg, 2002), pp. 51–68 (pp. 51–2).
11. *GM*, 8.1791, pp. 737–40.
12. *GM*, 7.1792, pp. 648, 653; 7.1795, p. 598; 7.1797, pp. 541–2, 552–4.
13. *GM*, 1.1798, p. 88; 7.1798, p. 636.
14. *GM*, 7.1794, p. 697.
15. *GM*, 7.1809, p. 679.
16. F.P. Lock, *Burke's Reflections on the Revolution in France* (London, 1985), pp. 156, 161.
17. John Keane, *Tom Paine: A Political Life* (paperback edition, London, 2009, 1st published 1995). Bridges were a popular subject for illustration in the *GM*, although by the 1790s correspondents were more interested in canals.
18. Letter in *Pennsylvania Journal*, 10.4.1776, quoted in Keane, *Tom Paine*, p. 23.
19. *GM*, 8.1791, p. 737.
20. Thomas Paine, *Rights of Man* (paperback edition, New York, 1999, 1st published 1791), p. 94.

21. Edmund Burke, *Reflections on the Revolution in France and on the Proceedings in Certain Societies in London Relative to that Event*, ed. Conor Cruise O'Brien (London, 1968, 1st published 1790), p. 125, fulsomely reviewed by Gough, *GM*, 11.1790, pp. 1021–32. For immediate reactions to Burke see Lock, *Burke's Reflections*, pp. 132–65.
22. See David Bindman, *The Shadow of the Guillotine: Britain and the French Revolution* (London, 1989), especially pp. 28, 49, 146.
23. *GM*, 12.1792, facing p. 1104; 1.1793, pp. 85–6.
24. *GM*, 7.1793, p.676; 1.1794, pp.89, 90, 91; 1.1799, p.78.
25. For the impact on newspapers, see Hannah Barker, *Newspapers, Politics and English Society, 1695–1855* (Harlow, 2000), pp. 171–95. Baer regards only the followers of Paine as radical, and 'the people' as broadly conservative (Marc Baer, *The Rise and Fall of Radical Westminster, 1780–1890* (London, 2012), p. 88). A warning against homogenizing class attitudes is impoverished Lancashire labourer, Benjamin Shaw, who recorded **both** participation in a mock trial and effigy-burning of Paine **and** dissatisfaction with the government in the same diary entry (Alan G. Crosby, ed., *The Family Records of Benjamin Shaw Mechanic of Dent, Dolphinholme and Preston* (Stroud, 1991) p. 27).
26. John Byng, 5th Viscount Torrington, *The Torrington Diaries: Containing the Tours through England and Wales of the Hon. John Byng, Later Fifth Viscount Torrington between the Years 1781 and 1794*, ed. C. Bruyn Andrews, 4 vols (reprint edition, New York, 1970, 1st published 1934–8), IV, p. 1.
27. *GM*, 12.1790, p. 110, review of Catherine Macaulay's hostile *Observations* on Burke's *Reflections*.
28. On contemporary thinking and usage of 'democrat' and its cognates, see Joanna Innes and Mark Philp, eds., *Re-imagining Democracy in the Age of Revolutions: America, France, Britain, Ireland 1750–1850* (Oxford, 2013).
29. *GM*, 1.1793, p.90; 1.1809, p. 18; 7.1813, pp.26-8.
30. For example letter from 'E.A.', *GM*, 1.1795, p. 29.
31. Arthur Burns and Joanna Innes, eds., *Rethinking the Age of Reform: Britain 1780–1850* (Cambridge, 2003), especially 'Introduction', pp. 1–70, and Boyd Hilton, *The Age of Atonement: The Influence of Evangelicalism on Social and Economic Thought, 1785–1865* (Oxford, 1986).
32. *GM*, 1.1811, pp. 30–4.
33. Thomas Gisborne, *An Enquiry into the Duties of Men: In the Higher and Middle Classes of Society in Great Britain, Resulting from their Respective Stations, Professions, and Employment* (London, 1794), p. 3.
34. *GM*, 1.1810, pp. 9–11 (the context opposition to Catholic emancipation).
35. *GM*, 7.1791, p. 669.
36. *GM*, 1.1803, pp. 4–5.
37. *GM*, 1.1804, p. 58.
38. *GM* wrapper, 8.1813.
39. 'The loyalist commercial model', Amanda Goodrich, *Debating England's Aristocracy in the 1790s: Pamphlets, Polemics, and Political Ideas* (Woodbridge, 2005), p. 144.
40. Henry Angelo, *Reminiscences of Henry Angelo: With Memoirs of his Late Father and Friends, Including Numerous Original Anecdotes and Curious Traits of the*

Most Celebrated Characters that Have Flourished During the Past Eighty Years (London, 1828), p. 536 (1803).

41. Linda Colley, *Britons: Forging the Nation, 1707–1837* (paperback edition 2005, 1st published Yale, 1992), p. 178.
42. *GM*, 1.1798, p. 73.
43. *GM*, 2.1809, pp. 177–9.
44. *GM*, 7.1809, pp. 654–5.
45. Richard Cumberland, *The Memoirs of Richard Cumberland*, ed. Richard J. Dircks, 2 vols (New York, 2002), II, p. 153.
46. Ian F.W. Beckett, *Amateur Military Tradition, 1558–1945* (Manchester, 1991), pp. 74–89.
47. Ibid., pp. 74–5.
48. *GM*, 7.1805, pp. 681–2.
49. *GM*, 7.1793, pp. 588–9.
50. *GM*, 7.1796, pp. 567–8, 608.
51. *GM*, 7.1800, pp. 679–82.
52. Cumberland, *Memoirs,* II, pp. 151–3.
53. Ibid., p. 153.
54. *GM*, 7.1801, pp. 588–9.
55. Gisborne, *Enquiry*, pp. 183–218.
56. There were two fatal duels under Deaths in *GM*, 1.1806, pp. 89–90, each using the term 'animosity'.
57. *GM*, 1.1803, pp. 63–4.
58. Revd Edward Mangin, 'Some Account of the Writer's Situation as Chaplain in the British Navy', in *Five Naval Journals, 1789–1817*, ed. Rear-Adm. H.G. Thursfield (London, 1951), pp. 4–39 (pp. 7–8, 22–5).
59. *GM*, 1.1799, pp. 60–1, 69.
60. *GM*, 1.1800, p. 86; 7.1800, p. 681.
61. See *ODNB* entry for reactions of fellow officers. Artist Joseph Farington (1747–1821) considered Nelson's marriage happy until his 'unfortunate acquaintance with Lady Hamilton' (Joseph Farington, *The Farington Diary*, ed. James Greig, 8 vols (London, 1922–8), III, p. 131). Naval wife Elizabeth Fremantle criticized Nelson's separation, thinking him a fool at his age and 'such a cripple' to dally with Emma (Anne Fremantle, ed., *The Wynne Diaries 1789–1820*, 3 vols (Oxford, 1982), III, p. 31).
62. *GM*, 3.1801, pp. 206–8 and 4.1801, pp. 297–8.
63. 'The Attitudes of Lady Hamilton', etching by Francesco Novelli, *c.*1791 (Victoria & Albert Museum: E.253-2000).
64. She gave birth to twins in January 1801.
65. Farington, *Diary*, III, p. 123. It was also recorded by Charles Fothergill, who wept (*Diary*, p. 217–8), Benjamin Haydon (Alexander P.D. Penrose, ed., *The Autobiography and Memoirs of Benjamin Robert Haydon, 1786–1846* (London, 1927), p. 27) and Matthew Oakes (Jane Fiske, ed., *The Oakes Diaries: Business, Politics and the Family in Bury St Edmunds 1778–1827*, 2 vols (Woodbridge, 1990), II, p. 72).
66. *GM*, 11.1805, pp. 1044–8.
67. *GM*, 1.1806, pp. 65–72.
68. Family patronage aided his start in the navy.
69. *GM*, 1.1806, pp. 92–3.

70. *GM*, 7.1796, pp. 617–18; 7.1812, p. 89; 1.1813, p. 83.
71. James Stanier Clarke and John M'Arthur, *The Life of Admiral Nelson, KB* (London, 1809); *GM*, 12.1810, pp. 556–63; 1.1811, pp. 46–9.
72. *GM*, 1.1790, pp. 9–11.
73. *GM*, 1.1800, pp. 3–4.
74. *GM*, 1.1801, pp. 66–7.
75. *GM*, 1800, Preface.
76. *GM*, 1.1809, pp. 18–19.
77. *GM*, 1.1802, p. 39.
78. *GM*, 7.1802, p. 607; 1.1803, pp. 5–6.
79. *GM*, 1.1799, p. 84; 7.1808, p. 659 (see too Ch. 3).
80. *GM*, 1.1795, pp. 84–5.
81. Ibid., p. 86; Joseph Brasbridge, *The Fruits of Experience: Or, Memoir of Joseph Brasbridge Written in his 80th and 81st Years* (2nd edition, London, 1824), pp. 161–4.
82. *GM*, 7.1793, p. 677; 7.1794, p. 672; 7.1795, p. 618; 7.1798, pp. 622–3; 7.1803, p. 696; 7.1807, p. 684.
83. *GM*, 6.1790, pp. 503–5; 7.1790, p. 613.
84. *GM*, 1800, Preface.
85. *GM*, 7.1808, pp. 613–4.
86. *GM*, 1.1813, pp. 49–51.
87. *GM*, 1.1793, p. 7; 1.1798, pp. 14–16.
88. *GM*, 1.1799, pp. 6–7.
89. Gordon Rimmer, *Marshalls of Leeds: Flax-Spinners, 1788–1886* (Cambridge, 1960), p. 67.
90. Brasbridge, *Fruits*, pp. 169, 311.
91. *GM*, 7.1792, p. 648.
92. Gisborne, *Enquiry*, pp. 571–2.
93. James Finlayson, ed., *The Sermons of Hugh Blair, Complete in Four Volumes: To which Is Prefixed, a Short Account of the Life and Character of the Author*, 4 vols (London, 1815).
94. *GM*, 7.1807, p. 684.
95. Sophie Bankes, 'James Lackington (1746–1815) and Reading in the Late Eighteenth Century' (unpublished PhD thesis, Open University, 2013), p. 239.
96. *GM*, 7.1814, pp. iii–iv.
97. *GM*, 7.1812, pp. 61–2, as 'not in his Works'.
98. *GM*, 1.1804, p. 93.
99. *GM*, 1.1791, pp. 89–901; 7.1795, p. 619; 1.1806, pp. 88–9; 1.1814, p. 101.
100. *GM*, 1814, Preface, pp. iii–iv.
101. *GM*, 1.1793, p. 13; 1.1800, p. 608; 1.1803, p. 64.
102. John Tosh, *A Man's Place: Masculinity and the Middle-Class Home in Victorian England* (New Haven, CT, 2007, 1st published 1999), p. 184.
103. *GM*, 1.1800, p. 94.
104. *GM*, 7.1797, ed. p. 546, fn.
105. *GM*, 7.1810, p. 8.
106. Penelope Peoples, 'The Folger Nichols Manuscript Collection: A Description and Analysis' (unpublished PhD thesis, University of Wisconsin-Milwaukee, 1980)', pp. 228–9.

107. *GM*, 1.1790, pp. 7–8. He presumably meant the Proclamation Society.

108. *GM*, 1.1805, pp. 28–30.

109. Farington, *Diary*, II, pp.54, 57.

110. *GM*, 7.1806, p. 605.

111. *GM*, 7.1795, p. 599; 1.1796, p. 66; Revd S. Bishop, *The Poetical Works of the Revd Samuel Bishop, to which Are Prefixed, Memoirs of the Life of the Author, by the Revd Thomas Clare* (London, 1796); *GM*, 1.1801, p. 68; 1.1807, pp. 4–7.

112. *GM*, 1.1799, pp. 6–7; 1.1801, p. 38; 1.1803, pp. 60–1.

113. *GM*, 9.1807, p. 831; 1.1808, p. 6. See also Carolyn D. Williams, *Pope, Homer and Manliness: Some Aspects of Eighteenth-Century Classical Learning* (London, 1993).

114. Anne Stott, *Wilberforce: Family and Friends* (Oxford, 2012).

115. *GM*, 1.1795, p. 72.

116. Faramerz Dabhoiwala, *The Origins of Sex: A History of the First Sexual Revolution* (London, 2012).

117. *GM*, 7.1798, p. 612.

118. *GM*, 7.1790, pp. 660–2; 8.1790, p. 703. See too Cindy McCreery, 'A Moral Panic in Eighteenth-Century London? The 'Monster' and the Press', in Lemmings, *Moral Panics,* pp. 195–220.

119. *GM*, 1.1792, pp. 23–4.

120. *GM*, 11.1802, p. 1062.

121. Ibid., p. 1063.

122. *GM*, 12.1792, pp. 1114–6; 1.1800, pp. 18–24.

123. *GM*, 11.1802, pp. 1013, 1062, 1157; Supplement 1802, p. 1209 by 'R.M.R., the Gentle Shepherd, of Witham, Essex'; 1.1803, p. 61 by T. Stott of Dromore; 3.1803, p. 260 by W. Cunningham also of Dromore (both men were in Bishop Percy's circle).

124. *Derby Mercury,* 28.10.1802; William Mudford, *Augustus and Mary: Or, The Maid of Buttermere, a Domestic Story* (London, 1803).

125. 'Poor Mary: Or, the Beauty of Buttermere', a song advertised at 1s by Weller's Music Warehouse, *MP*, 11.12.1802; for prints see NPG: D23538 (William Mineard Bennett) and D12793 (Gillray); Charles Dibdin, *Edward and Susan: Or, the Maid of Buttermere* (London, 1803) was performed at Sadler's Wells in April; A Short Hand Writer, *Report of the Proceedings on the Trial of John Hatfield* (London, 1803).

126. Portrait no. 679, advertisement in *MP*, 2.5.1803 (perhaps the original of the Bennett print).

127. *MP*, 4.1.1803; *Morning Chronicle,* 30.4.1803.

128. *MP*, 4.1.1803 and 21.12.1803; *Report of the Proceedings*; R.S. Kirby, *Kirby's Wonderful and Eccentric Museum: Or, Magazine of Remarkable Character* (London, 1820, 1st published 1803–20), pp. 309–31 (with portrait); *Bury & Norwich Post,* 24.8.1803.

129. *Report of the Proceedings,* p. 6.

130. *MP*, 11.10.1802.

131. *Hampshire Telegraph & Portsmouth Gazette,* 27.12.1802.

132. For execution see *GM*, 9.1803, p. 876; for pregnancy, birth and bigamy, *MP*, 18.12.1802; *Hampshire Telegraph,* 27.12.1802; *Southwark Election,* 14.6.1803 and *Kirby's*, pp. 325–6. Mary remained sufficiently well-known to earn a *GM* obituary (4.1837, pp. 444–5).

133. For 'complicity in the legal system' see Andrea McKenzie, ' " Useful and entertaining to the generality of Readers": Selecting the Select Trials, 1718–64', in *Crime, Courtrooms, and the Public Sphere in Britain, 1700–1850*, ed. David Lemmings (Farnham, 2012), pp. 43–69.

134. See Susan Lamb, *Bringing Travel Home to England: Tourism, Gender, and Imaginative Literature in the Eighteenth Century* (Newark, DE, 2009), p. 207.

135. *GM*, 1.1810, pp. 25–6.

136. Appendix 1.

137. *GM*, 1.1796, pp. 41–3.

138. Paul Romney, ed., *Diary of Charles Fothergill, 1805: An Itinerary to York, Flamborough and the North-Western Dales of Yorkshire* (Leeds, 1984) e.g. pp. 94–8, 121, 201, 230.

139. Lamb, *Bringing Travel Home*, p. 200.

140. *GM*, 2.1803, pp. 102–3.

141. *GM*, 1802, Supplement, p. 1209.

142. William Wordsworth, *The Fourteen-Book Prelude*, ed. W.J.B. Owen (Ithaca, NY, 1985), pp. 145–7, *ll.* 288–330. The 1768 Baltimore affair was recalled in this way in the anonymous *A Fortnight's Ramble though London* (1795), a warning guide to metropolitan vices purportedly by a farmer's son, who pointed out the window of the room in Baltimore House where Sarah Woodcock was held (p. 36).

143. S.J. Pratt, *The Poor, or, Bread: A Poem* (2nd edition, London, 1802), p. 50.

144. William Jones, *The Diary of the Revd William Jones 1777–1821, Curate and Vicar of Broxbourne and the Hamlet of Hoddesdon 1781–1821*, ed. O.F. Christie (London, 1929), p. 209.

145. Ibid., p. 147.

146. *GM*, 7.1792, p. 677; 7.1794, pp. 672–3.

147. *GM*, 1.1813, p. 40.

148. *GM*, 1.1790, p. 87; 7.1793, p. 674; 7.1798, p. 637.

149. In one instance, Mr James of Serjeant's Inn slit his throat dressed in his wedding clothes on receiving unpalatable information on his young milliner bride-to-be, *GM*, 7.1800, p. 596.

150. *GM*, 1.1795, p. 86.

151. See Elizabeth McKellar, *Landscapes of London: The City, the Country and the Suburbs 1660–1840* (New Haven, CT, 2013), pp. 169–203.

152. There were none in 1790–9, 11 in 1800–9 and 3 in 1810–15.

153. *GM*, 1.1798, p. 80.

154. *GM*, 1.1801, pp. 66–7.

155. *GM*, 1.1802, pp. 62–3.

156. *GM*, 7.1803, Preface.

157. See David Parkes' (1763–1833) description and illustration, *GM*, 3.1815, p. 201.

158. The original, probably by Moses Haughton, is lost. An engraving forms the frontispiece to Llewellynn Jewitt's 1872 edition of Hutton's *Life*.

159. *GM*, 1.1812, p. 62.

160. Charles Pigott, *A Political Dictionary: Explaining the True Meaning of Words, Illustrated and Exemplified in the Lives, Morals, Character and Conduct of the Following Most Illustrious Personages, among Many Others*, ed. Robert Rix (facsimile of 1795 edition, Ashgate, 2004), p. 3. See also

Goodrich, *Debating England's Aristocracy*, p. 123; and Iain McCalman, *Radical Underworld: Prophets, Revolutionaries and Pornographers in London, 1795–1840* (Cambridge, 1988).

161. *GM*, 7.1800, pp. 682–4.
162. An exception was the 1809 affair of Mary Anne Clarke, mistress of the Duke of York, and army commissions. *GM* coverage was primarily tucked away in 'Proceedings in Parliament' in February to May of that year. It pronounced the instigator of the inquiry, Col. Wardle MP, 'manly and independent' in 'attacking the hydra of corruption' (3.1809, p. 273).
163. See David Collings, *Monstrous Society: Reciprocity, Discipline, and the Political Uncanny, c.1780–1848* (Lewisburg, 2009) on this breakdown of reciprocity.
164. *GM*, 1.1810, pp. 25–6.
165. *GM*, 1.1802, pp. 9–12. 'The Projector' by Alexander Chalmers appeared in the *GM* from 1802 to 1809. In 1811 Nichols published the essays as a volume, in its 3rd edition by 1817. Johnson's *Dictionary* defined a projector as 'one who forms schemes or designs' or 'one who forms wild impracticable schemes'.
166. No. XIV, *GM*, 1.1803, pp. 11–15; no. LXXII, *GM*, 1.1807, pp. 612–5, (p. 613).
167. *GM*, 7.1809, p. 608.
168. *GM*, 1 and 2.1811, pp. 63–4, 158–9, later included in a volume published 1812 in aid of the Lincoln Lunatic Asylum.
169. *GM*, 7.1801, pp. 587–9; e.g. Gillray's 'Farmer Giles & his Wife Shewing off their Daughter Betty to their Neighbours on her Return from School', 1809 (NPG: D13117).
170. *GM*, 1.1814, pp. 30–2.
171. *GM*, 7.1798, p. 571.
172. Richard Polwhele, *The Old English Gentleman: A Poem* (London, 1797).
173. Richard Edgeworth, *Essays on Professional Education* (London, 1809), p. 259.
174. *GM*, 11.1782, p. 539 noted 'we do not apprehend that we have many fox-hunters among our readers'. See also Allyson N. May, *The Fox-hunting Controversy, 1781–2004: Class and Cruelty* (Farnham, 2013).
175. 7.1797, pp. 617–18 and Supplement, p. 1125 and Polwhele, *Old English Gentleman*, fn., p. 49. Polwhele's Sir Humphrey did hunt.
176. *GM*, 1.1801, p. 87.
177. *GM*, 7.1806, pp. 673–4.
178. *GM*, 1.1798, pp. 9–10.
179. *GM*, 12.1811, p. 527 in 'The Times' no. VI, by 'Aaron Bickerstaffe', the last of six humorous essays, again recalling Steele's *Tatler* and its authorial *persona* Isaac Bickerstaff; 1.1812, pp. 29–30.
180. *GM*, 7.1812, pp. 15–16.
181. See Robert Hole, *Pulpits, Politics and Public Order in England, 1760–1832* (Cambridge, 1989), pp. 138–40; and Thomas W. Laqueur, *Religion and Respectability: Sunday Schools and Working Class Culture, 1780–1850* (New Haven, CT, 1976), pp. 190–201.
182. *Torrington Diaries*, III, p. 211 (1793).
183. Farington, *Diary*, I, p. 224.
184. *GM*, 10.1797, pp. 819–20.
185. *GM*, 11.1797, pp. 940–2
186. *GM*, 1.1798, pp. 30–4.

187. P.J. Cain and A.G. Hopkins, *British Imperialism, 1688–2000* (2nd edition, Harlow, 2002, 1st published 1993).
188. Baer, *Radical Westminster*, p. 89.
189. *British Critic*, 7.1801, Preface, p. i.
190. Emily Lorraine de Montluzin, *The Anti-Jacobins, 1798–1800: The Early Contributors to the Anti-Jacobin Review* (Basingstoke, 1988) places the *GM* in the conservative camp with the *British Critic* and the more rabid *Anti-Jacobin Review*.
191. *British Critic*, 7.1801, p. i.
192. *GM*, 7.1808, pp. 572–4, reply to 'Clericus Buckinghamiensis" attack on dissenters as *inter alia* 'gloomy fanatics', 4.1808, pp. 314–15. An editorial footnote suggests 'Dissenter' regarded the magazine as 'peculiarly devoted to the Church of England'.

Conclusion

1. J.C.D. Clark, *English Society, 1688–1832: Religion, Ideology and Politics during the Ancien Regime* (Cambridge, 2000, 1st published 1985).
2. S.K. Tillyard, *Aristocrats: Caroline, Emily and Sarah Lennox, 1740–1832* (London, 1994), pp. 343, 352–3.
3. I am grateful for the thoughts of Prof. Penelope J. Corfield in 'Intimations of a Coming Meritocracy: Britain, 1780–1850', paper presented to Cambridge University Modern Cultural History Seminar, 23.10.2013.
4. *GM*, 1.1810, pp. 14–15.

Bibliography

1. Primary sources

The *Gentleman's Magazine*

Anon., 'The Autobiography of Sylvanus Urban', *GM*, 1856: July, pp. 3–9; August, pp. 131–40; September, pp. 267–77; November, pp. 531–41; December, pp. 667–77; 1857: January, pp. 3–10; February, pp. 149–57; March, pp. 282–9 and April, pp. 379–87.

Ayscough, Samuel, *General Index to Fifty-Six Volumes of the Gentleman's Magazine, 1731–86* (London, 1789).

Ayscough, Samuel and John Nichols, *General Index to the Gentleman's Magazine, 1787–1818*, 5 vols (London, 1818–21).

Bodleian Library: Blue wrappers from *Gentleman's* and *London Magazines* in the John Johnson Collection, An Archive of Printed Ephemera, Advertizers VI; Nichols Correspondence, MS.Eng.Lett.b.11–19, c.354–72.

British Library Manuscripts: Correspondence with Edward Cave, Stowe 748; Miscellaneous Correspondence, Add 4392; Correspondence with John Nichols, Add 63652, Vol. 2.

General Index to the First Twenty Volumes of the Gentleman's Magazine, in Five Parts: To Which Is Added, an Index to the First Volume of the Miscellaneous Correspondence (London, 1753).

Gentleman's Magazine

Gomme, G.L., A.B. Gomme, Lady A.C. Bickley, and F.A. Milne, F.A., eds, *The Gentleman's Magazine Library: Being a Classified Collection of the Chief Contents of the Gentleman's Magazine from 1731 to 1868*, 29 vols (London, 1883–1905).

Halliday, Francis, *Miscellanea Curiosa Mathematica: Or, The Literary Correspondence of Some Eminent Mathematicians in Great Britain and Ireland, Containing a Choice Collection of Mathematical Essays and Dissertations on What is Most Valuable and Really Useful* (London, 1745–55).

Kimber, Edward, *The Gentleman's Magazine, 1731–51: The Lists of Books, Collected with Annual Indexes and the Index to the First Twenty Years* (facsimile reprint London, 1966).

Miscellaneous Correspondence, Containing Essays, Dissertations, etc. on Various Subjects, Sent to the Author of the Gentleman's Magazine, Nos. I–IX (London, 1742–8).

Nichols Archive Database: contact Dr Julian Pooley FSA, The Nichols Archive Project, c/o Surrey History Centre, 130 Goldsworth Road, Woking, Surrey, GU21 6ND. jpooley@surreycc.gov.uk.

Nichols, J., 'A Prefatory Introduction Descriptive of the Rise and Progress of the Magazine, with Anecdotes of the Projector and his Early Associates' in Samuel Ayscough and John Nichols, *General Index to the Gentleman's Magazine, 1787–1818*, 5 vols (London, 1818–21), III, pp. iii–lxxx.

St Barbe, Charles, *A Complete List of the Plates and Wood-cuts in the Gentleman's Magazine, from the Commencement in the Year 1731 to 1818 Inclusive, and an Alphabetical Index Thereto* (London, 1821).

Walker, John, *A Selection of Curious Articles from the Gentleman's Magazine*, 4 vols (London, 1809).

Published diaries, journals, memoirs and letters

Angelo, Henry, *Reminiscences of Henry Angelo: With Memoirs of his Late Father and Friends, Including Numerous Original Anecdotes and Curious Traits of the Most Celebrated Characters that Have Flourished During the Past Eighty Years* (London, 1828).

Baker, John, *The Diary of John Baker: Being Extracts therefrom, Transcribed and Edited with an Introduction and Notes by Philip C. Yorke: A Record of Life, Family History and Society, 1751–78, in England (Mostly in Sussex and London) and the Leeward Islands, and of Two Travels Abroad*, ed. Philip C. Yorke (London, 1931).

Beattie, James, *James Beattie's London Diary, 1773*, ed. Ralph S. Walker (Aberdeen, 1946).

Beresford, John, ed., *The Diary of a Country Parson: The Reverend James Woodforde*, 5 vols (Oxford, 1924–31).

Brasbridge, Joseph, *The Fruits of Experience: Or, Memoir of Joseph Brasbridge Written in his 80th and 81st Years* (2nd edition, London, 1824).

Brockbank, W. and F. Kenworthy, eds, *The Diary of Richard Kay, 1716–51, of Baldingstone, near Bury, a Lancashire Doctor* (Manchester, 1968).

Byrom, John, *The Private Journal and Literary Remains of John Byrom*, ed. Richard Parkinson, 4 vols (Manchester, 1854–7).

Carter, Thomas, *Memoirs of a Working Man* (London, 1845).

Crosby, Alan G., ed., *The Family Records of Benjamin Shaw Mechanic of Dent, Dolphinholme and Preston* (Stroud, 1991).

Cumberland, Richard, *The Memoirs of Richard Cumberland*, ed. Richard J. Dircks, 2 vols (New York, 2002).

De La Rochefoucauld, François, *A Frenchman in England 1784: Being the 'Mélanges sur l'Angleterre' of François de la Rochefoucauld*, ed. Jean Marchand and trans. by S.C. Roberts (Cambridge, 1933).

Eagles, Robin, ed., *The Diaries of John Wilkes, 1770–9* (Woodbridge, 2014).

Emin, Joseph, *The Life and Adventures of J.E., an Armenian* (London, 1792).

Farington, Joseph, *The Farington Diary*, ed. James Greig, 8 vols (London, 1922–8).

Fiske, Jane, ed., *The Oakes Diaries: Business, Politics and the Family in Bury St Edmunds 1778–1827*, 2 vols (Woodbridge, 1990).

Fremantle, Anne, ed., *The Wynne Diaries 1789–1820*, 3 vols (Oxford, 1982).

Gibson, Donald, ed., *A Parson in the Vale of White Horse: George Woodward's Letters from East Hendred*, 1753–61 (Gloucester, 1983).

Holcroft, Thomas, *Memoirs of the Late Thomas Holcroft, Written by Himself, and Continued to the Time of his Death, from his Diary, Notes, and Other Papers*, ed. William Hazlitt (1852 reprint, 1st published London, 1816).

Hutton, William, *The Life of William Hutton, FASS* (reprint edition, 1998, 1st published London, 1816).

Jewitt, Llewellynn F., ed., *The Life of William Hutton, and the History of the Hutton Family, from the Original Manuscripts* (2nd edition, London, 1872).

Jones, William, *The Diary of the Revd William Jones 1777–1821, Curate and Vicar of Broxbourne and the Hamlet of Hoddesdon 1781–1821*, ed. O.F. Christie (London, 1929).

Kielmansegge, Count Frederick, *Diary of a Journey to England in the Years 1761–2*, trans. Countess Kielmansegg (London, 1902).

Lackington, James, *Memoirs of the First Forty-Five Years of the Life of James Lackington: Written by Himself, in a Series of Letters to a Friend* (London, 1791).

Lackington, James, *The Confessions of J. Lackington in a Series of Letters to a Friend: To Which are Added Two Letters on the Bad Consequences of Having Daughters Educated at Boarding-schools* (2nd edition, London, 1804).

Lewis, W. S., ed., *The Yale Edition of Horace Walpole's Correspondence*, 48 vols (New Haven, CT, 1937–83).

Linnell, C.D., ed., *The Diary of Benjamin Rogers, Rector of Carlton, 1720–71* (Streatley, 1950).

Low, D.M., ed., *Gibbon's Journal to January 28th, 1763, My Journal, I, II, & III and Ephemerides* (London, 1929).

Mahon, Lord, ed., *The Letters of Philip Dormer Stanhope, Earl of Chesterfield, Including Numerous Letters Now First Published from the Original Manuscripts*, 4 vols (London, 1845).

Matthews, William, ed., *The Diary of Dudley Ryder, 1715–16* (London, 1939).

Mitchell, L.G., ed., *The Purefoy Letters, 1735–53* (London, 1973).

Money, John, ed., *The Chronicles of John Cannon Excise Officer and Writing Master*, 2 vols (Oxford, 2010).

Oliver, Andrew, ed., *The Journal of Samuel Curwen, Loyalist*, 2 vols (Harvard, 1972).

Penrose, Alexander P.D., ed., *The Autobiography and Memoirs of Benjamin Robert Haydon, 1786–1846* (London, 1927).

Price, Jacob M., ed., *Joshua Johnson's Letterbook, 1771–4: Letters from a Merchant in London to his Partners in Maryland* (London, 1979).

Reynolds, E.E., ed., *The Mawhood Diary: Selections from the Diary Note-books of William Mawhood, Woollen-draper of London, for the Years 1764–90* (London, 1956).

Romney, Paul, ed., *The Diary of Charles Fothergill, 1805: An Itinerary to York, Flamborough and the North-Western Dales of Yorkshire* (Leeds, 1984).

Simond, L., *An American in Regency England: The Journal of a Tour in 1810–11*, ed. Christopher Hibbert (London, 1968).

Southey, Revd Charles Cuthbert, ed., *The Life and Correspondence of Robert Southey*, 6 vols (London, 1849–50).

Thompson, Stanbury, ed., *The Journal of John Gabriel Stedman, 1744–97, Soldier and Author, Including an Authentic Account of his Expedition to Surinam, in 1772* (London, 1962).

Thursfield, Rear-Adm. H.G., ed., *Five Naval Journals, 1789–1817* (London, 1951).

Torrington, John Byng, 5th Viscount, *The Torrington Diaries: Containing the Tours through England and Wales of the Hon. John Byng, Later Fifth Viscount Torrington between the Years 1781 and 1794*, ed. C. Bruyn Andrews, 4 vols (reprint edition, New York, 1970, 1st published 1934–8).

Whitworth, Rex, ed., *Gunner at Large: The Diary of James Wood R.A., 1746–65* (London, 1988).

Wilson, Beckles, ed., *The Life and Letters of James Wolfe* (London, 1909).

Other primary sources

A Letter on the Behaviour of the Populace, on a Late Occasion in the Procedure against a Noble Lord from a Gentleman to his Countryman Abroad (London, 1768).

A Letter to Lord B——, with an Address to the Town (London, 1768).

A Short Hand Writer, *Report of the Proceedings on the Trial of John Hatfield, for Forgery: At Carlisle, on August 15, 1803 with an Account of his Life* (London, 1803).

Anon. (attrib. Duncan Forbes), *Memoirs of the Life of Lord Lovat* (London, 1746).

Anon., *The Female Soldier: Or, The Surprising Life and Adventures of Hannah Snell* (London, 1750).

Anon., *The Life of the Famous William Stroud: Who Was Convicted at the Last Quarter-Sessions for the City and Liberty of Westminster, Sentenced to Six Months Imprisonment in Bridewell, together with the Substance of the Speech Justice Ledlard Made, Stroud's Own Speech, and His Behaviour on that Occasion* (London, 1752).

Anon., *Memoirs of the Life and Particular Actions of that Brave Man, General Blakeney: To Which Is Added, the Viscount D'Melun's Ghost, with the Political Creed of the French* (London, 1756).

Anon., *Memoirs of the Seraglio of the Bashaw of Merryland, by a Discarded Sultana* (London, 1768).

Anon., *Modern Chastity, or, The Agreeable Rape: A Poem, by a Young Gentleman of Sixteen in Vindication of the Right Hon. Lord B——e* (London, 1768).

Anon., *Considerations on the Causes of the Present Stagnation of Matrimony* (London, 1772).

Anon., *The Economist: Shewing in a Variety of Estimates, from Fourscore Pounds a Year to upwards of 800l., How a Family May Live with Frugality, for a Little Money* (15th edition, London, 1781).

Anon., *Letters on the Most Common, as Well as the Most Important Occasions in Life, by Cicero, Pliny, Voiture, Balzac, St Evremond, Locke, Lord Lansdowne, Lord Oxford, Lord Peterborough, Lord Bolingbroke, Sir William Temple, Sir W. Trumbell, Dryden, Atterbury, Garth, Addison, Steele, Pope, Gay, Swift, Berkeley, Rowe, and Other Writers of Distinguished Merit: With Many Original Letters and Cards, by the Editor, Who Has Also Prefixed, a Dissertation on the Epistolary Style, with Proper Directions for Addressing Persons of Rank and Eminence, for the Use of Young Gentlemen and Ladies* (London, 1786, 1st published 1756).

Anon., *A Fortnight's Ramble through London: Or, A Complete Display of All the Cheats and Frauds Practized in that Great Metropolis, With the Best Methods for Eluding Them, Being a Pleasing Narrative of the Adventures of a Farmer's Son Published at his Request for the Benefit of his Country* (London, 1795).

Bailey, N., *Dictionarium Britannicum: Or, A More Compleat Universal Etymological Dictionary than any Extant* (London, 1736).

Baltimore, Lord F., *A Tour to the East, in the Years 1763 and 1764* (London, 1767).

Bignon, Jean Paul, *The Adventures of Abdallah Son of Hanif: Who Was Sent by the Sultan of the Indies, to Discover the Fountain of Borico, Which Restores Past Youth, Intermix'd with Several Curious and Instructive Histories* (London, 1729).

Bishop, Revd S., *The Poetical Works of the Revd Samuel Bishop, to Which Are Prefixed, Memoirs of the Life of the Author, by the Revd Thomas Clare* (London, 1796).

Bond, D., *Friendship Strikingly Exhibited in a New Light: In Letters Between Messrs D. Henry and J. Nichols, Managing Proprietors of the Gentleman's Magazine, and*

D. Bond, Late Printer of that Monthly Miscellany, with an Introductory Narrative, Notes and Observations (London, 1781).

Boswell, James, *Life of Johnson: Together with a Journal of a Tour to the Hebrides and Johnson's Diary of a Journey into North Wales*, ed. George Birkbeck Hill, revd L.F. Powell, 6 vols (Oxford, 1934, 1st published 1791).

British Critic.

Brown, James Baldwin, *Memoirs of the Public and Private Life of John Howard, the Philanthropist* (London, 1818).

Brown, John, *An Estimate of the Manners and Principles of the Times* (London, 1757).

Burke, Edmund, *Reflections on the Revolution in France and on the Proceedings in Certain Societies in London Relative to that Event*, ed. Conor Cruise O'Brien (London, 1968, 1st published 1790).

Burney, Frances, *Evelina: Or, The History of a Young Lady's Entrance into the World*, ed. Edward A. Bloom (Oxford, 2002, 1st published London, 1778).

Campbell, R., *The London Tradesman* (facsimile reprint 1969, 1st published London, 1747).

Clarke, James Stanier and John M'Arthur, *The Life of Admiral Nelson, KB* (London, 1809).

Cleland, John, *Fanny Hill or Memoirs of a Woman of Pleasure* (paperback edition Harmondsworth, n.d., 1st published 1748–9).

Colman, George and David Garrick, *The Clandestine Marriage: A Comedy* (London, 1765).

Cowper, William, *The Task* (facsimile edition 1973, 1st published London, 1785).

Crown(e), J., *Sir Courtly Nice: Or, It Cannot Be. A Comedy, as It Is Acted by His Majesties Servants* (London, 1685).

Cumberland, Richard, *The West Indian: A Comedy* (London, 1771).

Defoe, Daniel, *The Compleat English Tradesman* (2nd edition, London, 1727).

Defoe, Daniel, *The Compleat English Gentleman*, ed. Karl D. Bülbring (London, 1890).

Dyche, T., *A Guide to the English Tongue* (London, 1707).

Edgeworth, Richard, *Essays on Professional Education* (London, 1809).

Fielding, Henry, *Miscellanies*, ed. Hugh Amory, 3 vols (Oxford, 1997).

Finlayson, James, ed., *The Sermons of Hugh Blair, Complete in Four Volumes: To which is Prefixed, a Short Account of the Life and Character of the Author*, 4 vols (London, 1815).

Foote, Samuel, *The Commissary: A Comedy in Three Acts* (4th edition, London, 1782).

Fordyce, David, *Dialogues Concerning Education*, 2 vols (London, 1745).

Friedman, Arthur, ed., *Collected Works of Oliver Goldsmith*, 5 vols (Oxford, 1966).

Gisborne, Thomas, *An Enquiry into the Duties of Men: In the Higher and Middle Classes of Society in Great Britain, Resulting from their Respective Stations, Professions, and Employment* (London, 1794).

Gisborne, Thomas, *An Enquiry into the Duties of the Female Sex* (London, 1797).

Grub Street Journal.

Gurney, Joseph, *The Trial of Frederick Calvert, Esq., Baron of Baltimore, in the Kingdom of Ireland: for a Rape on the Body of Sarah Woodcock: and of Elizabeth Griffinburg, and Ann Harvey* (London, 1768).

Hammond, James, *An Elegy to a Young Lady, in the Manner of Ovid ... With an Answer* (London, 1733).

Hatton, Edward, *The Merchant's Magazine: Or, Trades Man's Treasury* (6th edition, London, 1712).

Hawkins, Sir John, *The Life of Samuel Johnson, LLD*, ed. Bertram H. Davis (London, 1962, 1st published 1787).

Hazlitt, William, 'The St James's Chronicle–The Morning Chronicle–The Times–The New Times–The Courier, &c.–Cobbett's Weekly Journal–The Examiner–The Observer–The Gentleman's Magazine–The New Monthly Magazine–The London, &c. &c.', *Edinburgh Review: Or Critical Journal*, 38 (May 1823), pp. 349–78.

Hunter, Joseph, *Hallamshire: The History and Topography of the Parish of Sheffield in the County of York, with Historical and Descriptive Notices of the Parishes of Ecclesfield, Hansworth, Treeton, and Whiston, and of the Chapelry of Bradfield* (London, 1819).

Hurd, Richard, *Dialogues on the Uses of Foreign Travel, Considered as a Part of an English Gentleman's Education: Between Lord Shaftesbury and Mr Locke* (2nd edition, London, 1764).

Ives, Edward, *A Voyage from England to India, in the Year MDCCLIV and an Historical Narrative of the Operations of the Squadron and Army in India, under Watson and Clive, also, a Journey from Persia to England, by an Unusual Route, with an Appendix, Containing an Account of the Diseases Prevalent in Admiral Watson's Squadron, a Description of Most of the Trees, Shrubs, and Plants of India, Illustrated with a Chart, Maps, and Other Copper-plates* (London, 1773).

Jackson, W., *The Beauties of Nature: Displayed in a Sentimental Ramble through the Luxuriant Fields, with a Retrospective View of Her, to which is Added, a Choice Collection of Thoughts, Concluded with Poems on Various Occasions* (Birmingham, 1769).

Johnson, Samuel, *A Dictionary of the English Language: In which the Words are Deduced from their Originals, and Illustrated in their Different Significations by Examples from the Best Writers: To Which Are Prefixed, a History of the Language, and an English Grammar* (London, 1755).

Johnson, Samuel, *The Idler*, 2 vols (London, 1771).

Johnson, Samuel, *The Works of Samuel Johnson LLD*, 11 vols (London, 1787), II, *The Lives of the Most Eminent English Poets*.

Jones, Erasmus, *The Man of Manners: Or, Plebeian Polish'd, Being Plain and Familiar Rules for a Modest and Genteel Behaviour, on Most of the Ordinary Occasions of Life* (3rd edition, London, 1737).

Kirby, R.S., *Kirby's Wonderful and Eccentric Museum: Or, Magazine of Remarkable Character* (London, 1820, 1st published 1803–20).

Langhorne, John, *Country Justice: A Poem by one of His Majesty's Justices of the Peace for the County of Somerset* (London, 1774–7).

Lillo, George, *The London Merchant: Or, The History of George Barnwell* (London, 1731).

Lillo, George, *The Christian Hero: A Tragedy, as It Is Acted at the Theatre Royal in Drury Lane* (2nd edition, London, 1735).

Locke, John, *Some Thoughts Concerning Education* (London, 1693).*London Magazine*.

Mackenzie, Henry, *The Man of Feeling* (London, 1771).

Malcolm, James Peller, *Anecdotes of the Manners and Customs of London during the Eighteenth Century*, 2 vols (2nd edition, London, 1810).

Mandeville, Bernard, *The Fable of the Bee: Or, Private Vices, Public Benefits* (London, 1714).

Meriton, H. and J. Rogers, *A Circumstantial Narrative of the Loss of the Halsewell (East-Indiaman), Which Was Unfortunately Wrecked at Seacombe, 6th of January, 1786* (London, 1786).

Lady Mary Wortley Montagu, 'The Answer to the Foregoing Elegy' in James Hammond, *An Elegy to a Young Lady, in the Manner of Ovid ... With an Answer* (London, 1733).

Mudford, William, *Augustus and Mary: Or, The Maid of Buttermere, a Domestic Story* (London, 1803).

The Newgate Calendar: Comprising Interesting Memoirs of the Most Notorious Characters Who Have Been Convicted of Outrages on the Laws of England since the Commencement of the Eighteenth Century, with Anecdotes and Last Exclamations of Sufferers, 4 vols (London, 1824–6).

Nichols, John, *Literary Anecdotes of the Eighteenth Century*, 9 vols (London, 1812–16).

Nichols, John, *Illustrations of the Literary History of the Eighteenth Century: Consisting of Authentic Memoirs and Original Letters of Eminent Persons and Intended as a Sequel to the Literary Anecdotes*, 8 vols (London, 1817–58).

Paine, Thomas, *Rights of Man* (paperback edition, New York, 1999, 1st published 1791).

Pigott, Charles, *A Political Dictionary: Explaining the True Meaning of Words, Illustrated and Exemplified in the Lives, Morals, Character and Conduct of the Following Most Illustrious Personages, among Many Others*, ed. Robert Rix (facsimile of 1795 edition, Ashgate, 2004).

Pindar, Peter (pseudonym of John Wolcott), *A Benevolent Epistle to Sylvanus Urban Alias Master John Nichols, Printer, Common-councilman of Farringdon Ward, and Censor General of Literature: Not Forgetting Master William Hayley* (London, 1790).

Poll Book for Electing Two Representatives in Parliament, for the City and Liberty of Westminster, June 18, to July 4, 1818 (facsimile reprint, Exeter, 1996, 1st published London, 1818).

Polwhele, Richard, *The Old English Gentleman: A Poem* (London, 1797).

Pope, Alexander, *Epistle II*, 'To a Lady: Of the **Characters** of Women'* (1743).

Pratt, S.J., *The Poor, or, Bread: A Poem* (2nd edition, London, 1802).

Proceedings of the Old Bailey, 1674–1913, http://www.oldbaileyonline.org/

R-, P-, Sir, *The Life, Adventures, and Amours of Sir R- P- Who So Recently Had the Honour to Present the F— Address at the English Court* (London, 1770).

Richardson, Samuel, *The Apprentice's Vade Mecum: Or, Young Man's Pocket-Companion* (reprint edition 1975, 1st published London, 1734).

Richardson, Samuel, *Letters Written to and for Particular Friends: On the Most Important Occasions, Directing Not Only the Requisite Style and Forms to Be Observed in Writing Familiar Letters, but How to Think and Act Justly and Prudently, in the Common Concerns of Human Life* (London, 1741).

Richardson, Samuel, *Clarissa: Or, The History of a Young Lady*, ed. Angus Ross (London, 1985, 1st published 1747–8).

Richardson, Samuel, *The History of Sir Charles Grandison*, ed. Jocelyn Harris, 3 vols (Oxford, 1972, 1st published 7 vols, London, 1753–4).

Richardson, Samuel, *A Collection of the Moral and Instructive Sentiments* (New York, 1980, facsimile reprint of 1755 edition).

Smith, John Thomas, *A Book for a Rainy Day* (London, 1845).

Steele, Richard, *The Christian Hero: An Argument Proving that No Principles but Those of Religion Are Sufficient to Make a Great Man* (London, 1701).

Stretzer, Thomas, *A New Description of Merryland, Containing a Topographical, Geographical and Natural History of that Country* (London, 1740).

Thackeray, William Makepeace, *Vanity Fair*, ed. J.I.M Stewart (Harmondsworth, 1968, 1st published 3 vols, 1848).

Tillotson, John, *Twenty Discourses on the Most Important Subjects; Carefully Abridged, from the Works of Archbishop Tillotson, Adapted to the Meanest Capacities, with a View to their Being Dispersed by Those Who Are Charitably Inclined* (2nd edition, London, 1763).

Timperley, Charles Henry, *A Dictionary of Printers and Printing* (London, 1839).

Ward, R., *Anima'dversions of Warre; Or, A Militarie Magazine of the Truest Rules, and Ablest Instructions, for the Managing of Warre* (London, 1639).

Watts, Isaac, *The Improvement of the Mind: Or, A Supplement to the Art of Logic* (London, 1801, 1st published 1741).

Wesley, Samuel, *Poems on Several Occasions* (London, 1736).

Wordsworth, William, *The Fourteen-Book Prelude*, ed. W.J.B. Owen (Ithaca, NY, 1985).

2. Secondary works

Allan, David, *Commonplace Books and Reading in Georgian England* (Cambridge, 2010).

Altick, Richard D., *The English Common Reader: A Social History of the Mass Reading Public, 1800–1900* (Chicago, 1957).

Anderson, Benedict, *Imagined Communities: Reflections on the Origin and Spread of Nationalism* (London, revised edition 1991, 1st published 1983).

Andrew, Donna T., 'The Code of Honour and its Critics: The Opposition to Duelling in England, 1700–1850', *Social History*, 5 (1980), pp. 409–34.

Andrew, Donna T., *Philanthropy and Police: London Charity in the Eighteenth Century* (Princeton, 1989).

Andrew, Donna T., ed., *London Debating Societies, 1776–99* (London, 1994).

Andrew, Donna T. and Randall McGowen, *The Perreaus and Mrs Rudd: Forgery and Betrayal in Eighteenth-Century London* (Berkeley, CA, 2001).

Arnold, John H. and Sean Brady, eds, *What Is Masculinity? Historical Dynamics from Antiquity to the Contemporary World* (Basingstoke, 2011).

Baer, Marc, *The Rise and Fall of Radical Westminster, 1780–1890* (London, 2012).

Bailey, Joanne, *Parenting in England, 1760–1830: Emotion, Identity, and Generation* (Oxford, 2012).

Banister, Julia, 'The Court Martial of Admiral John Byng: Politeness and the Military Man in the Mid-Eighteenth Century', in *Masculinity and the Other: Historical Perspectives*, ed. Heather Ellis and Jessica Meyer (Newcastle, 2009), pp. 236–59.

Bankes, Sophie, 'James Lackington (1746–1815) and Reading in the Late Eighteenth Century' (unpublished PhD thesis, Open University, 2013).

Barker, Anthony D., 'Edward Cave, Samuel Johnson and the Gentleman's Magazine' (unpublished PhD thesis, University of Oxford, 1981).

Barker, Hannah, *Newspapers, Politics and English Society, 1695–1855* (Harlow, 2000).

Barker, Hannah and Elaine Chalus, eds, *Gender in Eighteenth-Century England: Roles, Representations and Responsibilities* (London, 1997).

Barker-Benfield, G.J., *The Culture of Sensibility: Sex and Society in Eighteenth-Century Britain* (Chicago, 1992).

Barnard, Toby, 'Reading in Eighteenth-Century Ireland: Public and Private Pleasures', in *The Experience of Reading: Irish Historical Perspectives*, ed. Bernadette Cunningham and Máire Kennedy (Dublin, 1999), pp. 60–77.

Barry, Jonathan and Christopher Brooks, eds, *The Middling Sort of People: Culture, Society and Politics in England, 1550–1800* (Basingstoke, 1994).

Bate, Jonathan, 'Parodies of Shakespeare', *Journal of Popular Culture*, 19 (1985), pp. 75–90.

Beckett, Ian F.W., *The Amateur Military Tradition, 1558–1945* (Manchester, 1991).

Berry, Helen, 'Rethinking Politeness in Eighteenth-Century England: Moll King's Coffee House and the Significance of 'Flash Talk': The Alexander Prize Lecture', *Transactions of the Royal Historical Society*, 6th series, 11 (2001), pp. 65–81.

Berry, Helen, *Gender, Society and Print Culture in Late-Stuart England: The Cultural World of the Athenian Mercury* (Aldershot, 2003).

Bindman, David, *The Shadow of the Guillotine: Britain and the French Revolution* (London, 1989).

Biographical Directory of the United States Congress, 1774 to Present (http://bioguide. congress.gov/scripts/biodisplay.pl?index=S001095).

Bizzocchi, Roberto, 'Cicisbei: Italian Morality and European Values in the Eighteenth Century', in *Italy's Eighteenth Century: Gender and Culture in the Age of the Grand Tour*, ed. Paula Findlen, Wendy Wassyng Roworth, and Catherine M. Sama (Stanford, 2009), pp. 35–58.

Black, Jeremy, *The English Press in the Eighteenth Century* (1991 reprint, 1st published London, 1987).

Black, Jeremy, *The British Abroad: The Grand Tour in the Eighteenth Century* (paperback edition 1997, 1st published Stroud, 1992).

Borsay, Peter, *The English Urban Renaissance: Culture and Society in the Provincial Town, 1660–1770* (Oxford, 1989).

Bourdieu, Pierre, *Masculine Domination*, trans. Richard Nice (Cambridge, 2001, 1st published Paris, 1998).

Brewer, John, *The Sinews of Power: War and the English State, 1683–1783* (London, 1989).

Brewer, John, *The Pleasures of the Imagination: English Culture in the Eighteenth Century* (London, 1997).

Brewer, John and Roy Porter, eds, *Consumption and the World of Goods* (London, 1993).

Briggs, Asa and Peter Burke, *A Social History of the Media* (2nd edition, Cambridge, 2005, 1st published 2002).

Bristow, Edward J., *Vice and Vigilance: Purity Movements in Britain since 1700* (Dublin, 1977).

Broughton, Trev Lynn and Helen Rogers, eds, *Gender and Fatherhood in the Nineteenth Century* (Basingstoke, 2007).

Bulloch, J.M., 'The Charitable Corporation', *Notes and Queries*, 160 (1931), pp. 237–41.

Burley, Stephen, *New College, Hackney (1786–96): A Selection of Printed and Archival Sources* (Dr Williams's Centre for Dissenting Studies, 2nd revised edition 2011, 1st published 2010 at http://www.english.qmul.ac.uk/drwilliams/pubs/Burley/DWL%20Online%20Publication.pdf).

Burnard, Trevor, *Mastery, Tyranny, and Desire: Thomas Thistlewood and his Slaves in the Anglo-Jamaican World* (Chapel Hill and London, 2004).

Burns, Arthur and Joanna Innes, eds, *Rethinking the Age of Reform: Britain 1780–1850* (Cambridge, 2003).

Cain, P.J. and A.G. Hopkins, *British Imperialism, 1688–2000* (2nd edition, Harlow, 2002, 1st published 1993).

Cardew, Alexander G., *A Memoir of the Reverend Cornelius Cardew, DD, Master of the Truro Grammar School and Rector of St Erme, Cornwall* (Truro, 1926).

Carlson, C. Lennart, *The First Magazine: A History of the Gentleman's Magazine* (Providence, RI, 1938).

Carlson, C. Lennart, 'Edward Cave's Literary Club, and its Project for a Literary Review', *Philological Quarterly*, 17 (1938), pp. 115–20.

Carter, Philip, 'James Boswell's Manliness', in *English Masculinities, 1660–1800*, ed. Tim Hitchcock and Michèle Cohen (London, 1999), pp. 111–30.

Carter, Philip, *Men and the Emergence of Polite Society, Britain, 1660–1800* (Harlow, 2001).

Cherry, Bridget, 'Edward Hatton's New View of London', *Architectural History*, 44 (2001), pp. 96–105.

Childs, John, *The British Army of William III, 1689–1702* (Manchester, 1987).

Clark, Anna, *The Struggle for the Breeches: Gender and the Making of the British Working Class* (London, 1995).

Clark, Anna, *Scandal: The Sexual Politics of the British Constitution* (Princeton, 2004).

Clark, J.C.D., *English Society, 1688–1832: Religion, Ideology and Politics during the Ancien Regime* (Cambridge, 2000, 1st published 1985).

Clark, Peter, *British Clubs and Societies, 1580–1800* (Oxford, 2000).

Cody, Lisa Forman, *Birthing the Nation: Sex, Science, and the Conception of Eighteenth-Century Britons* (Oxford, 2005).

Cohen, Michèle, 'The Grand Tour: Constructing the English Gentleman in Eighteenth-Century France', *History of Education*, 21 (1992), pp. 241–57.

Cohen, Michèle, *Fashioning Masculinity: National Identity and Language in the Eighteenth Century* (London, 1996).

Colclough, Stephen M., 'Procuring Books and Consuming Texts: The Reading Experience of a Sheffield Apprentice, 1798', *Book History*, 3 (2000), pp. 21–44.

Colley, Linda, 'The Apotheosis of George III: Loyalty, Royalty and the British Nation, 1760–1820', *Past & Present*, 102 (1984), pp. 94–129.

Colley, Linda, *Britons: Forging the Nation, 1707–1837* (paperback edition 2005, 1st published Yale, 1992).

Colley, Linda, *The Ordeal of Elizabeth Marsh: A Woman in World History* (London, 2007).

Collings, David, *Monstrous Society: Reciprocity, Discipline, and the Political Uncanny, c.1780–1848* (Lewisburg, 2009).

Connell, Raewyn, *Masculinities* (2nd edition, Cambridge, 2005, 1st published 1995).

Connell, R.W. and James W. Messerschmidt, 'Hegemonic Masculinity. Rethinking the Concept', *Gender & Society*, 19 (2005), pp. 829–59.

Conway, Stephen, *War, State, and Society in Mid-Eighteenth-Century Britain and Ireland* (Oxford, 2006).

Cookson, J.E., *The British Armed Nation, 1793–1815* (Oxford, 1997).

Corfield, Penelope J., *The Impact of English Towns, 1700–1800* (Oxford, 1982).

Corfield, Penelope J., 'Class by Name and Number in Eighteenth-Century Britain', *History*, 72 (1987), pp. 38–61.

Corfield, Penelope J., *Power and the Professions in Britain, 1700–1850* (London, 1995).

Corfield, Penelope J., 'The Rivals: Landed and Other Gentlemen', in *Land and Society in Britain, 1700–1914*, ed. Negley Harte and Roland Quinault (Manchester, 1996), pp. 1–33.

Corfield, Penelope J., 'History and the Challenge of Gender History', *Rethinking History*, 1 (1997), pp. 241–58.

Cox, Margaret, ed., *Grave Concerns: Death and Burial in England, 1700–1850*, (York, 1998).

Cranfield, G.A., *The Development of the Provincial Newspaper, 1700–60* (Oxford, 1962).

Cressy, David, *Literacy and the Social Order: Reading and Writing in Tudor and Stuart England* (Cambridge, 1980).

Cunningham, Bernadette and Máire Kennedy, eds, *The Experience of Reading: Irish Historical Perspectives* (Dublin, 1999).

Dabhoiwala, Faramerz, *The Origins of Sex: A History of the First Sexual Revolution* (London, 2012).

Darnton, Robert, *The Kiss of Lamourette: Reflections in Cultural History* (London, 1990).

Daunton, M.J., *Progress and Poverty: An Economic and Social History of Britain, 1700–1850* (Oxford, 1995).

Davidoff, Leonore and Catherine Hall, *Family Fortunes: Men and Women of the English Middle Class, 1780–1850* (London, revised edition 2002, 1st published 1987).

De Bolla, Peter, *The Discourse of the Sublime: Readings in History, Aesthetics and the Subject* (Oxford, 1989).

DeMaria, Robert, 'Samuel Johnson and the Reading Revolution', *Eighteenth-Century Life*, 16 (1992), pp. 86–102.

De Montluzin, Emily Lorraine, *Attributions of Authorship in the Gentleman's Magazine, 1731–1868: An Electronic Union List* (13.03.2003, http://etext.virginia.edu/bsuva/gm2/index.html).

De Montluzin, Emily Lorraine, *The Anti-Jacobins, 1798–1800: The Early Contributors to the Anti-Jacobin Review* (Basingstoke, 1988).

De Montluzin, Emily Lorraine, *Daily Life in Georgian England as Reported in the 'Gentleman's Magazine'* (New York, 2002).

De Montluzin, Emily Lorraine, 'Quicksilver Ladies, Odes to Turds, and Three-Seater Privies: The Scatological Underside of the *Gentleman's Magazine*', *ANQ*, 21 (2008), pp. 24–35.

Deutsch, Phyllis, 'Moral Trespass in Georgian London: Gaming, Gender, and Electoral Politics in the Age of George III', *Historical Journal*, 39 (1996), pp. 637–56.

De Vries, Jan, *The Industrious Revolution: Consumer Behavior and the Household Economy, 1650 to the Present* (Cambridge, 2008).

Dickie, Simon, *Cruelty and Laughter: Forgotten Comic Literature and the Unsentimental Eighteenth Century* (Chicago, 2011).

Dickinson, H.T., *The Politics of the People in Eighteenth-Century Britain* (Basingstoke, 1995).

Dictionary of Canadian Biography Online (2003–15, http://www.biographi.ca/en/index.php).

Doody, Margaret Anne, 'Samuel Richardson: Fiction and Knowledge', in *The Cambridge Companion to the Eighteenth-Century Novel*, ed. John Richetti (Cambridge, 1996), pp. 90–119.

Dooley, Brendan and Sabrina Baron, eds, *The Politics of Information in Early Modern Europe* (New York, 2001).

Dudink, Stefan, Karen Hagemann, and John Tosh, eds, *Masculinities in Politics and War: Gendering Modern History* (Manchester, 2004).

Earle, Peter, *The Making of the English Middle Class: Business, Society and Family Life in London, 1660–1730* (London, 1989).

Ellis, Heather, ' "Boys, Semi-Men and Bearded Scholars": Maturity and Manliness in Early Nineteenth-Century Oxford', in *What Is Masculinity? Historical Dynamics from Antiquity to the Contemporary World*, ed. John H. Arnold and Sean Brady (Basingstoke, 2011), pp. 263–82.

Ellis, Heather and Jessica Meyer, eds, *Masculinity and the Other: Historical Perspectives* (Newcastle, 2009).

Elsner, John and Roger Cardinal, eds, *The Cultures of Collecting* (London, 1994).

Erickson, Amy Louise, 'Married Women's Occupations in Eighteenth-Century London', *Continuity & Change*, 23 (2008), pp. 267–307.

Estabrook, Carl B., *Urbane and Rustic England: Cultural Ties and Social Spheres in the Provinces, 1660–1780* (Manchester, 1998).

Evans, Medford B., 'Johnson's Debates in Parliament' (unpublished PhD thesis, Yale University, 1933).

Fang, Karen Y., *Romantic Writing and the Empire of Signs: Periodical Culture and Post-Napoleonic Authorship* (Charlottesville, 2010).

Feather, John, *The Provincial Book Trade in Eighteenth-Century England* (Cambridge, 1985).

Fergus, Jan S., 'Women, Class and the Growth of Magazine Readership in the Provinces, 1746–80', *Studies in Eighteenth-Century Culture*, 16 (1986), pp. 41–56.

Fergus, Jan S., *Provincial Readers in Eighteenth-Century England* (Oxford, 2006).

Findlen, Paula, Wendy Wassing Roworth, and Catherine M. Sama, eds, *Italy's Eighteenth Century: Gender and Culture in the Age of the Grand Tour* (Stanford, 2009).

Flavell, Julie, *When London Was Capital of America* (New Haven, CT, 2010).

Fletcher, Anthony, *Gender, Sex and Subordination in England, 1500–1800* (Yale, 1995).

Foyster, Elizabeth A., *Manhood in Early Modern England: Honour, Sex and Marriage* (London, 1999).

Foyster, Elizabeth A., ' "Boys will be boys?" Manhood and Aggression, 1660–1800', in *English Masculinities 1660–1800*, ed. Tim Hitchcock and Michèle Cohen (London, 1999), pp. 151–66.

French, Henry R., 'The Search for the "Middle Sort of People" in England, 1600–1800', *Historical Journal*, 43 (2000), pp. 277–93.

French, Henry R., *The Middle Sort of People in Provincial England 1600–1750* (Oxford, 2007).

French, Henry R. and Mark Rothery, 'Hegemonic Masculinities, 1700–1900', in *What is Masculinity? Historical Dynamics from Antiquity to the Contemporary World*, ed. John H. Arnold and Sean Brady (Basingstoke, 2011), pp. 139–66.

French, Henry R. and Mark Rothery, *Man's Estate: Landed Gentry Masculinities, 1660–1900* (Oxford, 2012).

Fritz, Paul and Richard Morton, eds, *Woman in the Eighteenth Century and Other Essays* (Toronto, 1976).

Gaskell, Philip, *A New Introduction to Bibliography* (Oxford, 1972).

Gatrell, Vic, *City of Laughter: Sex and Satire in Eighteenth-Century London* (London, 2006).

George, M. Dorothy, *London Life in the Eighteenth Century* (Harmondsworth, 1966, 1st published London, 1925).

Ghosh, S.C., *The Social Condition of the British Community in Bengal, 1757–1800* (Leiden, 1970).

Glaisyer, Natasha, *The Culture of Commerce in England*, 1660–1720 (Woodbridge, 2006).

Gleadle, Kathryn, *Borderline Citizens: Women, Gender, and Political Culture in Britain, 1815–67* (Oxford, 2009).

Goldgar, Anne, *Impolite Learning: Conduct and Community in the Republic of Letters, 1680–1750* (New Haven, CT, 1995).

Goodrich, Amanda, *Debating England's Aristocracy in the 1790s: Pamphlets, Polemics, and Political Ideas* (Woodbridge, 2005).

Goody, Jack, ed., *Literacy in Traditional Societies* (Cambridge, 1968).

Graff, Harvey J., ed., *Literacy and Historical Development* (Carbondale, S. Illinois, 2007).

Greig, Hannah, *The Beau Monde: Fashionable Society in Georgian England* (Oxford, 2013).

Griffin, Robert J., ed., *The Faces of Anonymity: Anonymous and Pseudonymous Publication from the Sixteenth to the Twentieth Century* (Basingstoke, 2003).

Grubb, Farley, 'Growth of Literacy in Colonial America: Longitudinal Patterns, Economic Models, and the Direction of Future Research', in *Literacy and Historical Development*, ed. Harvey J. Graff (Carbondale, S. Illinois, 2007), pp. 272–98.

Habermas, Jürgen, *The Structural Transformation of the Public Sphere: An Inquiry into a Category of Bourgeois Society*, trans. Thomas Burger and Frederick Lawrence (Cambridge, 1989).

Hall, Edith and Fiona Macintosh, *Greek Tragedy and the British Theatre, 1660–1914* (Oxford, 2005).

Harding, Vanessa, 'Research Priorities: An Historian's Perspective', in *Grave Concerns: Death and Burial in England, 1700–1850*, ed. Margaret Cox (York, 1998), pp. 205–12.

Harris, Michael, *London Newspapers in the Age of Walpole: A Study of the Origins of the Modern English Press* (London, 1987).

Harris, Tim, 'Problematising Popular Culture', in *Popular Culture in England, c.1500–1850*, ed. Tim Harris (Basingstoke, 1995), pp. 1–27.

Harvey, Karen, ed., *History and Material Culture: A Student's Guide to Approaching Alternative Sources* (London, 2009).

Harvey, Karen and Alex Shepard, 'What Have Historians done with Masculinity? Reflections on Five Centuries of British History, circa 1550–1950', *Journal of British Studies*, 44 (2005), pp. 274–80.

Haywood, Ian and John Seed, eds, *The Gordon Riots: Politics, Culture and Insurrection in Late Eighteenth-Century Britain* (Cambridge, 2012).

Heller, Benjamin, 'Leisure and the Use of Domestic Space in Georgian London', *Historical Journal*, 53 (2010), pp. 623–45.

Herzog, Don, *Poisoning the Minds of the Lower Orders* (Princeton, 1998).

Hewitt, Regina and Pat Rogers, eds, *Orthodoxy and Heresy in Eighteenth-Century Society: Essays from the De Bartolo Conference* (Lewisburg, 2002).

Heyd, Uriel, *Reading Newspapers: Press and Public in Eighteenth-Century Britain and America* (Oxford, 2012).

Hibberd, J.L., 'Salomon Gessner's Idylls as Prose Poems', *Modern Language Review*, 68 (1973), pp. 569–76.

Hill, Bridget, *Women, Work, and Sexual Politics in Eighteenth-Century England* (Oxford, 1989).

Hillier, Bevis, *Early English Porcelain* (London, 1992).

Hilton, Boyd, *The Age of Atonement: The Influence of Evangelicalism on Social and Economic Thought, 1785–1865* (Oxford, 1986).

History of Parliament (n.d., http://www.historyofparliamentonline.org).

Hitchcock, Tim, *Down and Out in Eighteenth-Century London* (London, 2004).

Hitchcock, Tim and Michèle Cohen, eds, *English Masculinities, 1660–1800* (London, 1999).

Hoffmann, Léon-François, 'An Eighteenth-Century Exponent of Black Power: Moses Bon Sàam', *Caribbean Studies*, 15 (1975), pp. 149–61.

Hole, Robert, *Pulpits, Politics and Public Order in England, 1760–1832* (Cambridge, 1989).

Honeybone, Diana and Michael Honeybone, eds, *The Correspondence of the Spalding Gentlemen's Society, 1710–61* (Woodbridge, 2010).

Hoppit, Julian, *Risk and Failure in English Business, 1700–1800* (Cambridge, 1987).

Houston, Rab, 'The Literacy Myth? Illiteracy in Scotland, 1630–1760', in *Literacy and Historical Development*, ed. Harvey J. Graff (Carbondale, S. Illinois, 2007), pp. 183–206.

Howard, Stephen, ' "A bright pattern to all her sex": Representations of Women in Periodical and Newspaper Biography', in *Gender in Eighteenth-Century England: Roles, Representations and Responsibilities*, ed. Hannah Barker and Elaine Chalus (London, 1997), pp. 230–49.

Hunt, Margaret R., *The Middling Sort: Commerce, Gender, and the Family in England, 1680–1780* (Berkeley, CA, 1996).

Hunter, Jean E., 'The Eighteenth-Century Englishwoman: According to the *Gentleman's Magazine*' in *Woman in the Eighteenth Century and Other Essays*, ed. Paul Fritz and Richard Morton (Toronto, 1976), pp. 73–88.

Innes, Joanna, 'Legislation and Public Participation: Aspects of a Changing Relationship, 1760–1830' in *The British and Their Laws*, ed. David Lemmings (Woodbridge, 2005), pp. 102–32.

Innes, Joanna and Mark Philp, eds, *Re-imagining Democracy in the Age of Revolutions: America, France, Britain, Ireland, 1750–1850* (Oxford, 2013).

Ireland, Richard W., 'Howard and the Paparazzi: Painting Penal Reform in the Eighteenth Century', *Art, Antiquity & Law*, 4 (1999), pp. 55–62.

Jackson, Ian, 'Approaches to the History of Readers and Reading in Eighteenth-Century Britain', *Historical Journal*, 47 (2004), pp. 1041–54.

Jacob, W.M., *Lay People and Religion in the Early Eighteenth Century* (Cambridge, 1996).

Karremann, Isabel and Anja Müller, eds, *Mediating Identities in Eighteenth-Century England: Public Negotiations, Literary Discourses, Topography* (Farnham, 2011).

Kaufman, Paul, 'A Bookseller's Record of Eighteenth-Century Book-Clubs', *The Library*, 5th series, 15 (1960), pp. 278–87.

Kaufman, Paul, 'The Community Library: A Chapter in English Social History', *Transactions of the American Philosophical Society*, NS 57 (1967), pp. 1–67.

Kaufman, Paul, *Libraries and their Users: Collected Papers in Library History* (London, 1969).

Kaufman, Paul, 'Readers and their Reading in Eighteenth-Century Lichfield', *The Library*, 5th series, 28 (1973), pp. 105–15.

Keane, John, *Tom Paine: A Political Life* (paperback edition, London, 2009, 1st published 1995).

Kennedy, Catriona and Matthew McCormack, eds, *Soldiering in Britain and Ireland, 1750–1850: Men of Arms* (Basingstoke, 2012).

Kernan, Alvin B., *Printing Technology, Letters and Samuel Johnson* (Princeton, 1987).

Kimber, S.A., 'The "Relation of a Late Expedition to St Augustine", with Biographical and Bibliographical Notes on Isaac and Edward Kimber', *Papers of the Bibliographical Society of America*, 28 (1934), pp. 81–96.

Kimmel, Michael S., *The History of Men: Essays in the History of American and British Masculinities* (New York, 2005).

Kinkel, Sarah, 'Saving Admiral Byng: Imperial Debates, Military Governance and Popular Politics at the Outbreak of the Seven Years' War', *Journal for Maritime Research*, 13 (2011), pp. 3–19.

Klancher, Jon P., *The Making of English Reading Audiences, 1790–1832* (Madison, WI, 1987).

Klein, Lawrence E., 'Politeness and the Interpretation of the British Eighteenth Century', *Historical Journal*, 45 (2002), pp. 869–98.

Kuist, James M., 'The *Gentleman's Magazine*, 1754–1800: A Study of its Development as a Vehicle for the Discussion of Literature' (unpublished PhD thesis, Duke University, 1965).

Kuist, James M., ' "What, does she still adorn this dreary scene?" Nichols' Problems with Obituary Notices in the *Gentleman's Magazine*', *Eighteenth-Century Life*, 4 (1978), pp. 76–8.

Kuist, James M., *The Nichols File of the Gentleman's Magazine: Attributions of Authorship and Other Documentation in Editorial Papers at the Folger Library* (Madison, WI, 1982).

Kuist, James M., 'A Collaboration in Learning: The *Gentleman's Magazine* and its Ingenious Contributors', *Studies in Bibliography*, 44 (1991), pp. 302–17.

Lamb, Susan, *Bringing Travel Home to England: Tourism, Gender, and Imaginative Literature in the Eighteenth Century* (Newark, DE, 2009).

Langford, Paul, *A Polite and Commercial People: England, 1727–83* (Oxford, 1998, 1st published 1989).

Langford, Paul, 'The Uses of Politeness', *Transactions of the Royal Historical Society*, 12 (2002), pp. 311–31.

Laqueur, Thomas W., *Religion and Respectability: Sunday Schools and Working-Class Culture, 1780–1850* (New Haven, CT, 1976).

Laqueur, Thomas W., *Making Sex: Body and Gender from the Greeks to Freud* (Harvard, 1990).

Lemmings, David, ed., *The British and Their Laws* (Woodbridge, 2005).

Lemmings, David, ed., *Moral Panics, the Media and the Law in Early Modern England* (Basingstoke, 2009).

Lemmings, David, ed., *Crime, Courtrooms, and the Public Sphere in Britain, 1700–1850* (Farnham, 2012).

Levine, Philippa, ed., *Gender and Empire* (Oxford, 2004).

Linch, Kevin and Matthew McCormack, eds, *Britain's Soldiers: Rethinking War and Society, 1715–1815* (Liverpool, 2014).

Lock, F.P., *Burke's Reflections on the Revolution in France* (London, 1985).

Lonsdale, Roger, ed., *The New Oxford Book of Eighteenth Century Verse* (paperback edition 2009, 1st published Oxford, 1984).

MacDonald, Michael and Terence R. Murphy, *Sleepless Souls: Suicide in Early Modern England* (Oxford, 1990).

Marks, Sylvia Kasey, *Sir Charles Grandison: The Compleat Conduct Book* (Lewisburg, 1986).

Marshall, P.J., 'British Society in India under the East India Company', *Modern Asian Studies*, 31 (1997), pp. 89–108.

Maurer, Shawn L., *Proposing Men: Dialectics of Gender and Class in the Eighteenth-Century Periodical* (Stanford, CA, 1998).

May, Allyson N., *The Fox-Hunting Controversy, 1781–2004: Class and Cruelty* (Farnham, 2013).

Mayo, Robert D., *The English Novel in the Magazines, 1740–1815* (Evanston, 1962).

McCalman, Iain, *Radical Underworld: Prophets, Revolutionaries and Pornographers in London, 1795–1840* (Cambridge, 1988).

McCormack, Matthew, *The Independent Man. Citizenship and Gender Politics in Georgian England* (Manchester, 2005).

McCormack, Matthew, ed., *Public Men: Masculinity and Politics in Modern Britain* (Basingstoke, 2007a).

McCormack, Matthew, 'The New Militia: War, Politics and Gender', *Gender & History*, 19 (2007b), pp. 483–500.

McCormack, Matthew, ' "Married Men and the Fathers of Families": Fatherhood and Franchise Reform in Britain', in *Gender and Fatherhood in the Nineteenth Century*, ed. Trev Lynn Broughton and Helen Rogers (Basingstoke, 2007c), pp. 43–54.

McCormack, Matthew, 'Supporting the Civil Power: Citizen Soldiers and the Gordon Riots', *London Journal*, 37 (2012), pp. 27–41.

McCreery, Cindy, 'Keeping up with the *Bon Ton*: The *Tête à Tête* Series in the *Town and Country Magazine*', in *Gender in Eighteenth-Century England: Roles, Representations and Responsibilities*, ed. Hannah Barker and Elaine Chalus (London, 1997), pp. 207–29.

McCreery, Cindy, 'A Moral Panic in Eighteenth-Century London? The 'Monster' and the Press', in *Moral Panics, the Media and the Law in Early Modern England*, ed. David Lemmings (Basingstoke, 2009) pp. 195–220.

McGowen, Randall, 'Forgers and Forgery: Severity and Social Identity in Eighteenth-Century England', in *Moral Panics, the Media and the Law in Early Modern England*, ed. David Lemmings (Basingstoke, 2009), pp. 157–75.

McKellar, Elizabeth, *Landscapes of London: The City, the Country and the Suburbs, 1660–1840* (New Haven, CT, 2013).

McKendrick, Neil, John Brewer, and J.H. Plumb, *The Birth of a Consumer Society: The Commercialization of Eighteenth-Century England* (London, 1983, 1st published 1982).

McKenzie, Andrea, ' "Useful and entertaining to the generality of Readers": Selecting the Select Trials, 1718–1764', in *Crime, Courtrooms, and the Public Sphere in Britain, 1700–1850*, ed. David Lemmings (Farnham, 2012), pp. 43–69.

McKenzie, Donald F. and John C. Ross, eds, *A Ledger of Charles Ackers* (London, 1968).

McKeon, Michael, 'Historicizing Patriarchy: The Emergence of Gender Difference in England, 1660–1760', *Eighteenth-Century Studies*, 3 (1995), pp. 295–322.

McNairn, Alan, *Behold the Hero: General Wolfe and the Arts in the Eighteenth Century* (Liverpool, 1997).

Midgley, Clare, *Women against Slavery: The British Campaigns, 1780–1870* (paperback edition 1995, 1st published London, 1992).

Moore, Stephen, ' "A Nation of Harlequins"? Politics and Masculinity in Mid-Eighteenth-Century England', *Journal of British Studies*, 49 (2010), pp. 514–39.

Morrall, Andrew, 'Ornament as Evidence', in *History and Material Culture: A Student's Guide to Approaching Alternative Sources*, ed. Karen Harvey (London, 2009), pp. 47–66.

Muldrew, Craig, *The Economy of Obligation: The Culture of Credit and Social Relations in Early Modern England* (Basingstoke, 1998).

Newman, Gerald, *The Rise of English Nationalism: A Cultural History, 1740–1830* (revised edition 1997, 1st published London, 1987).

Obeyesekere, Gananath, *The Apotheosis of Captain Cook: European Mythmaking in the Pacific* (Princeton, 1992).

Ogborn, Miles, *Indian Ink: Script and Print in the Making of the English East India Company* (Chicago, 2007).

Oxford Dictionary of National Biography (Oxford, 2004), www.oup.com/oxforddnb.

Pailler, Albert, *Edward Cave et le "Gentleman's Magazine"*, 1731–54, 2 vols (Lille, 1975).

Peakman, Julie, *Lascivious Bodies: A Sexual History of the Eighteenth Century* (London, 1988).

Peakman, Julie, *Mighty Lewd Books: The Development of Pornography in Eighteenth-Century England* (Basingstoke, 2003).

Pearsall, Sarah M.S., *Atlantic Families: Lives and Letters in the Later Eighteenth Century* (Oxford, 2008).

Peoples, Penelope, 'The Folger Nichols Manuscript Collection: A Description and Analysis' (unpublished PhD thesis, University of Wisconsin-Milwaukee, 1980).

Phillips, Nicola, *The Profligate Son: or, A True Story of Family Conflict, Fashionable Vice, and Financial Ruin in Regency Britain* (Oxford, 2013).

Plomer, H.R., G.H. Bushnell, and E.R.M. McClintock, *A Dictionary of the Printers and Booksellers who were at Work in England, Scotland and Ireland from 1726 to 1775* (Oxford, 1932).

Poovey, Mary, 'Accommodating Merchants: Accounting, Civility, and the Natural Laws of Gender', *Differences: A Journal of Feminist Studies*, 8 (1996), pp. 1–20.

Poovey, Mary, *A History of the Modern Fact: Problems of Knowledge in the Sciences of Wealth and Society* (Chicago, 1998).

Porter, Roy, *English Society in the Eighteenth Century* (revised edition 1990, 1st published London, 1982).

Porter, Roy, 'Lay Medical Knowledge in the Eighteenth Century: The Evidence of the *Gentleman's Magazine*', *Medical History*, 29 (1985a), pp. 138–68.

Porter, Roy, ed., *Patients and Practitioners: Lay Perceptions of Medicine in Pre-Industrial Society* (Cambridge, 1985b).

Porter, Roy, *Enlightenment: Britain and the Creation of the Modern World* (London, 2000).

Ram, Titia, *Magnitude in Marginality: Edward Cave and the "Gentleman's Magazine", 1731–54*, trans. from Dutch by the author (Utrecht, 1999).

Raven, James, *Judging New Wealth: Popular Publishing and Responses to Commerce in England, 1750–1800* (Oxford, 1992).

Raven, James, 'From Promotion to Proscription: Arrangements for Reading and Eighteenth-Century Libraries', in *The Practice and Representation of Reading in England*, ed. James Raven, Helen Small, and Naomi Tadmor (Cambridge, 1996), pp. 175–201.

Raven, James, *Publishing Business in Eighteenth-Century England* (Woodbridge, 2014).

Raven, James, Helen Small, and Naomi Tadmor, eds, *The Practice and Representation of Reading in England* (Cambridge, 1996).

Reading Experience Database, 1450–1945 (http://www.open.ac.uk/Arts/RED/).

Retford, Kate, *The Art of Domestic Life: Family Portraiture in Eighteenth-Century England* (New Haven, CT, 2006).

Ribeiro, Aileen, *Dress in Eighteenth-Century Europe, 1715–89* (New Haven, CT, 2002).

Richetti, John, ed., *The Cambridge Companion to the Eighteenth-Century Novel* (Cambridge, 1996).

Ricoeur, Paul, *Time and Narrative*, trans. Kathleen McLaughlin and David Pellauer, 3 vols (Chicago, 1984–8).

Rimmer, G., *Marshalls of Leeds: Flax-Spinners, 1788–1886* (Cambridge, 1960).

Roberts, William, 'The *Gentleman's Magazine* and its Rivals', *Athenaeum* (1889), p. 560.

Rodger, N.A.M., *The Wooden World: An Anatomy of the Georgian Navy* (London, 1986).

Rogers, Nicholas, 'Brave Wolfe: The Making of a Hero', in *A New Imperial History: Culture, Identity and Modernity in Britain and the Empire, 1660–1840*, ed. Kathleen Wilson (Cambridge, 2004), pp. 239–59.

Roper, Michael, 'Slipping Out of View: Subjectivity and Emotion in Gender History', *History Workshop Journal*, 59 (2005), pp. 57–72.

Roper, Michael and John Tosh, eds, *Manful Assertions: Masculinities in Britain since 1800* (London, 1991).

Rose, Jonathan, 'Rereading the English Common Reader: A Preface to a History of Audiences', *Journal of the History of Ideas*, 53 (1992), pp. 47–70.

Rowland, Antony, Emma Liggins, and Eriks Uskalis, eds, *Signs of Masculinity: Men in Literature, 1700 to the Present* (Amsterdam, 1998).

Rudé, George F.E., *Wilkes and Liberty: A Social Study of 1763–74* (Oxford, 1962).

Rusnock, Andrea, 'Correspondence Networks and the Royal Society, 1700–50', *British Journal for the History of Science*, 32 (1999), pp. 155–69.

Sainsbury, John, *John Wilkes: The Lives of a Libertine* (Ashgate, 2006).

Schofield, R.S., 'The Measurement of Literacy in Pre-Industrial England' in *Literacy in Traditional Societies*, ed. Jack Goody (Cambridge, 1968), pp. 311–25.

Schofield, R.S., 'Dimensions of Illiteracy, 1750–1850', *Explorations in Economic History*, 10 (1973), pp. 437–54.

Scodel, Joshua, *The English Poetic Epitaph: Commemoration and Conflict from Jonson to Wordsworth* (Ithaca, NY, 1991).

Scott, Joan Wallach, 'Gender: A Useful Category of Historical Analysis', *American Historical Review*, 91 (1986), pp. 1053–75.

Scott, Joan Wallach, *Gender and the Politics of History* (revised edition 1999, 1st published New York, 1988).

Secord, Anne, 'Corresponding Interests: Artisans and Gentlemen in Nineteenth-Century Natural History', *British Journal for the History of Science*, 27 (1994), pp. 383–408.

Sennett, Richard, *The Fall of Public Man* (New York, 1977).

Sharpe, Kevin and Steven N. Zwicker, eds, *Reading, Society, and Politics in Early Modern England* (Cambridge, 2003).

Shepard, Alex, *Meanings of Manhood in Early Modern England* (Oxford, 2003).

Sheps, Arthur, 'Sedition, Vice and Atheism: The Limits of Toleration and the Orthodox Attack on Rational Religion in Late Eighteenth-Century England' in *Orthodoxy and Heresy in Eighteenth-Century Society: Essays from the De Bartolo Conference*, ed. Regina Hewitt and Pat Rogers (Lewisburg, 2002), pp. 51–68.

Sherbo, Arthur, *Letters to Mr Urban of the Gentleman's Magazine, 1751–1811* (New York, 1997).

Sherbo, Arthur, *Studies in the Johnson Circle* (West Cornwall, CT, 1998).

Shevelow, Kathryn, *Women and Print Culture: The Construction of Femininity in the Early Periodical* (London, 1989).

Shoemaker, Robert, *Gender in English Society 1650–1850: The Emergence of Separate Spheres?* (London, 1998).

Shoemaker, Robert, 'Reforming Male Manners: Public Insult and the Decline of Violence in London, 1660–1740', in *English Masculinities 1660–1800*, ed. Tim Hitchcock and Michèle Cohen (London, 1999), pp. 133–50.

Shugg, Wallace, 'The Baron and the Milliner: Lord Baltimore's Rape Trial as a Mirror of Class Tensions in Mid-Georgian London', *Maryland Historical Magazine*, 83 (1988), pp. 310–30.

Smith, Hilda L., *All Men and Both Sexes: Gender, Politics, and the False Universal in England, 1640–1832* (University Park, PA, 2002).

Snell, Esther, 'Trials in Print: Narratives of Rape Trials in the *Proceedings of the Old Bailey*', in *Crime, Courtrooms, and the Public Sphere in Britain, 1700–1850*, ed. David Lemmings (Farnham, 2012), pp. 23–41.

Solly, G.A. and others, eds, *The Rugby Register* (Rugby, 1933–57).

Sommerville, C. John, *The News Revolution in England: Cultural Dynamics of Daily Information* (Oxford, 1996).

Spector, Robert Donald, *English Literary Periodicals and the Climate of Opinion during the Seven Years' War* (The Hague, 1966).

Spufford, Margaret, *Small Books and Pleasant Histories: Popular Fiction and its Readership in Seventeenth-Century England* (Cambridge, 1985).

Spufford, Margaret, 'First Steps in Literacy: The Reading and Writing Experiences of the Humblest Seventeenth-Century Spiritual Autobiographers', in *Literacy and Historical Development*, ed. Harvey J. Graff (Carbondale, S. Illinois, 2007), pp. 207–37.

Stafford, William, 'Gentlemanly Masculinities as Represented by the Late Georgian *Gentleman's Magazine*', *History*, 93 (2008), pp. 47–68.

Stafford, William, 'Representations of the Social Order in *The Gentleman's Magazine*, 1785–1815', *Eighteenth-Century Life*, 33 (2009), pp. 64–91.

Starck, Nigel, *Life after Death: The Art of the Obituary* (Carlton, Vic., Australia, 2006).

St Clair, William, *The Reading Nation in the Romantic Period* (Cambridge, 2004).

Stephen, Sir Leslie, ed., *Dictionary of National Biography*, 63 vols (London, 1885–1903).

Stone, Lawrence, *The Family, Sex and Marriage in England, 1500–1800* (abridged edition, Harmondsworth, 1979, 1st published 1977).

Stott, Anne, *Wilberforce: Family and Friends* (Oxford, 2012).

Sullivan, Alvin, ed., *British Literary Magazines*, 4 vols (Westport, CT, 1983).

Sweet, Rosemary, *The English Town, 1680–1840* (Harlow, 1999).

Sweet, Rosemary, *Antiquaries: The Discovery of the Past in Eighteenth-Century Britain* (Hambledon and London, 2004).

Tadmor, Naomi, ' "In the even my wife read to me": Women, Reading and Household Life in the Eighteenth Century', in *The Practice and Representation of Reading in England*, ed. James Raven, Helen Small, and Naomi Tadmor (Cambridge, 1996), pp. 162–7.

Tadmor, Naomi, *Family and Friends in Eighteenth-Century England: Household, Kinship, and Patronage* (Cambridge, 2001).

Tarlow, Sarah, *Bereavement and Commemoration: An Archaeology of Mortality* (Oxford, 1999).

Thomas, Peter D.G., 'The Beginning of Parliamentary Reporting in Newspapers, 1768–74', *English Historical Review*, 74 (1959), pp. 623–36.

Thorne, R.G., The *House of Commons*, 1790–1820, 5 vols (London, 1986).

Tillyard, S.K., *Aristocrats: Caroline, Emily and Sarah Lennox, 1740–1832* (London, 1994).

Todd, William B., 'A Bibliographical Account of the Gentleman's Magazine, 1731–54', *Studies in Bibliography*, 18 (1965), pp. 81–109.

Tosh, John, *A Man's Place: Masculinity and the Middle-Class Home in Victorian England* (New Haven, CT, 2007, 1st published 1999).

Tosh, John, 'The Old Adam and the New Man: Emerging Themes in the History of English Masculinities, 1750–1850', in *Manliness and Masculinities in Nineteenth-Century Britain: Essays on Gender, Family and Empire*, ed. John Tosh (Harlow, 2005), pp. 61–82.

Tosh, John, ed., *Manliness and Masculinities in Nineteenth-Century Britain: Essays on Gender, Family and Empire* (Harlow, 2005).

Trumbach, R., *The Rise of the Egalitarian Family: Aristocratic Kinship and Domestic Relations in Eighteenth-Century England* (New York, 1978).

Turner, David M., *Fashioning Adultery: Gender, Sex and Civility in England, 1660–1740* (Cambridge, 2002).

Vickery, Amanda, 'Golden Age to Separate Spheres? A Review of the Categories and Chronology of English Women's History', *Historical Journal*, 36 (1993), pp. 383–414.

Vickery, Amanda, *The Gentleman's Daughter: Women's Lives in Georgian England* (Yale, 1998).

Vickery, Amanda, *Behind Closed Doors: At Home in Georgian England* (Yale, 2009).

Wahrman, Dror, 'National Society, Communal Culture: An Argument about the Recent Historiography of Eighteenth-Century Britain', *Social History*, 17 (1992), pp. 43–72.

Wahrman, Dror, *Imagining the Middle Class: The Political Representation of Class in Britain, c.1780–1840* (Cambridge, 1995).

Wahrman, Dror, *The Making of the Modern Self: Identity and Culture in Eighteenth-Century England* (Yale, 2006).

Wahrman, Dror, 'Change and the Corporeal in Seventeenth- and Eighteenth-Century Gender History: Or, Can Cultural History be Rigorous?', *Gender & History*, 20 (2008), pp. 584–602.

Wardaugh, Benjamin, *Poor Robin's Prophecies: A Curious Almanac, and the Everyday Mathematics of Georgian Britain* (Oxford, 2012).

Weatherill, Lorna, *Culture in Britain, 1660–1760* (2nd edition, London, 1996, 1st published 1988).

Wells, Andrew, 'Masculinity and its Other in Eighteenth-Century Racial Thought' in *Masculinity and the Other: Historical Perspectives*, ed. Heather Ellis and Jessica Meyer (Newcastle, 2009), pp. 85–113.

Western, J.R., *The English Militia in the Eighteenth Century: The Story of a Political Issue, 1660–1802* (London, 1965).

Whyman, Susan E., *The Pen and the People: English Letter Writers, 1660–1800* (Oxford, 2009).

Williams, Carolyn D., *Pope, Homer and Manliness: Some Aspects of Eighteenth-Century Classical Learning* (London, 1993).

Wilson, Kathleen, *The Sense of the People: Politics, Culture and Imperialism in England, 1715–85* (Cambridge, 1995).

Wilson, Kathleen, *The Island Race: Englishness, Empire and Gender in the Eighteenth Century* (London, 2003).

Wilson, Kathleen, ed., *A New Imperial History: Culture, Identity and Modernity in Britain and the Empire, 1660–1840* (Cambridge, 2004).

Wrightson, Keith, *English Society, 1580–1680* (London, 1982).

Yost, Calvin Daniel, *The Poetry of the Gentleman's Magazine: A Study in Eighteenth-Century Literary Taste* (Philadelphia, 1936).

Zemon Davis, Natalie, 'Remaking Impostors: From Martin Guerre to Sommersby', *Hayes Robinson Lecture Series*, 1 (1997, http://www.rhul.ac.uk/history/docu ments/pdf/events/hrzemon-davis.pdf).

Zwicker, Steven N., 'The Constitution of Opinion and the Pacification of Reading', in *Reading, Society, and Politics in Early Modern England*, ed. Kevin Sharpe and Steven N. Zwicker (Cambridge, 2003), pp. 295–316.

Index

Printed and bound in Great Britain by
CPI Group (UK) Ltd, Croydon, CR0 4YY